Sources and Documents

illustrating the

American Revolution

1764—1788

Dan Nelson

Sources and Documents

illustrating the

American Revolution

1764—1788

and the formation of the

Federal Constitution

Selected and Edited by

SAMUEL ELIOT MORISON

SOMETIME HAROLD VYVYAN HARMSWORTH PROFESSOR OF AMERICAN
HISTORY IN THE UNIVERSITY OF OXFORD
PROFESSOR OF HISTORY, HARVARD UNIVERSITY

SECOND EDITION

OXFORD UNIVERSITY PRESS

LONDON   OXFORD   NEW YORK

FIRST PUBLISHED BY THE CLARENDON PRESS, 1923
SECOND EDITION PUBLISHED, 1929
FIRST ISSUED AS AN OXFORD UNIVERSITY PRESS PAPERBACK, 1965
THIS REPRINT, 1967
PRINTED IN THE UNITED STATES OF AMERICA

PREFACE

THE plan of this book is to include (a) all the absolutely essential documents, such as the Declaration of Independence and the Federal Constitution, (b) the more important acts, resolves, state constitutions, royal instructions, &c., not easily obtainable elsewhere, (c) samples of the more human varieties of source material, such as debates, letters, pamphlets, Indian relations, and frontier petitions, which illustrate and often influenced public opinion. A large part of the book is devoted to the six years after the war, when the Revolution was logically completed by the Federal Constitution. Military and diplomatic subjects have been excluded, because it is the Revolution rather than the War of Independence that we are trying to elucidate; and certain economic aspects of the Revolution have been excluded because they are adequately dealt with in Professor Callender's *Selections from the Economic History of the United States*.[1]

Professors Alvord of the University of Minnesota, Becker of Cornell, Coupland and Egerton of Oxford, Merk and McIlwain of Harvard, and Van Tyne of Michigan have given the editor valuable suggestions which he gratefully acknowledges.

The documents are reproduced from the manuscript, or, in the case of those already printed, from the best available edition, without change in spelling. Conformity to modern use of capitals and italics has, however, been attempted. Authors' foot-notes are indicated by asterisks or daggers : the editor's, by numbers.

The Introduction is not a history of the Revolution, but a guide to the documents. Somewhat fuller treatment than this principle would permit has been given to the Western problem, which has received scant notice in the books that undergraduates are likely to read. Of such books the following are recommended :

Carl Becker's *The Beginnings of the American People* (Boston:

[1] Ginn and Co., 1909. Other sources that should be read in connexion with this book are the Parliamentary debates on American affairs in Hansard, especially Burke's speeches ; W. Knox, *Controversy Reviewed* (London, 1769) ; T. Paine, *Common Sense* (1776) ; the Constitution of Massachusetts (1780) ; and the *Federalist* (1788).

Houghton, Mifflin, 1915), a sound and brilliant essay on the colonial and revolutionary period. H. E. Egerton's *Causes and Character of the American Revolution* (Oxford : Clarendon Press, 1923, 207 pp.) ; by an English scholar who has a thorough knowledge of similar issues in the later British Empire.

E. Channing's *History of the United States*, vol. iii, 1761–89 (Macmillan, 1912, 585 pp.), is the best single volume covering the whole of the Revolutionary period, by the greatest living authority on American history.

C. H. Van Tyne's *Causes of the War of Independence* (Houghton, Mifflin, and Constable, 1922, 499 pp.) presents the results of important research during the last decade.

Sir G. O. Trevelyan's *American Revolution*, 6 vols. (Longmans, 1917), is the final edition of a work first published in many parts and titles. Its literary quality is pre-eminent ; its point of view is vigorously Whig.

In this revised edition no change has been made in the choice of documents ; but a number of misprints have been corrected, and an index has been added. I should also like to recommend Charles H. McIlwain's *American Revolution* (Macmillan, 1923), a most stimulating essay on the constitutional aspect ; *The Correspondence of George III* (5 vols., Macmillan, 1927–8), which with the pithy introductions of the editor, Sir John Fortescue, well presents the Tory point of view : Vernon L. Parrington's *The Colonial Mind* (Harcourt, Brace & Co., 1927) ; and volume i of C. A. and M. R. Beard's *Rise of American Civilization* (Macmillan, 1927), both brilliant works of interpretation, and A. F. Pollard's racy comment on the Revolution in his *Factors in American History* (Cambridge Univ. Press, 1925).

S. E. M.

Harvard College,
1 *October* 1928.

TABLE OF CONTENTS

INTRODUCTION

DOCUMENTS

INTRODUCTION

I. *The Taxation Question, 1764–70.*

THE roots of the American Revolution go far down into the
past. Geography and climate, institutional developments,
religion and race, and other factors beyond our ken, may have
made the separation inevitable. Only the immediate causes,
however, can be studied in these documents. Since 1688 the
colonies had been pushing toward a larger measure of self-
government, as indeed the dominions have done in the last
century. Then came an attempt to check this evolution ; to
create new institutional bonds between the colonies and
Great Britain, and to strengthen such as existed. It was a part
of the struggle between centralization and localism which runs
through all modern history ; and not the least interesting
phase were the attempted solutions through federalism—
unsuccessful in 1774–5, successful on a smaller scale in 1787–8.
The American Revolution belongs not only to America ; it is
an important part of the great liberal movement of the
eighteenth century, a portent of dominion home rule, and
a laboratory of imperial and federal problems.

In 1760, when the Seven Years' War closed in North
America, the English colonists were fairly satisfied with the
existing rough compromise between home rule and imperial
control. Although irritated with certain aspects of the old
colonial system, they were content that Parliament should
control imperial commerce, so long as it permitted them to
prosper ; and they had no criticism of a foreign policy which
had brought glorious results. No separatist movement existed.
In England, however, there was serious dissatisfaction with
this rough compromise. It was commonly believed that the

colonies had not done their proper share in the war (below, p. 21).[1] The colonists not only denied this, but asserted that they were pulling more than their own weight in imperial taxation (pp. 28-9, 33), and that the fruits of victory were imperial rather than local (pp. 7, 49-50).[2] It would be even more difficult to-day to strike a just mean between these opposing views, than to decide ' who won the war ' of 1914-18, or to settle debts and reparations. There was, and is, no agreed basis for the proper contribution of colonies to an imperial war ; and it depended entirely on future events whether England or the Thirteen Colonies would get the most out of Canada and the Floridas.

As early as 1762 the Newcastle ministry decided to retain in the colonies a garrison of 10,000 men (several times larger than the pre-war garrisons), and to tax the colonists for its support. The Grenville ministry had to find ways and means. The Revenue Act of 1764 [3] was the first important step in a new colonial policy. This law had a double purpose, to provide revenue, and to tighten the mercantile system by strengthening the Acts of Trade and Navigation.

Since the seventeenth century the colonists had not objected to the mercantile system as such. Scattered through the documents in this book are frequent admissions, as late as 1775, that Parliament was the proper body to regulate the trade of the entire empire. Nor is it true that the prohibition of direct trade with continental Europe had been complained

---

[1] This is argued in G. L. Beer, *British Colonial Policy, 1754-65*, and E. I. McCormac, *Colonial Opposition* (Berkeley, Calif., 1911), by adopting *a priori* standards of what the colonies should have done ; but they have at least shown that some did very much more than others, and that several had almost to be bribed to defend themselves.

[2] Franklin's letter of 7 January 1766 on the Stamp Act (in all editions of his writings) is a typical expression. Note quotation from Governor Bernard's letters in Burke, *Speeches on American Affairs* (Everyman ed.), 33. Channing (*United States*, iii. 33) prints a table of outstanding colonial war debts in 1766.

[3] 4 Geo. III, c. 15. Also called the Grenville Act, Sugar Act, &c. See marginal references in the Instructions of 1769, printed below.

of, or systematically evaded. The older laws had, however, left certain loopholes for free trade, which were now closed. The Molasses Act of 1733, imposing a prohibitory duty on molasses entering the English colonies from the foreign West Indies, had never been enforced; and one of the principal objections to the Revenue Act was its imposition of a lower but still onerous duty on such molasses.[1] ' The Act of Navigation is a good Act, so are all that exclude foreign manufactures from the plantations, and every honest man will readily subscribe to them,' wrote James Otis.[2] ' Right as to Europe : but for God's sake, must we have no trade with other colonies ? '

As yet few persons had cared to look into the constitutional relationship between colonies and mother country. It would have been better for imperial unity had none but humorists done so. But the Revenue Act taught colonial lawyers that ' broadening down from precedent to precedent ' might be disastrous. ' One single Act of Parliament ', wrote James Otis, ' has set people a-thinking, in six months, more than they had done in their whole lives before.' His pamphlet, *The Rights of the British Colonies*, is the first of numerous attempts by colonial publicists, following each forward move of the British Government from 1764 to 1774, to formulate a static theory of the colonial status. The short extracts here printed (pp. 4–9) will show his interesting presentation of the ' law of nature ' theory—the law above Parliament—which provided both a justification for the American Revolution and a basis for the State and Federal Constitutions.[3]

The preamble of the Revenue Act (p. 39) announcing that the new duties were levied for revenue purposes, was the point

[1] See documents printed in Callender, *Selections from Economic History*, chapter iii, and pp. 122–35 ; and G. L. Beer, *op. cit.*, chapter xiii.
[2] *Rights of the British Colonies* (1764), 55. Cf. Burke, *op. cit.*, 24.
[3] For the historical background to this theory, see C. H. McIlwain, *The High Court of Parliament* (Yale Univ. Press, 1910), and C. Becker, *Declaration of Independence* (New York : Harcourt, Brace, 1922).

on which colonial lawyers concentrated, for they saw in it the thin end of a wedge of 'taxation without representation'. *Principiis obsta* was the cry (p. 6). This thin-end-of-the-wedge argument we find running through the whole pre-revolutionary controversy. It is a fair question whether potential rather than actual oppression did not produce the ferment in America.

On 22 March 1765, before colonial opinion had been fairly mobilized against the Revenue Act, Parliament passed the Stamp Act.[1] This law extended to the colonies, where social conditions made stamp duties particularly onerous,[2] a system long prevalent in England. Stamp duties, in sterling, were required on all legal documents, on newspapers, pamphlets, and almanacs, playing cards and dice.

The wedge was entering fast, but it was now taking the form of direct internal taxation, against which it was easy to concentrate. The issue was no longer complicated with trade regulation, as in the Revenue Act ; and it touched the pride or interest of all classes in every colony, save Nova Scotia, which showed an abnormal docility. Virginia led off with Henry's speech (of which ascending versions have been given, to show how tradition is made), and defined the issue in the Resolves of 30 May (pp. 14–18). The Stamp Act Congress in New York, the first intercolonial meeting summoned by local initiative, adopted a more reasoned and moderate set of resolves than Henry's (p. 32). 'No taxation without representation' was the cry. But were the colonies not 'virtually' represented in Parliament ? Had a colonial government any higher status than an English corporation ? Would a grant of direct representation solve the difficulty ? Daniel Dulany's and Soame Jenyns's pamphlets (pp. 18–32) are good examples of the arguments used on both sides of the water : in the

---

[1] 5 Geo. III, c. 12. Digest in Macdonald, *Documentary Source Book*, 122.

[2] See quotations from William Sumner in Callender, *op. cit.*, 137.

periodical press, the clubs, county courts, market places, and wherever men gathered together.[1]

Colonial opinion was united against the Stamp Act as on no issue before or since. Royal officials were powerless to enforce it, and the new Rockingham ministry had it repealed. At the same time the Declaratory Act of 1766 [2] was passed, declaring that King and Parliament ' have full power and authority to make laws and statutes of sufficient force and validity to bind the colonies . . . in all cases whatsoever '. This was barely noticed in the colonies, and the Revenue Act was forgotten ; the repeal of the Stamp Act seemed completely satisfactory.

A new period of agitation began in 1767, with the passage of the Townshend Acts.[3] Parliament returned to the policy tentatively begun in 1764, that of raising a revenue through customs duties. To this end the colonial customs service was completely reorganized by the creation of a special American Board of Commissioners of the Customs, resident at Boston, and directly responsible to the Treasury ; and by the establishment of new vice-admiralty courts. New duties—the ' Townshend duties '—were levied on certain British manufactures, and on tea, when entering the colonies. The moneys thus raised in the colonies, instead of going to support the garrison, were to be used to create a colonial civil list (p. 51), and thus render the royal governors and judges independent of the assemblies.

In the Instructions issued by the new American Commissioners of the Customs to their subordinates (pp. 74–83),[4] we can find exactly what acts and regulations regarding colonial trade, navigation, and manufactures were in force in 1769. The newer regulations (p. 81, note) were probably necessary to prevent the systematic smuggling that had sprung up since

---

[1] See Channing, iii, chapter iii, and M. C. Tyler, *Literary History of the Revolution*, i, chapters iii–v, for the more important pamphlets.

[2] 6 Geo. III, c. 12 : almost a word-for-word copy of the Irish Declaratory Act of 1719, 6 Geo. I, c. 5.

[3] 7 Geo. III, c. 41, 46, 56 ; 8 Geo. III, c. 22.

[4] Channing, iii, chapter iv, should be read with this document.

1764. These regulations, in view of the problems of the present Federal Government with illicit trade, were remarkably successful; but they bore with excessive severity on the merchants and shipowners of the northern colonies, where trade was already slack, and the silver required for the new duties, hard to come by.[1] The Instructions, however, do not mention the Iron Act of 1750, the Currency Act of 1764, nor the fact that Parliament had practically abolished drawbacks on foreign goods re-exported to the colonies, and levied export duties on English textiles.[2] On the other hand, Parliament aided the readjustment of American commerce by removing the English import duties on colonial corn and whale fins, and granting bounties on colonial flax, hemp, and timber.[3]

To oppose the Townshend Acts, a new formulation of the colonial relationship was necessary—Daniel Dulany had admitted too much. John Dickinson, a country gentleman who had read law at the Temple, and practised it in Philadelphia, filled the need with his *Farmer's Letters* (pp. 34-54). Their influence was great, for they caught the contradictory spirit of the period: loyalty to King and Empire, but growing American unity; dislike of mob violence, but determination to pay no tax levied by Parliament, in whatever form.

William Knox wrote the most effective reply to the ' Pennsylvania Farmer '.[4]

The agitation that followed was marked by less violence than the period of the Stamp Act, except in Boston. Domestic manufactures were encouraged, and merchants combined with

---

[1] See Callender, 63-8, 140; Becker, *Political Parties in New York*, chapter iii; *Publications Colonial Society of Mass.*, xix. 181-91. Cf. Burke, *Speeches on American Affairs*, 29.

[2] G. L. Beer, *op. cit.*, 179-88, 282; 23 Geo. II, c. 29; 4 Geo. III, c. 34; 6 Geo. III, c. 52.

[3] 4 Geo. III, c. 26, 29; 5 Geo. III, c. 45; 6 Geo. III, c. 3; 7 Geo. III, c. 4. The old naval stores and indigo bounties remained, somewhat reduced in amount. 3 Geo. III, c. 25.

[4] *The Controversy Reviewed* (London, 1769); reprinted in *Old South Leaflets*, No. 210.

politicians in an agreement not to import the taxed articles from England.[1] Although little enforced in certain places, this ' non-importation agreement ' caused English exports to the colonies to fall off almost one-half by 1769. In 1770 the North ministry, concluding that colonial duties on English manufactures were preposterous, repealed all the Townshend duties except that on tea ; but all other duties and the commissioners of the customs remained. Radical leaders wished to continue the boycott, but the merchants were sick of it, and refused to do so. Colonial trade promptly adjusted itself to the new regulations ; prosperity returned ; and by the end of 1770 there was apparently a complete reconciliation between England and the colonies—except in Boston.

II. *The Western Problem, 1763-88.*[2]

The Western problem, the problem of the unsettled parts of the North American continent, with their aboriginal inhabitants and white invaders, is as old as European colonization in America. It may be likened to a rope of many strands, now twisted in a regular pattern, but more often tangled with each other and with strands from other ropes, or tortured into

[1] A. M. Schlesinger, *Colonial Merchants and the American Revolution* (New York : Longmans ; London : P. S. King, 1918).

[2] Five works of great value and interest deal with the Western problem in whole or in part. F. J. Turner, *Frontier in American History* (New York : Henry Holt, 1921), is a collection of Professor Turner's essays, which have established the frontier as the central force in American history. The first essay, at least, should be read by every student of American history. For the facts in this Introduction I am chiefly indebted to C. W. Alvord, *The Mississippi Valley in British Politics* (2 vols., Cleveland : A. H. Clark, 1917) ; the well-presented results of deep research on the efforts of the British Government to solve the Western problem. Theodore Roosevelt, *The Winning of the West* (6 vols., Putnam's, 1889, and many later editions), is a picturesque and fairly accurate history mainly of the combative aspects of the Westward movement from 1760 to 1807. Francis Parkman, *The Conspiracy of Pontiac* (2 vols., Boston, 1851, and many later editions), is classic. These two works have a quality that no subsequent work can have ; they were written by men of keen observation and historical imagination, who had actually lived with Indians and frontiersmen.

Gordian knots which only war could sever. Of these strands we may distinguish :

(*a*) The International problem : whether the North American West would be won by France, Spain, the British Empire, or the United States, or be partitioned among them. The Peace of 1763 was an important stage in this problem, eliminating France from the contest (save as a diplomatic factor), and dividing the West, by the Mississippi river, between the British and the Spanish empires. Her new acquisitions brought Britain face to face with other aspects of the Western problem, which are closely interwoven.[1]

(*b*) The problem of Indian *v.* Backwoodsman. Should the Indian hunting grounds be reserved for them in the interest of humanity and the fur trade ; or should the advance of the white frontier be favoured at the Indians' expense ? And how were the Indians, or the frontiersmen, to be protected in their rights ? This is really the great Western problem which met the English-speaking colonists at Jamestown and Plymouth rock. Given the conditions of American society, the problem could hardly have been solved otherwise than by gradually eliminating the Indians. As Roosevelt says, the sole alternative was to keep that ' vast continent as a game preserve for squalid savages '. That was the real reason why the new British policy of 1763, illustrated in our documents, was doomed to failure, apart from the conditions of British politics ; and why the later efforts of the United States Government failed, in the long run, to protect the aborigines.

Frederic L. Paxson, *History of the American Frontier, 1763–1893* (Boston : Houghton, Mifflin Co., 1924), is an excellent compendium of the whole movement in all its aspects.

[1] The same applies to Spain, which acquired the trans-Mississippi West from France. But Spain was an old hand at the Western problem. What Spain did to meet her new responsibilities is outside the scope of this book, though by no means outside the scope of the history of the United States, which later reaped the harvest of Spain's Western policies. The reader is referred, in the first instance, to H. E. Bolton, *The Spanish Borderlands* (' Chronicles of America ', v. 23), and to A. P. Whitaker, *The Spanish-American Frontier*: 1783–95 (Houghton, Mifflin Co., 1927).

With the different conditions that obtained in Canada—a strong government, a powerful fur-trading interest, a small white population, and autocratic traditions—the Indians might have been exterminated in a more kindly fashion, and the whites less brutalized in the process.

(c) The fur trade was a problem in itself. Should it be regulated, and if so by what authority, imperial, federal, or local; or should the Indians be left to the mercy of the traders?

(d) The public land problem. How should land acquired from the Indians be disposed of, and by what authority?

(e) The political problem. What degree of self-government should be allowed to the new settlements, and what should be their relationship to the older colonies, the Empire, and (after 1775) to the United States? We may subdivide this problem into distinct strands for most of the Thirteen Colonies and States: the internal problem of adjustment between an old-settled, aristocratic, and creditor seaboard, and a new-settled, democratic, and debtor interior. This sectional issue flared into armed conflict in the Carolinas before the Revolution, and in New England after it; combined with the public land problem it has permanently influenced the history of the United States.

In the years 1763–5 these diverse strands of the Western problem were mixed with the general colonial problem, and until 1775 with English politics; after 1775 they enter into the web of American development.

In 1754, when the Seven Years' War was imminent, the British Government endeavoured to induce the Thirteen Colonies to form a union for the purpose of defence, and directing Indian relations. These had been dangerously mismanaged by individual colonies. This effort came to naught through colonial particularism.[1] But the British Government,

---

[1] G. L. Beer, *British Colonial Policy, 1754–65*, chapter ii. The text of the Albany Plan of Union may be found in William Macdonald, *Select Charters*, 253.

as a war measure, placed Indian political relations within the competence of its commander-in-chief in America, General Braddock. That ill-starred soldier laid the foundations for an imperial western policy, in 1756, by appointing two highly capable colonists, Sir William Johnson, and later, John Stuart, as Superintendents of the northern and southern Indians.

This good beginning was largely undone by the tactlessness of General Amherst, who cut off the usual presents to the north-western Indians after victory seemed secure, by the trickery of private traders, and the aggressiveness of frontiersmen. In May 1763 came a serious Indian uprising under Pontiac. Colonel Bouquet's expedition broke the back of the rebellion that summer, but the Algonkian tribes between the Great Lakes and the Ohio river were not fairly pacified before 1766.

Pontiac's rebellion proved that something must be done about the Western problem. And in the meantime the ministry had decided to retain Canada and the Floridas instead of Guadeloupe and Havana.

The Royal Proclamation of 7 October 1763 (p. 1) was the announcement of a provisional Western policy, in order to placate the Indians. Even the boundaries of the three new provinces, Canada and the Floridas, were determined with a view to keeping settlers and Indians apart. The line of demarcation, as Mr. Alvord has proved, was not intended as a permanent barrier to Westward expansion. The colonists, apparently, understood this.[1] It was not until some years had elapsed, and the Proclamation had been deliberately distorted by the Grafton ministry into a permanent barrier (p. 70), that it helped to inflame colonial sentiment against the Government.

---

[1] In the ' Declaration ' preceding the ' Remonstrance ' (p. 9) of the Pennsylvania frontiersmen, on their colony's handling of the Pontiac rebellion, they state that ' the standing of the frontier settlements depended, under God, on the almost despaired of success of His Majesty's little army, whose valour the whole frontiers acknowledge with gratitude' —whilst no mention is made of the Proclamation of 1763.

The principles of the Proclamation of 1763 were developed, through correspondence between the Lords of Trade and the Indian Superintendents, into a detailed plan for the complete control of Indian relations and white settlement, which was submitted to the Crown on 10 July 1764.[1] This Plan of 1764 recommended a well-organized Indian service under the two Indian Superintendents, fixed tariffs for trade, licences and regulations for traders, and the repeal of all conflicting colonial laws. It suggested that only the Crown—not the colonial authorities—be permitted to acquire land from the Indians. As the enforcement of this plan was expected to cost £20,000 annually, it was not formally adopted.

The failure and repeal of the Stamp Act meant the adjournment of any real effort to solve the Western problem, which at this point diverges from those of colonial relations and taxation. The Rockingham ministry let it lie, and the Chatham-Grafton ministry adopted no definite Western policy until 1768.

In the meantime, the two able Indian Superintendents, Johnson and Stuart, were enforcing the Plan of 1764 so far as their limited funds permitted. They licensed traders, issued regulations, and began to build up an efficient Indian service. They mediated peace between warring tribes, and with Pontiac's followers. They established an almost continuous line of demarcation, considerably to the west of the line of 1763, between the Indians' hunting grounds and lands open to white settlement.[2] This was done by a series of ' talks ' or conferences between Indian chiefs, the Superintendents, and colonial governors. The minutes of an important ' talk ' are here printed (p. 54) as a sample of Indian diplomacy. A later conference the same year resulted in the Treaty of Fort

[1] Printed in Alvord and Carter, *The Critical Period* (Illinois Historical Collections, x), 273-81 ; Shortt and Doughty, 433. See Comments on the Plan in pp. 62-8 below, *American Historical Review*, xx. 815-31, and *English Historical Review*, xxxiii. 37-56.

[2] See map of this line in *American Historical Review*, x. 785.

Stanwix, 5 November 1768, which established that part of the line through central New York and Pennsylvania.

Most of this frontier line was actually surveyed and marked ; it was confirmed by the Crown, and intended to endure. But the Superintendents had neither power nor authority to make it respected by the frontiersmen. No important treaty between North American Indians and colonial, imperial, or federal authorities has been much more than a truce, or a death warrant for the Indians. Their political organization was so loose that the young braves could not be restrained from occasional scalping expeditions ; and no English or American Government has been strong enough to restrain its frontiersmen from bloody outrages and reprisals.

The backwoodsman's viewpoint is presented in the Remonstrance of 13 February 1764 here printed (p. 9), from the ' distressed and bleeding frontier inhabitants of Pennsylvania ' to their own Governor and Assembly : a document which may serve as a link between (b) the problem of Indian and backwoodsman, and (c) that of political adjustment between seaboard and interior. Pennsylvania was then controlled by an oligarchy composed of Philadelphia Quakers, with some of the older German families.[1] It was kept in power by manipulating the apportionment of assemblymen against the frontier counties. Although whiggish on the taxation question, this ruling class saw eye-to-eye with the imperial government on the Western problem, its Quaker pacifism being reinforced by an interest in the fur trade, in dear land, and in cheap labour.[2] The backwoodsmen, mainly Irish protestants, could get no support or protection from the Assembly, even during Pontiac's rebellion. In December 1763 a gang known as the

[1] C. H. Lincoln, *Revolutionary Movement in Pennsylvania* (New York : Appleton, 1901).

[2] See significant extracts in the *Farmer's Letters* (pp. 48–50, below), and message from the Assembly to the Governor, 13 January 1768, alluding to the ' horrid acts of barbarity ' and ' audacious encroachments ' of the backwoodsmen, and proposing a bill for their deportation. *Minutes of Provincial Council of Penn.*, ix. 408.

' Paxton Boys ' took a cowardly revenge by wiping out the peaceful survivors of the Conestogo Indians, whose ancestors had made the celebrated ' treaty that was never broken ' with William Penn.[1] The ' Boys ' then marched on Philadelphia, with the intention of putting more refugees to the hatchet, and were only dissuaded from their purpose by the Assembly adopting their demands as to scalp bounties (p. 13). The Pennsylvania frontiersmen joined the revolutionary movement in order to democratize Pennsylvania (in which they succeeded—see pp. 162–76), as well as to obtain freedom from transatlantic control.

Another document that illustrated the internal conflict in the Colonies, but without Indian complications, is the petition of North Carolina ' Regulators ' in 1769 (pp. 83–7).[2] In this province the physical, social, and religious differences between seaboard and frontier were even more pronounced than in Pennsylvania. The highlanders were mostly Germans and Ulstermen who had come in from the north, by following the folds of the Alleghanies. Their settlements were separated by a strip of pine barrens from the lowlands, where dwelt many slaveholding planters and merchants. The lowlanders, ardent champions of ' no taxation without representation ', had held bonfires of stamped paper in 1765. At the same time they exploited the highlanders with unfair taxation and representation, and by centrally appointed judges and local officials, who grew rich through various methods of judicial robbery. When redress could not be had, the people of the frontier counties formed associations ' for regulating public grievances ', which refused to pay taxes, and broke up court sessions. Their armed bands were defeated in the ' Battle of the Alamance ' on 16 May 1771 by North Carolinians, who afterwards became patriot leaders in the War of Independence ;

[1] Franklin's ' Narrative of the Massacres ', in his *Works* (Bigelow ed.), iii. 260–86.

[2] See Channing, *United States*, iii. 122, for bibliography of the Regulator movement, and *Amer. Hist. Rev.* xxi. 320–2.

whilst many of the Regulators became loyalists, and others
emigrated beyond the mountains to escape their oppressors.

Internal conditions in Pennsylvania and the Carolinas were
exceptional; but in all the colonies there was more or less
western or agrarian discontent, which in some instances gave
the final push toward independence; in others wrested
reforms from the gentry; and in New England, aggravated
by post-war conditions, broke out in Shays's rebellion (pp. 208–
22). That the newly settled regions were on the whole more
radical than the seaboard was appreciated by the Privy
Council, which on several occasions instructed royal governors
to refuse representation in the colonial assemblies to western
settlements (p. 158).

Of all the well-meaning English officials who were forced
into contact with colonial affairs, Lord Shelburne alone had
studied the Western problem. Gifted like Chatham with
a statesman's imagination, visions of the future would
occasionally flash across his mind; but unlike Chatham,
he had no power to project a vision beyond a state paper.
In 1767 he worked out in detail a new plan for the West,[1]
favouring the immediate establishment of new colonies
beyond the Appalachians (p. 69) provided the Indians could
be induced to cede the land. Shelburne knew it was impossible
to stop westward expansion; he would therefore use it to the
end of a greater Empire. Diffusion of population, he believed,
would not only extend the market for British manufactures,
but postpone the day when the colonists would find the Acts
of Trade intolerable. His policy was the logical development
of that momentous decision in 1762, to retain Canada and the
West, instead of Guadeloupe.

Lack of money was the main obstacle to carrying out the
Plan of 1764, and it made any such scheme of western de-

---

[1] Alvord, *Mississippi Valley*, i. 343–58; *Illinois Historical Collections*,
xi. 536.

velopment as Shelburne's out of the question. The Treasury begrudged the ten to twelve thousand pounds a year that Johnson and Stuart were spending. New western colonies would have had to draw on imperial funds for the support of their civil governments, as Georgia and Nova Scotia and the Floridas were still doing. Nothing substantial could be got from the promoters of new colonial projects,[1] and the execution of most of them would have precipitated an Indian war. Proceeds of the Townshend and other customs duties in the Colonies were earmarked for existing civil lists. Shelburne proposed to raise an American fund from quit-rents on land. But it was becoming more and more difficult to collect quit-rents from the older colonies ;[2] Westerners would never have paid them. Moreover, the West had been a disappointment from the mercantile viewpoint. English fur imports fell off instead of increasing with the conquest of Canada. This was partly due to the French and Spanish, who illicitly traded with the Illinois country from New Orleans and St. Louis ; but it was mainly due to geography. English fur-trading firms, using Fort Pitt (Pittsburg) as a base, sent truck down the Ohio and up into the Illinois ; but rather than transport their fur packs up stream, and across the mountains to Philadelphia, they found it much more easy and profitable to float them down stream to the great peltry market at New Orleans. Few of these furs found their way from New Orleans into Great Britain, a fact outrageous to mercantilism. As early as 1768 important people were saying that the West would never be of any use to England until Louisiana were annexed to it. If war had broken out with Spain in 1771 over the Falkland Islands question, the conquest of Louisiana would have been its main object. It was undoubtedly true that the Western problem could never be settled in its

---

[1] See below, p. 69, n. The Vandalia Company, however, was willing to support the entire charges of civil government in its territory.

[2] B. W. Bond, *Quit-Rent System in American Colonies* (Yale Univ. Press, 1919).

international aspect, until the whole of the Mississippi Valley should be controlled by a single power.

Besides these important reasons for imperial withdrawal from the West, we must remember that the general colonial problem was becoming acute in 1768, and engaged most of the time that the politicians could spare from place-hunting, fox-hunting, and gaming. Further, it is doubtful whether any proper regulations of the fur trade could have been enforced, except under conditions of autocratic government, isolation, and monopoly, such as the Hudson's Bay Company enjoyed.

The Report of the Board of Trade and Plantations, dated 7 March 1768 (pp. 62–73), was the outcome of these ideas and considerations. The policy it recommends was adopted by the Grafton ministry. Colonial governors were instructed by the Crown to enforce it, and the promoters of Western colonies remained unsatisfied. Even the Vandalia Company, skilfully promoted by Franklin, and by such stockholders as Lord Camden, Lord Hertford, Earl Temple, and the Walpoles, never obtained its coveted grant. Not improbably its defeat was due in part to the influence of Virginians like George Washington, Richard Henry Lee, and Patrick Henry, who had rival plans regarding the twenty million acres on the Western waters, for which the Vandalia Company proposed to pay the modest sum of ten thousand pounds.

The Report of 1768 was a well-thought-out document, on the basis of mercantilism. But there was a fundamental weakness in the policy that it defined. It proposed to divert the westward movement to the North, East, and South ; yet it dismantled the only possible machinery for such diversion, the Indian service, instead of strengthening it. The Lords of Trade naïvely assumed that if westward expansion were not encouraged, it would languish. What they really accomplished by the policy of 1768 was to clear the ring for a knock-down drag-out fight between Indians and backwoodsmen.

Things now went much harder with the Indians. The

frontiersmen were solving the Western problem in their own way. South of the Ohio river, between the Appalachians and the Mississippi, lay the ' dark and bloody ground ' of Kentucky, over which northern and southern Indians hunted and fought, but where none dared to dwell. At this point the boundary line of 1768 bent westward, in order to accommodate the Vandalia Company ; but others than the Vandalia stockholders reaped the benefit. The ' long hunters ', of whom Daniel Boone is the accepted type, had visited Kentucky every year since 1765, perhaps earlier, and had brought back tales of the enormous hardwood forests, clear streams, fertile river meads, blue-grass prairies, and enormous quantities of game. In 1769 a group of backwoodsmen settled on the Watauga headwaters, on land to which they had no title. Two young Virginians among them, John Sevier and James Robertson, organized their neighbours, in 1772, into a *de facto* state, the so-called Watauga government, and made their own treaty with the Cherokees. Settlers began to crowd the wilderness trail through the Appalachians. When the War of Independence broke out, the spear-head of the westward movement had passed the mountains ; and the force behind it was irresistible.

At the same time, Governor Dunmore of Virginia, in collusion with various patriots who were soon to deprive him of his livelihood, was recklessly making grants of crown lands near or beyond the Johnson-Stuart line of 1768, to holders of land warrants issued to soldiers of the Seven Years' War.[1] The North ministry endeavoured to check them by the additional Instructions of 3 February 1774 (p. 97). Threatening, as they did, to hamper both speculators and prospective settlers, these instructions caused much irritation in Virginia, and are alluded to as a grievance both in Jefferson's ' Summary

---

[1] See p. 86 for the abuses to which this system was liable. It worked particularly badly in Kentucky, where the surveys crossed each other in hopeless tangles, and litigation over titles continued well into the nineteenth century.

View ' and the Declaration of Independence (p. 158). Eleven years later similar principles were adopted by Congress (p. 209).

The last and most important act of British Western policy before the war was the Quebec Act of 1774 (p. 103).[1] Coming out as it did contemporaneously with the Coercive Acts, this law was believed by the patriots to be an attack on American liberty. They took particular exception to the religious clauses and to the great extension of the southern boundary of Quebec. The Act was primarily intended to correct mistakes in the Proclamation of 1763 and to secure the loyalty of French Canadians against French intrigues. But it did impair the practical interests of several colonies, by annexing to Quebec the North-west, including that part for which Virginia was then fighting the Shawnee Indians. It shut out the Philadelphia fur-traders from the Ohio country, to the profit of the Scots fur-traders of Montreal. Governor Carleton, by proclamation, put the Board of Trade's Plan of 1764 into effect throughout greater Quebec, and created an efficient Indian Department. The Scots traders then formed a sort of peltry trust for the Great Lakes region. By this means the Empire retained both the trade and the allegiance of the Indians as far south as the Ohio river, well into the nineteenth century.

During the War of Independence the international aspect of the Western problem again became prominent.[2] Spain let it be known that she would join the Franco-American Alliance of 1778 at the price of the Floridas and the country between the Ohio, the Mississippi, and the Appalachians. Congress refused to pay the price, but Spain entered the war as an ally of France, and captured the British posts in the Floridas and on the lower Mississippi. She hoped to obtain her object in the peace negotiations. The American commissioners stood out for the Mississippi boundary, and obtained it so far as

---

[1] R. Coupland, *The Quebec Act* (Clarendon Press, 1925).
[2] P. C. Phillips, *The West in the Diplomacy of the American Revolution.*

England was concerned; Spain, however, recovered the Floridas
and was able to close the Mississippi to Western commerce.
Curiously enough, there were influential Americans who hoped
she would keep it closed (p. 219). In the North-west the United
States demanded everything west and south of the old boundary of Quebec. Although a handful of Virginia frontiersmen
had captured the British posts in the Illinois country, the British
Government might well have insisted on Quebec retaining its
Ohio boundary of 1774. France encouraged it to do so, hoping
thereby to obtain compensation for Spain. But Lord Shelburne's ministry accepted the present American-Canadian
boundary as a compromise.

American independence meant, among other things, that
the same western problems which formerly vexed Whitehall
now had to be faced by Congress. As regards the Indians,
little was accomplished before 1790; but as regards the
opening up, disposal, and government of the Indians' former
hunting grounds, Congress showed foresight and statesman-
ship.

The western land problem [1] had, in the first place, an
important bearing on the Federal Government. There was
not an inch of the West between the Great Lakes and the
Ohio that was not claimed by one or more of seven out of the
Thirteen States, by virtue of their colonial charters. The
Articles of Confederation (p. 178), to go into effect, had to be
ratified by every State. It seemed unjust to the states with
definite western boundaries, that they should have no part
and share in the western domain which would be won with
their aid. Maryland withheld her ratification, pending provision for a federal territory. The New York legislature
broke the deadlock, early in 1780, by promising to cede its
western land claims to the United States; and Congress
urged the others to do likewise. On 10 October 1780 Congress

[1] Channing, *United States*, iii, chapter xvii

adopted a resolution announcing a western policy radically different from the colonial policy of any European power (p. 204). Maryland was then induced to ratify the Articles of Confederation. In 1784 Virginia, with a superb gesture, ceded to the United States her excellent claims to the country north of the Ohio; and the lesser claimants soon followed.

In 1784, then, Congress assumed responsibility for an immense domain, the North-west Territory; and by the Articles of Confederation (p. 183) it acquired the same jurisdiction over Indian relations that the British Government had claimed. Like that government, Congress was hampered by Indian hostility, frontier lawlessness, local interference, and lack of money.

Congress feebly attempted to regulate the fur trade. It obtained land cessions from the Iroquois and the North-west Indians, who in alliance with Britain had waged a terrible and relentless war against the backwoods settlements; but most of these treaties it was unable to enforce. New forts were built on the Ohio, and in 1787 a detachment of the United States army moved down the right bank, burning the cabins of frontiersmen who had staked out claims there by 'tomahawk right'; but it was not strong enough to prevent repeated Indian forays into Kentucky and Virginia. In the transmontane region south of the Ohio, where *de facto* state governments had been set up by the pioneers, and where no land claims had been made over to the Confederacy, the period 1785–8 was one of bitter race warfare. The westward movement had obtained such a start that even the stronger federal government of 1789 could do little more than give the Indians a breathing-space, pending their final removal or extinction.

In respect of the national domain north of the Ohio, the Congress of the Confederation did much to solve the land and local government problems. It was besieged by the same conflicting interests as its English predecessor. Veterans desired to cash their land warrants. Companies of speculators were anxious to buy millions of full-sized acres for thousands of depreciated dollars. Southerners wished to parcel out the land on the principle of first come first choice. New Englanders preferred to reproduce their beloved townships, with church and school. Certain gentlemen of influence hoped to renew the British policy of 1768 (p. 220). Out of this conflict of forces, Congress passed two important ordinances, which not only founded a national land system, but bridged the gap between wilderness and statehood, left open by the Resolution of 10 October 1780.

The Ordinance of 20 May 1785 [1] (p. 204) established the New England principle of rectangular survey prior to sale, as well as those methods of survey and allotment which have since been fundamental in the land system of the United States. The ' range ', the ' township ' six miles square, and the ' section ' of one square mile or 640 acres, have been the standard units of western settlement, from Pennsylvania to the Pacific. The system was a compromise between South and East ; between those who wanted quick sales to pay off the national debt, and those who wished to discourage the migration of labour. The principle of a reserve for purposes of education (p. 206) has provided many of the western States with valuable school funds.

Hostile Indians, and other causes, so delayed the surveys under this Ordinance that no land was placed on sale by the Confederation before 1787. In the meantime speculators approached Congress (as earlier they had Whitehall) with offers to purchase large tracts yet unsurveyed. Congress, desperately in need of money, was unable to resist ; and in order to provide the swarms of expected settlers with a government, it passed the famous Northwest Ordinance of 1787 (p. 226).

This Northwest Ordinance, based largely on an earlier report by Jefferson, belongs to the first rank of American

[1] Cf. the Royal Instructions of 1774 (p. 97).

constitutional documents. Noteworthy alike are the bill of rights, the provisions for representative government, for future statehood, and for the extinction of slavery. It provided the United States with a colonial system, on the basis of equal rights between new and old communities. It was the most important single step toward the solution of the Western problem, which never can be completely solved as long as the United States retains its agreeable diversity of races and sectional interests.[1]

III. *The Crisis, 1772–6.*

Constitutional calm, as we have seen, succeeded the agitation of 1767–70. Yet parliamentary taxation of the colonies was now an established fact. The unrepealed duties (pp. 79–80), including threepence a pound on tea, were being efficiently collected by the new American customs service, with the somewhat interested aid (p. 75) of the Royal Navy. In ten years from 1767, out of £257,000 taken in at colonial customs houses, £83,000 was remitted to England, and £32,000 expended on colonial civil lists.[2] This allocation had an important effect on the colonial governments (p. 93), especially in Massachusetts, where Governor Hutchinson, a royal official who was the more hated because of native stock, began to use a high hand with his assembly.[3] Yet prosperity was increasing, and most colonial leaders were

[1] In the Federal Convention of 1787 unsuccessful efforts were made by Gouverneur Morris and others to place restrictions on the admission of western territories to statehood. Subsequent efforts of rival interests, north and south, to obtain the support and control of the West ; struggles of the West to emancipate itself from dependence on eastern capital ; attempts of the Federal Government to deal justly with Indians and frontiersmen, and international rivalries for the fur trade, belong to later American history. See Turner and Merk, *References on the History of the West* (Harvard University Press, 1922).

[2] Statistics in Public Record Office, T. 1–482 ; summarized in Channing, iii. 89–90, 154.

[3] For the local situation see Palfrey, *New England*, v, chapter ix ; Hutchinson, *Massachusetts-Bay*, iii, chapter iii (London, 1828), and Alden Bradford (ed.), *Massachusetts State Papers* (Boston, 1824).

willing to let the future take care of itself. 'Our great security lies in our growing strength, both in numbers and wealth,' wrote Franklin to a Boston radical early in 1773.[1] 'Thence we may expect in a few years a total change of measures with regard to us.' Samuel Adams, however, believed the exact contrary. 'The people are paying the unrighteous tribute,' he wrote in 1771,[2] 'in hopes that the nation will at length revert to justice. But before that time comes, it is to be feared they will be so accustomed to bondage, as to forget they were ever free.' In order to arouse the province from its lethargy, he made a clever use of the Boston town meeting (pp. 87–96). First drawing the Governor's fire to obtain the appointment of a committee of correspondence, Adams and Warren drafted a statement of the 'Rights of the Colonists' with a 'List of Infringements', which were circulated in pamphlet form among the other Massachusetts towns. 'It told them a hundred rights, of which they had never heard before, and a hundred grievances which they had never before felt,' said Wedderburn. Chatham's comment was 'These worthy New Englanders ever feel as old Englanders ought to do'.[3]

Over seventy-five towns replied in kind, and appointed their committees of correspondence.[4] Their network soon covered New England; and, on Virginian initiative, it was completed by the appointment of standing committees of correspondence by the lower branches of colonial legislatures. The agitation simmered down during 1773; but in the committees of correspondence Samuel Adams had created a political machine which was to be of immense service when a real issue arose.

---

[1] *Works* (Bigelow ed.), v. 86.
[2] *Writings* (see p. 91), ii. 189.
[3] *Letters of Gov. Hutchinson* (2nd ed., London, 1774), 113; George Bancroft, *United States* (1854 ed.), vi. 434.
[4] For the political activities of a typical New England town at this period, see extracts from the Lexington records in *Old South Leaflets*, No. 156.

It was the 'Boston Tea-party' (16 December 1773) that brought on the next crisis. With the causes [1] of that momentous jettison we are not so much concerned here as with the results:—inflaming English public opinion, strengthening the 'die-hard' element in Cabinet and Parliament, and producing an unwise attempt at punishment and cure. The 'Coercive Acts', as they were called in America, included the Boston Port Act, the Massachusetts Government Act (p. 100), the Administration of Justice Act, and the Quartering Act,[2] of March–June 1774. All but the last had reference only to Massachusetts; but instead of isolating that province, as had been hoped, these Acts demonstrated a parliamentary power more dangerous to colonial liberty than mere taxing; and thus rallied twelve continental colonies to Massachusetts. On the invitation of the Virginia House of Burgesses, twelve colonies—or rather, twelve committees of correspondence—sent delegates to Philadelphia in September 1774, to consult as to what measures should be taken to procure a repeal of the Acts, and a redress of other outstanding grievances.[3] It was this Continental Congress which, beginning as an extra-legal consultative body, developed into the federal government of an independent republic.

As the Coercive Acts raised, constitutionally, no question of taxation, the distinctions of the Pennsylvania Farmer became obsolete. To meet this situation, the more advanced radicals created a theory of the British Empire which, boldly ignoring precedent, left the colonies entirely beyond parliamentary competence, connected with Great Britain only through the Crown. Of pamphlets presenting this view, the most logical was 'Considerations on the Legislative Authority of the British Parliament' (p. 104) by James Wilson, a Scots

[1] Channing, iii. 128–30, and Schlesinger, *Colonial Merchants*, 262 ff.

[2] 14 Geo. III, c. 19, 39, 45, 54. Cf. Introduction, part II, on Quebec Act.

[3] See resolutions of the local conventions and Assemblies appointing delegates, in *Journals of Continental Congress* (W. C. Ford, ed., Washington, 1904), i. 15–24.

graduate of the University of Edinburgh, who had read law with John Dickinson. It should be compared with the ' Summary View of the Rights of the British Colonies ' of Thomas Jefferson,[1] and with the ' Novanglus ' papers of John Adams (p. 125), the learned cousin of Samuel Adams. There was little likelihood of such a theory being accepted in England ; although Lord Camden, in speaking against the Declaratory Act of 1766, had pointed out the analogy of the Channel Islands.[2] Even Burke and Chatham were obsessed with the ' bugaboo of sovereignty '.

The Continental Congress found Wilson's doctrine too advanced. For a few days it played with Galloway's interesting Plan of Union (p. 116), then cast it aside as impracticable. The Declaration and Resolves passed by the Congress on 14 October 1774 (p. 118) were a compromise between the radical and the conservative delegates. They were followed by the Association (p. 122), a scheme of commercial retaliation to go into effect if the Coercive Acts were not soon repealed, and to be enforced by the committees of correspondence.

For the effect of these measures on English opinion, one should read the debates in the House of Commons from 20 January to 1 February 1775, on the motion to withdraw the troops from Boston, on the petitions of English merchants against the Coercive Acts, and on Chatham's bill for settling the troubles in America.[3] Was there any essential difference between the principles of Chatham's bill, as outlined in his speech of 1 February (or of Burke's famous speech of 22 March on conciliation with America), and the resolves of the Continental Congress ? However that may be, Chatham and Burke

[1] *Writings of Jefferson* (Ford ed.), i. 421 ; 4 Force's *American Archives*, i. 690 ; and contemporary pamphlet editions (Philadelphia and London, 1774).

[2] R. G. Adams, *Political Ideas of the American Revolution* (Univ. of N.C., 1922), 128. This excellent little book discusses the different attempts to restate imperialism in terms of dominion home rule.

[3] Hansard, *Parliamentary History*, xviii. 149–215.

did not prevail ; instead, Parliament on 27 February passed the ' Conciliatory Resolution ' of Lord North (p. 138, note) ; an unsatisfactory compromise—Burke's ' ransom by auction ' —on the taxation question, leaving the Coercive Acts in force.

War began on 19 April 1775, when the Boston garrison clashed with provincial militia at Lexington and Concord. On 10 May the Continental Congress reassembled. It represented all phases of colonial opinion except the out-and-out loyalists, who, owing to the drastic measures of local committees, were now becoming fairly numerous. Congress adopted the militia besieging Boston, as the continental army ; appointed Washington commander-in-chief, and issued the Declaration of Causes of taking up Arms (p. 141)— a joint product of the conservative Dickinson and the radical Jefferson. Many, but not all [1] of the radicals now believed independence to be the only solution ; but they were content to wait for public opinion to develop. The majority, both in Congress and the country, flattered itself that commercial pressure, combined with military success, would discredit the North ministry, produce a political crisis in England, and place Burke and Chatham in power. Independence sentiment gained ground very slowly. Between November 1775 and January 1776, four of the middle colonies instructed their delegates to oppose independence ; but before the end of the year Congress decided to seek French aid. [2]

By the opening of 1776 it became clear that the American policy was a failure. War had widened the chasm instead of closing the breach ; and the Association was hurting the colonies more than England. At this moment appeared at Philadelphia an amazing pamphlet by an Englishman with a stormy career before him. Thomas Paine's' Common

---

[1] See Warren's letters (p. 139), and cf. Jefferson's, of 25 August, in *Writings* (Ford ed.), i. 482, or *Hist. MSS. Comm., Dartmouth MSS.,* ii. 361.
[2] Callender, 163.

Sense '[1] was the first important republican tract to be issued in America, the first to turn colonial resentment against George III, and the first to present cogent arguments for independence. Provincial congresses began to instruct their Continental delegates in that sense (p. 146). On 6 April Congress declared American commerce open to the world. In May, it instructed the colonies to form State governments (p. 148). South Carolina had already done so (p. 146), and Virginia soon followed (pp. 149–56). Congress still hesitated before the final step ; the conservatives wished first to have a look at the terms that Admiral Lord Howe was rumoured to be bringing,[2] and the radicals were equally zealous to have independence an accomplished fact before that mission arrived. A political victory of the radical, frontier element in Pennsylvania over the local conservatives hastened matters. On 2 July a resolution for independence was passed by the Continental Congress, and on 4 July the famous Declaration (p. 157) was adopted.

Every one who studies the American Revolution must ask himself whether independence was, after all, the only way to avoid ' absolute tyranny '. The royal instructions to the peace commission of 1778 (p. 186) are relevant to this question. These were the most favourable terms the British Government could bring itself to offer, after Burgoyne's surrender, in the hope of averting the French alliance. Would they have satisfied America if proposed before 1776 ? Or, supposing they had been accepted as a compromise, would they have removed the causes of the conflict, and permitted colonial development toward dominion home rule, or independence by mutual consent ?

---

[1] To be found in numerous contemporary editions, in Paine's *Complete Works* (M. D. Conway, ed. Putnam's), and in a cheap edition published by Peter Eckler, New York.

[2] Lord Howe merely had power to issue pardons under the Prohibitory Act (16 Geo. III, c. 5, s. 44), and to use his good offices with Parliament for a redress of grievances.

IV. *The State and Federal Constitutions, 1776–88.*

' The manner in which free governments have been established in America ' (p. 355) is another remarkable phase of the Revolution. State and federal governments were substituted for the old colonial system ; and for their successful operation statesmen were found, and public opinion created. Self-government, under the colonial system, made this possible ; yet the colonists had had no experience with federalism, and no opportunity to draft charters, since the seventeenth century.

The transition from colonial to state government was, in most instances, carried out by the ' provincial congresses ' or ' conventions ' of 1775–6. These popularly elected bodies, which assumed legislative and executive authority in each colony [1] after the royal governors had dissolved the colonial assemblies, followed the recommendation of 15 May 1776 by the Continental Congress (p. 148), drafted state constitutions for their constituents, and put them into effect without popular ratification. Only three of the constitutions of 1776 contained any provision for subsequent amendment, and they gave the power to the state legislature.

Virginia's constitution of 1776 (pp. 149–56) was the first successful state constitution, and a model to most of the other states.

George Mason, a wealthy planter steeped in the traditions of English liberty, drafted both the Bill of Rights and the greater part of the Frame of Government. The latter was a compromise between the radical westerners, who favoured the wild constitutional notions of Paine's ' Common Sense ', and the conservative easterners, who desired a life senate and a strong governor. The convention was also much

---

[1] Rhode Island and Connecticut, however, were able to retain their seventeenth-century charters, on the joint-stock model, as state constitutions by a mere change of preamble.

influenced by John Adams's ' Thoughts on Government '.[1] On the whole the old-settled, slaveholding eastern section won, by obtaining a fixed basis of representation (ss. 5, 6, cf. p. 359), with no change in the franchise (s. 7) ; which meant, in general, that no one could vote unless he possessed fifty acres of improved, or one hundred of unimproved land. As a concession to popular prejudice against executive power, the governor was made a mere creature of the legislature. Nevertheless, the Virginia constitution was imitated by most of the states, and lasted until 1830.

The Pennsylvania constitution (p. 162) with its manhood suffrage, reflected the recent victory of the democratic element in that state, and incorporated two favourite notions of Benjamin Franklin, a unicameral legislature and a plural executive. Although the standard of the radicals, this constitution was a most unsuccessful experiment ; imitated only by the frontier state of Vermont, and superseded in Pennsylvania as early as 1790.

The War of Independence emphasized the faults of these early state constitutions. There was too much restraint on the executive and judiciary ; too little on the legislatures, who were not always composed of ' persons most noted for wisdom and virtue ' (p. 165). The New York constitution (1777) showed some improvement, but that of Massachusetts (1780) [2] was the more permanent. The town meetings of that state were so many debating societies of political theory during the war, and from one of them came the first recorded suggestion that a constitution should be drafted by a convention specially elected for that purpose, and submitted for approval to the people (p. 176). After a false start by the legislature, that mode was tried in 1779–80. The con-

---

[1] Adams's *Works*, iv. 185–203 ; cf. C. H. Ambler, *Sectionalism in Virginia* (Univ. of Chicago Press, 1910), and Eckenrode, *Revolution in Virginia* (Houghton, Mifflin, 1916).

[2] Printed in *Old South Leaflets*, No. 206, and in all volumes of the state laws. Cf. ' Struggle over adoption of the Constitution of Mass. in *Proceedings Mass. Hist. Society*, l. 353.

vention delegated to John Adams the actual drafting of the constitution. As a working government, it was a vast improvement over its predecessors, and has not yet been superseded ; it was a deliberate and successful attempt to further efficiency, safety, and order, even at the expense of liberty. The franchise was more restricted than under the colonial government, though not so much as in Virginia ; the governor was elected by the voters and given an appointive power and a suspensive veto ; the senate frankly represented wealth, being apportioned according to the taxable property of the state ; the judges of the supreme court were appointed by the governor, and held office during good behaviour. A more distinct religious establishment was adopted than in any other state save South Carolina ; separation of Church and State being the exception rather than the rule in American revolutionary constitutions.

Federal government was a different, and far more difficult, problem ; for the people of the states were of no mind to part with the powers they had taken over from Crown and Parliament. During the first two years of the war, the Continental Congress wielded considerable power without express authority. Constitutionally, it was little more than a supreme war council of thirteen allies. The Articles of Confederation (p. 178), drafted in 1777 but not ratified (for reasons connected with the Western problem) until 1781, legalized the existing situation. Congress, as organized in 1774, remained the sole organ of the Confederacy, and, in general, was granted only those powers which, before 1775, the Crown and Parliament had exercised without question. The states retained full control over taxation, commerce, and customs duties. This Confederation might have devoloped into an efficient federal government had not the process of amendment been so difficult, and the times out of joint.

To some extent the American Revolution was a social upheaval. It did not in any marked degree change the laws

of property, but through the confiscation of loyalists' estates
the distribution of property was changed; and the committees of correspondence gave thousands of poor men a
taste of power (p. 215).[1] Chattel slavery was abolished in
some of the northern states, relics of feudalism such as
titles of nobility, quitrents, entails, primogeniture, tithes,
and game laws were swept away (pp. 173-4, 226) in the
proprietary colonies and the south. Virginia's Statute of
Religious Liberty (p. 206), like Virginia's Bill of Rights,
was a milestone of freedom. Post-war economic depression [2]
widened the class and sectional divisions which the war had
partially concealed. Farmers of the interior, finding themselves in debt to the merchants, demanded cheap money.
Rhode Island yielded, with disastrous results; but in Massachusetts, where the distress was greater (pp. 208-10, 222),
the merchants controlled the state senate, and were thus
able to resist. In 1786 unlawful assemblies in the interior
counties began to break up sittings of the courts, in order
to prevent distraint for debts or taxes; and the people held
county conventions (p. 210) to present their demands. Loyal
militia put down the armed bands of Dan Shays, but not
before thinking men throughout the country had been alarmed
by the prospect of anarchy, or a second revolution (pp. 214-18,
221-3). The reports of the French chargé d'affaires (pp. 219-
25), a keen observer who later played a leading rôle in French
diplomacy, give an accurate picture of the events and the
atmosphere out of which came the Federal Convention of
1787.

The Federal Convention was an assembly of notables,
uniting the best intellects from the conservative groups,
north and south. Their grasp of political theory and the
realities of government is illustrated by the selections here
printed (pp. 233 ff.) from Madison's and Yates's notes of the
debates.

---

[1] Cf. Callender, 168-74.   [2] Callender, chapter v.

The Convention had been authorized only to prepare amendments to the Articles of Confederation.[1] Delegates from the larger states, who had most reason to be dissatisfied with the Confederation, introduced on the 29 May, the opening day of debate, the Randolph or Virginia Resolutions (p. 235), a plan for a new, and national government. For two weeks this plan was debated, and a national constitution was in process of formation, when the delegates of the smaller states (New York, New Jersey, Maryland, Connecticut, Delaware) countered with the New Jersey Plan (p. 251), a mere revamped Confederation. The small states did not object to nationalism as such ; indeed, their plan contained one of the strongest clauses in the Constitution (Art. VI, § 2) ; but they did object to losing the equality of representation they enjoyed in the Confederation. After Alexander Hamilton had communicated his nationalist ideas (p. 254), some important decentralizing amendments were made in the Virginia plan, and again it became the basis of discussion. Questions of detail frequently brought on a debate on fundamental principles, and the future development of America was prophesied (pp. 263–5). A deadlock between the large and the small states was broken on 16 July by the ' great compromise '—equal representation in the Senate, representation determined by the ' federal ratio ' (Art. II, s. II, § 3) in the House (cf. pp. 266–74). From 6 August to 10 September the Convention debated, clause by clause, a draft based upon the amended Virginia plan, submitted by the committee on detail. During this period the members were inclined to consider each question impartially, on its merits (pp. 274–81) ; but on questions involving local or economic interests they divided sectionally, the southern states and planting interest against the northern states and commercial interest (pp. 282–92). The resulting constitution (pp. 292–307), the result of compromise, was in Madison's phrase ' partly

[1] See Madison's paper on the ' Vices ' of the Confederation in his *Works* (Hunt ed.), ii. 361.

federal, partly national '. It was called the Federal rather than the National Constitution in order to disarm state prejudice against a ' consolidated ' government.

The process of ratification in the state conventions was long, and doubtful to the last.[1] In no state was the contest more severe, and the discussion more able than in Virginia, where political speculation was the chief intellectual occupation of the gentry. Patrick Henry presented the anti-federalist and state rights view, so cleverly appealing to popular prejudice that the federalists were placed on the defensive (pp. 317–21, 332). Madison's Speech of 6 June is one of the best brief statements of the nature of the Federal Union (p. 332). The speech of John Marshall, the future Chief Justice (p. 340), foretold the part of the Supreme Court in constitutional history. Finally, the contest resolved itself into the question whether Virginia would ratify with express reservations ; or unconditionally, with recommendation that a bill of rights be shortly added by amendment (p. 352). Although Patrick Henry invoked the spectre of slave emancipation (p. 353), in order to defeat ratification, he greatly contributed, with other anti-federalists, to the success of the Constitution by loyally accepting the majority decision (p. 361).

Virginia was the tenth state to ratify ; New York shortly followed ; but North Carolina and Rhode Island only joined the Union after Washington's inauguration (30 April 1789) as first President of the United States of America. Within three years a Federal Bill of Rights (pp. 363–4) was adopted by constitutional amendment.

[1] Summary in A. J. Beveridge, *John Marshall* (Houghton, Mifflin, 1916), i. Robert Livingston Schuyler, *The Constitution of the United States* (Macmillan, 1923), is the best short account of the constitutional movement.

SOURCES AND DOCUMENTS

FROM THE ROYAL PROCLAMATION ON NORTH AMERICA,[1] 7 OCTOBER 1763

BY THE KING. A PROCLAMATION. GEORGE, R.

WHEREAS we have taken into our royal consideration the extensive and valuable acquisitions in America secured to our Crown by the late definitive treaty of peace concluded at Paris the 10th day of February last ; and being desirous that all our loving subjects, as well of our kingdom as of our colonies in America, may avail themselves, with all convenient speed, of the great benefits and advantages which must accrue therefrom to their commerce, manufactures, and navigation ; we have thought fit, with the advice of our Privy Council, to issue this our Royal Proclamation, hereby to publish and declare to all our loving subjects that we have, with the advice of our said Privy Council, granted our letters patent under our Great Seal of Great Britain, to erect within the countries and islands ceded and confirmed to us by the said treaty, four distinct and separate governments, styled and called by the names of Quebec, East Florida, West Florida, and Grenada, and limited and bounded as follows, viz. :

First, the Government of Quebec, bounded on the Labrador coast by the river St. John, and from thence by a line drawn from the head of that river, through the lake St. John, to the south end of the lake Nipissim ; from whence the said line, crossing the river St. Lawrence and the lake Champlain in 45 degrees of north latitude, passes along the high lands which divide the rivers that empty themselves into the said river St. Lawrence from those which fall into the sea ; . . .

Secondly, the Government of East Florida, bounded to the westward by the gulf of Mexico and the Apalachicola river ; to the northward, by a line drawn from that part of the said river where the Chatahoochee and Flint rivers meet, to the

[1] *Annual Register* for 1763, pp. 208–13. Also printed in full, from the manuscript, in Shortt and Doughty, *Documents relating to Constitutional History of Canada* (1918 ed.), i. 163–5.

source of the St. Mary's river, and by the course of the said
river to the Atlantic Ocean : . . .

Thirdly, the Government of West Florida, bounded to the
. . . westward, by the lake Pontchartrain, the lake Maurepas,
and the river Mississippi ; to the northward, by a line
drawn due east from that part of the river Mississippi which
lies in 31 degrees north latitude, to the river Apalachicola or
Chatahoochee ; and to the eastward, by the said river. . . .

We have also, with the advice of our Privy Council aforesaid,
annexed to our Province of Georgia all the lands lying between
the rivers Altamaha and St. Mary's.

.   .   .   .

And whereas it is just and reasonable, and essential to our
interest and the security of our colonies, that the several
nations or tribes of Indians with whom we are connected, and
who live under our protection, should not be molested or
disturbed in the possession of such parts of our dominions and
territories as, not having been ceded to or purchased by us,
are reserved to them, or any of them, as their hunting-grounds ;
we do therefore, with the advice of our Privy Council, declare
it to be our royal will and pleasure, that no Governor or
commander in chief, in any of our colonies of Quebec, East
Florida, or West Florida, do presume, upon any pretence
whatever, to grant warrants of survey, or pass any patents
for lands beyond the bounds of their respective governments,
as described in their commissions ; as also that no Governor
or commander in chief of our other colonies or plantations in
America do presume for the present, and until our further
pleasure be known, to grant warrants of survey or pass patents
for any lands beyond the heads or sources of any of the rivers
which fall into the Atlantic Ocean from the west or north-
west ; or upon any lands whatever, which, not having been
ceded to or purchased by us, as aforesaid, are reserved to
the said Indians, or any of them.

And we do further declare it to be our royal will and
pleasure, for the present as aforesaid, to reserve under our
sovereignty, protection, and dominion, for the use of the said
Indians, all the land and territories not included within the
limits of our said three new governments, or within the limits
of the territory granted to the Hudson's Bay Company; as also
all the land and territories lying to the westward of the sources
of the rivers which fall into the sea from the west and north-

west as aforesaid ; and we do hereby strictly forbid, on pain of our displeasure, all our loving subjects from making any purchases or settlements whatever, or taking possession of any of the lands above reserved, without our special leave and license for that purpose first obtained.

And we do further strictly enjoin and require all persons whatever, who have either wilfully or inadvertently seated themselves upon any lands within the countries above described, or upon any other lands which, not having been ceded to or purchased by us, are still reserved to the said Indians as aforesaid, forthwith to remove themselves from such settlements.

And whereas great frauds and abuses have been committed in the purchasing lands of the Indians, to the great prejudice of our interests, and to the great dissatisfaction of the said Indians ; in order, therefore, to prevent such irregularities for the future, and to the end that the Indians may be convinced of our justice and determined resolution to remove all reasonable cause of discontent, we do, with the advice of our Privy Council, strictly enjoin and require, that no private person do presume to make any purchase from the said Indians of any lands reserved to the said Indians within those parts of our colonies where we have thought proper to allow settlement ; but that if at any time any of the said Indians should be inclined to dispose of the said lands, the same shall be purchased only for us, in our name, at some public meeting or assembly of the said Indians, to be held for that purpose by the Governor or commander in chief of our colony respectively within which they shall lie : and in case they shall lie within the limits of any proprietary government, they shall be purchased only for the use and in the name of such proprietaries, conformable to such directions and instructions as we or they shall think proper to give for that purpose. And we do, by the advice of our Privy Council, declare and enjoin, that the trade with the said Indians shall be free and open to all our subjects whatever, provided that every person who may incline to trade with the said Indians do take out a license for carrying on such trade, from the Governor or commander in chief of any of our colonies respectively where such person shall reside, and also give security to observe such regulations as we shall at any time think fit, by ourselves or commissaries to be appointed for this purpose, to direct and appoint for the benefit of the said trade. And we do hereby authorize, enjoin, and require the Governors and commanders in chief of all our colonies respectively, as well those under our immediate government as those under the government and direction of proprietaries, to grant such licenses without fee or reward, taking especial care to insert therein a condition that such license shall be void, and the security forfeited, in case the person to whom the same is granted shall refuse or neglect to observe such regulations as we shall think proper to prescribe as aforesaid.

And we do further expressly enjoin and require all officers whatever, as well military as those employed in the management and direction of Indian affairs within the territories reserved as aforesaid, for the use of the said Indians, to seize and apprehend all persons whatever who, standing charged with treasons, misprisions of treason, murders, or other felonies or misdemeanors, shall fly from justice and take refuge in the said territory, and to send them under a proper guard to the colony where the crime was committed of which they shall stand accused, in order to take their trial for the same.

Given at our Court at St. James's, the 7th day of October 1763, in the third year of our reign.

FROM JAMES OTIS'S ' RIGHTS OF THE COLONIES '

The Rights of the British Colonies asserted and proved. By James Otis, Esq., Boston, 1764.

[p. 8] It is, however, true in fact and experience, as the great, the incomparable Harrington has most abundantly demonstrated in his *Oceana*, and other divine writings, that Empire follows the balance of property : 'Tis also certain that property in fact generally confers power, tho' the possessor of it may not have much more wit than a mole or a musquash. And this is too often the cause, that riches are sought after, without the least concern about the right application of them. But is the fault in the riches, or the general law of nature, or the unworthy possessor ? It will never follow from all this, that government is rightfully founded on property, alone. What shall we say then ? Is not government founded on grace ? No. Nor on force ? No. Nor on compact ? Nor property ? Not altogether on either. Has it any solid foundation ? any chief corner stone, but what accident, chance or confusion may lay one moment and destroy the next? I think it has an everlasting foundation in the unchangeable will of God, the author of nature, whose laws never vary. The same omniscient, omnipotent, infinitely good and gracious Creator of the universe, who has been pleased to make it necessary that what we call matter should gravitate, for the celestial bodies to roll round their axes, dance their orbits and perform their various revolutions in that beautiful order and concert, which we all admire, has made it equally necessary that from Adam and Eve to these degenerate days, the different sexes should sweetly attract each other, form societies of single families, of which larger bodies and communities are as naturally, mechanically, and necessarily combined, as the dew of Heaven and the soft distilling rain is collected by the all enliv'ning heat of the sun. Government is therefore most evidently founded on the necessities of our nature. It is by no means an arbitrary thing, depending merely on compact or human will for its existence.

[p. 30] 'The natural liberty of man is to be free from any superior power on earth, and not to be under the will or legislative authority of man, but only to have the law of nature for his rule.' This is the liberty of independant states; this is the liberty of every man out of society, and who has a mind to live so; which liberty is only abridged in certain instances, not lost to those who are born in or voluntarily enter into society; this gift of God cannot be annihilated.

The Colonists being men, have a right to be considered as equally entitled to all the rights of nature with the Europeans, and they are not to be restrained in the exercise of any of these rights, but for the evident good of the whole community. By being or becoming members of society, they have not renounced their natural liberty in any greater degree than other good citizens, and if 'tis taken from them without their consent, they are so far enslaved.

[p. 32] I also lay it down as one of the first principles from whence I intend to deduce the civil rights of the British colonies that all of them are subject to, and dependent on Great Britain; and that therefore as over subordinate governments, the Parliament of Great Britain has an undoubted power and lawful authority to make Acts for the general good, that by naming them, shall and ought to be equally binding, as upon the subjects of Great Britain within the realm. This principle,

I presume, will be readily granted on the other side the Atlantic. It has been practised upon for twenty years to my knowledge, in the province of the Massachusetts-Bay ; and I have ever received it, that it has been so from the beginning, in this and the sister provinces, thro' the continent.

. . . .

[p. 39] The power of Parliament is uncontroulable, but by themselves, and we must obey. They only can repeal their own Acts. There would be an end of all government, if one or a number of subjects or subordinate provinces should take upon them so far to judge of the justice of an Act of Parliament, as to refuse obedience to it. If there was nothing else to restrain such a step, prudence ought to do it, for forceably resisting the Parliament and the King's laws, is high treason. Therefore let the Parliament lay what burthens they please on us, we must, it is our duty to submit and patiently bear them, till they will be pleased to relieve us. And 'tis to be presumed the wisdom and justice of that august assembly, always will afford us relief by repealing such Acts, as through mistake, or other human infirmities, have been suffered to pass, if they can be convinced that their proceedings are not constitutional, or not for the common good. . . .

[p. 41] Reasons may be given, why an Act ought to be repeal'd, and yet obedience must be yielded to it till that repeal takes place. If the reasons that can be given against an Act are such as plainly demonstrate that it is against natural equity, the executive courts will adjudge such Act void. It may be questioned by some, tho' I make no doubt of it, whether they are not obliged by their oaths to adjudge such Act void. . . .

[p. 42] I cannot but observe here, that if the Parliament have an equitable right to tax our trade, 'tis indisputable that they have as good an one to tax the lands, and everything else. . . . There is no foundation for the distinction some make in England, between an internal and an external tax on the colonies. By the first is meant a tax on trade, by the latter a tax on land, and the things on it. A tax on trade is either a tax of every man in the province, or 'tis not. If 'tis not a tax on the whole, 'tis unequal and unjust, that a heavy burden should be laid on the trade of the colonies, to maintain an army of soldiers, custom-house officers, and fleets of guard-ships ; all which, the incomes of both trade and land would not furnish

means to support so lately as the last war, when all was at
stake, and the colonies were reimbursed in part by Parliament.
How can it be supposed that all of a sudden the trade of the
colonies alone can bear all this terrible burden. The late
acquisitions in America, as glorious as they have been, and as
beneficial as they are to Great-Britain, are only a security to
these colonies against the ravages of the French and Indians.
Our trade upon the whole is not, I believe, benefited by them
one groat. . . .

. . . .

[p. 47] To say the Parliament is absolute and arbitrary is
a contradiction. The Parliament cannot make 2 and 2, 5 :
Omnipotency cannot do it. The supreme power in a state is
ius dicere only :—*ius dare*, strictly speaking, belongs alone to
God. Parliaments are in all cases to declare what is for the
good of the whole; but it is not the declaration of Parliament
that makes it so : There must be in every instance a higher
authority, viz. God. Should an Act of Parliament be against
any of His natural laws, which are immutably true, their
declaration would be contrary to eternal truth, equity, and
justice, and consequently void : and so it would be adjudged
by the Parliament itself, when convinced of their mistake.
Upon this great principle, Parliaments repeal such Acts, as soon
as they find they have been mistaken, in having declared them
to be for the public good, when in fact they were not so. When
such mistake is evident and palpable, as in the instances in the
appendix, the judges of the executive courts have declared the
Act ' of a whole Parliament void '. See here the grandeur of
the British constitution ! See the wisdom of our ancestors !
The supreme legislative, and the supreme executive, are
a perpetual check and balance to each other. If the supreme
executive errs, it is informed by the supreme legislative in
Parliament : If the supreme legislative errs, it is informed by
the supreme executive in the King's courts of law. Here, the
King appears, as represented by his judges, in the highest
lustre and majesty, as supreme executor of the Commonwealth;
and he never shines brighter, but on his throne, at the head of
the supreme legislative. This is government ! This is a constitution ! to preserve which, either from foreign or domestic
foes, has cost oceans of blood and treasure in every age ; and
the blood and the treasure have upon the whole been well spent.

. . . .

[p. 62] Sometimes we have been considered only as the corporations in England : and it may be urged that it is no harder upon us to be taxed by Parliament for the general cause than for them, who besides are at the expence of their corporate subordinate government. I answer, (1) those corporations are represented in Parliament ; (2) the colonies are and have been at great expence in raising men, building forts, and supporting the King's civil government here. Now I read of no governors and other officers of His Majesty's nomination, that the city of London taxes its inhabitants to support ; I know of no forts and garrisons that the city of London has lately built at its own expence, or of any annual levies that they have raised for the King's service and the common cause. These are things very fitting and proper to be done by a subordinate dominion, and 'tis their duty to do all they are able ; but it seems but equal they should be allowed to assess the charges of it themselves. The rules of equity and the principles of the constitution seem to require this. Those who judge of the reciprocal rights that subsist between a supreme and subordinate state of dominion, by no higher rules than are applied to a corporation of button-makers, will never have a very comprehensive view of them. . . .

[p. 64] The sum of my argument is, that civil government is of God : that the administrators of it were originally the whole people : that they might have devolved it on whom they pleased : that this devolution is fiduciary, for the good of the whole ; that by the British constitution, this devolution is on the King, lords and commons, the supreme, sacred and uncontroulable legislative power, not only in the realm, but thro' the dominions : that by the abdication, the original compact was broken to pieces : that by the revolution, it was renewed, and more firmly established, and the rights and liberties of the subjects in all parts of the dominions more fully explained and confirmed : that in consequence of this establishment, and the Acts of Succession and Union, His Majesty George III is rightful king and sovereign, and with his Parliament, the supreme legislative of Great Britain, France, and Ireland, and the dominions thereto belonging : that this constitution is the most free one, and by far the best, now existing on earth : that by this constitution, every man in the dominions is a free man : that no parts of His Majesty's dominions can be taxed without their consent : that every part has a right to be represented in the supreme or some subordinate legislature : that the refusal of this would seem to be a contradiction in practice to the theory of the constitution : that the colonies are subordinate dominions, and are now in such a state, as to make it best for the good of the whole, that they should not only be continued in the enjoyment of subordinate legislation, but be also represented in some proportion to their number and estates, in the grand legislature of the nation : that this would firmly unite all parts of the British empire, in the greatest peace and prosperity ; and render it invulnerable and perpetual.

A REMONSTRANCE FROM THE PENNSYLVANIA FRONTIER [1]

13 February 1764

To the Honourable John Penn, Esquire, Governor of the Province of *Pennsylvania* and of the Counties of *New Castle, Kent,* and *Sussex,* on *Delaware,* and to the Representatives of the Freemen of the said Province, in General Assembly met :

WE, Matthew Smith and James Gibson, in behalf of ourselves and His Majesty's faithful and loyal subjects, the inhabitants of the frontier counties of Lancaster, York, Cumberland, Berks, and Northampton, humbly beg leave to remonstrate and to lay before you the following grievances, which we submit to your wisdom for redress.

1. We apprehend that as freemen and English subjects, we have an indisputable title to the same privileges and immunities with His Majesty's other subjects who reside in the interior counties of Philadelphia, Chester, and Bucks, and therefore ought not to be excluded from an equal share with them in the very important privilege of legislation. Nevertheless, contrary to the Proprietor's Charter and the acknowledged principles of common justice and equity, our five counties are restrained

---

[1] *A Declaration and Remonstrance of the distressed and bleeding Frontier Inhabitants of the Province of Pennsylvania, . . . shewing the Causes of their late Discontent and the Grievances under which they have laboured.* [Philadelphia], 1764, pp. 10–18 (copy in New York Historical Society). Also printed in *Minutes of the Provincial Council of Pennsylvania* (often cited as *Colonial Records of Pennsylvania*), ix. 138–42.

from electing more than ten representatives, viz., four for Lancaster, two for York, two for Cumberland, one for Berks, and one for Northampton ; while the three counties (and city) of Philadelphia, Chester, and Bucks, elect twenty-six. This we humbly conceive is oppressive, unequal, and unjust, the cause of many of our grievances, and an infringement of our natural privileges of freedom and equality ; wherefore we humbly pray that we may be no longer deprived of an equal number with the three aforesaid counties, to represent us in Assembly.

2. We understand that a bill is now before the House of Assembly, wherein it is provided that such persons as shall be charged with killing any Indians in Lancaster County, shall not be tried in the county where the fact was committed, but in the counties of Philadelphia, Chester, or Bucks. This is manifestly to deprive British subjects of their known privileges, to cast an eternal reproach upon whole counties, as if they were unfit to serve their country in the quality of jurymen, and to contradict the well-known laws of the British nation in a point whereon life, liberty, and security essentially depend, namely, that of being tried by their equals in the neighborhood where their own, their accusers', and the witnesses' character and credit, with the circumstances of the fact, are best known, and instead thereof putting their lives in the hands of strangers who may as justly be suspected of partiallity to, as the frontier counties can be of prejudices against Indians ; and this, too, in favour of Indians only, against His Majesty's faithful and loyal subjects. Besides, it is well known that the design of it is to comprehend a fact [1] committed before such a law was thought of. And if such practices were tolerated, no man could be secure in his most valuable interests. We are also informed to our great surprize, that this bill has actually received the assent of a majority of the House, which we are persuaded could not have been the case had our frontier counties been equally represented in Assembly. However, we hope that the Legislature of this Province will never enact a law of so dangerous a tendency, or take away from His Majesty's good subjects a privilege so long esteemed sacred by Englishmen.

3. During the late and present Indian wars, the frontiers of this Province have been repeatedly attacked and ravaged by

[1] The Conestogo massacre. See Introduction.

skulking parties of the Indians, who have with the most savage cruelty murdered men, women, and children without distinction, and have reduced near a thousand families to the most extream distress. It grieves us to the very heart to see such of our frontier inhabitants as have escaped savage fury with the loss of their parents, their children, their wives or relatives, left destitute by the public, and exposed to the most cruel poverty and wretchedness while upwards of an hundred and twenty of the savages who are with great reason suspected of being guilty of these horrid barbarities under the mask of friendship, have procured themselves to be taken under the protection of the government, with a view to elude the fury of the brave relatives of the murdered, and are now maintained at the public expence. Some of these Indians now in the barracks of Philadelphia, are confessedly a part of the Wyalusing Indians, which tribe is now at war with us, and the others are the Moravian Indians, who, living amongst us under the cloak of friendship, carried on a correspondence with our known enemies on the Great Island. We cannot but observe with sorrow and indignation that some persons in this Province are at pains to extenuate the barbarous cruelties practised by these savages on our murdered brethren and relatives, which are shocking to human nature, and must pierce every heart but that of the hardened perpetrators or their abettors, nor is it less distressing to hear others pleading that although the Wyalusing tribe is at war with us, yet that part of it which is under the protection of the government may be friendly to the English and innocent. In what nation under the sun was it ever the custom that when a neighboring nation took up arms, not an individual should be touched but only the persons that offered hostilities ? Who ever proclaimed war with a part of a nation, and not with the whole ? Had these Indians disapproved of the perfidy of their tribe, and been willing to cultivate and preserve friendship with us, why did they not give notice of the war before it happened, as it is known to be the result of long deliberations, and a preconcerted combination amongst them ? Why did they not leave their tribe immediately, and come amongst us before there was ground to suspect them, or war was actually waged with their tribe ? No, they stayed amongst them, were privy to their murders and ravages, until we had destroyed their provisions ; and when they could no longer subsist at home, they come not as deserters, but as friends to be maintained through the winter, that they may be able to scalp and butcher us in the spring.

And as to the Moravian Indians,[1] there are strong grounds at least to suspect their friendship, as it is known they carried on a correspondence with our enemies on the Great Island. We killed three Indians going from Bethlehem to the Great Island with blankets, ammunition, and provisions, which is an undeniable proof that the Moravian Indians were in confederacy with our open enemies. And we cannot but be filled with indignation to hear this action of ours painted in the most odious and detestable colours, as if we had inhumanly murdered our guides who preserved us from perishing in the woods, when we only killed three of our known enemies, who attempted to shoot us when we surprized them. And besides all this, we understand that one of these very Indians is proved by the oath of Stenton's widow, to be the very person that murdered her husband. How then comes it to pass that he alone, of all the Moravian Indians, should join with the enemy to murder that family? Or can it be supposed that any enemy Indians, contrary to their known custom of making war, should penetrate into the heart of a settled country to burn, plunder and murder the inhabitants, and not molest any houses in their return, or ever be seen or heard of? Or how can we account for it, that no ravages have been committed in Northampton County, since the removal of the Moravian Indians, when the Great Cove has been struck since? These things put it beyond doubt with us that the Indians now at Philadelphia are His Majesty's perfidious enemies, and therefore to protect and maintain them at the public expence, while our suffering brethren on the frontiers are almost destitute of the necessaries of life and are neglected by the public, is sufficient to make us mad with rage, and tempt us to do what nothing but the most violent necessity can vindicate. We humbly and earnestly pray, therefore, that those enemies of His Majesty may be removed as soon as possible out of the Province.

4. We humbly conceive that it is contrary to the maxims of good policy, and extreamly dangerous to our frontiers, to

---

[1] The Moravian Indians were an Algonkian tribe converted to Christianity, pacifism, and agriculture by German Moravian missionaries. Their pathetic attempts to keep neutral between their savage brethren and the backwoodsmen, and their eventual extermination by the latter, are described in Roosevelt's *Winning of the West.*

suffer any Indians of what tribe soever to live within the inhabited parts of this Province while we are engaged in an Indian war ; as experience has taught us that they are all perfidious, and their claim to freedom and independency puts it in their power to act as spies, to entertain and give intelligence to our enemies, and to furnish them with provisions and warlike stores. To this fatal intercourse between our pretended friends and open enemies, we must ascribe the greatest of the ravages and murders that have been committed in the course of this and the last Indian war. We therefore pray that this grievance be taken under consideration and remedied.

5. We cannot help lamenting that no provision has been hitherto made, that such of our frontier inhabitants as have been wounded in defence of the Province, their lives and liberties, may be taken care of and cured of their wounds at the publick expence. We therefore pray that this grievance may be redressed.

6. In the late Indian war this Province, with others of His Majesty's Colonies, gave rewards for Indian scalps, to encourage the seeking them in their own country, as the most likely means of destroying or reducing them to reason ; but no such encouragement has been given in this war, which has damped the spirits of many brave men who are willing to venture their lives in parties against the enemy. We therefore pray that public rewards may be proposed for Indian scalps, which may be adequate to the dangers attending enterprizes of this nature.

7. We daily lament that numbers of our nearest and dearest relatives are still in captivity among the savage heathen, to be trained up in all their ignorance and barbarity, or to be tortured to death with all the contrivances of Indian cruelty, for attempting to make their escape from bondage. We see they pay no regard to the many solemn promises which they have made to restore our friends who are in bondage amongst them. We therefore earnestly pray that no trade may hereafter be permitted to be carried on with them, until our brethren and relatives are brought home to us.

8. We complain that a certain Society [1] of people in this Province, in the late Indian war, and at several treaties held by the King's representatives, openly loaded the Indians with presents, and that J. P., a leader of the said Society, in defiance

[1] The Society of Friends.

of all government, not only abetted our Indian enemies, but kept up a private intelligence with them, and publickly received from them a belt of wampum, as if he had been our Governor or authorized by the King to treat with his enemies. By this means the Indians have been taught to despise us as a weak and disunited people, and from this fatal source have arose many of our calamities under which we groan. We humbly pray therefore that this grievance may be redressed, and that no private subject be hereafter permitted to treat with, or carry on a correspondence with our enemies.

9. We cannot but observe with sorrow that Fort Augusta, which has been very expensive to this Province, has afforded us but little assistance during this or the last war. The men that were stationed at that place neither helped our distressed inhabitants to save their crops, nor did they attack our enemies in their towns, or patrole on our frontiers. We humbly request that proper measures may be taken to make that garrison more serviceable to us in our distress, if it can be done.

N.B. We are far from intending any reflection against the Commanding Officer stationed at Augusta, as we presume his conduct was always directed by those from whom he received his orders.

SIGNED on behalf of ourselves, and by appointment of a great number of the frontier inhabitants.

MATTHEW SMITH.
JAMES GIBSON.

February 13th, 1764.

THE VIRGINIA RESOLVES ON THE STAMP ACT
30 May 1765

1. PATRICK HENRY'S SPEECH INTRODUCING THE RESOLVES

(a) *From the contemporary diary of a French traveller.*[1]

May the 30th. Set out early from half-way house in the chair and broke fast at York, arived at Williamsburg at 12,

---

[1] This diary, which was recently discovered in the Archives de la Marine, Paris, is printed in the *American Historical Review*, xxvi. 726–47, xxvii. 70–89. The writer has not been identified. Apparently he was an agent of the French Government, possibly the Chevalier d'Anne-mours.

where I saw three negroes hanging at the galous for haveing robed Mr. Waltho of 300 pounds. I went imediately to the Assembly which was seting, where I was entertained with very strong debates concerning dutys that the Parlement wants to lay on the American colonys, which they call or stile stamp dutys. Shortly after I came in, one of the members stood up and said he had read that in former times Tarquin and Julus had their Brutus, Charles had his Cromwell, and he did not doubt but some good American would stand up in favour of his Country ; but (says he) in a more moderate manner, and was going to continue, when the Speaker of the House rose and, said he, the last that stood up had spoke traison, and was sorey to see that not one of the members of the House was loyal enough to stop him before he had gone so far. Upon which the same member stood up again (his name is Henery) and said that if he had afronted the Speaker or the House, he was ready to ask pardon, and he would shew his loyalty to His Majesty King George the third at the expence of the last drop of his blood ; but what he had said must be attributed to the interest of his country's dying liberty which he had at heart, and the heat of passion might have lead him to have said something more than he intended ; but, again, if he said any thing wrong, he beged the Speaker and the House's pardon. Some other members stood up and backed him, on which that afaire was droped.

May the 31th. I returned to the Assembly to-day, and heard very hot debates stil about the stamp dutys. The whole House was for entering resolves on the records but they differed much with regard the contents or purport thereof. Some were for shewing their resentment to the highest. One of the resolves that these proposed, was that any person that would offer to sustain that the Parlement of England had a right to impose or lay any tax or dutys whatsoever on the American colonys, without the consent of the inhabitants therof, should be looked upon as a traitor, and deemed an enemy to his country : there were some others to the same purpose, and the majority was for entring these resolves ; upon which the Governor disolved the Assembly, which hinderd their proceeding.

(b) From a private letter from Virginia, dated 21 June 1765.[1]

Mr. —— has lately blazed out in the Assembly, where he compared —— to a Tarquin, a Caesar, a Charles the First, threatening him with a Brutus, or an Oliver Cromwell; yet Mr. —— was not sent to the Tower: but having prevailed to get some ridiculous violent Resolves passed, rode off in triumph.

(c) From John Burk's History of Virginia, *1805.*[2]

' Caesar ', said he, ' had his Brutus, Charles his Cromwell, and (pausing) George the third (here a cry of treason, treason was heard, supposed to issue from the chair, but with admirable presence of mind he proceeded) may profit by their examples. Sir, if this be treason ', continued he, ' make the most of it.'

(d) From William Wirt's Life of Patrick Henry, *1817.*[3]

It was in the midst of this magnificent debate, while he was descanting on the tyranny of the obnoxious Act, that he exclaimed, in a voice of thunder, and with the look of a god, ' Caesar had his Brutus—Charles the first, his Cromwell— and George the third—(" Treason," cried the Speaker— " treason, treason ", echoed from every part of the House.— It was one of those trying moments which is decisive of character.—Henry faltered not an instant; but rising to a loftier attitude, and fixing on the Speaker an eye of the most determined fire, he finished his sentence with the firmest emphasis) *may profit by their example.* If *this* be treason, make the most of it.'

I had frequently heard the above anecdote of the cry of treason, but with such variations of the concluding words, that I began to doubt whether the whole might not be fiction. With a view

---

[1] Quoted in *Amer. Hist. Rev.,* xxvi. 727, from the *London Gazetteer,* 13th August 1765.

[2] iii. 309. Burk also gives a version of the entire speech, which Henry's biographers believe to be apocryphal. A manuscript History of Virginia by Edmund Randolph, written just before or just after Burk, gives the following version of Henry's retort: ' " Treason, sir," exclaimed the Speaker; to which Mr. Henry instantly replied, " and George the Third, may he never have either." '

[3] Text from the second edition, Philadelphia, 1818, p. 65. The matter in smaller type is Wirt's foot-note. Both Tyler and Jefferson heard Henry's speech.

to ascertain the truth, therefore, I submitted it to Mr. Jefferson, as it had been given to me by judge Tyler, and this is his answer. ' I well remember the cry of treason, the pause of Mr. Henry at the name of George the Third and the presence of mind with which he closed his sentence, and baffled the charge vociferated.' The incident, therefore, becomes authentic history.

2. THE RESOLVES [1]

Resolved, That the first adventurers and settlers of this His Majesty's Colony and Dominion of Virginia brought with them, and transmitted to their posterity, and all other His Majesty's subjects since inhabiting in this His Majesty's said Colony, all the liberties, privileges, franchises, and immunities, that have at any time been held, enjoyed, and possessed, by the people of Great Britain.

Resolved, That by two royal charters, granted by King James the First, the colonists aforesaid are declared entitled to all liberties, privileges, and immunities of denizens and natural subjects, to all intents and purposes, as if they had been abiding and born within the realm of England.

Resolved, That the taxation of the people by themselves, or by persons chosen by themselves to represent them, who can only know what taxes the people are able to bear, or the easiest method of raising them, and must themselves be affected by every tax laid on the people, is the only security against a burthensome taxation, and the distinguishing characteristick of British freedom, without which the ancient constitution cannot exist.

Resolved, That His Majesty's liege people of this his most ancient and loyal Colony have without interruption enjoyed the inestimable right of being governed by such laws, respecting their internal polity and taxation, as are derived from their own consent, with the approbation of their sovereign, or his substitute ; and that the same hath never been forfeited or yielded up, but hath been constantly recognized by the kings and people of Great Britain.

Resolved therefore, That the General Assembly of this Colony have the only and sole exclusive right and power to lay taxes

[1] *Journals of the House of Burgesses of Virginia, 1761–5* (J. P. Kennedy, ed. Richmond, 1907), pp. 360, lxvii, and frontispiece. The last two resolves were certainly not, and the fifth probably not, passed by the Assembly ; but all seven were published in the newspapers of Boston and elsewhere. See *Amer. Hist. Rev.* xxvi. 746, note.

and impositions upon the inhabitants of this Colony, and that every attempt to vest such power in any person or persons whatsoever other than the General Assembly aforesaid has a manifest tendency to destroy British as well as American freedom.

Resolved, That His Majesty's liege people, the inhabitants of this Colony, are not bound to yield obedience to any law or ordinance whatever, designed to impose any taxation whatsoever upon them, other than the laws or ordinances of the General Assembly aforesaid.

Resolved, That any person who shall, by speaking or writing, assert or maintain that any person or persons other than the General Assembly of this Colony, have any right or power to impose or lay any taxation on the people here, shall be deemed an enemy to His Majesty's Colony.

SOAME JENYNS'S 'OBJECTIONS CONSIDER'D'[1]

The Objections to the Taxation of our American Colonies by the Legislature of Great Britain, briefly consider'd
London, 1765.

THE right of the Legislature of Great Britain to impose taxes on her American colonies, and the expediency of exerting that right in the present conjuncture, are propositions so indisputably clear that I should never have thought it necessary to have undertaken their defence, had not many arguments been lately flung out both in papers and conversation, which with insolence equal to their absurdity deny them both. As these are usually mixt up with several patriotic and favorite words such as liberty, property, Englishmen, etc., which are apt to make strong impressions on that more numerous part of mankind who have ears but no understanding, it will not, I think, be improper to give them some answers. To this, therefore, I shall singly confine myself, and do it in as few words as possible, being sensible that the fewest will give least trouble to myself, and probably most information to my reader.

The great capital argument which I find on this subject, and which, like an elephant at the head of a Nabob's army,

---

[1] Soame Jenyns, the minor poet and M.P. for Dunwich, was a member of the Board of Trade and Plantations when he wrote this pamphlet.

being once overthrown must put the whole into confusion, is this ; that no Englishman is, or can be taxed, but by his own consent : by which must be meant one of these three propositions ; either that no Englishman can be taxed without his own consent as an individual ; or that no Englishman can be taxed without the consent of the persons he chuses to represent him ; or that no Englishman can be taxed without the consent of the majority of all those who are elected by himself and others of his fellow subjects to represent them. Now let us impartially consider whether any one of these propositions are in fact true : if not, then this wonderful structure which has been erected upon them falls at once to the ground, and like another Babel, perishes by a confusion of words, which the builders themselves are unable to understand.

First then, that no Englishman is or can be taxed but by his own consent as an individual : this is so far from being true, that it is the very reverse of truth ; for no man that I know of is taxed by his own consent, and an Englishman, I believe, is as little likely to be so taxed as any man in the world.

Secondly, that no Englishman is or can be taxed but by the consent of those persons whom he has chose to represent him. For the truth of this I shall appeal only to the candid representatives of those unfortunate counties which produce cyder, and shall willingly acquiesce under their determination.[1]

Lastly, that no Englishman is or can be taxed without the consent of the majority of those who are elected by himself and others of his fellow subjects to represent them. This is certainly as false as the other two ; for every Englishman is taxed, and not one in twenty represented : copyholders, leaseholders, and all men possessed of personal property only, chuse no representatives ; Manchester, Birmingham, and many more of our richest and most flourishing trading towns send no members to Parliament, consequently cannot consent by their representatives, because they chuse none to represent them ; yet are they not Englishmen ? or are they not taxed ?

I am well aware that I shall hear Lock, Sidney, Selden, and many other great names quoted to prove that every Englishman, whether he has a right to vote for a repre-

[1] A reference to the unpopular cider tax of 1764.

sentative or not, is still represented in the British Parliament, in which opinion they all agree. On what principle of common-sense this opinion is founded I comprehend not, but on the authority of such respectable names I shall acknowledge its truth ; but then I will ask one question, and on that I will rest the whole merits of the cause. Why does not this imaginary representation extend to America as well as over the whole Island of Great Britain ? If it can travel three hundred miles, why not three thousand ? if it can jump over rivers and mountains, why cannot it sail over the ocean ? If the towns of Manchester and Birmingham, sending no representatives to Parliament, are notwithstanding there represented, why are not the cities of Albany and Boston equally represented in that Assembly ? Are they not alike British subjects ? are they not Englishmen ? or are they only Englishmen when they sollicit for protection, but not Englishmen when taxes are required to enable this country to protect them ?

But it is urged that the colonies are by their charters placed under distinct Governments each of which has a legislative power within itself, by which alone it ought to be taxed ; that if this privilege is once given up, that liberty which every Englishman has a right to, is torn from them, they are all slaves, and all is lost.

The liberty of an Englishman is a phrase of so various a signification, having within these few years been used as a synonymous term for blasphemy, bawdy, treason, libels, strong beer, and cyder, that I shall not here presume to define its meaning ; but I shall venture to assert what it cannot mean ; that is, an exemption from taxes imposed by the authority of the Parliament of Great Britain ; nor is there any charter that ever pretended to grant such a privilege to any colony in America ; and had they granted it, it could have had no force ; their charters being derived from the Crown, and no charter from the Crown can possibly supersede the right of the whole legislature. Their charters are undoubtedly no more than those of all corporations, which impower them to make bye-laws, and raise duties for the purposes of their own police, for ever subject to the superior authority of Parliament ; and in some of their charters the manner of exercising these powers is specifyed in these express words, ' according to the course of other corporations

in Great Britain '.   And therefore they can have no more
pretence .to plead an exemption from this parliamentary
authority, than any other corporation in England.

It has been moreover alledged, that though Parliament
may have power to impose taxes on the colonies, they have
no right to use it, because it would be an unjust tax ; and no
supreme or legislative power can have a right to enact any
law in its nature unjust.   To this, I shall only make this
short reply, that if Parliament can impose no taxes but what
are equitable, and if the persons taxed are to be the judges
of that equity, they will in effect have no power to lay any
tax at all.   No tax can be imposed exactly equal on all, and
if it is not equal it cannot be just, and if it is not just, no
power whatever can impose it ; by which short syllogism all
taxation is at end ; but why it should not be used by Englishmen on this side the Atlantic as well as by those on the other,
I do not comprehend.

Thus much for the right.   Let us now a little inquire into
the expediency of this measure, to which two objections have
been made ; that the time is improper, and the manner
wrong.

As to the first, can any time be more proper to require
some assistance from our colonies, to preserve to themselves
their present safety, than when this country is almost undone
by procuring it ?   Can any time be more proper to impose
some tax upon their trade, than when they are enabled to
rival us in our manufactures, by the encouragement and protection which we have given them ?   Can any time be more
proper to oblige them to settle handsome incomes on their
Governors, than when we find them unable to procure a subsistence on any other terms than those of breaking all their
instructions, and betraying the rights of their sovereign ?
Can there be a more proper time to compel them to fix certain
salaries on their judges, than when we see them so dependent
on the humours of their Assemblies, that they can obtain
a livelihood no longer than *quam diu se male gesserint ?*   Can
there be a more proper time to force them to maintain an
army at their expence, than when that army is necessary for
their own protection, and we are utterly unable to support
it ?   Lastly ; can there be a more proper time for this mother
country to leave off feeding out of her own vitals these
children whom she has nursed up, than when they are arrived

at such strength and maturity as to be well able to provide for themselves, and ought rather with filial duty to give some assistance to her distresses?

As to the manner; that is, the imposing taxes on the colonies by the authority of Parliament, it is said to be harsh and arbitrary; and that it would have been more consistent with justice, at least with maternal tenderness, for administration here to have settled quotas on each of the colonies, and have then transmitted them with injunctions that the sums allotted should be immediately raised by their respective legislatures, on the penalty of their being imposed by Parliament in case of their non-compliance. But was this to be done, what would be the consequence? Have their Assemblies shewn so much obedience to the orders of the Crown, that we could reasonably expect that they would immediately tax themselves on the arbitrary command of a minister? Would it be possible here to settle those quotas with justice, or would any one of the colonies submit to them, were they ever so just? Should we not be compared to those Roman tyrants, who used to send orders to their subjects to murder themselves within so many hours, most obligingly leaving the method to their own choice, but on their disobedience threatening a more severe fate from the hands of an executioner? And should we not receive votes, speeches, resolutions, petitions, and remonstrances in abundance, instead of taxes? In short, we either have a right to tax the colonies, or we have not. If Parliament is possessed of this right, why should it be exercised with more delicacy in America than it has ever been even in Great Britain itself? If on the other hand, they have no such right, sure it is below the dignity as well as justice of the Legislature to intimidate the colonies with vain threats, which they have really no right to put in execution.

One method indeed has been hinted at, and but one, that might render the exercise of this power in a British Parliament just and legal, which is the introduction of representatives from the several colonies into that body; but as this has never seriously been proposed, I shall not here consider the impracticability of this method, nor the effects of it if it could be practised; but only say that I have lately seen so many specimens of the great powers of speech of which these American gentlemen are possessed, that I should be much afraid that the sudden importation of so much eloquence at once, would greatly endanger the safety and government of this country ; or in terms more fashionable, though less understood, this our most excellent Constitution. If we can avail ourselves of these taxes on no other condition, I shall never look upon it as a measure of frugality ; being perfectly satisfyed that in the end it will be much cheaper for us to pay their army than their orators.

I cannot omit taking notice of one prudential reason which I have heard frequently urged against this taxation of the colonies, which is this : That if they are by this means impoverished, they will be unable to purchase our manufactures, and consequently we shall lose that trade from which the principal benefit which we receive from them must arise. But surely, it requires but little sagacity to see the weakness of this argument ; for should the colonies raise taxes for the purposes of their own government and protection, would the money so raised be immediately annihilated ? What some pay, would not others receive ? Would not those who so receive it, stand in need of as many of our manufactures, as those who pay ? Was the army there maintained at the expence of the Americans, would the soldiers want fewer coats, hats, shirts, or shoes than at present ? Had the judges salaries ascertained to them, would they not have occasion for as costly perriwigs, or robes of as expensive scarlet, as marks of their legal abilities, as they now wear in their present state of dependency ? Or had their Governors better incomes settled on them for observing their instructions, than they can now with difficulty obtain for disobeying them, would they expend less money in their several Governments, or bring home at their return less riches to lay out in the manufactories of their native country ?

It has been likewise asserted that every shilling which our colonies can raise either by cultivation or commerce, finally centers in this country ; and therefore it is argued we can acquire nothing by their taxation, since we can have no more than their all ; and whether this comes in by taxes or by trade, the consequence is the same. But allowing this assertion to be true, which it is not, yet the reasoning upon it is glaringly false : for surely it is not the same whether the wealth derived from these colonies flows immediately into the coffers of the public, or into the pockets of individuals from whence it must be squeezed by various domestic taxes before it can be rendered of any service to the nation. Surely it is by no means the same, whether this money brought in by taxes enables us to diminish part of that enormous debt contracted by the last expensive war, or whether coming in by trade it enables the merchant, by augmenting his influence together with his wealth, to plunge us into new wars and new debts for his private advantage.

From what has been here said, I think that not only the right of the legislature of Great Britain to impose taxes on her colonies, not only the expediency, but the absolute necessity of exercising that right in the present conjuncture, has been so clearly though concisely proved, that it is to be hoped that in this great and important question all parties and factions, or in the more polite and fashionable term, all connections will most cordially unite ; that every member of the British Parliament, whether in or out of humour with Administration, whether he has been turned out because he has opposed, or whether he opposes because he has been turned out, will endeavour to the utmost of his power to support this measure. A measure which must not only be approved by every man who has any property or common sense, but which ought to be required by every English subject of an English Administration.

FINIS

FROM DANIEL DULANY'S ' CONSIDERATIONS ' [1]

Considerations on the Propriety of imposing Taxes in the British Colonies, for the purpose of Raising a Revenue, by Act of Parliament.

Second edition. Annapolis, 1765.

IN the Constitution of England, the three principal forms of government, monarchy, aristocracy, and democracy, are blended together in certain proportions ; but each of these orders, in the exercise of the legislative authority, hath its peculiar department from which the other are excluded. In

[1] Dulany was a Maryland lawyer, educated at Eton, Clare, and the Temple. He never changed his position as to the legality of external taxation by Parliament, and eventually became a loyalist.

this division, the granting of supplies or laying taxes is deemed to be the province of the House of Commons, as the representative of the people. All supplies are supposed to flow from their gift ; and the other orders are permitted only to assent, or reject generally, not to propose any modification, amendment, or partial alteration of it.

This observation being considered, it will undeniably appear that in framing the late Stamp Act, the Commons acted in the character of representatives of the colonies. They assumed it as the principle of that measure, and the propriety of it must therefore stand or fall as the principle is true or false : for the preamble sets forth that the Commons of Great Britain had resolved to give and grant the several rates and duties imposed by the Act ; but what right had the Commons of Great Britain to be thus munificent at the expence of the Commons of America ? To give property not belonging to the giver, and without the consent of the owner, is such evident and flagrant injustice in ordinary cases, that few are hardy enough to avow it ; and therefore when it really happens, the fact is disguised and varnished over by the most plausible pretences the ingenuity of the giver can suggest. But it is alledged that there is a *virtual*, or *implied representation* of the colonies springing out of the Constitution of the British Government. And it must be confessed on all hands, that as the representation is not actual, it is virtual, or it doth not exist at all ; for no third kind of representation can be imagined. The colonies claim the privilege which is common to all British subjects, of being taxed only with their own consent given by their representatives, and all the advocates for the Stamp Act admit this claim. Whether therefore . . . the imposition of the stamp duties is a proper exercise of constitutional authority or not, depends upon the single question, whether the Commons of Great Britain are *virtually* the representatives of the Commons of America or not.

The advocates for the Stamp Act admit in express terms, that ' the colonies do not chuse members of Parliament ', but they assert that ' the colonies are virtually represented in the same manner with the non-electors resident in Great Britain '.

How have they proved this position ? Where have they defined, or precisely explained what they mean by the expression, *virtual representation* ?

• • • • • • • • • • •

They argue, that ' the right of election being annexed to certain species of property, to franchises, and inhabitancy in some particular places, a very small part of the land, the property, and the people of England, is comprehended in those descriptions. All landed property not freehold, and all monied property are excluded. The merchants of London, the proprietors of the public funds, the inhabitants of Leeds, Halifax, Birmingham, and Manchester, and that great corporation of the East India Company, none of them chuse their representatives, and yet are they all represented in Parliament, and the colonies being exactly in their situation, are represented in the same manner.'

.   .   .   .

The notion of a *virtual representation* of the colonies . . . is a mere cob-web, spread to catch the unwary, and intangle the weak. I would be understood. I am upon a question of propriety, not of power ; and, though some may be inclined to think it is to little purpose to discuss the one, when the other is irresistible, yet are they different considerations ; and, at the same time that I invalidate the claim upon which it is founded, I may very consistently recommend a submission to the law, whilst it endures. . . .

Lessees for years, copyholders, proprietors of the public funds, inhabitants of Birmingham, Leeds, Halifax, and Manchester, merchants of the City of London, or members of the corporation of the East India Company, are, *as such*, under no personal incapacity to be electors ; for they may acquire the right of election, and there are actually not only a considerable number of electors in each of the classes of lessees for years, &c., but in many of them, if not all, even members of Parliament. The interests therefore of the non-electors, the electors, and the representatives, are individually the same ; to say nothing of the connection among neighbours, friends, and relations. The security of the non-electors against oppression, is that their oppression will fall also upon the electors and the representatives. The one can't be injured, and the other indemnified.

Further, if the non-electors should not be taxed by the British Parliament, they would not be taxed at all ; and it would be iniquitous, as well as a solecism in the political system, that they should partake of all the benefits resulting from the imposition and application of taxes, and derive an immunity from the circumstance of not being qualified to vote. Under this Constitution then, a double or virtual representation may be reasonably supposed. The electors, who are inseparably connected in their interests with the non-electors, may be justly deemed to be the representatives of the non-electors, at the same time they exercise their personal privilege in their right of election, and the members chosen, therefore, the representatives of both. This is the only rational explanation of the expression, *virtual representation*. . . .

It is an essential principle of the English Constitution that the subject shall not be taxed without his consent, which hath not been introduced by any particular law, but necessarily results from the nature of that mixed Government; for without it the order of democracy could not exist.

. . . .

[p. 10]. There is not that intimate and inseparable relation between the electors of Great Britain and the inhabitants of the colonies which must inevitably involve both in the same taxation; on the contrary, not a single actual elector in England might be immediately affected by a taxation in America, imposed by a statute which would have a general operation and effect upon the properties of the inhabitants of the colonies. The latter might be oppressed in a thousand shapes, without any sympathy, or exciting any alarm in the former. Moreover, even Acts oppressive and injurious to the colonies in an extreme degree might become popular in England, from the promise or expectation that the very measures which depressed the colonies, would give ease to the inhabitants of Great Britain. It is indeed true that the interests of England and the colonies are allied, and an injury to the colonies produced into all its consequences, will eventually affect the mother-country; yet these consequences being generally remote, are not at once forseen, they do not immediately alarm the fears and engage the passions of the English electors; the connection between a freeholder of Great Britain and a British American being deducible only through a train of reasoning which few will take the trouble . . . to investigate; wherefore a relation between the British Americans and the English electors is a knot too infirm to be relied on. . . .

. . . .

[p. 13. In answer to the argument that the colonies are no more than common corporations, and no more entitled to exemption from parliamentary taxation, than London.]

The colonies have a compleat and adequate legislative authority, and are not only represented in their Assemblies, but in no other manner. The power of making bye-laws vested in the Common Council is inadequate and incompleat, being bounded by a few particular subjects ; and the Common Council are actually represented too, by having a choice of members to serve in Parliament. How then can the reason of the exemption from internal parliamentary taxations claimed by the colonies, apply to the citizens of London ?

The power described in the provincial charters is to make laws, and in the exercise of that power the colonies are bounded by no other limitations than what result from their subordination to and dependence upon Great Britain. The term bye-laws is as novel and improper when applied to the Assemblies, as the expression Acts of Assembly would be, if applied to the Parliament of Great Britain, and it is as absurd and insensible to call a colony a common corporation, because not an independant kingdom, . . . as it would be to call Lake Erie a duck-puddle, because not the Atlantic Ocean.

The Colonies are dependent upon *Great Britain*, and the supreme Authority vested in the King, Lords, and Commons, may justly be exercised to secure, or preserve their dependence, whenever necessary for that Purpose. This Authority results from, and is implied in the idea of the relation subsisting between England and her Colonies. . . . In what the superior may rightfully controul or compel, and in what the inferior ought to be at liberty to act without controul or compulsion, depends upon the nature of the dependence, and the degree of the subordination : and, these being ascertained, the measure of obedience and submission, and the extent of the authority and superintendence, will be settled. When powers, compatible with the relation between the superior and inferior, have, by express Compact, been granted to and accepted by the latter, and have been, after that Compact, repeatedly recognized by the former ;—when they may be exercised effectually upon every occasion without any injury to that relation, the authority of the superior can't properly interpose : for by the powers vested in the inferior, is the superior limited.

.   .   .   .   [p. 26]   .   .   .   .   .

The truth is that a vast revenue arises to the British nation from taxes paid by the colonies *in Great Britain,* and even the most ignorant British cottager, not imposed upon by infamous misrepresentation, must perceive that it is of no consequence to his ease and relief, whether the duties raised upon America are paid there, and thence afterwards remitted to Great Britain, or paid at first upon the produce of the colonies in Great Britain.

In the article of tobacco, for instance, the planter pays a tax upon that produce of his land and labour consumed in Great Britain, more than six times the clear sum received by him for it, besides the expences of freight, commission, and other charges, and double freight, commission and charges upon the tobacco re-exported, by which the British merchants, mariners, and other British subjects are supported— a tax at least equal to what is paid by any farmer of Great Britain, possessed of the same degree of property ; and moreover the planter must contribute to the support of the expensive internal Government of the colony in which he resides.

Is it objected that the duties charged upon tobacco fall ultimately upon the consumers of this commodity in the consequential price set upon it ? Be it so, and let the principle be established that all taxes upon a commodity are paid by the consumers of it, and the consequence of this principle be fairly drawn and equally applied.

The British consumers, therefore, ultimately pay the high duties laid upon tobacco, in proportion to the quantity of that commodity which they consume. The colonies therefore, in proportion to their consumption of British manufactures, pay also the high duties of custom and excise with which the manufacturers are charged in the consequential price set upon their consumptions. In their passage, moreover, from the British manufacturers to the American importers, the commodities go thro' a great many hands, by which their costs are enhanced ; the factors, the carriers, the shopkeepers, the merchants, the brokers, the porters, the watermen, the mariners and others, have their respective profits, from which they derive their subsistence and the support of their families, and are enabled to pay the high duties of customs and excise in the price of their consumptions.

The policy of the late regulations of the colonies is of the same character with their justice and lenity. The produce of their lands, the earnings of their industry, and the gains of their commerce, center in Great Britain, support the artificers, the manufactories, and navigation of the nation, and with them the British landholders too.

. . . . . [p. 34] . . . . .

It appears to me that there is a clear and necessary Distinction between an Act imposing a tax for *the single purpose of revenue*, and those Acts which have been made for the *regulation of trade*, and have produced some revenue in consequence of their effect and operation as regulations of trade.

The colonies claim the privileges of British subjects. It has been proved to be inconsistent with those privileges to tax them without their own consent, and it hath been demonstrated that a tax imposed by Parliament is a tax without their consent.

The subordination of the colonies, and the authority of the Parliament to preserve it, have been fully acknowledged. Not only the welfare, but perhaps the existence of the mother country as an independent kingdom, may rest upon her trade and navigation, and these so far upon her intercourse with the colonies, that if this should be neglected, there would soon be an end to that commerce whence her greatest wealth is derived, and upon which her maritime power is principally founded. From these considerations, the right of the British Parliament to regulate the trade of the colonies, may be justly deduced ; a denial of it would contradict the admission of the subordination, and of the authority to preserve it, resulting from the nature of the relation between the mother country and her colonies. It is a common and frequently the most proper method to regulate trade by duties on imports and exports. The authority of the mother country to regulate the trade of the colonies being unquestionable, what regulations are the most proper, are to be of course submitted to the determination of the Parliament ; and if an incidental revenue should be produced by such regulations, these are not therefore unwarrantable.

A right to impose an internal tax on the colonies without their consent *for the single purpose of revenue* is denied ; a right to regulate their trade without their consent is admitted. The imposition of a duty may, in some instances, be the proper regulation. If the claims of the mother country and the colonies should seem on such an occasion to interfere, and

the point of right to be doubtful (which I take to be otherwise) it is easy to guess that the determination will be on the
side of power, and that the inferior will be constrained to
submit.

.   .   .   .   [p. 47]   .   .   .   .   .

Any oppression of the colonies would intimate an opinion
of them I am persuaded they don't deserve, and their security
as well as honour ought to engage them to confute. When
contempt is mixed with injustice, and insult with violence,
which is the case when an injury is done to him who hath
the means of redress in his power ; if the injured hath one
inflammable grain of honour in his breast, his resentment
will invigorate his pursuit of reparation, and animate his
efforts to obtain an effectual security against a repetition of
the outrage.

If the case supposed should really happen, the resentment
I should recommend would be a legal, orderly, and prudent
resentment, to be expressed in a zealous and vigorous *
industry, in an immediate use and unabating application of
the advantages we derive from our situation,—a resentment
which could not fail to produce effects as beneficial to the
mother country as to the colonies, and which a regard to her
welfare as well as our own, ought to inspire us with on such
an occasion.

The general assemblies would not, I suppose, have it in
their power to encourage by laws, the prosecution of this
beneficial, this necessary measure ; but they might promote
it almost as effectually by their example. I have in my
younger days seen fine sights, and been captivated by their
dazzling pomp and glittering splendor ; but the sight of our
representatives, all adorned in compleat dresses of their own
leather and flax and wool, manufactured by the art and
industry of the inhabitants of Virginia, would excite, not
the gaze of admiration, the flutter of an agitated imagination,
or the momentary amusement of a transient scene, but

* The ingenious Mr. Hume observes, in his *History of James I,*
that the English fine cloth was in so little credit even at home, that
the king was obliged to seek expedients by which he might engage
the people of fashion to wear it, and the manufacture of fine linen
was totally unknown in the kingdom. What an encouragement to
industry ! This very penetrating gentleman also recommends a mild
Government, as a proper measure for preserving the dominion of
England over her colonies.

a calm, solid, heartfelt delight.   Such a sight would give me more pleasure than the most splendid and magnificent spectacle the most exquisite taste ever painted, the richest fancy ever imagined, realized to the view—as much more pleasure as a good mind would receive from the contemplation of virtue, than of elegance ; of the spirit of patriotism, than the ostentation of opulence.

Not only ' as a friend to the colonies ', but as an inhabitant, having my all at stake upon their welfare,[1] I desire an ' Exemption from taxes imposed without my consent ', and I have reflected longer than ' a moment upon the consequences ' : I value it as one of the dearest privileges I enjoy : I acknowledge dependence on Great Britain, but I can perceive a degree of it without slavery, and I disown all other.   I do not expect that the interests of the colonies will be discovered by some men, but in subserviency to other regards.   The effects of luxury and venality and oppression, posterity may perhaps experience, and sufficient for the day will be the evil thereof.

RESOLUTIONS OF THE STAMP ACT CONGRESS [2]

19 October 1765

THE members of this Congress, sincerely devoted with the warmest sentiments of affection and duty to His Majesty's person and Government, inviolably attached to the present happy establishment of the Protestant succession, and with minds deeply impressed by a sense of the present and impending misfortunes of the British colonies on this continent ; having considered as maturely as time will permit the circumstances of the said colonies, esteem it our indispensible duty to make the following declarations of our humble opinion respecting the most essential rights and liberties of the colonists, and of the grievances under which they labour, by reason of several late Acts of Parliament.

I. That His Majesty's subjects in these colonies owe the same allegiance to the Crown of Great Britain that is owing from his subjects born within the realm, and all due sub-

---

[1] [John Campbell] *The Regulations lately made* (London, 1765), p. 111.
[2] *Collection of Interesting, Authentic Papers relative to the Dispute between Great Britain and America* (John Almon, ed., London, 1777, usually cited as ' Prior Documents '), p. 27.   The Congress also adopted separate petitions to King, Lords, and Commons.

ordination to that august body the Parliament of Great Britain.

II. That His Majesty's liege subjects in these colonies are intitled to all the inherent rights and liberties of his natural born subjects within the kingdom of Great Britain.

III. That it is inseparably essential to the freedom of a people, and the undoubted right of Englishmen, that no taxes be imposed on them but with their own consent, given personally or by their representatives.

IV. That the people of these colonies are not, and from their local circumstances cannot be, represented in the House of Commons in Great Britain.

V. That the only representatives of the people of these colonies are persons chosen therein by themselves, and that no taxes ever have been, or can be constitutionally imposed on them, but by their respective legislatures.

VI. That all supplies to the Crown being free gifts of the people, it is unreasonable and inconsistent with the principles and spirit of the British Constitution, for the people of Great Britain to grant to His Majesty the property of the colonists.

VII. That trial by jury is the inherent and invaluable right of every British subject in these colonies.

VIII. That the late Act of Parliament, entitled *An Act for granting and applying certain stamp duties, and other duties, in the British colonies and plantations in America, etc.,* by imposing taxes on the inhabitants of these colonies ; and the said Act, and several other Acts, by extending the jurisdiction of the courts of Admiralty beyond its ancient limits, have a manifest tendency to subvert the rights and liberties of the colonists.

IX. That the duties imposed by several late Acts of Parliament, from the peculiar circumstances of these colonies, will be extremely burthensome and grievous ; and from the scarcity of specie, the payment of them absolutely impracticable.

X. That as the profits of the trade of these colonies ultimately center in Great Britain, to pay for the manufactures which they are obliged to take from thence, they eventually contribute very largely to all supplies granted there to the Crown.

XI. That the restrictions imposed by several late Acts of Parliament on the trade of these colonies will render them unable to purchase the manufactures of Great Britain.

XII. That the increase, prosperity, and happiness of these colonies depend on the full and free enjoyments of their rights and liberties, and an intercourse with Great Britain mutually affectionate and advantageous.

XIII. That it is the right of the British subjects in these colonies to petition the King or either House of Parliament.

Lastly, That it is the indispensible duty of these colonies to the best of sovereigns, to the mother country, and to themselves, to endeavour by a loyal and dutiful address to His Majesty, and humble applications to both Houses of Parliament, to procure the repeal of the Act for granting and applying certain stamp duties, of all clauses of any other Acts of Parliament, whereby the jurisdiction of the Admiralty is extended as aforesaid, and of the other late Acts for the restriction of American commerce.

FROM DICKINSON'S FARMER'S LETTERS, 1767–8

Letters from a Farmer in Pennsylvania to the Inhabitants of the British Colonies.[1]

LETTER I

MY DEAR COUNTRYMEN,

I am a farmer, settled after a variety of fortunes near the banks of the river Delaware, in the province of Pennsylvania. I received a liberal education and have been engaged in the busy scenes of life, but am now convinced, that a man may be as happy without bustle as with it. My farm is small, my servants are few and good, I have a little money at interest, I wish for no more, my employment in my own affairs is easy, and with a contented, grateful mind, undisturbed by worldly hopes or fears relating to myself, I am completing the number of days allotted to me by divine goodness.

Being generally master of my time, I spend a good deal of it in a library, which I think the most valuable part of my small estate ; and being acquainted with two or three gentlemen of abilities and learning who honour me with their friendship,

---

• From the Philadelphia edition of 1768, as reprinted in *The Writings of John Dickinson* (P. L. Ford, ed.), *Memoirs of the Historical Society of Pennsylvania*, xiv (Philadelphia, 1895). They first appeared in the newspapers, Letter I being dated November 5, 1767.

I have acquired, I believe, a greater knowledge in history and the laws and constitution of my country, than is generally attained by men of my class, many of them not being so fortunate as I have been in the opportunities of getting information.

From my infancy I was taught to love humanity and liberty. Enquiry and experience have since confirmed my reverence for the lessons then given me, by convincing me more fully of their truth and excellence. Benevolence towards mankind excites wishes for their welfare, and such wishes endear the means of fulfilling them. These can be found in liberty only, and therefore her sacred cause ought to be espoused by every man on every occasion, to the utmost of his power. As a charitable but poor person does not withhold his mite because he cannot relieve all the distresses of the miserable, so should not any honest man suppress his sentiments concerning freedom, however small their influence is likely to be. Perhaps he ' may touch some wheel ' that will have an effect greater than he could reasonably expect.

These being my sentiments, I am encouraged to offer to you, my countrymen, my thoughts on some late transactions that appear to me to be of the utmost importance to you. Conscious of my own defects, I have waited some time, in expectation of seeing the subject treated by persons much better qualified for the task; but being therein disappointed, and apprehensive that longer delays will be injurious, I venture at length to request the attention of the public, praying that these lines may be read with the same zeal for the happiness of British America, with which they were wrote.

With a good deal of surprize I have observed that little notice has been taken of an Act of Parliament, as injurious in its principle to the liberties of these colonies, as the Stamp Act was : I mean the act for suspending the legislation of New York.[1]

---

[1] The Quartering Act of 1765 (5 Geo. III, c. 33) required colonial local authorities to provide the king's troops with barracks or billets, and to furnish them gratis with candles, firing, bedding, cooking utensils, salt and vinegar, and five pints of small beer or cider, or a gill of rum per man, per diem. The New York Assembly, on 3 July 1766, voted to fulfil all these requirements, save the salt, vinegar, and liquor, for about eleven hundred men. This was deemed insufficient by the Lords of Trade, and, as the Assembly refused to incur an additional ' ruinous and insupportable ' expense, Parliament, by 7 Geo. III,

The Assembly of that Government complied with a former Act of Parliament, requiring certain provisions to be made for the troops in America, in every particular, I think, except the articles of salt, pepper, and vinegar. In my opinion they acted imprudently, considering all circumstances, in not complying so far as would have given satisfaction, as several colonies did. But my dislike of their conduct in that instance has not blinded me so much that I cannot plainly perceive that they have been punished in a manner pernicious to American freedom, and justly alarming to all the colonies.

If the *British* Parliament has a legal authority to issue an order that we shall furnish a single article for the troops here, and to compel obedience to *that* order, they have the same right to issue an order for us to supply those troops with arms, cloths, and every necessary ; and to compel obedience to *that* order also ; in short, to lay any burthens they please upon us. What is this but taxing us at a certain sum, and leaving to us only the manner of raising it ? How is this mode more tolerable than the Stamp Act ? Would that Act have appeared more pleasing to Americans, if being ordered thereby to raise the sum total of the taxes, the mighty privilege had been left to them, of saying how much should be paid for an instrument of writing on paper, and how much for another on parchment ?

An Act of Parliament commanding us to do a certain thing, if it has any validity, is a tax upon us for the expence that accrues in complying with it ; and for this reason, I believe, every colony on the continent, that chose to give a mark of their respect for Great Britain in complying with the Act relating to the troops, cautiously avoided the mention of that Act, lest their conduct should be attributed to its supposed obligation.

The matter being thus stated, the Assembly of New York either had, or had not a right to refuse submission to that Act. If they had, and I imagine no American will say they had not, then the Parliament had no right to compel them to execute it. If they had not *that right*, they had *no right* to punish them for not executing it ; and therefore no right to

c. 59, declared all Acts, &c., of the New York Assembly to be null and void until it should comply in full with the Quartering Act. The Assembly of 1769 gave in. For an explanation of the local conditions which produced this unexpected result, see C. L. Becker, *Political Parties in the Province of New York* (Madison, Wis., 1909).

suspend their legislation, which is a punishment. In fact, if the people of New York cannot be legally taxed but by their own representatives, they cannot be legally deprived of the privilege of legislation, only for insisting on that exclusive privilege of taxation. If they may be legally deprived in such a case of the privilege of legislation, why may they not with equal reason be deprived of every other privilege ? Or why may not every colony be treated in the same manner, when any of them shall dare to deny their assent to any impositions that shall be directed ? Or what signifies the repeal of the Stamp Act, if these colonies are to lose their other privileges, by not tamely surrendering that of taxation ?

There is one consideration arising from this suspension, which is not generally attended to, but shews its importance very clearly. It was not necessary that this suspension should be caused by an Act of Parliament. The Crown might have restrained the Governor of New York, even from calling the Assembly together, by its prerogative in the royal governments. This step, I suppose, would have been taken, if the conduct of the Assembly of New York had been regarded as an act of disobedience to the Crown alone ; but it is regarded as an act of disobedience to the authority ' of the *British Legislature* '. This gives the suspension a consequence vastly more affecting. It is a parliamentary assertion of the *supreme authority* of the *British* Legislature over these colonies in *the point of taxation*, and is intended to *compel* New York into a submission to that authority. It seems therefore to me as much a violation of the liberty of the people of that province, and consequently of all these colonies, as if the Parliament had sent a number of regiments to be quartered upon them till they should comply. For it is evident that the suspension is meant as a compulsion ; and the method of compelling is totally indifferent. It is indeed probable that the sight of red coats and the hearing of drums would have been most alarming, because people are generally more influenced by their eyes and ears than by their reason. But whoever seriously considers the matter, must perceive that a dreadful stroke is aimed at the liberty of these colonies. I say of these colonies ; for the cause of one is the cause of all. If the Parliament may lawfully deprive New York of any of her rights, it may deprive any, or all the other colonies of their rights ; and nothing can possibly so much encourage such attempts as a mutual inattention to the interests of each other. To divide and thus to destroy is the first political maxim in attacking those who are powerful by their union. He certainly is not a wise man who folds his arms and reposes himself at home, viewing with unconcern the flames that have invaded his neighbour's house, without using any endeavours to extinguish them. When Mr. Hampden's ship money cause for three shillings and fourpence was tried, all the people of England, with anxious expectations, interested themselves in the important decision ; and when the slightest point touching the freedom of *one* colony is agitated, I earnestly wish that all the rest may with equal ardour support their sister. Very much may be said on this subject ; but I hope more at present is unnecessary.

With concern I have observed that two Assemblies of this Province have sat and adjourned, without taking any notice of this Act. It may perhaps be asked, what would have been proper for them to do ? I am by no means fond of inflammatory measures ; I detest them. I should be sorry that anything should be done which might justly displease our sovereign or our mother country. But a firm, modest exertion of a free spirit should never be wanting on public occasions. It appears to me that it would have been sufficient for the Assembly to have ordered our agents to represent to the King's ministers, their sense of the Suspending Act, and to pray for its repeal. Thus we should have borne our testimony against it ; and might therefore reasonably expect that, on a like occasion, we might receive the same assistance from the other colonies.

Concordia res parvæ crescunt.
Small things grow great by concord.

A FARMER.

LETTER II

MY DEAR COUNTRYMEN,

There is another late Act of Parliament, which appears to me to be unconstitutional and as destructive to the liberty of these colonies, as that mentioned in my last letter ; that is, the Act for granting the duties on paper, glass, etc.[1]

The Parliament unquestionably possesses a legal authority

[1] The Townshend duties. A long foot-note, giving a digest of previous acts of trade and navigation, is omitted.

to regulate the trade of Great Britain and all her colonies.
Such an authority is essential to the relation between a mother
country and her colonies ; and necessary for the common good
of all. He, who considers these provinces as States distinct
from the British Empire, has very slender notions of justice,
or of their interests. We are but parts of a whole ; and
therefore there must exist a power somewhere to preside,
and preserve the connexion in due order. This power is lodged
in the Parliament ; and we are as much dependent on Great
Britain as a perfectly free people can be on another.

I have looked over every statute relating to these colonies,
from their first settlement to this time ; and I find every one
of them founded on this principle till the Stamp Act administration. All before are calculated to regulate trade and
preserve or promote a mutually beneficial intercourse between
the several constituent parts of the Empire; and though many
of them imposed duties on trade, yet those duties were always
imposed with design to restrain the commerce of one part, that
was injurious to another, and thus to promote the general
welfare. The raising a revenue thereby was never intended.
Thus the king, by his judges in his courts of justice, imposes
fines which all together amount to a very considerable sum and
contribute to the support of government : but this is merely
a consequence arising from restrictions that only meant to
keep peace and prevent confusion; and surely a man would
argue very loosely, who should conclude from hence that the
king has a right to levy money in general upon his subjects.
Never did the British Parliament, till the period above
mentioned, think of imposing duties in America *for the purpose
of raising a revenue.* Mr. Grenville first introduced this
language, in the preamble to the 4 Geo. III, c. 15, which has
these words : ' And whereas it is just and necessary that
a revenue be raised in Your Majesty's said dominions in
America, for defraying the expences of defending, protecting,
and securing the same : We, Your Majesty's most dutiful and
loyal subjects, the Commons of Great Britain, in Parliament
assembled, being desirous to make some provision in this
present session of Parliament, towards raising the said revenue
in America, have resolved to give and grant unto Your Majesty
the several rates and duties herein after mentioned,' etc.

A few months after came the Stamp Act, which reciting this,
proceeds in the same strange mode of expression, thus : ' And

whereas it is just and necessary that provision be made for raising a further revenue within Your Majesty's dominions in America, towards defraying the said expences, we Your Majesty's most dutiful and loyal subjects, the Commons of Great Britain, etc., give and grant,' etc., as before.

The last Act, granting duties upon paper, etc., carefully pursues these modern precedents. The preamble is, ' Whereas it is expedient that a revenue should be raised in Your Majesty's dominions in America, for making a more certain and adequate provision for defraying the charge of the administration of justice, and the support of civil government in such provinces, where it shall be found necessary ; and towards the further defraying the expences of defending, protecting, and securing the said dominions, we Your Majesty's most dutiful and loyal subjects, the Commons of Great Britain, etc., give and grant,' etc., as before.

Here we may observe an authority expressly claimed and exerted to impose duties on these colonies ; not for the regulation of trade ; not for the preservation or promotion of a mutually beneficial intercourse between the several constituent parts of the Empire, heretofore the sole objects of parliamentary institutions ; but for the single purpose of levying money upon us.

This I call an innovation ; and a most dangerous innovation. It may perhaps be objected that Great Britain has a right to lay what duties she pleases upon her exports, and it makes no difference to us whether they are paid here or there. To this I answer : these colonies require many things for their use, which the laws of Great Britain prohibit them from getting anywhere but from her. Such are paper and glass. That we may legally be bound to pay any general duties on these commodities relative to the regulation of trade, is granted ; but we being obliged by the laws to take from Great Britain any special duties imposed on their exportation to us only, with intention to raise a revenue from us only, are as much taxes upon us as those imposed by the Stamp Act.

What is the difference in substance and right whether the same sum is raised upon us by the rates mentioned in the Stamp Act, on the use of paper, or by these duties on the importation of it ? It is only the edition of a former book, shifting a sentence from the end to the beginning.

Suppose the duties were made payable in Great Britain.

It signifies nothing to us, whether they are to be paid here or there. Had the Stamp Act directed that all the paper should be landed at Florida, and the duties paid there before it was brought to the British colonies, would the Act have raised less money upon us, or have been less destructive of our rights ? By no means : for as we were under a necessity of using the paper, we should have been under the necessity of paying the duties. Thus, in the present case, a like necessity will subject us, if this Act continues in force, to the payment of the duties now imposed.

Why was the Stamp Act then so pernicious to freedom ? It did not enact, that every man in the colonies should buy a certain quantity of paper—No : It only directed that no instrument of writing should be valid in law if not made on stamped paper.

The makers of that Act knew full well that the confusions that would arise from the disuse of writings would compel the colonies to use the stamped paper, and therefore to pay the taxes imposed. For this reason the Stamp Act was said to be a law that would execute itself. For the very same reason, the last Act of Parliament, if it is granted to have any force here, will execute itself, and will be attended with the very same consequences to American liberty.

Some persons perhaps may say that this Act lays us under no necessity to pay the duties imposed, because we may ourselves manufacture the articles on which they are laid ; whereas by the Stamp Act no instrument of writing could be good, unless made on British paper, and that too stamped.

. . . .

Great Britain has prohibited the manufacturing iron and steel in these colonies, without any objection being made to her right of doing it. The like right she must have to prohibit any other manufacture among us. Thus she is possessed of an undisputed precedent on that point. This authority, she will say, is founded on the original intention of settling these colonies ; that is, that we should manufacture for them, and that they should supply her with materials. The equity of this policy, she will also say, has been universally acknowledged by the colonies, who never have made the least objections to statutes for that purpose ; and will further appear by the mutual benefits flowing from this usage ever since the settlement of these colonies.

Our great advocate Mr. Pitt, in his speeches on the debate concerning the repeal of the Stamp Act, acknowledged that Great Britain could restrain our manufactures. His words are these : ' This kingdom, as the supreme governing and legislative power, has always bound the colonies by her regulations and restrictions in trade, in navigation, in manufactures—in everything, except that of taking their money out of their pockets, without their consent.' Again he says : ' We may bind their trade, confine their manufactures, and exercise every power whatever, except that of taking their money out of their pockets, without their consent.'

Here then, my dear countrymen, ROUSE yourselves, and behold the ruin hanging over your heads. If you ONCE admit that Great Britain may lay duties upon her exportations to us, *for the purpose of levying money on us only*, she then will have nothing to do but to lay those duties on the articles which she prohibits us to manufacture—and the tragedy of American liberty is finished. We have been prohibited from procuring manufactures, in all cases, anywhere but from Great Britain (excepting linens, which we are permitted to import directly from Ireland). We have been prohibited in some cases from manufacturing for ourselves, and may be prohibited in others. We are therefore exactly in the situation of a city besieged, which is surrounded by the works of the besiegers in every part but one. If that is closed up, no step can be taken, but to surrender at discretion. If Great Britain can order us to come to her for necessaries we want, and can order us to pay what taxes she pleases before we take them away, or when we land them here, we are as abject slaves as France and Poland can show in wooden shoes and with uncombed hair.

Perhaps the nature of the necessities of dependent states, caused by the policy of a governing one, for her own benefit, may be elucidated by a fact mentioned in history. When the Carthaginians were possessed of the island of Sardinia, they made a decree, that the Sardinians should not raise corn, nor get it any other way than from the Carthaginians. Then, by imposing any duties they would upon it, they drained from the miserable Sardinians any sums they pleased ; and whenever that oppressed people made the least movement to assert their liberty, their tyrants starved them to death or submission. This may be called the most perfect kind of political necessity.

LETTER III

. . . .

The cause of liberty is a cause of too much dignity to be sullied by turbulence and tumult. It ought to be maintained in a manner suitable to her nature. Those who engage in it should breathe a sedate, yet fervent spirit, animating them to actions of prudence, justice, modesty, bravery, humanity, and magnanimity.

To such a wonderful degree were the ancient Spartans, as brave and free a people as ever existed, inspired by this happy temperature of soul, that rejecting even in their battles the use of trumpets and other instruments for exciting heat and rage, they marched up to scenes of havoc and horror with the sound of flutes, to the tunes of which their steps kept pace— ' exhibiting,' as Plutarch says, ' at once a terrible and delightful sight, and proceeding with a deliberate valor, full of hope and good assurance, as if some divinity had sensibly assisted them.'

I hope, my dear countrymen, that you will, in every colony, be upon your guard against those who may at any time endeavour to stir you up under pretences of patriotism, to any measures disrespectful to our Sovereign and our mother country. Hot, rash, disorderly proceedings, injure the reputation of a people as to wisdom, valor and virtue, without procuring them the least benefit. I pray God that he may be pleased to inspire you and your posterity to the latest ages, with a spirit of which I have an idea that I find a difficulty to express. To express it in the best manner I can, I mean a spirit that shall so guide you that it will be impossible to determine whether an American's character is most distinguishable for his loyalty to his Sovereign, his duty to his mother country, his love of freedom, or his affection for his native soil.

. . . .

When the appeal is made to the sword, highly probable is it that the punishment will exceed the offence ; and the calamities attending on war outweigh those preceding it. These considerations of justice and prudence will always have great influence with good and wise men.

To these reflections on this subject it remains to be added, and ought for ever to be remembered, that resistance, in the case of colonies against their mother country, is extremely different from the resistance of a people against their prince. A nation may change their king, or race of kings, and, retaining their antient form of government, be gainers by changing. Thus Great Britain, under the illustrious house of Brunswick, a house that seems to flourish for the happiness of mankind, has found a felicity, unknown in the reigns of the Stewarts. But if once we are separated from our mother country what new form of government shall we adopt, or where shall we find another Britain to supply our loss? Torn from the body, to which we are united by religion, liberty, laws, affections, relation, language and commerce, we must bleed at every vein.

In truth—the prosperity of these provinces is founded in their dependence on Great Britain; and when she returns to her ' old good humour, and her old good nature ', as Lord Clarendon expresses it, I hope they will always think it their duty and interest, as it most certainly will be, to promote her welfare by all the means in their power.

We cannot act with too much caution in our disputes. Anger produces anger; and differences that might be accommodated by kind and respectful behavior, may by imprudence be enlarged to an incurable rage. In quarrels between countries, as well as in those between individuals, when they have risen to a certain height the first cause of dissension is no longer remembered, the minds of the parties being wholly engaged in recollecting and resenting the mutual expressions of their dislike. When feuds have reached that fatal point, all considerations of reason and equity vanish; and a blind fury governs, or rather confounds all things. A people no longer regards their interest, but the gratification of their wrath. The sway of the Cleons and Clodius's,* the designing and detestable flatterers of the prevailing passion, becomes confirmed. Wise and good men in vain oppose the storm, and may think themselves fortunate, if in attempting to preserve their ungrateful fellow citizens they do not ruin themselves. Their prudence will be called baseness; their moderation will be called guilt; and if their virtue does not lead them to destruction, as that of many other great and excellent persons has done, they may survive to receive from their expiring country the mournful glory of her acknowledgment that their counsels, if regarded, would have saved her.

* Cleon was a popular firebrand of Athens, and Clodius of Rome; each of whom plunged his country into the deepest calamities.

The constitutional modes of obtaining relief are those which I wish to see pursued on the present occasion ; that is, by petitions of our assemblies, or, where they are not permitted to meet, of the people, to the powers that can afford us relief.

We have an excellent prince, in whose good dispositions towards us we may confide. We have a generous, sensible, and humane nation, to whom we may apply. They may be deceived. They may by artful men be provoked to anger against us. I cannot believe they will be cruel or unjust ; or that their anger will be implacable. Let us behave like dutiful children, who have received unmerited blows from a beloved parent. Let us complain to our parent ; but let our complaints speak at the same time the language of affliction and veneration.

If however it shall happen by an unfortunate course of affairs that our applications to His Majesty and the Parliament for redress prove ineffectual, let us then take another step, by withholding from Great Britain all the advantages she has been used to receive from us. Then let us try if our ingenuity, industry and frugality, will not give weight to our remonstrances. Let us all be united with one spirit, in one cause. Let us invent, let us work, let us save, let us continually keep up our claim, and incessantly repeat our complaints—but above all let us implore the protection of that infinitely good and gracious Being, ' by whom kings reign and princes decree justice.'

> *Nil desperandum.*
> Nothing is to be despaired of.

A Farmer.

LETTER IV

My dear Countrymen,

An objection, I hear, has been made against my second letter, which I would willingly clear up before I proceed. ' There is,' say these objectors, ' a material difference between the Stamp Act and the late Act for laying a duty on paper, etc., that justifies the conduct of those who opposed the former, and yet are willing to submit to the latter. The duties imposed by the Stamp Act were internal taxes ; but the present are external, and therefore the Parliament may have a right to impose them.'

To this I answer, with a total denial of the power of

Parliament to lay upon these colonies any ' tax ' whatever. This point, being so important to this, and to succeeding generations, I wish to be clearly understood.

To the word ' tax ', I annex that meaning which the Constitution and history of England require to be annexed to it ; that is—that it is an imposition on the subject, for the sole purpose of levying money.

In the early ages of our monarchy certain services were rendered to the Crown for the general good. These were personal ; but in process of time such institutions being found inconvenient, gifts and grants of their own property were made by the people, under the several names of aids, tallages, tasks, taxes and subsidies, etc. These were made, as may be collected even from the names, for public service upon ' need and necessity '. All these sums were levied upon the people by virtue of their voluntary gift. Their design was to support the national honor and interest. Some of those grants comprehended duties arising from trade ; being imposts on merchandizes. These Lord Chief Justice Coke classes under ' subsidies ' and ' parliamentary aids '. They are also called ' customs '. But whatever the name was, they were always considered as gifts of the people to the Crown, to be employed for public uses.

Commerce was at a low ebb, and surprizing instances might be produced how little it was attended to for a succession of ages. The terms that have been mentioned, and, among the rest, that of ' tax ', had obtained a national, parliamentary meaning, drawn from the principles of the Constitution, long before any Englishman thought of imposition of duties, for the regulation of trade.

Whenever we speak of taxes among Englishmen, let us therefore speak of them with reference to the principles on which, and the intentions with which they have been established. This will give certainty to our expression and safety to our conduct : but if, when we have in view the liberty of these colonies, we proceed in any other course, we pursue a Juno * indeed, but shall only catch a cloud.

In the national, parliamentary sense insisted on, the word *tax* †

* The Goddess of Empire, in the heathen mythology ; according to an ancient fable, Ixion pursued her, but she escaped in a cloud.

† In this sense Montisquieu uses the word *tax* in his 13th book of *Spirit of Laws.*

was certainly understood by the Congress at New York, whose resolves may be said to form the American Bill of Rights.

The third, fourth, fifth, and sixth resolves are thus expressed. [See above, p. 33.]

Here is no distinction made between internal and external taxes. It is evident, from the short reasoning thrown into these resolves, that every imposition ' to grant to His Majesty the property of the colonies ', was thought a ' tax ' ; and that every such imposition, if laid any other way than ' with their consent, given personally, or by their representatives ', was not only ' unreasonable, and inconsistent with the principles and spirit of the British Constitution ', but destructive ' to the freedom of a people '.

LETTER VI

. . . .

It is true that impositions for raising a revenue may be hereafter called regulations of trade : but names will not change the nature of things. Indeed we ought firmly to believe, what is an undoubted truth, confirmed by the unhappy experience of many states heretofore free, that unless the most watchful attention be exerted, a new servitude may be slipped upon us, under the sanction of usual and respectable terms.

Thus the Caesars ruined the Roman liberty, under the titles of tribunical and dictatorial authorities, old and venerable dignities, known in the most flourishing times of freedom. In imitation of the same policy, James II when he meant to establish popery, talked of liberty of conscience, the most sacred of all liberties ; and had thereby almost deceived the dissenters into destruction.

All artful rulers who strive to extend their power beyond its just limits, endeavour to give to their attempts as much semblance of legality as possible. Those who succeed them may venture to go a little further ; for each new encroachment will be strengthened by a former. ' That which is now supported by examples, growing old, will become an example itself,' * and thus support fresh usurpations.

A free people therefore can never be too quick in observing, nor too firm in opposing the beginnings of alteration either

* Tacitus.

in form or reality, respecting institutions formed for their security. The first kind of alteration leads to the last : yet, on the other hand, nothing is more certain, than that the forms of liberty may be retained, when the substance is gone. In government, as well as in religion, ' The letter killeth, but the spirit giveth life.'

I will beg leave to enforce this remark by a few instances. The Crown by the Constitution has the prerogative of creating peers. The existence of that order in due number and dignity is essential to the constitution ; and if the Crown did not exercise that prerogative, the peerage must have long since decreased so much as to have lost its proper influence. Suppose a prince, for some unjust purposes, should, from time to time, advance so many needy, profligate wretches to that rank, that all the independence of the House of Lords should be destroyed ; there would then be a manifest violation of the Constitution, under the appearance of using legal prerogative.

The House of Commons claim the privilege of forming all money bills, and will not suffer either of the other branches of the Legislature to add to or alter them ; contending that their power simply extends to an acceptance or rejection of them. This privilege appears to be just : but under pretence of this just privilege, the House of Commons has claimed a licence of tacking to money bills clauses relating to things of a totally different kind, and thus forcing them in a manner on the King and Lords. This seems to be an abuse of that privilege, and it may be vastly more abused. Suppose a future House, influenced by some displaced, discontented demagogues in a time of danger, should tack to a money bill something so injurious to the King and peers, that they would not assent to it, and yet the Commons should obstinately insist on it ; the whole kingdom would be exposed to ruin by them, under the appearance of maintaining a valuable privilege.

LETTER VIII

.   .   .   .

. . . But the Act now objected to, impose duties upon British colonies, ' to defray the expences of defending, protecting, and securing His Majesty's dominions in America.'
. . . not only the British colonies, but also the conquered

provinces of Canada and Florida, and the British garrisons of Nova Scotia ; for these do not deserve the name of colonies.

What justice is there in making us pay for ' defending, protecting, and securing ' these places ? What benefit can we, or have we ever derived from them ? None of them was conquered for us ; nor will ' be defended, protected, or secured ' for us.

In fact, however advantageous the subduing or keeping any of these countries may be to Great Britain, the acquisition is greatly injurious to these colonies. Our chief property consists in lands. These would have been of much greater value, if such prodigious additions had not been made to the *British* territories on this continent. The natural increase of our own people, if confined within the colonies, would have raised the value still higher and higher every fifteen or twenty years. Besides we should have lived more compactly together, and have been therefore more able to resist any enemy. But now the inhabitants will be thinly scattered over an immense region, as those who want settlements will chuse to make new ones, rather than pay great prices for old ones.[1]

These are the consequences to the colonies, of the hearty assistance they gave to Great Britain in the late war—a war undertaken solely for her own benefit. The objects of it were, the securing to herself the rich tracts of land on the back of these colonies, with the Indian trade ; and Nova Scotia, with the fishery. These and much more, has that kingdom gained ; but the inferior animals that hunted with the lion, have been amply rewarded for all the sweat and blood their loyalty cost them, by the honor of having sweated and bled in such company.

I will not go so far as to say that Canada and Nova Scotia are curbs on New England ; the chain of forts through the backwoods, on the Middle Provinces ; and Florida, on the rest : but I will venture to say that if the products of Canada, Nova Scotia, and Florida, deserve any consideration, the two first of them are only rivals of our Northern Colonies, and the other of our Southern.

. . . .

So that the British colonies are to be drained of the rewards of their labor, to cherish the scorching sands of Florida, and

[1] Cf. the reasoning in the Report of the Lords of Trade in 1768, below, pp. 70-3.

the icy rocks of Canada and Nova Scotia, which never will
return to us one farthing that we send to them.

Great Britain—I mean the ministry in Great Britain, has
cantoned Canada and Florida out into five or six governments,
and may form as many more. There now are fourteen or
fifteen regiments on this continent ; and there soon may be
as many more. To make ' an adequate provision ' for all
these expences, is, no doubt, to be the inheritance of the
colonies.

Can any man believe that the duties upon paper, etc., are
the last that will be laid for these purposes ? It is in vain to
hope that because it is imprudent to lay duties on the exportation of manufactures from a mother country to colonies, as
it may promote manufactures among them, that this consideration will prevent such a measure.

Ambitious, artful men have made it popular, and whatever
injustice or destruction will attend it in the opinion of the
colonists, at home it will be thought just and salutary.

The people of Great Britain will be told, and have been
told, that they are sinking under an immense debt—that
great part of this debt has been contracted in defending the
colonies—that these are so ungrateful and undutiful, that
they will not contribute one mite to its payment—nor even
to the support of the army now kept up for their ' defence
and security '—that they are rolling in wealth, and are of
so bold and republican a spirit that they are aiming at independence—that the only way to retain them in ' obedience '
is to keep a strict watch over them and to draw off part of
their riches in taxes—and that every burden laid upon them
is taking off so much from Great Britain—these assertions
will be generally believed, and the people will be persuaded
that they cannot be too angry with their colonies, as that
anger will be profitable to themselves.

In truth, Great Britain alone receives any benefit from
Canada, Nova Scotia, and Florida ; and therefore she alone
ought to maintain them. The old maxim of the law is drawn
from reason and justice, and never could be more properly
applied than in this case.

Qui sentit commodum, sentire debet et onus.
They who feel the benefit, ought to feel the burden.

A FARMER.

LETTER X

MY DEAR COUNTRYMEN,

The consequences, mentioned in the last letter, will not be the utmost limits of our misery and infamy, if the late Act is acknowledged to be binding upon us. We feel too sensibly, that any ministerial measures relating to these colonies, are soon carried successfully through the Parliament. Certain prejudices operate there so strong against us that it may be justly questioned whether all the provinces united will ever be able effectually to call to an account before the Parliament any minister who shall abuse the power by the late Act given to the Crown in America. He may divide the spoils torn from us in what manner he pleases, and we shall have no way of making him responsible. If he should order that every Governor shall have a yearly salary of 5,000*l.* sterling ; every chief Justice of 3,000*l.* ; every inferior officer in proportion ; and should then reward the most profligate, ignorant, or needy dependents on himself or his friends with places of the greatest trust, because they were of the greatest profit, this would be called an arrangement in consequence of the ' adequate provision for defraying the charge of the administration of justice and the support of the civil government '. And if the taxes should prove at any time insufficient to answer all the expences of the numberless offices which ministers may please to create, surely the members of the House of Commons will be so ' modest ' as not to ' contradict a minister ' who shall tell them it is become necessary to lay a new tax upon the colonies for the laudable purposes of defraying the charges of the ' administration of justice and support of civil government ' among them. Thus in fact we shall be taxed by ministers. In short, it will be in their power to settle upon us any civil, ecclesiastical, or military establishment which they choose.

We may perceive, by the example of Ireland, how eager ministers are to seize upon any settled revenue, and apply it in supporting their own power. Happy are the men, and happy the people, who grow wise by the misfortunes of others. Earnestly, my dear countrymen, do I beseech the author of all good gifts, that you may grow wise in this manner ; and if I may be allowed to take such a liberty, I beg leave to recommend to you in general, as the best

method of attaining this wisdom, diligently to study the
histories of other countries. You will there find all the arts
that can possibly be practiced by cunning rulers or false
patriots among yourselves, so fully delineated, that, changing
names, the account would serve for your own times.

It is pretty well known on this continent that Ireland has
with a regular consistency of injustice, been cruelly treated
by ministers in the article of pensions ; but there are some
alarming circumstances relating to that subject which I wish
to have better known among us.

The revenue of the Crown there arises principally from
the excise granted ' for pay of the army and defraying other
public charges, in defence and preservation of the kingdom '
—from the tonnage and additional poundage granted ' for
protecting the trade of the kingdom at sea, and augmenting
the public revenue '—from the hearth money granted—as
a ' public revenue, for a public charge and expences '. There
are some other branches of the revenue, concerning which
there is not any express appropriation of them for public
service, but which were plainly so intended.

Of these branches of the revenue the Crown is only trustee
for the public. They are unalienable. They are inapplicable
to any other purposes but those for which they were established ; and therefore are not legally chargeable with pensions.

There is another kind of revenue which is a private revenue.
This is not limited to any public uses ; but the Crown has
the same property in it that any person has in his estate.
This does not amount, at the most, to fifteen thousand
pounds a year, probably not to seven, and is the only revenue
that can be legally charged with pensions.

If ministers were accustomed to regard the rights or happiness of the people, the pensions in Ireland would not exceed
the sum just mentioned : but long since have they exceeded
that limit ; and in December 1765 a motion was made in the
House of Commons in that kingdom, to address His Majesty
on the great increase of pensions on the Irish establishment,
amounting to the sum of 158,685*l.* in the last two years. . . .

From this conduct towards Ireland in open violation of
law we may easily foresee what we may expect when a minister
will have the whole revenue of America in his own hands to
be disposed of at his own pleasure. For all the monies raised
by the late act are to be ' applied by virtue of warrants under
the sign manual, countersigned by the high treasurer or any

three of the commissioners of the Treasury '. The ' residue ' indeed is to be ' paid into the receipt of the exchequer, and to be disposed of by Parliament '. So that a minister will have nothing to do but to take care that there shall be no ' residue ', and he is superior to all controul.

Besides the burden of pensions in Ireland, which have enormously encreased within these few years, almost all the offices in that poor kingdom have been since the commencement of the present century, and now are bestowed upon strangers. For tho' the merit of persons born there justly raises them to places of high trust when they go abroad, as all Europe can witness, yet he is an uncommonly lucky Irishman who can get a good post in his native country.

When I consider the manner in which that island has been uniformly depressed for so many years past with this pernicious particularity of their Parliament continuing as long as the Crown pleases, I am astonished to observe such a love of liberty still animating that loyal and generous nation ; and nothing can rise higher my idea of the integrity and public spirit of a people who have preserved the sacred fire of freedom from being extinguished, tho' the altar on which it burnt has been overturned. . . .

LETTER XII

Let these truths be indelibly impressed on our minds— that we cannot be happy without being free—that we cannot be free without being secure in our property—that we cannot be secure in our property if without our consent others may as by right take it away—that taxes imposed on us by Parliament do thus take it away—that duties laid for the sole purpose of raising money are taxes—that attempts to lay such duties should be instantly and firmly opposed—that this opposition can never be effectual unless it is the united effort of these Provinces—that therefore benevolence of temper towards each other and unanimity of councils are essential to the welfare of the whole—and lastly, that for this reason, every man amongst us who in any manner would encourage either dissension, diffidence, or indifference between these colonies is an enemy to himself and to his country.

To discharge this double duty to yourselves and to your posterity you have nothing to do but to call forth into use the good sense and spirit of which you are possessed. You have nothing to do but to conduct your affairs peaceably—prudently—firmly—jointly. By these means you will support the character of freemen without losing that of faithful subjects—a good character in any government—one of the best under a British Government. You will prove that Americans have that true magnanimity of soul that can resent injuries without falling into rage ; and that tho' your devotion to Great Britain is the most affectionate, yet you can make proper distinctions and know what you owe to yourselves as well as to her. You will at the same time that you advance your interests advance your reputation. You will convince the world of the justice of your demands and the purity of your intentions. While all mankind must, with unceasing applauses, confess that you indeed deserve liberty, who so well understand it, so passionately love it, so temperately enjoy it, and so wisely, bravely and virtuously assert, maintain and defend it.

Certe ego libertatem, quae mihi a parente meo tradita est, experiar ; Verum id frustra an ob rem faciam, in vestra manu situm est, quirites. For my part I am resolved to contend for the liberty delivered down to me by my ancestors ; but whether I shall do it effectually or not, depends on you, my countrymen.

' How little soever one is able to write, yet when the liberties of one's country are threatened, it is still more difficult to be silent.'   A FARMER.

FINIS

INDIAN DIPLOMACY

Proceedings of a General Congress of the Six Nations, etc. ; *the Chiefs of* Coghnawagey *and of the* Seven Confederate Nations of Canada *and the Deputys sent from the* Cherokee Nation *to treat of Peace with the former before Sir* William Johnson, *Baronet, at Johnson Hall in March 1768.*[1]

THE Cherokee Deputy's arrived the 29 December 1767, on which Sir William sent Belts and Messages to the Six Nations, etc., who did not arrive until the 2nd of March by reason of the inclemency of the weather and other impediments.

[1] Public Record Office, London, C.O. 5, 69, pp. 329–48. Printed in full in *Documents relative to the Colonial History of New York,* viii. 38–53.

AT A CONGRESS with the above mentioned Nations at Johnson Hall, March 4, 1768,

PRESENT—

Sir William Johnson, Baronet.
Sir John Johnson, Knight.
Daniel Claus ⎱ Esquires, Deputy Agents for Indian
Guy Johnson ⎰   Affairs.
Lieut. Frazier.
Mr. Michaell Byrne, Commissary of Indian Affairs.
Mr. Robert Adems.
Mr. Daniell Denniston.
John Butler, Esq. ⎱ Interpreters for the Six Nations and
Mr. Perthies   ⎰ Canada Indians.
Mr. John Walls, Cherokee Interpreter.

Being all seated, Sir William open'd the Congress as follows—

BRETHEREN OF THE SIX NATIONS AND CANADA CON-FEDERACY :—I give you all a most cordial welcome to this place, where I wish our mutual proceedings may be conducted with the strictest candour and sincerity.

It is with no small concern that I am to condole with you on account of the late act of cruelty exercised on some of your friends within the Province of Pensilvania. Whatever might have been the provocation given to that bad man who was the author of the deaths of ten of your Confederacy, you may rest assured that all His Majesties subjects hold that act in the greatest abhorence, and that he will certainly be punished with the death he so justly deserves whenever he is apprehended. On this disagreeable subject I am particularly authorised to speak to you by the Governor and people of the Province where that act was perpetrated, which you shall hear in due time. At present I am on the part of His Majesty and all his subjects to assure you that he and they are much concerned at it, that it is hoped you are all satisfied of its being the private act of a profligate individual and his accom-plice without the knowledge or consent of any others, and that every possible means is making use of for apprehending him in order to bring him to the punishment which the crime deserves. I do therefore, on the part of His Majesty and all his subjects, with this 3 strings of Wampum wipe away and dry up the tears which you have shed upon this occasion, clearing your sight that you may be enabled to look chearfully upon us,—With this string I clear the passage of your throats that you may speak to us freely and without any difficulty, and with this, I wipe away the blood of the slain from about your habitations that the same may appear no more to offend your eyes.   *Gave 3 strings of Wampum.*

BROTHERS,—With this Belt I take the hatchet out of your heads, with which you were struck by that villain who was regardless of the friendship subsisting between us, and I request you to remember that he and his accomplice only were guilty in that point, and that notwithstanding the order of our Government and the goodness of our laws, we must expect to have some bad men amongst us, whose conduct and inclinations may differ widely from that of the rest of the people.   *Gave a large Black Belt.*

BROTHERS,—With this Belt I pull up the largest pine tree by the roots, under which I bury the axe that gave you the blow, placeing the tree over it in its former position so that the axe may no more be found.

Gave a large White Belt with Black figures.

BROTHERS,—This is the first opportunity my son (Sir John) has had for shaking you by the hand since his arrival from England, where he was not unmindfull of your affairs, he will now say something to you upon the occasion.

Then Sir John (after shaking hands with the Chiefs) said :—

BROTHERS,—I am happy at finding you all here in health at this time and sincerely wish that your proceedings may be conducted to the public satisfaction. It is with pleasure I can inform you that I have had an opportunity of hearing His Majesty's favourable opinion of all good Indians, and his steady resolution to redress your grievances, and do you strict justice, to this end your affairs are now under consideration, and the boundary line between the white inhabitants and you, which is considered so necessary for the preservation of your hunting grounds, will speedily be settled.

BROTHERS,—I heartily thank you for your frequent enquirys after me during my absence in England, and I shall be at all times glad to convince you of my sincerity and good wishes for your several Confederacies.

Gave a White Belt with Black figures.

Sir William then address'd them in the following manner :—

BROTHERS,—I have now gone through the business of condolance with you, and hope it will prove agreeable, and ease your minds. Tomorrow I shall proceed to the business for which you are now assembled.

So soon as Sir William had ended, each of the Nations present gave the Yo-hah, or shout of approbation, after which they received pipes, tobacco, and a dram each. And after a short consultation amongst the Chiefs, Conoghquiesor Chief of Oneida arose, and haveing repeated according to custom all that had been said with the several strings and belts to the Six Nations, etc., he addressed Sir William on their behalf as follows :—

BROTHER GORAH WARRAGHIYAGEY : [1]—We give thanks to the Great Spirit for enableing us to meet this day after so many accidents as have befallen us, and we thank you for what you have said to us, which we have hearkened to with great attention. We feel ourselves something easier since you spoke to us, and according to the manner of our forefathers removed those objects from before our eyes which have given us pain. Brother, we and our dependants have been for some time like giddy people not knowing what to do, wherever we turned about we saw our blood, and when our young men wanted to go a hunting the wild beasts in our country, they found it covered with fences, so that they were weary crossing them, neither can they get venison to eat, or bark to make huts ; for the beasts are run away and the trees cut down. The French told us this would come to pass, and when our young men sit down hungry in hot weather, and find no trees to shelter them, it makes them soon get drunk. Brother, we have got a great deal to say about these things, but as you have remembered our old ceremonys, taken the hatchet out of our heads, and given us such good words, we will do in like manner by you. Then went thro the ceremony of condolance with strings and belts, and buried the axe, but did not as usual take it out of the heads of the English. After which the Speaker said,

BROTHER,—We return the Great Spirit our best thanks for giving us the pleasure of seeing your son safe returned and of hearing good friendly words he spoke to us ; we have had our neck stretched out this long time endeavouring to see him. We now congratulate you on his safe arrival over the

[1] Sir William's nickname, meaning ' Rays of the Sun Enlightening the Earth '.

dangerous lake, and we heartily thank him for his love for us and for the good things he has said to us, which makes us all easier in our minds. Then the Chiefs all arose, and shaking Sir John by the hand, welcomed him to America. After which adjourned till next morning.

At night Sir William had some private conferences with several of the Chiefs, to whom he spoke on the subject of their neglecting to take the axe out of the heads of the English, which indicated resentment. His discourse had a good deal of effect upon them, and they withdrew to have a conference amongst themselves.

5 March

The Cherokees refusing to open their embassy from a superstitious notion that as it was noon, the day was too far advanced for a work of peace, according to the opinion of the Southern Nations. The Six Nations, having been late assembling, at length addressed Sir William by their speaker, who made an apology for their omission of the preceding day, and then in a speech for that purpose took the hatchet out of the heads of the English, and buried it, giving a Belt of Wampum, then agreeing to meet earlyer next morning, adjourned. After which the day was spent in private conferences with Sir William, and at night they had a feast and dance.

6 March

Sir William on entering the Council room introduced the Cherokee deputys to the rest of the Indians, and then addressed the Six Nations, etc., as follows :—

BROTHERS,—I am now to speak on the subject for which you have been here assembled, and I desire you will pay due regard and attention to my words. [He urges them to make peace with the Six Nations.] . . . *Gave a Large White Belt.*

Sir William then told the Cherokee Chiefs they might begin, when Ouconastota [1] stood up, ranged all his Belts, Calumets of Peace, etc., in order, and then spoke as follows :—

BROTHERS,—Hearken to me and give attention to what I have to say. We come from Chotte [2] where the Wise House, the House of Peace is erected, to Charlestown and from thence

---

[1] The Chief who visited England in the days of George II.
[2] Chota was five miles above the ruins of Fort Loudon, at the junction of the Tellico and Little Tennessee rivers, on the south-west frontier of the State of Tennessee.

by water to New York in our way to this place, it being recommended to us by Mr. Stuart our Superintendant to go by water lest we should meet with opposition, or to be attacked if we travelled by land thro' the woods, and Mr. Stuart told us that our Father, Sir William Johnson, would assist us in sending for our brothers the Northern Indians to meet about peace. *Gave 3 Strings.*

[Belts are presented to each of the Six Nations, and a calumet to Sir William Johnson.] . . .

BROTHERS,—We now present a Belt from our women to yours, and we know that they will hear us, for it is they who undergo the pains of childbirth and produce men, surely therefore they must feel mothers' pains for those killed in war, and be desirous to prevent it. *A Belt.*

BROTHERS,—Here is a Belt from our boys to you, who are now but small, and therefore their speech must be childish untill they arrive at manhood. All they desire is that they may be once more enabled to venture out to hunt birds and rabbits without the risk of being carried away or killed, and therefore all they beg is peace. *A Small Belt.*

BROTHERS,—With this Belt we clear and open the road, removing all things out of it that may hurt us. It was not us that stopped it, but our elder brothers the English and French, who in their dispute felled a great tree across it in the path ; but as the tree is now rotten the path is now open. *A Belt.*

SACHEMS AND CHIEFS, you have heard what we had to say, we beg you to agree to it, and that you will send some of your people with us to open the path between your towns and Chotte, that all our doors may once more be opened, so that we may be at peace and that our young people may pass and repass as their occasions require, without being in danger of being scratched or wounded by the briars along the road. *A Belt.*

[On 7 March the Chief of the Oneidas replies in kind, and on 8 March, Sir William Johnson addresses the entire assembly, urging the tribes to conclude a boundary treaty, and frankly to communicate their grievances.] . . .

P. M. The Indians having had a private conference amongst themselves assembled, and by their Speaker answered the speech of this morning as follows :—

BROTHER,—We thank the Great Spirit above for the present meeting, and we shall honestly answer you on the subject of your speech, and declare the causes of our uneasyness which we confess to have arrived at a great pitch—and we beg in our turn you will open your ears and hearken to what we have to say, and endeavour to obtain that redress for us which is the only sure way of securing the peace.

BROTHER,—We have often put you in mind of the many promises which were made to us at the beginning of the late war by the Generals, Governors, and by yourself, from all which we had the strongest reason to expect that the event of your success would have proved greatly to our benefit, that we should be favored and noticed, that we should not be wronged of our lands or of our peltry, that every encroachment should be removed, and we should live in peace, and travel about without molestation or hindrance. At the same time the French told us that what was said was not true, nor from your hearts; and that the day you got the better of them would be the first day of our misfortunes. You persuaded us not to believe them, but we have found it since too true. We soon found ourselves used ill at the posts, on the frontiers, and by the traders. The people who had formerly wronged us, and who did not choose to venture before to take possession of our rights, then rose up to crush us. The rum bottles hung at every door to steal our lands, and instead of the English protecting us as we thought they would do, they employed their superior cunning to wrong us, they murdered our people in Pensilvania, Virginia, and all over the country, and the traders began more and more to deceive, and now neither regard their own character, or the officers sent to take care of the trade, so that if we are wronged, who is to help us? We cant ramble over the country for justice, and if we did, we begin now to grow old and wise, we see that your wise men in the towns will be always against us. Your people came from the sun, rising up our rivers to the west, and now they begin to come upon us from the south, they have got already almost to Fort Pitt, but nothing is done to drive them away. You cant say that we have not often complained of this, and if you are not able or willing to do it we can, and must do so soon or they will eat us up, for your people want to chuse all the best of our lands, tho' there is enough within your part with your own marks upon it, without any inhabitants. Brother, this is very hard upon us, but it is not all, for the road thro' the country is no longer safe, the Pensilvanians and Virginians murder all those of our people they can meet, without any reason, and instead of leaving off as you told us they would, they have murdered ten the other day, two of which are our own people, the rest are our younger brothers and nephews that depend upon us. Yet you wont take the murderer or do any thing to him. You are wise, you have a Government and laws, but you dont prevent this ; you often tell us we dont restrain our people and that you do so with yours, but, brother, your words differ more from your actions than ours do. We have large wide ears and we can hear that you are going to settle great numbers in the heart of our country, and our necks are stretched out, and our faces set to the sea shore to watch their motions. Brother, you that are wise and have laws and say you can make your people do what they are desired, should prevent all this, and if they wont let us alone, you should shake them by the head. We believe that you are wise and that you can do all this, but we begin to think you have no mind to hinder them. If you will say you cant, we will do it for you, our legs are long, and our sight so good that we can see a great way thro' the woods, we can see the blood you have spilled and the fences you have made, and surely it is but right that we should punish those who have done all this mischief. Brother, this is the truth, it comes from our hearts. Why should we hide it from you ? If you wont do justice to our fathers the Mohawks who are going to lose the land at their very doors, if you wont keep the people away from the rivers near Ohio, and keep the road open, making Pensylvania and Virginia quiet, we must get tired of looking to you, and turn our faces another way. *Gave a Large Belt.*

BROTHER,—We heartily thank the Great King for his intentions, and for what he is going to do about the boundary line, but, brother, we hear bad news, the Cherokees have told us that the line was run in their country last year, and that it has surrounded them so that they cannot stir ; we beg that you will think of this, for our heads will be quite turned if that is to be our case, we therefore think that the line we talked of last should not go beyond Fort Augusta.

[Sir William relates the efforts that have been made to apprehend the murderers, and informs them that £2,500 have been voted by the Province of Pennsylvania to the tribes of the victims. The treaty between the Northern Indians and the Cherokees is then concluded.]

FROM THE REPORT OF THE BOARD OF TRADE AND PLANTATIONS ON THE WESTERN PROBLEM[1]

7 March 1768

To the King's Most Excellent Majesty.

May it please your Majesty,

In obedience to your Majesty's commands signified to us by a letter from the Earl of Shelburne, one of your Majesty's principal Secretaries of State, dated the 5th of October last, we have taken into our most serious consideration the several memorials, letters, and other papers therewith referred to us, containing objections to, and observations upon the present Plan[2] for the management of our commerce and connexions with the Indians in North America ; stating the great expense attending as well that branch of service, as the present disposition of the troops for Indian purposes, and urging the expediency and propriety, in various lights, of establishing certain new governments upon the Mississippi, the Ohio, and at the Detroit, between the Lakes Erie and Huron. We have also conferred, upon this occasion, with such of your Majesty's military servants, as have been employed in North America, and with such merchants and others as are most intelligent in the North American and Indian trade.

Whereupon we humbly beg leave to represent to your Majesty,

That the subject matter, to which these papers refer, and the questions arising thereupon, stated to us in the Earl of Shelburne's letter, appear to us to lead to a consideration of no less consequence and importance, than what system it may be now proper for your Majesty to pursue, with respect to that vast and extensive country in North America, which, on account of the Indian War raging within it, was made by the Proclamation of the 7 October 1763, the object of mere provisional arrangement.

The advantages arising from the Treaty of Paris, are in no

[1] Public Record Office, C.O. 5, 69, pp. 119–71. Printed in *Documents relative to the Colonial History of New York*, viii. 19–31. As this report is drawn up in the excessively redundant style affected by the Lords of Trade, it has been pruned by the editor as much as was possible without affecting the substance.

[2] The Plan of 1764. See Introduction.

part of it more distinguished than in those stipulations, which by obtaining from France and Spain cessions to your Majesty of those important possessions in North America, which, by their situation, gave most alarm and annoyance to the British Colonies, laid the foundation of lasting security to your Majesty's Empire in North America, and of relief to this country by a reduction of that heavy expense, with which it was necessarily burthen'd for the defence and protection of those colonies. And, although the unfavourable impressions left upon the minds of the Indians by the event of the war, and the representations of the French that we meant to extirpate them, did for sometime involve us in a war with them, that rendered necessary the continuance of a large military establishment; yet, that war being happily ended, the Treaties of Peace and Friendship to which all the various tribes have acceded, having been finally concluded, it is now become of immediate importance to examine, how far the alteration which has thus taken place in the state of your Majesty's Dominion in North America, may require or admit of any proportionable alteration in the system, by which that part of your Majesty's service is to be carried on for the future.

The parts of the Service for which we are more immediately called upon by the Earl of Shelburne's letter to give our attention, are, (1) the present Civil Establishment regarding the Indians ; (2) the disposition of the troops for Indian purposes ; and lastly, the establishment of certain new colonies.

. . . We are directed to state our opinion, how far the present expense of the civil establishment regarding the Indians may with safety and propriety be reduced, by entrusting the Indian trade, and all other Indian affairs, to the management of the several colonies.

In considering this question it may be proper to observe, that the institution of Superintendants for the affairs of Indians appears to have been a measure originally adopted principally with a view to counteract the designs of the French in 1754, who by sowing the seeds of jealousy amongst the Indians, and exciting them to resent injuries, for redress of which they had in vain solicited the colonies, had well nigh entirely weaned them from the British interest, and at the same time by uniting the force and conducting the enterprizes of the savages, had rendered them an overmatch for your Majesty's colonies standing single and disunited.

. . . Upon a carefull examination into the state of Indian affairs after the conclusion of peace, it appears that the two principall causes of the discontent, that still rankled in the minds of the Indians and influenced their conduct, were the encroachments made upon lands which they claimed as their property, and the abuses committed by Indian traders and their servants. The necessity which appeared . . . induced the Proclamation of October 1763 ; which very prudently restrained all persons from trading with the Indians without licence ; and forbid, by the strongest prohibitions, all settlement beyond the limits therein described as the boundary of the Indian hunting ground, putting both their commerce and property under the protection of officers acting under your Majesty's immediate authority, and making their intervention necessary in every transaction with those Indians.

These, however, being, as we have before observed, mere provisional arrangements adapted to the exigence of the time, it is become now necessary to consider what may be more permanently requisite in both the cases to which they apply.

The giving all possible redress to the complaints of the Indians in respect to encroachments on their lands, and a steady and uniform attention to a faithful execution of whatever shall be agreed upon for that salutary purpose, is a consideration of very great importance. It is a service of a general nature, in which your Majesty's interest, as Lord of the Soil of all ungranted lands which the Indians may be inclined to give up, is deeply and immediately concerned, and with which the general security of your Majesty's possessions there is in some measure connected. It is an object comprehensive of a variety of cases, to which the separate authority and jurisdiction of the respective colonies is not competent, and it depends upon negotiation, which has always been carried on between Indians and officers acting under your Majesty's immediate authority, and has reference to matters which the Indians would not submit to the discussion of particular colonies.

For these reasons we are of opinion, that the execution of all measures and services, respecting the complaints of the Indians touching their lands, should be continued to be entrusted to the Superintendants at present acting under commission from your Majesty, reserving to the Governor and Council of every particular colony, which may be interested in any measure that has reference to this general service, a right to interpose their advice, and making their concurrence necessary to the ratification of every compact that shall be provisionally made, until your Majesty's pleasure shall be known upon it.

In a plan for the management of Indian affairs prepared by this Board in 1764, the fixing a boundary between the settlements of your Majesty's subjects and the Indian country was proposed to be established by compact with the Indians, as essentially necessary to the gaining their good will and affection, and to preserving the tranquility of the colonies.

This plan having been communicated to the Superintendants, they have in the consequence thereof made the proposition of such a boundary line an object of their particular attention, and of negotiation and discussion with the several tribes of Indians interested therein.

[A description of the then incomplete negotiations for a boundary line follows.]

Upon the whole it does appear to us, that it will be greatly for your Majesty's interest as well as for the peace, security, and advantage of the colonies, that this boundary line should as speedily as possible be ratified by your Majesty's authority, and that the Superintendants should be instructed and impowered to make treaties in your Majesty's name with the Indians for that purpose, and enabled to make such presents to the Indians as the nature and extent of the concessions on their part shall appear to require. Care, however, should be taken in the settlement of this business, that the agreement for a boundary line be left open to such alterations as, by the common consent, and for the mutual interests of both parties, may hereafter be found necessary and expedient.

. . . We humbly submit whether it may not be further necessary that the colonies should be required to give every sanction to the measure in their power and to provide by proper laws for the punishment of all persons, who shall endanger the publick peace of the community, by extending settlements or occupying lands beyond such line.

. . . We humbly submit, that there are other branches of duty and service, which . . . require the intervention of officers acting under your Majesty's immediate authority ; and which . . . cannot be provided for by the Provincial Laws. Such are the renewal of antient compacts or covenant-chains made between the Crown and the principal tribes of savages in that country ; the reconciling differences and disputes between one body of Indians and another ; the agreeing with them for the sale or surrender of lands for public purposes not lying within the limits of any particular colony ; and the holding interviews with them for these and a variety of other general purposes, which are merely objects of negotiation between your Majesty and the Indians. . . .

Antecedent to the establishment of the present plan of Superintendants, the management of these interests was entrusted to the Governors of the colonies which were principally connected with the Indians. But when we consider the dependent state of such Governors ; that the other duties of their stations must interfere with this very important one ; how greatly the objects of this service are increased by alliances with those numerous nations heretofore under the dominion of France ; and how necessary it is that a constant watch should be kept upon their motions and designs ; and that your Majesty's servants should be constantly and regularly informed of the true state of affairs and of all transactions in the Indian country ; we cannot but be of opinion . . . that the office of Superintendants should for the present be continued for these purposes ; and that they should be enabled by a stated annual establishment confined to a certain sum, to make such presents as have been usual and customary [and] therefore . . . absolutely necessary upon all occasions of treaties held with the Indians for publick purposes ; the expence of which, including salaries to the two Superintendants, need not, according to the calculations and estimates made by them, exceed eight thousand pounds annually. . . .

It must be admitted that a proper plan of trade with the Indians is an object deserving great attention not only from the commercial benefit resulting from it, but also from the effect that it . . . must have upon the temper and disposition of the savages. . . . We are convinced, however, upon the whole of this consideration,

1. That no one general plan of commerce and policy is or can be applicable to all the different nations of Indians of different interests and in different situations.

2. That the confining trade to certain posts and places, which is the spirit and principal of the present system, however expedient and effectual with respect to the southern

Indians, is of doubtfull policy with respect to those Indians more particularly connected with New York and Pensylvania ; and that it is evidently disadvantageous, inconvenient, and even dangerous with respect to the much larger body of Indians, who possess the country to the westward, and with whom your Majesty's subjects in Quebec in particular do carry on so extensive a commerce.

3. That independent of this objection, and of any doubt that might attend the practicability of its execution in its full extent, the whole Plan does consist of such a variety of establishments, and necessarily leads to such extensive operations, as to bring on an increasing expence which in point of commerce, may exceed the value of the object to which it applies, and being greater than the trade can bear, must, if the present Plan should be permanent, either fall upon the colonies (in which case it will be impracticable to settle the proportion each colony should bear), or become a burthen upon this country, which we humbly conceive would be both unreasonable and highly inconvenient.

For these reasons therefore and under these circumstances, we are humbly of opinion that the laying aside that part of the present Plan which relates to the Indian trade, and intrusting the entire management of that trade to the colonies themselves, will be of great advantage to your Majesty's service, as a means of avoiding much difficulty, and saving much expense both at present and in future.

It is certainly true, that while the management of this trade was in the hands of the colonies antecedent to the establishment of Superintendants, many abuses were committed by the traders, little care was taken to subject them to proper regulations, and the misconduct of the colonies in this particular contributed not a little to involve us in the enormous expences of an Indian war.

. . . But we trust, that the experience which the old colonies have had of the ill effects of such inattention and neglect, will induce all of them to use more caution and better management for the future ; and particularly to adopt such of the regulations established by the present Superintendants as have evidently operated to the benefitt of the trade, and to the giving that satisfaction and content to the Indians. . . .

. . . We beg leave . . . to represent it to your Majesty as our humble opinion, that it will be in the highest degree expedient to reduce all such posts in the interior country, as are not immediately subservient to the protection of the Indian commerce and to the defeating of French and Spanish machinations among the Indians, or which . . . cannot be maintained but at an expence disproportioned to the degree of their utility. . . .

[Mention is made of the illicit trade between Louisiana and the Choctaws], and as their commerce both from Louisiana and the British colonies is carried on through a great variety of paths and routs, and does not depend upon rivers and lakes, . . . it is evident that . . . neither the trade of your Majesty's subjects can be protected, nor the connection and intercourse between Louisiana and the Indians prevented, by forts or military establishments.

In the Northern District the principal Indians form themselves into two great Confederacies ; the one composed of the Six Nations and their allies and dependants, the other, called the Western Confederacy, composed of a great variety of powerfull tribes occupying that extensive country which lyes about the Lakes Huron, Michigan, and Superior, and to the West and Northwest.

The commerce and connection with the first of these bodies of Indians was, antecedent to the war, confined chiefly to the Province of New York, upon the teritories of which their principal hunting ground lyes, and the trade was carried on at fortified truck-houses upon the Lake Ontario. Since the peace a large share of this trade is carried on from Pennsylvania by the channel of the Ohio, and from thence by Venango and Rivière-aux-Bœufs into Lake Erie. The commerce and connection with those Indians which form the Western Confederacy, were . . . altogether confined to the French in Canada, and is now principally carried on from thence by your Majesty's subjects there, through the channel of the Ottawa River and by the lakes.

. . . It does appear to us that the keeping up military establishments at Detroit, Michilimacinac, and Niagara, and the having two, or at most three armed vessels on the Lakes Erie, Huron, Michigan, and Superior, may be necessary for keeping up and preserving that good correspondence with the Indians, which is essential to the safety, improvement, and extension of the trade with them.

.   .   .   .

All such forts as shall be judged necessary to be kept up for the security of your Majesty's dominions against a foreign enemy, or for forcing obedience to and a due execution of the Laws of Trade, ought to be garrisoned by troops in your Majesty's pay, commanded by officers appointed by your Majesty ; as it would in our humble opinion be dangerous to publick safety, and inconsistent with the true principles of this Government, that forts and military establishments intended to answer such important objects, should be entrusted to any other hands. . . .

This consideration therefore naturally leads us to the last head of inquiry referred to us by the Earl of Shelburne's letter, viz. How far the establishment of new governments on the Mississippi, the Ohio, and at Detroit, would contribute to answer the purpose of lessening either the present civil or military expence or would procure the several other important advantages set forth in the papers referred to us.

Now, although it does not appear from the papers referred to us, that propositions have been made for the establishment of more than three new governments or colonies in the interior parts of America ; viz. one at the Detroit between Lakes Erie and Huron ; [1] one at or near the mouth of the Ohio ; [2] and one in the Illinois country at or near the mouth of the river of that name ; [3] and therefore by the strict letter of his lordship's reference, the present consideration seems to be confined to these only ; yet as it does appear . . . that they are meant to support the utility of colonizing in the interior country, as a general principle of policy ; and that in fact they have nothing less in view than the entire possession and peopling of all that country, which has communications with the rivers Mississippi and St. Lawrence, it does in our humble opinion, open a much wider field of discussion than might at the first glance seem to be necessary.

[1] Promoted by Major Thomas Mant and 59 other officers who had served in Pontiac's rebellion. They proposed to transport 624 families to a land grant covering more than the present State of Michigan.

[2] The plan of General Phineas Lyman and a group of former officers and others, called the ' Military Adventurers '. They asked for most of Kentucky and half of Tennessee.

[3] A plan promoted by Benjamin Franklin, Sir William Johnson, and other leading colonists, embracing most of Illinois and Wisconsin. A map showing these three schemes is in Alvord, *Mississippi Valley*, i. 318. The Vandalia or Walpole scheme is not mentioned here, as the period of its organized activity came later.

The proposition of forming inland colonies in America is, we humbly conceive, entirely new ; it adopts principles in respect to American settlements different from what has hitherto been the policy of this kingdom ; and leads to a system which, if pursued through all its consequences, is in the present state of this country of the greatest importance.[1]

The great object of colonizing upon the Continent of North America has been to improve and extend the commerce, navigation, and manufactures of this Kingdom, upon which its strength and security depend : (1) by promoting the advantageous fishery carried on upon the northern coast ; (2) by encouraging the growth and culture of naval stores, and of raw materials to be transported hither in exchange for perfect manufacture and other merchandize ; (3) by securing a supply of lumber, provisions, and other necessaries for the support of our establishments in the American islands.

In order to answer these salutary purposes it has been the policy of this Kingdom to confine her settlements as much as possible to the sea coast and not to extend them to places unacessible to shipping and consequently more out of the reach of commerce, a plan which at the same time . . . had the further political advantage of guarding against all interfering of foreign powers and of enabling this Kingdom to keep up a superior naval force in those seas, by the actual possession of such rivers and harbours as were proper stations for fleets in time of war.

Such, may it please your Majesty, have been the considerations inducing that plan of policy hitherto pursued in the settlement of your Majesty's American colonies, with which the private interest and sagacity of the settlers co-operated from the first establishments. . . . It was upon these principles and with these views, that Government undertook the settling of Nova Scotia in 1749 ; and . . . that it was so liberally supported by the aid of Parliament.

The same motives . . . did, as we humbly conceive, induce the forming the colonies of Georgia, East Florida, and West Florida to the south, and the making those provisional arrangements in the Proclamation in 1763, by which the interior country was left to the possession of the Indians. . . .

[1] The rest of the Report, beginning with this paragraph, is quoted with approval in the Report of the Board of Trade and Plantations on the Vandalia scheme.   Franklin, *Works* (Bigelow ed.), v. 5-17.

It is well known that, antecedent to the year 1749, all that part of the sea coast of the British Empire in America which extends north-east from the Province of Main to Cançeau in Nova Scotia, and from thence north to the mouth of St. Lawrence's River, lay waste and neglected, though naturally affording or capable by art of producing every species of naval stores, the seas abounding with whale, cod, and other valuable fish, and having many great rivers, bays, and harbours fit for the reception of ships of war. . . . [These considerations] induced that Plan for the settlement of Nova Scotia, to which we have before referred. . . .

The establishment of Government in this part of America . . . induced a zeal for migration ; and associations were formed for taking up lands and making settlements in this Province by principal persons residing at those colonies. In consequence of these associations upwards of 10,000 souls have passed from those colonies into Nova Scotia, who have either engaged in the fisheries, or become exporters of lumber and provisions to the West Indies ; and further settlements to the extent of 21 townships of 100,000 acres each, have been engaged to be made there by many of the principal persons in Pennsylvania, whose names and association for that purpose now lye before your Majesty in Council.

The Government of Massachusets Bay, as well as the proprietors of large tracts to the eastward of the Province of Main, excited by the success of these settlements, are giving every encouragement to the like settlements in that valuable country lying between them and Nova Scotia ; and the proprietors of twelve townships, lately laid out there by the Massachusets Government, now solicit your Majesty for a confirmation of their title.

Such, may it please your Majesty, is the present state of the progress making in the settlement of the northern parts of the sea coasts of North America, in consequence of what appears to have been the policy adopted by this Kingdom ; and many persons of rank and substance here are proceeding to carry into execution the Plan, which your Majesty (pursuing the same principles of commercial policy) has approved for the settlement of the islands of St. John and Cape Breton, and of the new established colonies to the south ; and therefore . . . we cannot be of opinion that it would . . . be adviseable to divert your Majesty's subjects in America from the

persuit of these important objects, by adopting measures of
a new policy at an expence to this Kingdom, which, in its
present state, it is unable to bear. . . .

The several arguments urged in support of the particular
establishments now recommended, . . . appear to us reducible
to the following general propositions, viz. : (1) that such
colonies will promote population, and increase the demands
for, and consumption of, British manufactures ; (2) that they
will secure the furr trade, and prevent all illicit trade, or
interfering of French or Spaniards with the Indians ; (3) that
they will be a defence and protection to the old colonies
against the Indians ; (4) that they will contribute to lessen
the present heavy expence of supplying provisions to the
distant forts and garrisons ; lastly, that they are necessary
in respect to the inhabitants already residing in those places
where they are proposed to be established, who require some
form of civil government. . . .

We admit, as an undeniable principle of true policy, that,
with a view to prevent manufactures, it is necessary and
proper to open an extent of territory for colonization proportioned to the increase of people ; as a large number of
inhabitants, cooped up in narrow limits, without a sufficiency
of land for produce, would be compelled to convert their
attention and industry to manufactures.   But we submit
whether the encouragement given to the settlement of the
colonies upon the sea-coast, . . . has not already effectually
provided for this object as well as for . . . consumption of
British manufactures ;   an advantage which, in our humble
opinion, would not be promoted by these new colonies, which
being proposed to be established at the distance of above
fifteen hundred miles from the sea, and in places which upon
the fullest evidence are found to be utterly inaccessible to
shipping, will, from their inability to find returns wherewith
to pay for the manufactures of Great Britain, be probably
led to manufacture for themselves ; . . . The settlement of
that extensive tract of sea-coast hitherto unoccupied, . . .
together with the liberty that the . . . middle colonies will
have (in consequence of the proposed boundary line with the
Indians) of gradually extending themselves backwards, will
more effectually and beneficially answer the object of encouraging population and consumption, than the erection of
new governments. Such gradual extension might, through

the medium of a continued population upon even the same extent of territory, preserve a communication of mutual commercial benefits between its extremest parts and Great Britain, impossible to exist in colonies separated by immense tracts of unpeopled desart. As to the effect which it is supposed the colonies may have to increase and promote the furr trade, and to prevent all contraband trade or intercourse between the Indians under your Majesty's protection and the French or Spaniards, it does appear to us : that the extension of the furr trade depends entirely upon the Indians being undisturbed in the possession of their hunting grounds ; that all colonizing does in its nature, and must in its consequences operate to the prejudice of that branch of commerce ; and that the French and Spaniards would be left in possession of a great part of what remained, as New Orleans would still continue the best and surest markett. As to the protection which it is supposed these new colonies may be capable of affording to the old ones, it will in our opinion appear upon the slightest view of their situation, that, so far from affording protection to the old colonies, they will stand most in need of it themselves. . . .

The present French inhabitants in the neighbourhood of the lakes will, in our humble opinion, be sufficient to furnish with provisions whatever posts may be necessary to be continued there. . . . There never has been an instance of a government instituted merely with a view to supply a body of troops with suitable provisions ; nor is it necessary in these instances for the settlements already existing as above described ; which . . . do not, in our humble opinion, require any other superintendance than that of the military commanding at these posts.

All which is most humbly submitted

CLARE	THOMAS ROBINSON
SOAME JENYNS	WM. FITZHERBERT
Whitehall, March 7, 1768.	ED. ELIOT.

THE ACTS OF TRADE AND NAVIGATION IN FORCE, FEBRUARY 1769

Instructions by the Commissioners of His Majesty's Customs in America, to [John Mascarene, Esquire] who is appointed [Comptroller] of the Customs at the Port of [Salem and Marblehead] in America.[1]

I. [Oaths of office.]

II. You are to be diligent in the execution of the powers and authorities given you by several Acts of Parliament for visiting and searching of ships, and for seiz-
4 Geo. III, c. 15, ss. 36–8; 7 Geo. III, c. 46, s. 10. ing, securing, and bringing on shore any goods prohibited to be imported into, or exported out of the said plantations; or for which any duties are payable, or ought to have been paid, by any Act of Parliament; as also for entering any houses or warehouses to search for and seize any such goods, observing that you are not to enter any house, shop, cellar, or warehouse, but in the day time, and taking with you a writ of assistants,[2] and a constable, headborough, or other civil officer next inhabiting.

III. . . . Persons assisting in the conveyance, concealment, or rescue of any goods, or in the hinderance or resistance of yourself or any other officer in the performance of your or their duties, are subject to the like penalties as are provided by the Act of 14 Ch. II [c. 11], in similar cases in Great Britain; and the like assistance is to be given to you and the other officers in the execution of your and their duties, as by the 14 Ch. II is provided for officers in Great Britain; and in case you or they shall be sued or molested for anything done in the execution of your office, you are to plead the general issue, giving that Act and the 4 Geo. III in evidence, and claim the like priviledges and advantages as are allowed to officers of His Majesty's customs in Great Britain.

IV. You are to take notice that for the further encourage-

[1] Printed pamphlet in Massachusetts Historical Society, 40 pages. The words in brackets in heading are inserted in writing.

[2] A writ of assistance was a general warrant. For James Otis's argument on the unconstitutionality of writs of assistance in 1761, see any history of the Revolution.

ment of officers to make seizures and prosecute offences against the revenue laws, all penalties and forfeitures recovered in America on any Act of Parliament relating to trade, or the revenue of the customs, are by the 4 Geo. III, after deducting the charges of prosecution from the gross produce thereof, to

4 Geo. III, c. 15, ss. 42–6.

be divided as follows : one-third of the nett produce to be paid into the collector's hands for the use of His Majesty, his heirs and successors : one-third to the governor of the colony or plantation where the offence shall be committed : and one-third part to such person or persons as shall sue for the same, excepting such seizures as shall be made at sea by commanders or officers of His Majesty's ships duly authorized to make seizures. And that no person can be admitted to enter a claim to any ship or goods seized untill sufficient security be first given in court in the penalty of sixty pounds, to answer the costs and charges of prosecution ; in default of giving which security the ship and goods will be condemned ; and where any dispute shall arise whether the duties have been paid,

4 Geo. III, c. 15, s. 44.

or the same have been lawfully imported or exported ; or concerning the growth, product, or manufacture of such goods, or the place from whence they were brought, the proof is to lie upon the owner or claimer of such ship or goods ; and it being provided that if the produce of any seizure shall not be sufficient to answer the expences of condemnation and sale ; or if upon tryal a verdict or sentence shall be given for the claimant, the charges of prosecution may with our consent be paid out of the revenue of customs in America. . . .

VI. No goods or commodities whatsoever can be imported into, or exported from, any of the British plantations, but in vessels built in, and owned by people of Great-Britain, Ireland, Guernsey, Jersey, or the said plantations, and navigated by a master

12 Ch. II, c. 18, ss. 1, 7, 10, 11, 13 ; 14 Ch. II, c. 11, ss. 6–8 ; 7 & 8 Wm. III, c. 22, ss. 1, 2.

and three-fourths of the mariners of the said places ; except such ships only as are or shall be taken as prize, and condemned in the Courts of Admiralty. And to be qualified so to trade, such vessel must be provided with a proper register, under forfeiture of the vessel and cargo, and the number of mariners are to be accounted according to what they shall have been during the whole voyage. And no ship or vessel is to lade or unlade any goods, until the master hath made known to the Governor or such officer as shall be by him thereunto appointed, the arrival of the said ship or vessel, with her name, and have shewn that she is English built and navigated, and delivered a perfect invoice of her lading, with the place or places at which such goods were laden, under the pain of the loss of such ship or vessel with all her tackle, apparel, &c., and of all such goods of the growth, product or manufacture of Europe, as were not laden in Great-Britain.

15 Ch. II, c. 7. s. 8.

VII. No goods or commodities whatsoever, of the growth, produce, or manufacture of any part of Europe or the East Indies, can be imported into the British colonies but from Great-Britain, under forfeiture thereof, and of the vessel, excepting salt for the fisheries, wines from Maderia and the Azores or Western Islands ; and servants, horses, victuals, and linens from Ireland.

Of goods.   15 Ch. II, c. 7, ss. 5–7 ; 3 Anne, c. 8, s. 1.

VIII. With regard to vessels that arrive in any British Colony or Plantation in America, you are to take notice that the master, before he proceeds with his vessel to the place of unlading, is to come directly to the custom-house for the port or district where he arrives, and make a just and true entry upon oath, before the Collector and Comptroller or other principal officer, and answer upon oath to such questions as shall be demanded of him by them, upon forfeiture of one hundred pounds sterling for every default or neglect.

7 Geo. III, c. 46, s. 9.

IX. You are to take notice that the master of every ship or vessel, before he suffers any goods to be taken on board, is to enter and report outwards his said vessel, and before he departs with his vessel out of any Colony or Plantation, shall bring and deliver unto the collector and comptroller a content in writing, under his hand, of the name of every merchant or other person, who shall have put on board his vessel any goods, together with the marks and numbers of such goods ; and both at coming in and going out of any British Colony or Plantation, whether his ship or vessel shall be laden or in ballast or otherwise, shall likewise publickly, in the open custom-house, answer upon oath to all such questions as shall be demanded of him by the collector and comptroller, or other principal officer of the customs, upon forfeiture of one hundred pounds for every neglect or default.

X. You are to take notice that no goods whatsoever are to be shipped or laden from one British Colony to another, without a sufferance or warrant first had and obtained from the proper officers of the customs, at the port where the goods are intended to be shipped, and that before the same be carried out of the port of lading the master is to take out a cocket or cockets for the same, expressing the quantity and quality of the goods, and marks of the packages, with the merchants' names by whom shipped, and to whom consigned, and if liable to duty, either on importation or exportation, the cockets to specify that the duties have been paid, referring to the times or dates of payment, and by whom paid, according to the specimen annexed. The master of every vessel is to produce to the Collector and Comptroller of the port where his vessel shall arrive, the cockets for his goods on board, before any part of them are unladen or put on shore. And if any goods are shipped without such sufferance, as is before mentioned, or the vessel departs without such cocket, or the goods are landed before the cockets are produced, or not agreeing in all respects therewith, the goods in all such cases are forfeited, and the officers of the customs are impowered to stop all vessels bound as aforesaid, which shall be discovered within two leagues of the shore of any such British Colonies or Plantations, and to seize all goods on board, for which no such cocket or cockets shall be produced ; but you are to take notice that this does not extend to require any person to take out any sufferance or cocket for any goods of the growth, product, or manufacture of the said Colonies, not liable to any duties, nor prohibited to be exported from thence, which shall be laden in any boat or other vessel without a deck, not exceeding twenty tons, and shall be carried within any river, lake, or other inland water, within the said Colonies, and not further than one league from the shore.

XI. You are to take notice that all goods concealed, and found on board any ship or vessel, after report shall have been made by the master, and not comprized in his report, are forfeited ; and that the master or person having the charge of

5 Geo. III, c. 45, s. 25.

4 Geo. III, c. 15, s. 29.

4 Geo. III, c. 15, s. 36.

the ship, if he was privy to the concealment, forfeits treble the value of the goods so found.

XII. You are to take notice that all goods and commodities of the growth, produce, or manufacture of the British Colonies are distinguished as *enumerated* and *non-enumerated*. The *enumerated* consisting of

12 Ch. II, c. 18, ss. 18, 19 ; 25 Ch. II, c. 7, s. 3 ; 23 Ch. II, c. 2, s. 10–12 ; 3 & 4 Anne, c. 5, s. 12, c. 10, s. 8 ; 12 Anne, c. 9, s. 1 ; 8 Geo. 1, c. 15, s. 24, c. 18, s. 22 ; 4 Geo. III, c. 15, s. 27.

Tobacco,
Cotton wool,
Indigo,
Ginger,
Fustick, or other dying
    wood,
Melasses,
Hemp,
Copper ore,
Beaver skins, or other furs,
Pitch,
Tar,
Turpentine,

Masts,
Yards,
Bowsprits,
Sugar,
Rice,
Coffee,
Piemento,
Cocoa nutts,
Whale fins,
Raw silk,
Hides and skins,
Pot and pearl
    ashes,

are not to be laden on board of any vessel until the master with one surety shall enter into a bond (if in Great-Britain to the chief officers of the custom house of such port or place from whence the said ship shall sail ; if in the Plantations to the Governor of such Plantation) in the penalty of one thousand pounds sterling if his vessel is under one hundred tons, and of two thousand pounds sterling if above that tonnage, with condition that the said goods shall be landed in some British Colony, or in Great-Britain, under a forfeiture of the said goods and vessel.

EXCEPTIONS

12 Geo. II, c. 30.
4 Geo. III, c. 12.

Sugar may be exported to the southward of Cape-Finisterre upon the master's entering into bond, and observing the regulations prescribed by law.

3 Geo. II, c. 28 ;
8 Geo. II, c. 18 ;
4 Geo. III, c. 27 ;
7 Geo. III, c. 35.

Rice also may be exported to the southward of Cape-Finisterre in like manner, and to foreign plantations in America, on payment of the duties, and under the regulations prescribed by law.

XIII. The *non-enumerated* goods, consisting of all other goods or commodities of the growth, produce or manufacture of the British Colonies, are not to be loaded on board of any vessel until the master with one surety hath entered into the like bond to the Collector or other principal officer of the customs at the port where the goods are taken on board,   6 Geo. III, c. 52, ss. 30, 31; 7 Geo. III, c. 2. conditional that the said goods shall not be carried to any part of Europe, northward of Cape-Finisterre, except to Great-Britain or Ireland, under forfeiture of such goods and vessel.

XIV. By the Act of 4 Geo. III, c. 15, the non-enumerated goods, iron and lumber, were not to be loaded on board any vessel until the master with one surety had entered into a bond in the penalty of double the value of the goods, and conditional that the same should not be landed in any part of Europe except in Great-Britain, but by a subsequent Act of 5 Geo. III, c. 45, the said non-enumerated article of iron may be landed in Ireland, and lumber may be landed in Ireland, the Madeiras, the Western Islands, or any part of Europe southward of Cape-Finisterre, subject to the bond and penalties afore mentioned.

XV. Annexed you have a state of the duties payable on goods in the British Colonies in America.

Articles subject to duty on exportation from one British American Colony to another.

	£	s.	d.	
Tobacco the pound	0	0	1	
Indigo, ditto	0	0	2	
Ginger per cwt.	0	1	0	25 Ch. II, c. 7,
Logwood, ditto	5	0	0	s. 2.
Fustick, and all other dying wood, per cwt.	0	0	6	
Cocoa nutts the pound . . .	0	0	1	

Articles subject to duty on importation from Great-Britain.[1]

	£	s.	d.	
Spanish, Portugal, and all other wines except French, per ton .	0	10	0	4 Geo. III, c. 15.
White glass per cwt.	0	4	8	7 Geo. III, c. 46.
Green glass, ditto	0	1	2	
Red lead, ditto	0	2	0	
White lead, ditto	0	2	0	
Painters' colours, ditto . . .	0	2	0	
Teas per lb.	0	0	3	
Paper, *vide* duty on each species in the Act of 7 Geo. III, c. 46.				

[1] All except the first are the Townshend duties of 1767, which, except for that on tea, were repealed in 1770.

Articles subject to duty on importation from British Plantations in America.

		£	s.	d.
6 Geo. III, c. 52.	Melasses the gallon	0	0	1
	Coffee the cwt.	0	7	0
	Piemento per lb.	0	0	0½

N.B. Melasses imported from Dominica with a certificate of the duties being paid there, is not subject to duty on importation.

British coffee and piemento are not subject to duty upon importation, provided that upon landing they are deposited in warehouses at the expence of the importer, under the care and inspection of the Collector and Comptroller, and shipped from thence within twelve months for Great-Britain, or some other British Colony in America, under the securities and restrictions required by law.

Articles subject to duty of importation from foreign plantations, viz.

		£	s.	d.
	Wines from Madeira, and the Western			
4 Geo. III, c. 15.	Islands, per ton	7	0	0
	White or clay'd sugar per cwt. .	1	7	0
	Other sugars, ditto	0	5	0
	Indigo per lb.	0	0	6
	Coffee per cwt.	2	19	9
6 Geo. III, c. 52, ss. 4, 29.	Melasses per gallon	0	0	1

Foreign sugar, coffee, and indigo, are not subject to duty upon importation, provided that upon landing they are secured in warehouses at the expence of the importer under the care and inspection of the Collector and Comptroller, and reshipped for exportation within twelve months, under the securities and restrictions required by law. The sugars to be exported either directly to Great-Britain or some part of Europe to the southward of Cape-Finisterre. 6 Geo. III, c. 52, ss. 15, 16. The indigo to be exported to Great-Britain only ; and the exporter of the coffee before it is taken out of the warehouse for exportation, is to become bound with sufficient security in the penalty of five pounds for every hundred weight of coffee that it shall all be truly exported, and not brought back or relanded in any part of the British Dominions in America. . . .

XVI. If any goods or merchandize subject to duty shall

be laden on board any ship or vessel outward bound, or be unshipped or landed from any ship or vessel inward bound, before the respective duties due thereon are paid ; or if any prohibited goods what- 4 Geo. III, c. 15, soever are imported into, or exported out s. 37. of any of the British Colonies or Plantations in America, every person concerned therein shall forfeit treble the value of the goods, and all the boats, carriages, and cattle employed therein are forfeited and lost.

XVII. You are to take notice that no rum or spirits of the produce or manufacture of any foreign Colony or Plantation in America, can be imported into any of His Majesty's Dominions in America, upon 4 Geo. III, c. 15, forfeiture of all such rum or spirits, together s. 18. with the ship or vessel in which the same shall be imported.

XVIII. You are to take notice that every person loading on board any ship or vessel any rum or spirits, sugar or paneles, melasses or syrups, is to deliver to the Collector at the loading port before the clearing out of the ship or vessel an affidavit by the grower, maker or shipper, of the quality of the goods, the number and denomination of the packages, and the Collector is to grant the master a certificate of his having received such affidavit, and the master on his arrival at his port of discharge, is to deliver the certificate to the Collector or other principal officer of the customs, and make oath of the identity of the goods, on penalty of one hundred pounds. And if any such 4 Geo. III, c. 15, goods are imported or found on board not s. 20. certified for, the same are to be deemed foreign goods, and subject to the same duties, regulations, and penalties as such foreign goods would be liable to by law.

XIX. You are to take notice that for all rum or other spirits that shall be shipped or laden on board any ship or vessel in any British 5 Geo. III, c. 39, Colony or Plantation in America, the master s. 5. must produce a certificate that bond hath been given by himself and one surety, that the same should not be carried to or landed in the Isle of Man ; and if any vessel loaded therewith, has not a certificate to shew that such bond had been given, the vessel and goods are forfeited.[1]

---

[1] The Merchants of Boston complain, in their *Observations on Several Acts of Parliament* (Boston, 1769), pp. 9–15, that the bonds mentioned

XX. Whenever you receive information of any quantity of goods run, and of the place where they are lodged, if you are apprehensive of any opposition, or that any attempt will be made to rescue the goods after seizure, you are in such cases to take with you the neighbouring officers, and other sufficient assistance, in order to secure the goods and guard them to the warehouse ; and if any military forces are quartered in your parts, you are likewise, when necessary, to apply to the Commanding Officer for their aid. . . . And in case you are obstructed or abused in your duty, you are to mention the same with the names of the offenders if known, acquainting your Collector and Comptroller therewith, that proper measures may be used to punish the offenders. . . .

XXI. [In case of successful smuggling, obtain all possible information.]

XXII. . . . If the Informer desires to be concealed, you need not mention his name, and you are at the same time to send or deliver an account in writing to the register of seizures, . . . and you are not, on any pretence, to treat upon any proposal for a composition . . . or otherwise stop or delay proceeding against any offender, . . . without first obtaining our approbation. . . .

XXIII. It being enacted by the Act of the 10 and 11 Wm. III, c. 10, s. 19, that no wool, woolfells, shortlings, mortlings, woolflocks, bay or woollen yarn, cloth bays, sarge kersies, says, frizes, druggets, cloth serges, shalloons, or any other drapery stuffs, or woollen manufactures whatsoever, made or mixt with wool or woolflocks, being of the product or manufacture of any of the British Plantations in America, shall be laden on board any ship or vessel in any place or parts within any of the said British Plantations, upon any pretence whatsoever ; . . . [or] loaden upon any horse, cart, or carriage, to the intent and purpose to be . . . conveyed out of the said British Plantations, . . . under forfeiture of the goods, with the ship, vessel, boat or other bottom what-

in sections xii–xiv and xix, and the papers mentioned in x, were then required not only for vessels in foreign trade, but for coasting craft. In addition, every coasting vessel had to enter and clear at a royal custom house, which might be fifty miles distant from the place where it wished to load lumber or fish. These regulations were somewhat ameliorated as to coasting craft, but the bonds were still being required of them in 1773. See D. D. Wallace, *Life of Henry Laurens*, chapters xii, xiii, and *Proceedings Am. Antiquarian Society* for April 1922.

soever employed therein, and the penalty of five hundred pounds to every offender for every offence, and forty pounds to every master, mariner, waggoner, porter, carrier or boatman concerned therein. You are to take care and use your best endeavours to carry the said Act into execution.

XXIV. The exporting and transporting of hatts and felts dyed or undyed, finished or unfinished, out of any British Colony or Plantation in America being prohibited, under the forfeiture of the goods,   5 Geo. II, c. 22. and the like penalties upon the persons concerned therein as is provided for woollen manufactures, you are to take care and use your best endeavours to prevent . . . the same.

XXV. You shall not [engage in] . . . trade as a merchant for yourself, or as a factor, . . . nor keep a victualing house, or house of public entertainment. . . .

XXVI. . . . Observing that by 4 Geo. III, c. 15, s. 38, every officer of the customs who shall receive any bribe, . . . will for each and every offence forfeit five hundred pounds, and be rendered incapable of serving the Crown in any office or employment, civil or military. . . .

XXX. [An appendix of twenty pages follows, with digest of Acts of Parliament, special instructions for the coasting trade, &c.]   [28 February 1769

Custom-house,   WM. BURCH,
Boston.   HEN. HULTON,
                      J. TEMPLE.
                      CHAS. PAXTON.][1]

THE REGULATOR MOVEMENT IN NORTH CAROLINA.
PETITION OF A FRONTIER COUNTY [2]
9 October 1769

MR. SPEAKER AND GENTLEMEN OF THE ASSEMBLY:

The Petition of the Inhabitants of Anson County, being part of the Remonstrance of the Province of North Carolina,

HUMBLY SHEWETH, That the Province in general labour under general grievances, and the western part thereof under particular ones ; which we not only see but very sensibly feel,

---

[1] In manuscript on the copy used for text.
[2] Printed from the State Archives in *Colonial Records of North*

being crouch'd beneath our sufferings : and, notwithstanding our sacred priviledges, have too long yielded ourselves slaves to remorseless oppression. Permit us to conceive it to be our inviolable right to make known our grievances, and to petition for redress ; as appears in the Bill of Rights pass'd in the reign of King Charles the first, as well as the Act of Settlement of the Crown of the Revolution. We therefore beg leave to lay before you a specimen thereof, that your compassionate endeavours may tend to the relief of your injured constituents, whose distressed condition calls aloud for aid. The alarming cries of the oppressed possibly may reach your ears ; but without your zeal how shall they ascend the throne. How relentless is the breast without sympathy, the heart that cannot bleed on a view of our calamity ; to see tenderness removed, cruelty stepping in ; and all our liberties and priviledges invaded and abridg'd by (as it were) domesticks who are conscious of their guilt and void of remorse. O how daring ! how relentless ! whilst impending judgments loudly threaten and gaze upon them, with every emblem of merited destruction.

A few of the many grievances are as follows, viz.,

1. That the poor inhabitants in general are much oppress'd by reason of disproportionate taxes, and those of the western counties in particular ; as they are generally in mean circumstances.

2. That no method is prescribed by law for the payment of the taxes of the western counties in produce (in lieu of a currency) as is in other counties within this province ; to the peoples great oppression.

3. That lawyers, clerks, and other pentioners, in place of being obsequious servants for the country's use, are become a nuisance, as the business of the people is often trausacted without the least degree of fairness, the intention of the law evaded, exorbitant fees extorted, and the sufferers left to mourn under their oppressions.

4. That an attorney should have it in his power, either for the sake of ease or interest or to gratify their malevolence and spite, to commence suits to what courts he pleases, how-

Carolina (Raleigh : Josephus Daniels, 1890), viii. 75–80. Cf., in same volume, petitions of Orange and Rowan counties, pp. 81, 231, and account of breaking up the session of the County Court at Hillsborough, p. 241.

ever inconvenient it may be to the defendant : is a very
great oppression.

5. That all unlawful fees taken on indictment, where the
defendant is acquitted by his country (however customary it
may be) is an oppression.

6. That lawyers, clerks, and others extorting more fees
than is intended by law : is also an oppression.

7. That the violation of the King's instructions to his
delegates, their artfulness in concealing the same from him ;
and the great injury the people thereby sustains : is a manifest oppression.

And for remedy whereof, we take the freedom to recommend the following mode of redress, not doubting audience
and acceptance ; which will not only tend to our relief, but
command prayers as a duty from your humble petitioners.

1. That at all elections each suffrage be given by ticket
and ballot.

2. That the mode of taxation be altered, and each person
to pay in proportion to the profits arising from his estate.

3. That no future tax be laid in money, untill a currency
is made.

4. That there may be established a Western as well as
a Northern and Southern District, and a Treasurer for the
same.

5. That when a currency is made it may be let out by
a loan office on land security,[1] and not to be call'd in by a tax.

6. That all debts above 40s. and under £10 be tried and
determined without lawyers, by a jury of six freeholders
impanneled by a Justice, and that their verdict be enter'd by
the said Justice, and be a final judgment.

7. That the Chief Justice have no perquisites, but a sallary
only.

8. That clerks be restricted in respect to fees, costs, and
other things within the course of their office.

---

[1] This demand for cheap money has been a typical device of frontier
debtor communities in the United States from the early eighteenth
century to the present. It was tried in Massachusetts in 1739, and in
Rhode Island in 1786, with disastrous results ; the refusal of the
Massachusetts Legislature to grant it in 1786 precipitated Shays's
Rebellion ; a clause was inserted in the Constitution (Art. I, s. x, § 1)
to prevent it. The Greenback party and the free silver movement
had fundamentally the same idea as basis ; and the radical agrarian
movement of 1923 is making the same demand.

9. That lawyers be effectually barr'd from exacting and extorting fees.

10. That all doubts may be removed in respect to the payment of fees and costs on indictments where the defendant is not found guilty by the jury, and therefore acquitted.

11. That the Assembly make known by remonstrance to the King, the conduct of the cruel and oppressive Receiver of the Quit Rents, for omitting the customary easie and effectual method of collecting by distress, and pursuing the expensive mode of commencing suits in the most distant courts.

12. That the Assembly in like manner make known that the Governor and Council do frequently grant lands to as many as they think proper without regard to head rights,[1] notwithstanding the contrariety of His Majesties instructions ; by which means immense sums has been collected, and numerous patents granted, for much of the most fertile lands in this Province, that is yet uninhabited and uncultivated, environed by great numbers of poor people who are necessitated to toil in the cultivation of bad lands whereon they hardly can subsist, who are thereby deprived of His Majesties liberality and bounty : nor is there the least regard paid to the cultivation clause in said patent mentioned, as many of the said Council as well as their friends and favorites enjoy large quantities of lands under the above-mentioned circumstances.

13. That the Assembly communicates in like manner the violation of His Majesties instructions respecting the Land Office by the Governor and Council, and of their own rules, customs and orders ; if it be sufficiently proved that after they had granted warrants for many tracts of land, and that the same was in due time survey'd and return'd, and the patent fees timely paid into the said office ; and that if a private Council was called on purpose to avoid spectators, and peremptory orders made that patents should not be granted ; and warrants by their orders arbitrarily to have issued in the names of other persons for the same lands, and if when intreated by a solicitor they refus'd to render so

---

[1] The head right system, which originated in Virginia, was that of granting a man so many acres of land gratis for every person he brought into the colony. Such land was supposed to be forfeited if not brought under cultivation within a certain period.

much as a reason for their so doing, or to refund any part of the money by them extorted.

14. That some method may be pointed out that every improvement on lands in any of the proprietor's part [1] be proved when begun, by whom, and every sale made, that the eldest may have the preference of at least 300 Acres.

15. That all taxes in the following counties be paid as in other counties in the Province, i. e. in the produce of the country and that warehouses be erected as follows, viz. in Anson County, at Isom Haley's ferry landing on Pe Dee river; in Rowan and Orange, . . . Cumberland . . . Mecklenburg . . . and in Tryon County. . . .

16. That every denomination of people may marry according to their respective mode, ceremony, and custom, after due publication or licence.

17. That Doctr Benjamin Franklin or some other known patriot be appointed agent, to represent the unhappy state of this Province to His Majesty, and to solicit the several Boards in England :—

[260 signatures.]

Dated October the 9th 1769.

PROCEEDINGS OF THE TOWN OF BOSTON [2]

October–November 1772

At a meeting of the freeholders and other inhabitants of the Town of Boston, duly qualified and legally warned, in public town meeting assembled at Faneuil Hall, on Wednesday the 28th day of October 1772.

The Hon. John Hancock, Esq., was chosen Moderator. . . . It was moved and seconded—That a decent and respectful application from this meeting be made to his Excellency the Governor, acquainting him that the Town has been alarm'd

[1] This clause is a demand that the earliest 'squatter' on a given section of the Granville Propriety be given a pre-emption right over other possible purchasers.

[2] *Boston Town Records*, 1770–7 (18th Report of Boston Record Commissioners, 1887), pp. 88–108. These proceedings, which show the methods of Samuel Adams and the Boston 'Sons of Liberty', were also published at Boston in a contemporary pamphlet, *Votes and Proceedings of the Freeholders and other Inhabitants of the Town of Boston*, which was reprinted in Dublin and in London, 1773.

with the reports that stipends are affixed to the office of the Judges of the Superior Court of Judicature of this Province, whereby they are rendered intirely independent of the grants and acts of the General Assembly for their support, which the Town is apprehensive will be attended with the most fatal consequences, and therefore humbly and earnestly to pray his Excellency, that he would be pleased to inform them, whether his Excellency has received any advice relative to this matter in any way from whence he has reason to apprehend that such an establishment has or will be made. And the question being put, it passed in the affirmative by a vast majority.

Also *voted* that Mr. Samuel Adams, Dr. Joseph Warren, Dr. Benjamin Church, be a committee to draw up an address to the Governor on the aforegoing subject and to report at the adjournment.

[That afternoon the address was adopted.

On October 30 the committee reported to the Town Meeting the Governor's written reply :]

GENTLEMEN,—It is by no means proper for me to lay before the inhabitants of any town whatsoever, in consequence of their votes and proceedings in a town meeting, any part of my correspondence as Governor of this Province, or to acquaint them whether I have received any advice relating to the public affairs of government. This reason alone, if your address to me had been in other respects unexceptionable, would have been sufficient to restrain me from complying with your desire.

I shall always be ready to gratify the inhabitants of the Town of Boston upon every regular application to me on business of public concernment to the Town, as far as I shall have it in my power, consistent with fidelity to the trust which His Majesty has reposed in me.

T. HUTCHINSON.

The aforegoing answer having been considered, it was moved and the question put—Whether application shall be now made to his Excellency by the Town that he would be pleased to permit the General Assembly to meet at the time to which they stand prorogued, which passed in the affirmative, *nem. con.*

It was then *voted* that the Hon. James Otis, Esq., Mr. Samuel

Adams, the Hon. Thomas Cushing, Esq., be a committee to prepare a petition to his Excellency for the purpose aforesaid.

[That afternoon the petition was reported and accepted. It complains of the reported fixed stipends for the judges, and their holding their commissions *bene placitu*, and concludes as follows :]

It is therefore their earnest and humble request that your Excellency would be pleased to allow the General Assembly to meet at the time to which they now stand prorogued ; in order that in that *constitutional* body, with whom it is to enquire into grievances and redress them, the joint wisdom of the Province may be employed in deliberating, and determine on a matter so important and alarming.

[On November 2 the committee laid before the Town Meeting the Governor's reply :]

GENTLEMEN,—The Royal Charter reserves to the Governor full power and authority from time to time, as he shall judge necessary, to adjourn, prorogue, and dissolve the General Assembly. In the exercise of this power, both as to time and place, I have always been governed by a regard to His Majesty's service and to the interest of the Province. It did not appear to me necessary for these purposes that the Assembly should meet at the time to which it now stands prorogued, and before I was informed of your Address, I had determined to prorogue it to a further time. The reasons which you have advanced have not altered my opinion. If, notwithstanding, I should alter my determination and meet the Assembly, contrary to my own judgment, at such a time as you judge necessary, I should in effect yield to you the exercise of that part of the prerogative, and should be unable to justify my conduct to the King. There would, moreover, be danger of encouraging the inhabitants of the other towns in the Province to assemble from time to time in order to consider of the necessity and expediency of a session of the General Assembly, or to debate and transact other matters which the law that authorizes towns to assemble, does not make the business of a Town Meeting.

T. HUTCHINSON.

The foregoing reply having been read several times and duly considered, it was moved and the question accordingly put—Whether the same be satisfactory to the Town; which passed in the negative, *nem. con.* And thereupon,

Resolved as the opinion of the inhabitants of this Town that they have ever had, and ought to have, a right to petition the King or his representatives for the redress of such grievances as they feel, or for preventing of such as they have reason to apprehend, and to communicate their sentiment to other towns.

It was then moved by Mr. Samuel Adams that a Committee of Correspondence be appointed, to consist of twenty-one persons, to state the Rights of the Colonists and of this Province in particular, as men, as Christians,[1] and as subjects; to communicate the same to the several towns in this Province, and to the World, as the sense of this Town, with the infringements and violations thereof that have been, or from time to time may be made—also requesting of each Town a free communication of their sentiments on this subject. And the question being accordingly put, passed in the affirmative, *nem. con.*

Also *voted*, that the Hon. James Otis, Esq., Mr. Samuel Adams, Dr. Joseph Warren [and eighteen others] be, and hereby are appointed a Committee for the purpose aforesaid.

[On November 20 the Committee of Correspondence reports. The first part of their report, 'The State of the Rights of the Colonists', is accepted *nem. con.*; the second part, a 'List of Infringements and Violations of Rights', is recommitted for additions, and accepted in the afternoon session, as is a Letter to other towns. It is voted that the aforegoing proceedings be printed, and copies sent to the selectmen of every town in the Province. The concluding

---

[1] Adams wrote Elbridge Gerry, 14 November 1772, 'The word you object to in our resolves was designed to introduce into our State of Grievances the " Church innovations, and the establishment of those tyrants in religion, bishops ", which as you observe will probably take place. I cannot but hope, when you consider how indifferent too many of the clergy are to our just and righteous cause, that some of them are the adulators of our oppressors, and even some of the best of them are extremely cautious of recommending (at least in their publick performances) the rights of their country to the protection of Heaven, lest they should give offence to the little gods on earth, you will judge it quite necessary that we should assert and vindicate our rights as Christians as well as men and subjects.' *Writings*, ii. 349.

paragraph of the ' Rights of the Colonists ', and an abridge-
ment of the ' Infringements ', follow : [1]]

The inhabitants of this country in all probability in a few
years will be more numerous than those of Great Britain
and Ireland together ; yet it is absurdly expected by the
promoters of the present measures, that these, with their
posterity to all generations, should be easy while their property shall be disposed of by a House of Commons at three
thousand miles distant from them ; and who cannot be
supposed to have the least care or concern for their real
interest : who have not only no natural care for their interest,
but must be in effect bribed against it ; as every burden they
lay on the colonists is so much saved or gained to themselves.
Hitherto many of the colonists have been free from quit
rents ; but if the breath of a British House of Commons can
originate an Act for taking away all our money, our lands
will go next, or be subject to rack rents from haughty and
relentless landlords who will ride at ease, while we are trodden
in the dirt. The colonists have been branded with the odious
names of traitors and rebels, only for complaining of their
grievances ; how long such treatment will, or ought to be
born, is submitted.

A List of Infringements and Violations of Rights

We cannot help thinking, that an enumeration of some of
the most open infringments of our rights, will by every candid
person be judged sufficient to justify whatever measures have
been already taken, or may be thought proper to be taken,
in order to obtain a redress of the grievances under which
we labour. . . .

1. The British Parliament have assumed the power of
legislation for the colonists in all cases whatsoever, without
obtaining the consent of the inhabitants, which is ever
essentially necessary to the right establishment of such a
legislative.

2. They have exerted that assumed power, in raising
a revenue in the colonies without their consent ; thereby
depriving them of that right which every man has to keep

[1] The whole may be found in the *Writings of Samuel Adams* (H. A.
Cushing, ed.), ii. 350–74 ; and the ' Rights ' in *Old South Leaflets*,
No. 173.

his own earnings in his own hands until he shall in person, or by his Representative, think fit to part with the whole or any portion of it. . . .

3. A number of new officers, unknown in the charter of this Province, have been appointed to superintend this revenue, whereas by our charter the Great and General Court or Assembly of this Province has the sole right of appointing all civil officers, excepting only such officers, the election and constitution of whom is in said charter expressly excepted ; among whom these officers are not included.

4. These officers are by their commission invested with powers altogether unconstitutional, and entirely destructive to that security which we have a right to enjoy ; and to the last degree dangerous, not only to our property, but to our lives. For the Commissioners of His Majesty's Customs in America, or any three of them, are by their commission impowered, ' by writing under their hands and seales to constitute and appoint inferior officers in all and singular the ports within the limits of their commissions '. Each of these petty officers so made is intrusted with power more absolute and arbitrary than ought to be lodged in the hands of any man or body of men whatsoever. . . .[1]

Thus our houses and even our bed chambers are exposed to be ransacked, our boxes, chests, and trunks broke open, ravaged and plundered by wretches, whom no prudent man would venture to employ even as menial servants ; whenever they are pleased to say they *suspect* there are in the house wares, etc., for which the dutys have not been paid. Flagrant instances of the wanton exercise of this power, have frequently happened in this and other seaport towns. By this we are cut off from that domestick security which renders the lives of the most unhappy in some measure agreable. . . .

5. Fleets and armies have been introduced to support these unconstitutional officers in collecting and managing this unconstitutional revenue ; and troops have been quarter'd in this metropolis for that purpose. Introducing and quartering standing armies in a free country in times of peace without the consent of the people either by themselves or by their representatives, is, and always has been deemed a violation of their rights as freemen ; and of the charter or compact made between the King of Great Britain, and the people of

[1] See the instructions by the Commissioners, above, pp. 74–83.

this province, whereby all the rights of British subjects are confirmed to us.

6. The Revenue arising from this tax unconstitutionally laid, and committed to the management of persons arbitrarily appointed and supported by an armed force quartered in a free city, has been in part applyed to the most destructive purposes. It is absolutely necessary in a mixt government like that of this Province, that a due proportion or balance of power should be established among the several branches of legislative. Our ancestors received from King William and Queen Mary a charter by which it was understood by both parties in the contract, that such a proportion or balance was fixed; [1] and therefore everything which renders any one branch of the legislative more independent of the other two than it was originally designed, is an alteration of the constitution as settled by the charter; and as it has been untill the establishment of this revenue, the constant practise of the General Assembly to provide for the support of government, so it is an essential part of our constitution, as it is a necessary means of preserving an equilibrium, without which we cannot continue a free state.

In particular it has always been held that the dependence of the Governor of this Province upon the General Assembly for his support, was necessary for the preservation of this equilibrium; nevertheless His Majesty has been pleased to apply fifteen hundred pounds sterling annually out of the American revenue, for the support of the Governor of this Province independent of the Assembly, whereby the ancient connection between him and this people is weakened, the confidence in the Governor lessened and the equilibrium destroyed, and the constitution essentially altered.

And we look upon it highly probable from the best intelligence we have been able to obtain, that not only our Governor and Lieuvetenant Governor, but the Judges of the Superior Court of Judicature, as also the King's Attorney and Solicitor General are to receive their support from this grievous tribute. This will if accomplished compleat our slavery. . . .

7. We find ourselves greatly oppressed by instructions sent to our Governor from the Court of Great Britain, whereby the first branch of our legislature is made merely a ministerial

[1] Of course the charter of 1691 was in no sense a contract, and the original balance of it had long since been destroyed.

engine. And the Province has already felt such effects from these instructions, as we think justly intitle us to say that they threaten an entire destruction of our liberties, and must soon, if not checked, render every branch of our government a useless burthen upon the people. We shall point out some of the alarming effects of these instructions which have already taken place.

In consequence of instructions, the Governor has called and adjourned our General Assemblies to a place highly inconvenient to the members, and grately disadvantageous to the interest of the Province, even against his own declared intention.

In consequence of instructions, the Assembly has been prorogued from time to time, when the important concerns of the Province required their meeting.

In obedience to instructions, the General Assembly was anno 1768 dissolved by Governor Bernard, because they would not consent to rescind the resolution of a former house, and thereby sacrifise the rights of their constituents.

By an instruction, the honourable His Majesty's Council are forbid to meet and transact matters of publick concern as a Council of advice to the Governor, unless called by the Governor ; and if they should from a zealous regard to the interest of the Province so meet at any time, the Governor is ordered to negative them at the next election of Councellors. . . .

His Excellency has also pleaded instructions for giving up the provincial fortress, Castle William, into the hands of troops, over whom he had declared he had no controul, and that at a time when they were menaceing the Slaughter of the inhabitants of the Town, and our streets were stained with the blood which they had barbariously shed. . . .

8. The extending the power of the Courts of Vice Admirality to so enormous a degree as deprives the people in the colonies in a great measure of their inestimable right to tryals by juries : which has ever been justly considered as the grand bulwark and security of English property. . . .

9. The restraining us from erecting slitting mills for manufacturing our iron, the natural produce of this country, is an infringement of that right with which God and nature have invested us, to make use of our skill and industry in procuring the necessaries and conveniences of life. And we

look upon the restraint laid upon the manufacture and transportation of hatts to be altogether unreasonable and grievous.
Although by the charter all havens, rivers, ports, waters, etc.,
are expressly granted the inhabitants of the Province and their
successors, to their only proper use and behoof forever, yet
the British Parliament passed an Act, whereby they restrain
us from carrying our wool, the produce of our own farms,
even over a ferry; whereby the inhabitants have often been
put to the expence of carrying a bag of wool near an hundred
miles by land, when passing over a river or water of one quarter
of a mile, of which the Province are the absolute proprietors,
would have prevented all that trouble.[1]

10. The Act passed in the last session of the British Parliament, intitled, An Act for the better preserving his Majestys
Dock Yards, Magizines, Ships, Ammunition and Stores, is,
as we apprehend a violent infringement of our rights.[2] By
this Act any one of us may be taken from his family, and
carried to any part of Great Britain, there to be tried whenever it shall be pretended that he has been concerned in burning or otherwise destroying any boat or vessel, or any materials
for building, etc., any naval or victualling store, etc., belonging to His Majesty. . . .

11. As our Ancestors came over to this Country that they
might not only enjoy their civil but their religious rights,
and particularly desired to be free from the prelates, who in
those times cruilly persecuted all who differed in sentiment
from the established Church ; we cannot see without concern
the various attempts which have been made and are now
making, to establish an American Episcopate. Our Episcopal
brethren of the colonies do enjoy, and rightfully ought ever
to enjoy, the free exercise of their religeon, we cannot help
fearing that they who are so warmly contending for such an
establishment, have views altogether inconsistent with the
universal and peaceful enjoyment of our Christian privileges.
And doing or attempting to do anything which has even
the remotest tendency to endanger this enjoyment, is justly
looked upon a great grievance, and also an infringement of
our rights, which is not barely to exercise, but peaceably
and securely to enjoy, that liberty wherewith Christ has
made us free.

And we are further of Opinion that no power on Earth can

[1] See p. 82, and 23 Geo. II, c. 29.   [2] 12 Geo. III, c. 24.

justly give either temporal or spiritual jurisdiction within
this Province, except the Great and General Court. We
think therefore that every design for establishing the jurisdiction of a bishop in this Province, is a design both against
our civil and religeous rights. And we are well informed, that
the more candid and judicious of our brethren of the Church
of England in this and the other colonies, both clergy and
laity, conceive of the establishing an American Episcopate
both unnecessary and unreasonable.[1]

12. Another grievance under which we labour is the frequent
alteration of the bounds of the colonies by decisions before
the King and Council, explanatory of former grants and
charters. This not only subjects men to live under a constitution to which they have not consented, which in itself
is a great grievance; but moreover under color that the
right of soil is affected by such declarations, some governors,
or ministers, or both in conjunction, have pretended to grant
in consequence of a mandamus many thousands of acres of
lands appropriated near a century past; and rendered
valuable by the labors of the present cultivators and their
ancestors. There are very notable instances of setlers, who
having first purchased the soil of the natives, have at considerable expence obtained confermation of title from this
Province; and on being transferred to the jurisdiction of
the Province of New Hampshire have been put to the trouble
and cost of a new grant or confermation from thence; and
after all this there has been a third declaration of royal will,
that they should thenceforth be considered as pertaining to
the Province of New York.[2] The troubles, expences, and
dangers which hundreds have been put to on such occasions,
cannot here be recited; but so much may be said, that they
have been most cruelly harrassed, and even threatned with
a military force, to dragoon them into a compliance with
the most unreasonable demands.

[1] Van Tyne, *Causes of War of Independence*, chapter xiii; A. L. Cross,
Anglican Episcopate and American Colonies, Harvard Historical
Studies, ix.

[2] This refers particularly to the ' New Hampshire Grants ', which
later became the State of Vermont. Massachusetts had suffered from
Colonial boundary decisions, but it had also authorized settlements in
territories to which it had no colour of right.

ADDITIONAL INSTRUCTIONS TO THE ROYAL GOVERNORS [1]

3 February 1774

GEORGE R.

Additional Instructions to Our Trusty and Wellbeloved Our Captain General and Governor in Cheif in and over Our Province of , and the Islands and Territories thereunto belonging in America ; Or to the Commander in Chief of Our said Province for the time being, Given at Our Court at St. James's the third day of February 1774, in the Fourteenth Year of Our Reign.

WHEREAS by Our Commission to you under our Great Seal of Great Britain, bearing date the   day of   in the   year of our reign, you are authorized and impowered, with the advice and consent of our Council for our said Province of   under your Government, to settle and agree with the inhabitants of our said Province for such lands, tenements and hereditaments, as now are or hereafter shall be in our power to dispose of, and them to grant to any person or persons, upon such terms, and under such moderate quit rents, services, and acknowledgements to be thereupon reserved unto us, as you, by and with the advice aforesaid, shall think fit ; and whereas the usual directions for the due execution of the said powers . . . have been found to be inadequate, improper and inconvenient. . . . We do hereby revoke and annul all and every part of the said Instructions . . . as they relate to the laying out and passing grants of land within our said Provinces, and to the terms and conditions upon which the said grants are to be made. And it is our further will and pleasure, and We do hereby direct and appoint that the following Rules and Regulations be henceforth strictly and punctually observed in the laying out, allotting, and granting such lands, tenements and hereditaments, as now are, or hereafter shall be in our power to dispose of, within our said Province. That is to say.

1. That you Our said Governor, . . . with the advice and assistance of Our Lieutenant Governor of our said Province,

[1] Public Record Office, C. O. 5, 241, pp. 511–24. The blanks in this copy are filled in for Nova Scotia.

Our Surveyor General of Lands for the northern District of North America, Our Secretary, Our Surveyor General of Our Lands and Our Receiver General of Our quit-rents for our said Province of   or any three of them, do from time to time, and at such times as you shall, with the advice aforesaid judge most convenient, cause actual surveys to be made of such parts of our said Province, not already granted or disposed of, the settlement and improvement whereof you shall think will be most advantageous to the public interest and welfare ; taking care, that such Districts, so to be surveyed and laid out as aforesaid, be divided into such a number of lots (each lot to contain not less than one hundred nor more than one thousand acres) as our said Surveyor General shall judge best adapted to the nature and situation of the District so to be surveyed.[1]

2. That when the said Survey shall have been made, a map of the District so surveyed, with the several lots marked and number'd thereon, be hung up in our Secretary's Office within our said Province, and duplicates thereof transmitted to us by one of our Principal Secretary's of State, and to our Commissioners of our Treasury, accompanied with a report in writing signed by our said Surveyor General, descriptive of the nature and advantages not only of the whole District in general, but also of each particular Lot.

3. That so soon as the said Survey shall have been made and returned, as aforesaid, you our said Governor or Commander in Chief of our said Province for the time being do, with the advice of our Council of our said Province and of the Officers herein before mentioned, appoint such time and place for the sale and disposal of the lands, contained within the said Survey, to the best bidder, as you and they shall judge most convenient and proper, giving previous notice thereof at least four months before such sale by printed advertisements to be published, not only within our said Province, but also in the other neighbouring Provinces ; and that you do proceed to

---

[1] This system of prior survey was founded on the system by which the New England colonies had extended their frontier of settlement. Judge William Smith of New York had recommended the application of it to the West in his *Historical Account* of the Bouquet expedition (Philadelphia, 1766), and Governor William Franklin made the same suggestion in his 'Reasons for Establishing a Colony in the Illinois' (*Illinois Hist. Collections*, xi. 252). See above, p. xxvii, and the Ordinance of Congress of 1785, below.

such Sales at the times appointed, unless you shall first receive directions from us to the contrary under our signet and sign manual, or by our Order in our Privy Council.

4. That you Our said Governor, or Our Governor, or Commander in Chief of Our said Province for the time being do, with the advice and assistance aforesaid, fix the price per Acre, at which the several Lots shall be put up to sale, according to the quality and condition thereof, taking care, that no Lot is put up to such sale at a less price than six pence per Acre, and all such Lots are to be sold subject to a reservation to Us, Our Heirs and Successors of an annual Quitrent of one halfpenny Sterling per acre.

5. That the printed advertisement containing notice of the time and place of sale, so to be published, as aforesaid, be as full and explicit as may be, as well in respect to the number and contents of the lots to be sold, as the terms and conditions, on which they are to be put up to sale, and the general situation of the lands, and the advantages and conveniency thereof.

6. That the person, who at such sale shall bid most for any lot, shall be the purchaser, and shall upon payment of the purchase money into the hands of Our Receiver General or his deputy, who is to attend at such sales, receive from him a bill of sale of the lot or lots so purchased, upon producing whereof to you our Governor, . . . he shall be forthwith entitled to a grant in fee simple of the land so purchased as aforesaid by Letters Patent under our public seal of our said Province, subject to no conditions or reservations whatever, other than except the payment to us, our heirs, and successors of the annual quit rent of one halfpenny her acre, as aforesaid and also of all mines of gold, silver or precious stones.

7. That the fees to be paid by purchasers of land, in manner herein before recited be such as are allowed by law and no other, . . .

And it is our further will and pleasure, that neither you our Governor . . . do, upon any pretence whatever, presume to grant any lands, tenements or hereditaments within our said Province, which are in our power to dispose of, upon any other terms, or in any other manner, than as herein before recited, without our express authority for that purpose, under our Signet, and Sign Manual, or by our Order in our Privy Council, except only in the case of such commission officers and soldiers, as are entitled to grants of lands in virtue of our Royal

Proclamation of the 7 October 1763, to whom such grants are to be made and passed in the proportions, and under the conditions prescribed in the said Proclamation.

And it is our further will and pleasure, that in all Districts, which shall hereafter be surveyed, in order to a sale of the lands in manner herein before recited, there be a reservation of such parts thereof, as shall appear from the report of the Surveyor, to be necessary for public uses.

And it is our further will and pleasure, that you our said Governor, . . . do from time to time, and as often as any Survey or sales of land shall be made in manner before mentioned, make a full and particular Report to us, by one of our principal Secretaries of State, of all proceedings in regard thereto, together with a state of the expences attending the said Survey and sales, and your or their opinion of the allowances it may be proper to make on that account to the end and intent, that we may take such order therein as shall appear to be reasonable and proper.

G. R.

A like Instruction and of the same date to the following Governors : New Hampshire, New York, Virginia, North Carolina, South Carolina, Georgia, East Florida, West Florida.

FROM THE MASSACHUSETTS GOVERNMENT ACT [1]

20 May 1774

An Act for the better regulating the Government of the Province of the Massachusetts-Bay in New England.

[WHEREAS, the method of electing the Councillors of this Province, under the Charter of 1691,[2]] hath, for some time past been such as had the most manifest tendency to obstruct, and in great measure defeat the execution of the laws ; to weaken the attachment of His Majesty's well-disposed subjects in the said Province to His Majesty's government, and to

---

[1] 14 Geo. III, c. 45.
[2] Unlike the other colonies, where the Council or Upper House was appointed by the royal Governor, the Council of Massachusetts-Bay was annually elected by the whole legislature (General Court). Consequently it reflected the opinions of the Whig majority.

encourage the ill-disposed among them to proceed even to acts of direct resistance to and defiance of His Majesty's authority. ... Be it therefore enacted [that so much of the said Charter which relates to the election of Councillors] is hereby revoked, ... [and that from 1 August 1774] the Council, or Court of Assistants of the said Province for the time being, shall be composed of such of the inhabitants or proprietors of lands within the same as shall be thereunto nominated and appointed by His Majesty, his heirs and successors, from time to time, by warrant under his or their signet or sign manual, and with the advice of the Privy Council, agreeable to the practice now used in respect to the appointment of Counsellors in such of His Majesty's other colonies in America, the Governors whereof are appointed by commission under the great seal of Great Britain : provided, that the number of the said Assistants or Counsellors shall not, at any one time, exceed thirty-six, nor be less than twelve.

2. And it is hereby further enacted, that the said Assistants or Counsellors, ... shall hold their offices respectively, for and during the pleasure of His Majesty. ...

3. It shall and may be lawful for His Majesty's Governor ... of the said Province, ... to nominate and appoint, under the seal of the Province, from time to time, and also to remove, without the consent of the Council, all judges of the inferior courts of common pleas, commissioners of oyer and terminer, the attorney general, provosts, marshals, justices of the peace, and other officers to the Council or courts of justice belonging ; and ... [5] to nominate and appoint the sheriffs without the consent of the Council, and to remove such sheriffs with such consent, and not otherwise.

6. ... Upon every vacancy of the offices of Chief Justice and Judges of the Superior Court of the said Province, ... the Governor for the time being, or, in his absence, the Lieutenant Governor, without the consent of the Council, shall have full power and authority to nominate and appoint the persons to succeed to the said offices, who shall hold their commission during the pleasure of His Majesty. ...

7. And whereas, by several acts of the General Court, ...the freeholders and inhabitants of the several townships ... are authorized to assemble together annually or occasionally, upon notice given, in such manner as the said acts direct, for the choice of selectmen, constables, and other officers, and for the

making and agreeing upon such necessary rules, orders, and bye-laws, for the directing, managing, and ordering, the prudential affairs of such townships : . . . and whereas a great abuse has been made of the power of calling such meetings, and the inhabitants have, contrary to the design of their institution, been misled to treat upon matters of the most general concern, and to pass many dangerous and unwarrantable resolves : for remedy whereof, be it enacted, That no meeting shall be called . . . without the leave of the Governor, or in his absence of the Lieutenant-Governor, in writing expressing the special business of the said meeting, first had and obtained, except the annual meeting in the months of March or May for the choice of select men, constables, and other officers, or except for the choice of persons to fill up the offices aforesaid, . . . and also, except any meeting for the election of a representative or representatives in the General Court ; and that no other matter shall be treated of at such meetings, except the election of their aforesaid officers or representatives, nor at any other meeting, except the business expressed in the leave given by the Governor, or, in his absence, by the Lieutenant-Governor.

8. And whereas the method at present used in the Province of Massachusetts-Bay, in America, of electing persons to serve on grand juries, and other juries, by the freeholders and inhabitants of the several towns, affords occasion for many evil practices, and tends to pervert the free and impartial administration of justice : for remedy whereof, be it further enacted . . . the jurors to serve at the superior courts of judicature, courts of assize, general gaol delivery, general sessions of the peace, and inferior court of common pleas, in the several counties within the said Province, . . . shall be summoned and returned by the sheriffs of the respective counties within the said Province. . . .

FROM THE QUEBEC ACT [1]

22 June 1774

An Act for making more effectual provision for the Government of the Province of Quebec *in* North America.

WHEREAS His Majesty, by his Royal Proclamation bearing date the seventh day of October in the third year of his reign, thought fit to declare the provisions which had been made in respect to certain countries, territories and islands in America, ceded to His Majesty by the definitive Treaty of Peace, concluded at Paris on the tenth day of February 1763 : And whereas by the arrangements made by the said Royal Proclamation, a very large extent of country, within which there were several colonies and settlements of the subjects of France, who claimed to remain therein under the faith of the said Treaty, was left without any provision being made for the administration of civil government therein ; . . . be it enacted. . .

That all the territories, islands and countries in North America belonging to the Crown of Great Britain, bounded on the South by a line from the Bay of Chaleurs, along the high lands which divide the rivers that empty themselves into the river Saint Lawrence from those which fall into the sea, to a point in forty-five degrees of northern latitude, on the eastern bank of the river Connecticut, keeping the same latitude directly west, through the lake Champlain, until, in the same latitude, it meets the river Saint Lawrence ; from thence up the eastern bank of the said river to the Lake Ontario ; thence through the Lake Ontario, and the river commonly called Niagara ; and thence along by the eastern and south-eastern bank of Lake Erie, following the said bank, until the same shall be intersected by the northern boundary granted by the charter of the Province of Pensylvania, in case the same shall be so intersected ; and from thence along the said northern and western boundaries of the said Province, until the said western boundary strike the Ohio ; . . . and along the bank of the said river, westward to the banks of the Mississippi, and northward to the southern boundary of the territory granted to the Merchants Adventurers of England

---

[1] 14 Geo. III, c. 83. Full text in 4 Force's *American Archives*, i. 216–20, and Shortt and Doughty, *Documents rel. to Constitutional History of Canada* (1907 ed.), pp. 401–5.

trading to Hudson's Bay ; . . . are hereby, during His Majesty's pleasure, annexed to and made part and parcel of the Province of Quebec. . . .

Provided always, that nothing herein contained relative to the boundary of the Province of Quebec shall in any wise affect the boundaries of any other colony.

.   .   .   .

And . . . it is hereby declared, that His Majesty's subjects professing the religion of the Church of Rome of and in the said Province of Quebec, may have, hold and enjoy the free exercise of the religion of the Church of Rome, subject to the King's Supremacy ; . . . and that the clergy of the said Church may hold, receive and enjoy their accustomed dues and rights, with respect to such persons only as shall profess the said religion.

FROM JAMES WILSON'S ' CONSIDERATIONS ON THE AUTHORITY OF PARLIAMENT '[1]

August 1774

Considerations on the Nature and Extent of the Legislative Authority of the British Parliament. Philadelphia, 1774.

ADVERTISEMENT

THE following sheets were written during the late non-importation agreement : [2] but that agreement being dissolved before they were ready for the press, it was then judged unseasonable to publish them. Many will, perhaps, be surprised to see the legislative authority of the British Parliament over the colonies denied in every instance. Those the writer informs, that, when he began this piece, he would probably have been surprised at such an opinion himself ; for that it was the *result*, and not the *occasion*, of his disquisitions. He entered upon them with a view and expectation of being able to trace some constitutional line between those cases in which we ought, and those in which we ought not, to acknowledge the power of Parliament over us. In the prosecution of his inquiries, he became fully convinced that such a line does not exist ; and that there can be no medium between

[1] *Works of James Wilson* (J. De W. Andrews, ed.), Chicago, 1896. ii. 504, 522–43.   [2] In 1770.

acknowledging and denyng that power in *all* cases. Which of these two alternatives is most consistent with law, with the principles of liberty, and with the happiness of the colonies, let the public determine. To them the writer submits his sentiments, with that respectful deference to their judgment, which, in all questions affecting them, every individual should pay.

August 17th, 1774.

.   .   .   .

But from what source does this mighty, this uncontrolled authority of the House of Commons flow ? From the collective body of the commons of Great Britain. This authority must, therefore, originally reside in them ; for whatever they convey to their representatives must ultimately be in themselves. And have those, whom we have hitherto been accustomed to consider as our fellow-subjects, an absolute and unlimited power over us ? Have they a natural right to make laws, by which we may be deprived of our properties, of our liberties, of our lives ? By what title do they claim to be our masters ? What act of ours has rendered us subject to those, to whom we were formerly equal ? Is British freedom denominated from the soil, or from the people of Britain ? If from the latter, do they lose it by quitting the soil ? Do those, who embark freemen in Great Britain, disembark slaves in America ? Are those who fled from the oppression of regal and ministerial tyranny, now reduced to a state of vassalage to those who then equally felt the same oppression ? Whence proceeds this fatal change ? Is this the return made us for leaving our friends and our country—for braving the danger of the deep—for planting a wilderness inhabited only by savage men and savage beasts—for extending the dominions of the British Crown—for increasing the trade of the British merchants— for augmenting the rents of the British landlords—for heightening the wages of the British artificers ? Britons should blush to make such a claim : Americans would blush to own it.

It is not, however, the ignominy only, but the danger also, with which we are threatened, that affects us. The many and careful provisions which are made by the British Constitution, that the electors of Members of Parliament may be prevented from choosing representatives who would betray them : and that the representatives may be prevented from betraying their constituents with impunity, sufficiently evince that such precautions have been deemed absolutely necessary for securing and maintaining the system of British liberty.

How would the commons of Great Britain startle at a proposal to deprive them of their share in the legislature, by rendering the House of Commons independent of them! With what indignation would they hear it! What resentment would they feel and discover against the authors of it! Yet the commons of Great Britain would suffer less inconvenience from the execution of such a proposal, than the Americans will suffer from the extension of the legislative authority of Parliament over them.

The Members of Parliament, their families, their friends, their posterity, must be subject as well as others to the laws. Their interest, and that of their families, friends, and posterity, cannot be different from the interest of the rest of the nation. A regard to the former will therefore direct to such measures as must promote the latter. But is this the case with respect to America? Are the legislators of Great Britain subject to the laws which are made for the colonies? Is their interest the same with that of the colonies? If we consider it in a large and comprehensive view we shall discern it to be undoubtedly the same, but few will take the trouble to consider it in that view; and of those who do, few will be influenced by the consideration. Mankind are usually more affected with a near though inferior interest than with one that is superior, but placed at a greater distance. As the conduct is regulated by the passions it is not to be wondered at if they secure the former, by measures which will forfeit the latter. Nay, the latter will frequently be regarded in the same manner as if it were prejudicial to them. It is with regret that I produce some late regulations of Parliament as proofs of what I have advanced. We have experienced what an easy matter it is for a minister with an ordinary share of art to persuade the Parliament and the people that taxes laid on the colonies will ease the burthens of the mother country; which, if the matter is considered in a proper light, is in fact to persuade them that the stream of national riches will be increased by closing up the fountain from which they flow. . . .

Let us pause here a little. Does neither the love of gain, the love of praise, nor the love of honor influence the members of the British Parliament in favor of the Americans? On what principles then, on what motives of action can we depend for the security of our liberties, of our properties, of everything dear to us in life, of life itself ? Shall we depend on their veneration for the dictates of natural justice ? A very little share of experience in the world, a very little degree of knowledge in the history of men, will sufficiently convince us that a regard to justice is by no means the ruling principle in human nature. He would discover himself to be a very sorry statesman who would erect a system of jurisprudence upon that slender foundation. ' He would make ', as my Lord Bacon says, ' imaginary laws for imaginary commonwealths ; and his discourses, like the stars, would give little light, because they are so high.'

But this is not the worst that can justly be said concerning the situation of the colonies, if they are bound by the acts of the British Legislature. So far are those powerful springs of action, which we have mentioned, from interesting the members of that Legislature in our favor, that, as has been already observed, we have the greatest reason to dread their operation against us. While the happy commons of Great Britain congratulate themselves upon the liberty which they enjoy, and upon the provisions—infallible, as far as they can be rendered so by human wisdom—which are made for perpetuating it to their latest posterity ; the unhappy Americans have reason to bewail the dangerous situation to which they are reduced, and to look forward with dismal apprehension to those future scenes of woe, which in all probability will open upon their descendants.

What has been already advanced will suffice to show that it is repugnant to the essential maxims of jurisprudence, to the ultimate end of all governments, to the genius of the British Constitution, and to the liberty and happiness of the colonies, that they should be bound by the legislative authority of the Parliament of Great Britain. Such a doctrine is not less repugnant to the voice of her laws. In order to evince this, I shall appeal to some authorities from the books of the law, which show expressly, or by a necessary implication, that the colonies are not bound by the Acts of the British Parliament ; because they have no share in the British Legislature.

The first case I shall mention was adjudged in the second year of Richard the Third. It was a solemn determination of all the judges of England, met in the exchequer chamber, to consider whether the people in Ireland were bound by an Act of Parliament made in England. They resolved, ' that they were not, as to such things as were done in Ireland ; but that what they did out of Ireland must be conformable to the laws of England, because they were the subjects of England. Ireland,' said they, ' has a Parliament, who make laws ; and our statutes do not bind them ; *because they do not send knights to Parliament ;* but their persons are the subjects of the king, in the same manner as the inhabitants of Calais, Gascoigne, and Guienne ' *

From this authority it follows that it is by no means a rule, that the authority of Parliament extends to all the subjects of the Crown. The inhabitants of Ireland were the subjects of the king as of his Crown of England ; but it is expressly resolved, in the most solemn manner, that the inhabitants of Ireland are not bound by the statutes of England. Allegiance to the King and obedience to the Parliament are founded on very different principles. The former is founded on protection ; the latter, on representation. An inattention to this difference has produced, I apprehend, much uncertainty and confusion in our ideas concerning the connexion, which ought to subsist between Great Britain and the American colonies.

The last observation which I shall make on this case is, that if the inhabitants of Ireland are not bound by Acts of Parliament made in England, *a fortiori*, the inhabitants of the American colonies are not bound by them. There are marks of the subordination of Ireland to Great Britain, which cannot be traced in the colonies. A writ of error lies from the King's Bench in Ireland,† to the King's Bench, and consequently to the House of Lords, in England ; by which means the former kingdom is subject to the control of the courts of justice of the latter kingdom. But a writ of error does not lie in the King's Bench, nor before the House of Lords, in England, from the colonies of America. The proceedings in their courts of justice can be reviewed and controlled only on an appeal to the King in Council.**

The foregoing important decision, favorable to the liberty of all the dominions of the British Crown that are not repre-

---

* 4 Mod. 255 ; 7 Rep. 22 b, Calvin's case. [But note later reversal of this decision, A. F. Pollard, *Henry VII*, iii. 292.]

† 4 Ins. 356.   ** 1 Bl. Com. 108, 231.

sented in the British Parliament, has been corroborated by subsequent adjudications.[1]

. . . .

I must not be so uncandid as to conceal, that in Calvin's case, where the above-mentioned decision of the judges in the exchequer chamber concerning Ireland, is quoted, it is added by way of explanation of that authority, ' which is to be understood, unless it (Ireland) be especially named.' Nor will I conceal that the same exception is taken notice of, and seems to be allowed, by the judges in the other cases relating to America. To any objection that may, hence, be formed against my doctrine, I answer, in the words of the very accurate Mr. Justice Foster, that ' general rules thrown out in argument, and carried farther than the true state of the case then in judgment requireth, have, I confess, no great weight with me '.

The question before the judges in the cases I have reasoned from, was not how far the naming of persons in an Act of Parliament would affect them ; though, unless named, they would not be bound by it : the question was, whether the legislative authority of Parliament extended over the inhabitants of Ireland or Jamaica or Virginia. To the resolution of the latter question the resolution of the former was by no means necessary, and was, therefore, wholly impertinent to the point of the adjudication.

But farther, the reason assigned for the resolution of the latter question is solid and convincing : the American colonies are not bound by the Acts of the British Parliament, because they are not represented in it. But what reason can be assigned why they should be bound by those acts in which they are specially named ? Does naming them give those who do them that honor, a right to rule over them ? Is this the source of the supreme, the absolute, the irresistible, the uncontrolled authority of Parliament ? These positions are too absurd to be alleged ; and a thousand judicial determinations in their favor would never induce one man of sense to subscribe his assent to them.

. . . .

I am sufficiently aware of an objection that will be made to what I have said concerning the legislative authority of the British Parliament. It will be alleged that I throw off all

[1] He cites Blankard *v.* Galdy, 4 Mod. 215, Salk. 411. See, however, Campbell *v.* Hall, 20 Howell's State Trials, 239.

dependence on Great Britain. This objection will be held forth in its most specious colors, by those who, from servility of soul or from mercenary considerations would meanly bow their necks to every exertion of arbitrary power : it may likewise alarm some who entertain the most favorable opinion of the connection between Great Britain and her colonies, but who are not sufficiently acquainted with the nature of that connection which is so dear to them. Those of the first class, I hope, are few ; I am sure they are contemptible, and deserve to have very little regard paid to them : but for the sake of those of the second class, who may be more numerous, and whose laudable principles atone for their mistakes, I shall take some pains to obviate the objection, and to show that a denial of the legislative authority of the British Parliament over America is by no means inconsistent with that connection which ought to subsist between the mother country and her colonies, and which, at the first settlement of those colonies, it was intended to maintain between them ; but that, on the contrary, that connection would be entirely destroyed by the extension of the power of Parliament over the American plantations.

Let us examine what is meant by a *dependence* on Great Britain : for it is always of importance clearly to define the terms that we use. Blackstone, who, speaking of the colonies, tells us, that ' they are no part of the mother country, but distinct (though dependent) dominions ', explains dependence in this manner. ' Dependence is very little else, but an obligation to conform to the will or law of that superior person or state, upon which the inferior depends. The original and true ground of this superiority, in the case of Ireland, is what we usually call, though somewhat improperly, the right of conquest ; a right allowed by the law of nations, if not by that of nature ; but which, in reason and civil policy, can mean nothing more than that, in order to put an end to hostilities, a compact is either expressly or tacitly made between the conqueror and the conquered, that if they will acknowledge the victor for their master he will treat them for the future as subjects, and not as enemies.' *

The original and true ground of the superiority of Great Britain over the American colonies is not shown in any book of the law, unless, as I have already observed, it be derived

* 1 Bl. Com. 107, 103.

from the right of conquest. But I have proved, and I hope
satisfactorily, that this right is altogether inapplicable to the
colonists. The original of the superiority of Great Britain
over the colonies is, then, unaccounted for ; and when we
consider the ingenuity and pains which have lately been
employed at home on this subject, we may justly conclude
that the only reason why it is not accounted for is that it
cannot be accounted for. The superiority of Great Britain
over the colonies ought therefore to be rejected ; and the
dependence of the colonies upon her, if it is to be construed into
' an obligation to conform to the will or law of the superior
state,' ought, in *this* sense, to be rejected also.

My sentiments concerning this matter are not singular.
They coincide with the declarations and remonstrances of the
colonies against the statutes imposing taxes on them. It was
their unanimous opinion that the Parliament have no right to
exact obedience to those statutes ; and consequently, that the
colonies are under no obligation to obey them. The dependence
of the colonies on Great Britain was denied in those instances ;
but a denial of it in those instances is, in effect, a denial of it in
all other instances. For, if dependence is an obligation to
conform to the will or law of the superior state, any exceptions
to that obligation must destroy the dependence. If, therefore,
by a dependence of the colonies on Great Britain, it is meant
that they are obliged to obey the laws of Great Britain, reason,
as well as the unanimous voice of the Americans, teaches us to
disown it. Such a dependence was never thought of by those
who left Britain in order to settle in America, nor by their
sovereigns who gave them commissions for that purpose.
Such an obligation has no correspondent right : for the
Commons of Great Britain have no dominion over their equals
and fellow-subjects in America ; they can confer no right to
their delegates to bind those equals and fellow-subjects by laws.

There is another, and a much more reasonable meaning,
which may be intended by the dependence of the colonies
on Great Britain. The phrase may be used to denote the
obedience and loyalty which the colonists owe to the kings
of Great Britain. If it should be alleged that this cannot be
the meaning of the expression, because it is applied to the
kingdom and not to the King, I give the same answer that my
Lord Bacon gave to those who said that allegiance related to the
the kingdom and not to the King, because in the statutes there

are these words—' born within the allegiance of England,' and again, ' born without the allegiance of England.' ' There is no trope of speech more familiar,' says he, ' than to use the place of addition for the person. So we say commonly, the line of York, or the line of Lancaster, for the lines of the duke of York, or the duke of Lancaster. So we say the possessions of Somerset or Warwick, intending the possessions of the dukes of Somerset, or earls of Warwick. And in the very same manner, the statute speaks, allegiance of England, for allegiance of the King of England.' *

Dependence on the mother country seems to have been understood in this sense, both by the first planters of the colonies, and also by the most eminent lawyers at that time in England.

Those who launched into the unknown deep, in quest of new countries and habitations, still considered themselves as subjects of the English monarchs, and behaved suitably to that character ; but it nowhere appears that they still considered themselves as represented in an English Parliament, or that they thought the authority of the English Parliament extended over them. They took possession of the country in the *king's* name : they treated, or made war with the Indians by *his* authority : they held the lands under *his* grants, and paid *him* the rents reserved upon them : they established governments under the sanction of *his* prerogative, or by virtue of *his* charters :—no application for those purposes was made to the Parliament : no ratification of the charters or letters patent was solicited from that assembly, as is usual in England with regard to grants and franchises of much less importance.

My Lord Bacon's sentiments on this subject ought to have great weight with us. His immense genius, his universal learning, his deep insight into the laws and constitution of England, are well known and much admired. Besides, he lived at that time when settling and improving the American plantations began seriously to be attended to, and successfully to be carried into execution. Plans for the government and regulation of the colonies were then forming : and it is only from the first general idea of these plans, that we can unfold, with precision and accuracy, all the more minute and intricate parts of which they now consist. ' The settlement of colonies,'

* 4 Ld. Bac. 192, 193, Case of the postnati of Scotland.

says he, ' must proceed from the option of those who will settle them, else it sounds like an exile : they must be raised by the leave, and not by the command of the King. At their setting out they must have their commission, or letters patent, from the king, that so they may acknowledge their dependency upon the crown of England, and under his protection.' In another place he says, ' that they still must be subjects of the realm.' ' In order to regulate all the inconveniences which will insensibly grow upon them,' he proposes, ' that the King should erect a subordinate council in England, whose care and charge shall be to advise and put in execution all things which shall be found fit for the good of those new plantations ; who, upon all occasions, shall give an account of their proceedings to the king or the council board, and from them receive such directions as may best agree with the government of that place.' It is evident from these quotations that my Lord Bacon had no conception that the Parliament would or ought to interpose,* either in the settlement or the government of the colonies. The only relation in which he says the colonists must still continue is that of subjects : the only dependency which they ought to acknowledge is a dependency on the Crown.

This is a dependence which they have acknowledged hitherto ; which they acknowledge now ; and which, if it is reasonable to judge of the future by the past and the present, they will continue to acknowledge hereafter. It is not a dependence like that contended for on Parliament, slavish and unaccountable, or accounted for only by principles that are false and inapplicable : it is a dependence founded upon the principles of reason, of liberty and of law. Let us investigate its sources.

The colonists ought to be dependent on the King, because they have hitherto enjoyed, and still continue to enjoy, his protection. Allegiance is the faith and obedience which every subject owes to his prince. This obedience is founded on the protection derived from government : for protection and allegiance are the reciprocal bonds which connect the prince and his subjects. Every subject, so soon as he is born, is under the royal protection, and is entitled to all the advantages

* It was chiefly during the confusions of the republic, when the king was in exile, and unable to assert his rights, that the House of Commons began to interfere in colony matters.

arising from it. He therefore owes obedience to that royal power, from which the protection which he enjoys is derived. But while he continues in infancy and nonage he cannot perform the duties which his allegiance requires. The performance of them must be respited till he arrive at the years of discretion and maturity. When he arrives at those years, he owes obedience not only for the protection which he now enjoys, but also for that which from his birth he has enjoyed ; and to which his tender age has hitherto prevented him from making a suitable return. Allegiance now becomes a duty founded upon principles of gratitude, as well as on principles of interest : it becomes a debt, which nothing but the loyalty of a whole life will discharge. As neither climate, nor soil, nor time entitle a person to the benefits of a subject, so an alteration of climate, of soil, or of time cannot release him from the duties of one. An Englishman who removes to foreign countries, however distant from England, owes the same allegiance to his King there which he owed him at home ; and will owe it twenty years hence as much as he owes it now. Wherever he is, he is still liable to the punishment annexed by law to crimes against his allegiance ; and still entitled to the advantages promised by law to the duties of it : it is not cancelled, and it is not forfeited. ' Hence all children born in any part of the world, if they be of English parents continuing at that time as liege subjects to the King, and having done no act to forfeit the benefit of their allegiance, are *ipso facto* naturalized : and if they have issue, and their descendants intermarry among themselves, such descendants are naturalized to all generations.' * . . .

Now we have explained the dependence of the Americans. They are the subjects of the King of Great Britain. They owe him allegiance. They have a right to the benefits which arise from preserving that allegiance inviolate. They are liable to the punishments which await those who break it. This is a dependence which they have always boasted of. The principles of loyalty are deeply rooted in their hearts ; and there they will grow and bring forth fruit while a drop of vital blood remains to nourish them. Their history is not stained with rebellious and treasonable machinations : an inviolable attachment to their sovereign and the warmest zeal for his glory shine in every page.

* 4 Ld. Bac. 192. Case of the postnati of Scotland.

From this dependence, abstracted from every other source, arises a strict connection between the inhabitants of Great Britain and those of America. They are fellow-subjects ; they are under allegiance to the same prince ; and this union of allegiance naturally produces a union of hearts. It is also productive of a union of measures through the whole British dominions. To the King is intrusted the direction and management of the great machine of government. He therefore is fittest to adjust the different wheels and to regulate their motions in such a manner as to co-operate in the same general designs. He makes war, he concludes peace, he forms alliances, he regulates domestic trade by his prerogative, and directs foreign commerce by his treaties with those nations with whom it is carried on. He names the officers of government, so that he can check every jarring movement in the administration. He has a negative on the different legislatures throughout his dominions, so that he can prevent any repugnancy in their different laws.

The connection and harmony between Great Britain and us, which it is her interest and ours mutually to cultivate, and on which her prosperity, as well as ours, so materially depends, will be better preserved by the operation of the legal prerogatives of the Crown, than by the exertion of an unlimited authority by Parliament.*

* After considering, with all the attention of which I am capable, the foregoing opinion—that all the different members of the British Empire are distinct states, independent of each other, but connected together under the same sovereign in right of the same Crown—I discover only one objection that can be offered against it. But this objection will, by many, be deemed a fatal one. ' How, it will be urged, can the trade of the British Empire be carried on, without some power, extending over the whole, to regulate it ? The legislative authority of each part, according to your doctrine, is confined within the local bounds of that part : how, then, can so many interfering interests and claims, as must necessarily meet and contend in the commerce of the whole, be decided and adjusted ? '

Permit me to answer these questions by proposing some others in my turn. How has the trade of Europe—how has the trade of the whole globe, been carried on ? Have those widely extended plans been formed by one superintending power ? Have they been carried into execution by one superintending power ? Have they been formed—have they been carried into execution, with less conformity to the rules of justice and equality, than if they had been under the direction of one superintending power ?

It has been the opinion of some politicians, of no inferior note, that all regulations of trade are useless ; that the greatest part of them are

JOSEPH GALLOWAY'S PLAN OF UNION [1]

Submitted to the Continental Congress, 28 September 1774

Resolved, That this Congress will apply to His Majesty for a redress of grievances, under which his faithful subjects in America labour, and assure him that the colonies hold in abhorrence the idea of being considered independent communities on the British Government, and most ardently desire the establishment of a political union, not only among themselves, but with the mother state, upon those principles of safety and freedom which are essential in the constitution of all free governments, and particularly that of the British

hurtful; and that the stream of commerce never flows with so much beauty and advantage, as when it is not diverted from its natural channels. Whether this opinion is well founded or not, let others determine. Thus much may certainly be said, that commerce is not so properly the object of laws, as of treaties and compacts. In this manner, it has been always directed among the several nations of Europe.

But if the commerce of the British Empire must be regulated by a general superintending power, capable of exerting its influence over every part of it, why may not this power be intrusted to the King, as a part of the royal prerogative? By making treaties, which it is his prerogative to make, he directs the trade of Great Britain with the other states of Europe : and his treaties with those states have, when considered with regard to his subjects, all the binding force of laws upon them (1 Bl. Com. 252). Where is the absurdity in supposing him vested with the same right to regulate the commerce of the distinct parts of his dominions with one another, which he has to regulate their commerce with foreign states? If the history of the British Constitution, relating to this subject, be carefully traced, I apprehend we shall discover, that a prerogative in the Crown, to regulate trade, is perfectly consistent with the principles of law. We find many authorities that the King cannot lay impositions on traffic ; and that he cannot restrain it altogether, nor confine it to monopolists ; but none of the authorities, that I have had an opportunity of consulting, go any farther. Indeed many of them seem to imply a power in the Crown to regulate trade, where that power is exerted for the great end of all prerogative—the public good.

If the power of regulating trade be, as I am apt to believe it to be, vested, by the principles of the Constitution, in the Crown, this good effect will flow from the doctrine : a perpetual distinction will be kept up between that power, and a power of laying impositions on trade. The prerogative will extend to the former : it can, under no pretence, extend to the latter : as it is given, so it is limited, by the law.

[1] *Journals of the Continental Congress* (Ford ed.), i. 49–51. The Plan was defeated by a majority of one colony.

Legislature. And as the colonies from their local circumstances cannot be represented in the Parliament of Great Britain, they will humbly propose to His Majesty, and his two Houses of Parliament, the following plan, under which the strength of the whole Empire may be drawn together on any emergency ; the interests of both countries advanced ; and the rights and liberties of America secured.

A Plan of a proposed Union between Great Britain and the Colonies of . . .

That a British and American Legislature, for regulating the administration of the general affairs of America, be proposed and established in America, including all the said colonies ; within and under which government, each colony shall retain its present constitution and powers of regulating and governing its own internal police in all cases whatsoever.

That the said government be administered by a President-General to be appointed by the King, and a Grand Council to be chosen by the representatives of the people of the several colonies in their respective Assemblies, once in every three years.

That the several Assemblies shall choose members for the Grand Council in the following proportions, viz. : . . . who shall meet at the city of   for the first time, being called by the President-General as soon as conveniently may be after his appointment. That there shall be a new election of members for the Grand Council every three years ; and on the death, removal, or resignation of any member, his place shall be supplied by a new choice at the next sitting of Assembly of the colony he represented.

That the Grand Council shall meet once in every year if they shall think it necessary, and oftener if occasions shall require, at such time and place as they shall adjourn to at the last preceding meeting, or as they shall be called to meet at, by the President-General on any emergency.

That the Grand Council shall have power to choose their Speaker, and shall hold and exercise all the like rights, liberties, and privileges as are held and exercised by and in the House of Commons of Great Britain.

That the President-General shall hold his office during the pleasure of the King, and his assent shall be requisite to all Acts of the Grand Council, and it shall be his office and duty to cause them to be carried into execution.

That the President-General, by and with the advice and consent of the Grand Council, hold and exercise all the legislative rights, powers, and authorities, necessary for regulating and administering all the general police and affairs of the colonies, in which Great Britain and the colonies, or any of them, the colonies in general, or more than one colony, are in any manner concerned, as well civil and criminal as commercial.

That the said President-General and Grand Council be an inferior and distinct branch of the British Legislature, united and incorporated with it for the aforesaid general purposes ; and that any of the said general regulations may originate, and be formed and digested, either in the Parliament of Great Britain or in the said Grand Council ; and being prepared, transmitted to the other for their approbation or dissent ; and that the assent of both shall be requisite to the validity of all such general Acts and Statutes.

That in time of war, all bills for granting aids to the Crown, prepared by the Grand Council and approved by the President-General, shall be valid and passed into a law, without the assent of the British Parliament.

DECLARATION AND RESOLVES OF THE FIRST CONTINENTAL CONGRESS [1]

14 October 1774

WHEREAS, since the close of the last war, the British Parliament, claiming a power, of right, to bind the people of America by statutes in all cases whatsoever, hath, in some acts, expressly imposed taxes on them, and in others, under various pretences, but in fact for the purpose of raising a revenue, hath imposed rates and duties payable in these colonies, established a board of commissioners with unconstitutional powers, and extended the jurisdiction of courts of admiralty, not only for collecting the said duties, but for the trial of causes merely arising within the body of a county.

And whereas, in consequence of other statutes, judges who before held only estates at will in their offices, have been made dependent on the Crown alone for their salaries, and

[1] *Journals of the Continental Congress* (Ford ed.), i. 63–73.

standing armies kept in times of peace. And it has lately been resolved in Parliament, that by force of a statute made in the thirty-fifth year of the reign of King Henry the Eighth, colonists may be transported to England, and tried there upon accusations for treasons and misprisions, or concealments of treasons committed in the colonies; and by a late statute, such trials have been directed in cases therein mentioned.

And whereas, in the last session of Parliament, . . . [the Boston Port Act, the Massachusetts Government Act, the Administration of Justice Act, and the Quebec Act were passed] . . . All which statutes are impolitic, unjust, and cruel, as well as unconstitutional, and most dangerous and destructive of American rights.

And whereas, Assemblies have been frequently dissolved, contrary to the rights of the people, when they attempted to deliberate on grievances; and their dutiful, humble, loyal, and reasonable petitions to the Crown for redress, have been repeatedly treated with contempt, by His Majesty's ministers of State:

The good people of the several colonies of New-Hampshire, Massachusetts-Bay, Rhode-Island and Providence Plantations, Connecticut, New-York, New-Jersey, Pennsylvania, Newcastle Kent and Sussex on Delaware, Maryland, Virginia, North-Carolina, and South-Carolina, justly alarmed at these arbitrary proceedings of Parliament and administration, have severally elected, constituted, and appointed deputies to meet, and sit in general Congress, in the city of Philadelphia, in order to obtain such establishment, as that their religion, laws, and liberties, may not be subverted.

Whereupon the deputies so appointed being now assembled, in a full and free representation of these colonies, taking into their most serious consideration the best means of attaining the ends aforesaid, do in the first place, as Englishmen their ancestors in like cases have usually done, for asserting and vindicating their rights and liberties, *declare,*

That the inhabitants of the English Colonies in North America, by the immutable laws of nature, the principles of the English Constitution, and the several charters or compacts, have the following rights:

1. That they are entitled to life, liberty, and property, and they have never ceded to any sovereign power whatever, a right to dispose of either without their consent.

2. That our ancestors, who first settled these colonies, were at the time of their emigration from the mother country, entitled to all the rights, liberties, and immunities of free and natural-born subjects within the realm of England.

3. That by such emigration they by no means forfeited, surrendered, or lost any of those rights, but that they were, and their descendants now are entitled to the exercise and enjoyment of all such of them, as their local and other circumstances enable them to exercise and enjoy.

4. That the foundation of English liberty, and of all free government, is a right in the people to participate in their legislative council: and as the English colonists are not represented, and from their local and other circumstances, cannot properly be represented in the British Parliament, they are entitled to a free and exclusive power of legislation in their several provincial legislatures, where their right of representation can alone be preserved, in all cases of taxation and internal polity, subject only to the negative of their sovereign, in such manner as has been heretofore used and accustomed. But, from the necessity of the case, and a regard to the mutual interest of both countries, we cheerfully consent to the operation of such Acts of the British Parliament, as are bona fide restrained to the regulation of our external commerce, for the purpose of securing the commercial advantages of the whole empire to the mother country, and the commercial benefits of its respective members ; excluding every idea of taxation, internal or external, for raising a revenue on the subjects in America without their consent.

5. That the respective colonies are entitled to the common law of England, and more especially to the great and inestimable privilege of being tried by their peers of the vicinage, according to the course of that law.

6. That they are entitled to the benefit of such of the English statutes, as existed at the time of their colonization ; and which they have, by experience, respectively found to be applicable to their several local and other circumstances.

7. That these, His Majesty's Colonies, are likewise entitled to all the immunities and privileges granted and confirmed to them by royal charters, or secured by their several codes of provincial laws.

8. That they have a right peaceably to assemble, consider of their grievances, and petition the king ; and that all

prosecutions, prohibitory proclamations, and commitments for the same, are illegal.

9. That the keeping a standing army in these colonies, in times of peace, without the consent of the legislature of that colony in which such army is kept, is against law.

10. It is indispensably necessary to good government, and rendered essential by the English Constitution, that the constituent branches of the legislature be independent of each other ; that, therefore, the exercise of legislative power in several colonies, by a council appointed during pleasure, by the Crown, is unconstitutional, dangerous, and destructive to the freedom of American legislation.

All and each of which the aforesaid deputies, in behalf of themselves, and their constituents, do claim, demand, and insist on, as their indubitable rights and liberties ; which cannot be legally taken from them, altered or abridged by any power whatever, without their own consent, by their representatives in their several provincial legislatures.

In the course of our inquiry, we find many infringements and violations of the foregoing rights, which, from an ardent desire that harmony and mutual intercourse of affection and interest may be restored, we pass over for the present, and proceed to state such acts and measures as have been adopted since the last war, which demonstrate a system formed to enslave America.

Resolved, That the following Acts of Parliament are infringements and violations of the rights of the colonists ; and that the repeal of them is essentially necessary, in order to restore harmony between Great Britain and the American colonies, viz. :

The several Acts of 4 Geo. III, c. 15, 34 ; 5 Geo. III, c. 25 ; 6 Geo. III, c. 52 ; 7 Geo. III, c. 41, 46 ; 8 Geo. III, c. 22 ; which impose duties for the purpose of raising a revenue in America, extend the powers of the admiralty courts beyond their ancient limits, deprive the American subject of trial by jury, authorize the judge's certificate to indemnify the prosecutor from damages that he might otherwise be liable to, requiring oppressive security from a claimant of ships and goods seized before he shall be allowed to defend his property ; and are subversive of American rights.

Also the 12 Geo. III, c. 24, ' For the better preserving His Majesty's dockyards, etc.', which declares a new offense in

America, and deprives the American subject of a constitutional trial by jury of the vicinage. . . .

Also the three Acts passed in the last session of Parliament, for stopping the port and blocking up the harbour of Boston, for altering the charter and government of the Massachusetts-Bay, and that which is entitled 'An Act for the better administration of Justice'.

Also the Act passed the same session for establishing the Roman Catholick religion in the Province of Quebec, abolishing the equitable system of English laws, and erecting a tyranny there, to the great danger, from so great a dissimilarity of religion, law, and government, of the neighbouring British colonies. . . .

Also the Act passed the same session for the better providing suitable quarters for officers and soldiers in His Majesty's service in North America.

Also, that the keeping a standing army in several of these colonies in time of peace, without the consent of the legislature of that colony in which the army is kept, is against law.

To these grievous Acts and measures Americans cannot submit, but in hopes that their fellow-subjects in Great Britain will, on a revision of them, restore us to that state in which both countries found happiness and prosperity, we have for the present only resolved to pursue the following peaceable measures: (1) To enter into a non-importation, non-consumption, and non-exportation agreement or association. (2) To prepare an Address to the people of Great Britain, and a Memorial to the inhabitants of British America, and (3) To prepare a loyal Address to His Majesty, agreeable to resolutions already entered into.

THE ASSOCIATION [1]

20 October 1774

WE, His Majesty's most loyal subjects, the delegates of the several colonies . . . deputed to represent them in a Continental Congress, . . . to obtain redress of these grievances, which threaten destruction of the lives, liberty, and property of His Majesty's subjects in North America, we are of opinion that a non-importation, non-consumption, and non-exporta-

---

[1] *Journals of the Continental Congress* (Ford ed.), i. 75–80. Callender, *Selections from the Economic History of the U S.*, 151–5.

tion agreement, faithfully adhered to, will prove the most speedy, effectual and peaceable measure ; and therefore we do, for ourselves, and the inhabitants of the several colonies whom we represent, firmly agree and associate, under the sacred ties of virtue, honour, and love of country, as follows :

1. That from and after the first day of December next, we will not import into British America from Great Britain or Ireland, any goods, wares, or merchandise whatsoever, or from any other place, any such goods, wares, or merchandise, as shall have been exported from Great Britain or Ireland ; nor will we after that day import any East-India tea from any part of the world ; nor any molasses, syrups, paneles, coffee, or pimento from the British plantations or from Dominica ; nor wines from Madeira or the Western Islands ; nor foreign indigo.

2. We will neither import nor purchase any slave imported after the first day of December next ; after which time we will wholly discontinue the slave trade, . . .

3. . . . from this day, we will not purchase or use any tea, imported on account of the East India Company, . . . and after the first day of March next, we will not purchase or use any East India tea whatever ; nor will we . . . purchase or use any of those goods, wares, or merchandise we have agreed not to import, . . .

4. The earnest desire we have not to injure our fellow-subjects in Great Britain, Ireland, or the West Indies, induces us to suspend a non-exportation, until the tenth day of September 1775 ; at which time, if the said Acts and parts of Acts of the British Parliament hereinafter mentioned are not repealed, we will not directly or indirectly export any merchandise or commodity whatsoever to Great Britain, Ireland, or the West Indies, except rice to Europe.

5. [Merchants to send no more orders to Great Britain.

6. Shipowners to order their masters to lade no prohibited goods.]

7. We will use our utmost endeavours to improve the breed of sheep, and increase their number to the greatest extent ; and to that end, we will kill them as seldom [1] as may be, especially those of the most profitable kind ; nor will we export any to the West Indies or elsewhere ; and those of us who are or may become overstocked with, or can conveniently

---

[1] Altered to ' sparingly ' in the pamphlet edition.

spare any sheep, will dispose of them to our neighbours, especially to the poorer sort, on moderate terms.

8. We will, in our several stations, encourage frugality, economy, and industry, and promote agriculture, arts and the manufactures of this country, especially that of wool ; and will discountenance and discourage every species of extravagance and dissipation, especially all horse-racing, and all kinds of gaming, cock-fighting, exhibitions of shews, plays, and other expensive diversions and entertainments ; and on the death of any relation or friend, none of us, or any of our families, will go into any further mourning-dress, than a black crape or ribbon on the arm or hat, for gentlemen, and a black ribbon and necklace for ladies, and we will discontinue the giving of gloves and scarves at funerals.

9. [Profiteers in stocks on hand will be boycotted.]

10. In case any merchant, trader, or other person, shall import any goods or merchandise, after the first day of December, and before the first day of February next, the same ought forthwith, at the election of the owner, to be either re-shipped or delivered up to the committee of the county or town wherein they shall be imported, to be stored at the risque of the importer until the non-importation agreement shall cease, or be sold under the direction of the committee aforesaid. . . .

11. That a committee be chosen in every county, city, and town, by those who are qualified to vote for representatives in the legislature, whose business it shall be attentively to observe the conduct of all persons touching this association ; and when it shall be made to appear, to the satisfaction of a majority of any such committee, that any person within the limits of their appointment has violated this association, that such majority do forthwith cause the truth of the case to be published in the gazette ; to the end, that all such foes to the rights of British-America may be publicly known, and universally contemned as the enemies of American liberty ; and thenceforth we respectively will break off all dealings with him or her.

12. That the committee of correspondence, in the respective colonies, do frequently inspect the entries of their custom-houses, and inform each other, from time to time, of the true state thereof, and of every other material circumstance that may occur relative to this association.

13. That all manufactures of this country be sold at reasonable prices, so that no undue advantage be taken of a future scarcity of goods.

14. And we do further agree and resolve, that we will have no trade, commerce, dealings or intercourse whatsoever, with any colony or province in North America, which shall not accede to, or which shall hereafter violate this association, but will hold them as unworthy of the rights of freemen, and as inimical to the liberties of their country.

And we do solemnly bind ourselves and our constituents, under the ties aforesaid, to adhere to this Association until [the Acts of Parliament complained of at the end of the Declaration and Resolves above] are repealed. And we recommend it to the provincial conventions and to the committees in the respective colonies to establish such farther regulations as they may think proper, for carrying into execution this association.

> PEYTON RANDOLPH, *President.*
> [Signed by all the members.]

In CONGRESS, PHILADELPHIA,
  October 20, 1774.

FROM JOHN ADAMS'S 'NOVANGLUS', NO. VII[1]

January 1775

AFTER a long discourse, which has nothing in it but what has been answered already, he [' Massachusettensis '] comes to a great subject indeed, the British Constitution, and undertakes to prove, that ' the authority of Parliament extends to the colonies '.

Why will not this writer state the question fairly ? The Whigs allow that from the necessity of a case not provided for by common law, and to supply a defect in the British dominions which there undoubtedly is, if they are to be governed only by that law, America has all along consented, still consents and ever will consent, that Parliament, being the most powerful legislature in the dominions, should regulate

---

[1] *Works of John Adams* (1851), iv. 99–116. The ' Novanglus ' papers were written in answer to a series of articles by Judge Daniel Leonard, a loyalist, which were appearing in a Boston newspaper over the signature ' Massachusettensis '.

the trade of the dominions. This is founding the authority of Parliament to regulate our trade upon *compact* and *consent* of the colonies, not upon any principle of common or statute law ; not upon any original principle of the English Constitution ; not upon the principle that Parliament is the supreme and sovereign legislature over them in all cases whatsoever. The question is not, therefore, whether the authority of Parliament extends to the colonies in any case, for it is admitted by the Whigs that it does in that of commerce ; but whether it extends in all cases. . . .

We are then detained with a long account of the three simple forms of government ; and are told, that ' the British Constitution, consisting of king, lords, and commons, is formed upon the principles of monarchy, aristocracy, and democracy, in due proportion ; that it includes the principal excellences, and excludes the principal defects of the other kinds of government—the most perfect system that the wisdom of ages has produced, and Englishmen glory in being subject to, and protected by it '.

Then we are told, ' that the colonies are a part of the British Empire '. But what are we to understand by this ? Some of the colonies, most of them indeed were settled before the kingdom of Great Britain was brought into existence. The union of England and Scotland was made and established by Act of Parliament in the reign of Queen Anne, and it was this union and statute which erected the kingdom of Great Britain. The colonies were settled long before, in the reigns of the Jameses and Charleses. What authority over them had Scotland ? Scotland, England, and the colonies were all under one king before that ; the two crowns of England and Scotland united on the head of James I, and continued united on that of Charles I, when our first charter was granted. Our charter, being granted by him who was king of both nations, to our ancestors, most of whom were *post nati*, born after the union of the two crowns, and consequently (as was adjudged in Calvin's case) free, natural subjects of Scotland as well as England—had not the king as good a right to have governed the colonies by his Scottish as by his English parliament, and to have granted our charters under the seal of Scotland as well as that of England ?

But to waive this. If the English Parliament were to govern us, where did they get the right without our consent, to take the Scottish parliament into a participation of the government over us ? When this was done, was the American share of the democracy of the Constitution consulted ? If not, were not the Americans deprived of the benefit of the democratical part of the Constitution ? And is not the democracy as essential to the English Constitution as the monarchy or aristocracy ? Should we have been more effectually deprived of the benefit of the British or English Constitution, if one or both Houses of Parliament, or if our House and Council, had made this union with the two Houses of Parliament in Scotland, without the king ?

If a new constitution was to be formed for the whole British dominions, and a supreme legislature coextensive with it, upon the general principles of the English Constitution, an equal mixture of monarchy, aristocracy, and democracy, let us see what would be necessary. England has six millions of people, we will say ; America had three. England has five hundred members in the House of Commons, we will say ; America must have two hundred and fifty. Is it possible she should maintain them there, or could they at such a distance know the state, the sense, or exigencies of their constituents ? Ireland, too, must be incorporated, and send another hundred or two of members. The territory in the East Indies and West India Islands must send members. And after all this, every navigation act, every act of trade must be repealed. America, and the East and West Indies, and Africa too, must have equal liberty to trade with all the world, that the favored inhabitants of Great Britain have now. Will the ministry thank Massachusettensis for becoming an advocate for such a union, and incorporation of all the dominions of the King of Great Britain ? Yet, without such a union, a legislature which shall be sovereign and supreme in all cases whatsoever, and coextensive with the empire, can never be established upon the general principles of the English Constitution which Massachusettensis lays down, namely, an equal mixture of monarchy, aristocracy, and democracy. Nay, further, in order to comply with this principle, this new government, this mighty colossus which is to bestride the narrow world, must have a House of Lords, consisting of Irish, East and West Indian, African, American, as well as English and Scottish noblemen ; for the nobility ought to be scattered about all the dominions, as well as the representatives of the commons.

If in twenty years more America should have six millions of inhabitants, as there is a boundless territory to fill up, she must have five hundred representatives. Upon these principles, if in forty years she should have twelve millions, a thousand ; and if the inhabitants of the three kingdoms remain as they are, being already full of inhabitants, what will become of your supreme legislative ? It will be translated, crown and all, to America. This is a sublime system for America. It will flatter those ideas of independency which the Tories impute to them, if they have any such, more than any other plan of independency that I have ever heard projected.

' The best writers upon the law of nations tell us, that when a nation takes possession of a distant country, and settles there, that country, though separated from the principal establishment or mother country, naturally becomes a part of the state equal with its ancient possessions.' We are not told who these ' best writers ' are. I think we ought to be introduced to them. But their meaning may be no more than that it is best they should be incorporated with the ancient establishment by contract, or by some new law and institution, by which the new country shall have equal right, powers, and privileges, as well as equal protection, and be under equal obligations of obedience, with the old. Has there been any such contract between Britain and the colonies ? Is America incorporated into the realm ? Is it a part of the realm ? Is it a part of the kingdom ? Has it any share in the legislative of the realm ? The Constitution requires that every foot of land should be represented in the third estate, the democratical branch of the Constitution. How many millions of acres in America, how many thousands of wealthy landholders, have no representatives there ?

But let these ' best writers ' say what they will, there is nothing in the law of nations, which is only the law of right reason applied to the conduct of nations, that requires that emigrants from a state should continue, or be made, a part of the state.

The practice of nations has been different. The Greeks planted colonies, and neither demanded nor pretended any authority over them ; but they became distinct, independent commonwealths. The Romans continued their colonies under the jurisdiction of the mother commonwealth, but nevertheless they allowed them the privileges of cities. Indeed, that sagacious city seems to have been aware of difficulties similar to those under which Great Britain is now laboring. She seems to have been sensible of the impossibility of keeping colonies planted at great distances, under the absolute control of her *senatus-consulta*. Harington tells us, that ' the commonwealth of Rome, by planting colonies of its citizens within the bounds of Italy, took the best way of propagating itself and naturalizing the country ; whereas, if it had planted such colonies without the bounds of Italy, it would have alienated the citizens, and given a root to liberty abroad, that might have sprung up foreign, or savage, and hostile to her ; wherefore it never made any such dispersion of itself and its strength till it was under the yoke of the emperors, who, disburdening themselves of the people, as having less apprehension of what they could do abroad than at home, took a contrary course '. But these Italian cities, although established by decrees of the senate of Rome, to which the colonist was always party, either as a Roman citizen about to emigrate, or as a conquered enemy treating upon terms, were always allowed all the rights of Roman citizens, and were governed by senates of their own. It was the policy of Rome to conciliate her colonies by allowing them equal liberties with her citizens. Witness the example of the Privernates. . . .

Having mentioned the wisdom of the Romans, for not planting colonies out of Italy, and their reasons for it, I cannot help recollecting an observation of Harington : ' For the colonies in the Indies,' says he, ' they are yet babes, that cannot live without sucking the breasts of their mother cities, but such as I mistake, if, when they come of age, they do not wean themselves, which causes me to wonder at princes that delight to be exhausted in that way.' This was written one hundred and twenty years ago ; the colonies are now nearer manhood than ever Harington foresaw they would arrive in such a period of time. Is it not astonishing, then, that any British minister should ever have considered this subject so little as to believe it possible for him to new-model all our governments, to tax us by an authority that never taxed us before, and subdue us to an implicit obedience to a legislature that millions of us scarcely ever thought any thing about ?

I have said, that the practice of free governments alone can be quoted with propriety to show the sense of nations. But the sense and practice of nations is not enough. Their practice must be reasonable, just, and right, or it will not govern Americans.

Absolute monarchies, whatever their practice may be, are nothing to us; for, as Harington observes, ' Absolute monarchy, as that of the Turks, neither plants its people at home nor abroad, otherwise than as tenants for life or at will; wherefore, its national and provincial government is all one.'

I deny, therefore, that the practice of free nations, or the opinions of the best writers upon the law of nations, will warrant the position of Massachusettensis,[1] that, ' when a nation takes possession of a distant territory, that becomes a part of the state equally with its ancient possessions '. The practice of free nations and the opinions of the best writers are in general on the contrary.

I agree, that ' two supreme and independent authorities cannot exist in the same state ', any more than two supreme beings in one universe; and, therefore, I contend, that our provincial legislatures are the only supreme authorities in our colonies. Parliament, notwithstanding this, may be allowed an authority supreme and sovereign over the ocean, which may be limited by the banks of the ocean, or the bounds of our charters; our charters give us no authority over the high seas. Parliament has our consent to assume a jurisdiction over them. And here is a line fairly drawn between the rights of Britain and the rights of the colonies, namely, the banks of the ocean, or low-water mark; the line

[1] ' The colonies are a part of the British Empire. The best writers upon the law of nations tell us, that when a nation takes possession of a distant country, and settles there, that country, though separated from the principal establishment, or mother country, naturally becomes a part of the state, equal with its ancient possessions. Two supreme or independent authorities cannot exist in the same state. It would be what is called *imperium in imperio*, the height of political absurdity. The analogy between the political and human body is great. Two independent authorities in a state would be like two distinct principles of volition and action in the human body, dissenting, opposing, and destroying each other. If, then, we are a part of the British Empire, we must be subject to the supreme power of the state, which is vested in the estates of parliament, notwithstanding each of the colonies have legislative and executive powers of their own, delegated or granted to them, for the purposes of regulating their own internal police, which are subordinate to, and must necessarily be subject to the checks, control, and regulation of the supreme authority.'

of division between common law, and civil or maritime law. If this is not sufficient—if Parliament are at a loss for any principle of natural, civil, maritime, moral, or common law, on which to ground any authority over the high seas, the Atlantic especially, let the colonies be treated like reasonable creatures, and they will discover great ingenuity and modesty. The Acts of Trade and Navigation might be confirmed by provincial laws, and carried into execution by our own courts and juries, and in this case, illicit trade would be cut up by the roots forever. I knew the smuggling Tories in New York and Boston would cry out against this, because it would not only destroy their profitable game of smuggling, but their whole place and pension system. But the Whigs, that is, a vast majority of the whole continent, would not regard the smuggling Tories. In one word, if public principles, and motives, and arguments were alone to determine this dispute between the two countries, it might be settled forever in a few hours ; but the everlasting clamors of prejudice, passion, and private interest drown every consideration of that sort, and are precipitating us into a civil war.

' If, then, we are a part of the British Empire, we must be subject to the supreme power of the state, which is vested in the estates in Parliament.'

Here, again, we are to be conjured out of our senses by the magic in the words ' British Empire ', and ' supreme power of the state '. But, however it may sound, I say we are not a part of the British Empire ; because the British Government is not an empire. The governments of France, Spain, &c., are not empires, but monarchies, supposed to be governed by fixed fundamental laws, though not really. The British Government is still less entitled to the style of an ' empire '. It is a limited monarchy. If Aristotle, Livy, and Harington knew what a republic was, the British Constitution is much more like a republic than an empire. They define a republic to be a government of laws, and not of men. If this definition be just, the British Constitution is nothing more nor less than a republic, in which the King is first magistrate. This office being hereditary, and being possessed of such ample and splendid prerogatives, is no objection to the government's being a republic, as long as it is bound by fixed laws which the people have a voice in making, and a right to defend. An empire is a despotism, and an emperor a despot, bound by no law or limitation but his own will; it is a stretch of tyranny beyond absolute monarchy. For, although the will of an absolute monarch is law, yet his edicts must be registered by parliaments. Even this formality is not necessary in an empire. There the maxim is *quod principi placuit legis habet vigorem*, even without having that will and pleasure recorded. There are but three empires now in Europe, the German or Holy Roman, the Russian, and the Ottoman.

There is another sense, indeed, in which the word ' empire ' is used, in which it may be applied to the government of Geneva, or any other republic, as well as to monarchy or despotism. In this sense it is synonymous with government, rule, or dominion. In this sense we are within the dominion, rule, or government of the King of Great Britain.

The question should be, whether we are a part of the kingdom of Great Britain. This is the only language known in English laws. We are not, then, a part of the British kingdom, realm, or state; and therefore the supreme power of the kingdom, realm, or state is not, upon these principles, the supreme power of us. That ' supreme power over America is vested in the estates in Parliament ', is an affront to us; for there is not an acre of American land represented there; there are no American estates in Parliament.

To say, that we ' must be ' subject, seems to betray a consciousness that we are not by any law, or upon any principles but those of mere power; and an opinion that we ought to be, or that it is necessary that we should be. But if this should be admitted for argument's sake only, what is the consequence? The consequences that may fairly be drawn are these; that Britain has been imprudent enough to let colonies be planted, until they are become numerous and important, without ever having wisdom enough to concert a plan for their government, consistent with her own welfare; that now it is necessary to make them submit to the authority of Parliament; and, because there is no principle of law, or justice, or reason, by which she can effect it, therefore she will resort to war and conquest—to the maxim, *delenda est Carthago*. These are the consequences, according to this writer's idea. We think the consequences are, that she has, after one hundred and fifty years, discovered a defect in her government, which ought to be supplied by some just and reasonable means, that is, by the consent of the colonies;

for metaphysicians and politicians may dispute forever, but they will never find any other moral principle or foundation of rule or obedience, than the consent of governors and governed. She has found out that the great machine will not go any longer without a new wheel. She will make this herself. We think she is making it of such materials and workmanship as will tear the whole machine to pieces. We are willing, if she can convince us of the necessity of such a wheel, to assist with artists and materials in making it, so that it may answer the end. But she says, we shall have no share in it ; and if we will not let her patch it up as she pleases, her Massachusettensis and other advocates tell us, she will tear it to pieces herself, by cutting our throats. To this kind of reasoning, we can only answer, that we will not stand still to be butchered. We will defend our lives as long as Providence shall enable us.

' It is beyond doubt, that it was the sense both of the *parent country* and *our ancestors*, that they were to remain subject to Parliament.'

This has been often asserted, and as often contradicted and fully confuted. The confutation may not, however, have come to every eye which has read this newspaper.

. . . .

That the authority of Parliament ' has been exercised almost ever since the first settlement of the country ', is a mistake ; for there is no instance, until the first Navigation Act, which was in 1660, more than forty years after the first settlement. This Act was never executed nor regarded until seventeen years afterwards, and then it was not executed as an Act of Parliament, but as a law of the colony, to which the king agreed.

This ' has been expressly acknowledged by our provincial legislatures '. There is too much truth in this. It has been twice acknowledged by our House of Representatives, that Parliament was the supreme legislative ; but this was directly repugnant to a multitude of other votes, by which it was denied. This was in conformity to the distinction between taxation and legislation, which has since been found to be a distinction without a difference.

When a great question is first started, there are very few, even of the greatest minds, which suddenly and intuitively comprehend it, in all its consequences.

It is both ' our interest and our duty to continue subject to the authority of Parliament ', as far as the regulation of our trade, if it will be content with that, but no longer.

' If the colonies are not subject to the authority of Parliament, Great Britain and the colonies must be distinct states, as completely so as England and Scotland were before the union, or as Great Britain and Hanover are now.' There is no need of being startled at this consequence. It is very harmless. There is no absurdity at all in it. Distinct states may be united under one king. And those states may be further cemented and united together by a treaty of commerce. This is the case. We have, by our own express consent, contracted to observe the Navigation Act, and by our implied consent, by long usage and uninterrupted acquiescence, have submitted to the other acts of trade, however grievous some of them may be. This may be compared to a treaty of commerce, by which those distinct states are cemented together, in perpetual league and amity. And if any further ratifications of this pact or treaty are necessary, the colonies would readily enter into them, provided their other liberties were inviolate.

That ' the colonies owe no allegiance to any imperial crown ', provided such a crown involves in it a house of lords and a house of commons, is certain. Indeed, we owe no allegiance to any crown at all. We owe allegiance to the person of His Majesty, King George III, whom God preserve. But allegiance is due universally, both from Britons and Americans to the person of the king, not to his crown ; to his natural, not his politic capacity, as I will undertake to prove hereafter, from the highest authorities, and the most solemn adjudications, which were ever made within any part of the British dominions.

If His Majesty's title to the crown is ' derived from an act of Parliament, made since the settlement of these colonies ', it was not made since the date of our charter. Our charter was granted by King William and Queen Mary, three years after the revolution ; and the oaths of allegiance are established by a law of the province. So that our allegiance to His Majesty is not due by virtue of any Act of a British Parliament, but by our own charter and province laws. It ought to be remembered that there was a revolution here, as well as in England, and that we, as well as the people of England, made an original, express contract with King William.

If it follows from thence, that he appears ' King of Massachusetts, King of Rhode Island, King of Connecticut, &c. ', this is no absurdity at all. He will appear in this light, and does appear so, whether Parliament has authority over us or not. He is King of Ireland, I suppose, although Parliament is allowed to have authority there. As to giving His Majesty those titles, I have no objection at all ; I wish he would be graciously pleased to assume them.

The only proposition in all this writer's long string of pretended absurdities, which he says follows from the position that we are distinct states, is this : That ' as the King must govern each state by its Parliament, those several Parliaments would pursue the particular interest of its own state ; and however well disposed the king might be to pursue a line of interest that was common to all, the checks and control that he would meet with would render it impossible '. Every argument ought to be allowed its full weight ; and therefore candor obliges me to acknowledge, that here lies all the difficulty that there is in this whole controversy. There has been, from the first to last, on both sides of the Atlantic, an idea, an apprehension, that it was necessary there should be some superintending power, to draw together all the wills, and unite all the strength of the subjects in all the dominions, in case of war, and in the case of trade. The necessity of this, in case of trade, has been so apparent, that, as has often been said, we have consented that Parliament should exercise such a power. In case of war, it has by some been thought necessary. But in fact and experience, it has not been found so. What though the proprietary colonies, on account of disputes with the proprietors, did not come in so early to the assistance of the general cause in the last war as they ought, and perhaps one of them not at all ? The inconveniences of this were small, in comparison of the absolute ruin to the liberties of all which must follow the submission to Parliament, in all cases, which would be giving up all the popular limitations upon the government. These inconveniences fell chiefly upon New England. She was necessitated to greater exertions ; but she had rather suffer these again and again than others infinitely greater. However, this subject has been so long in contemplation, that it is fully understood now in all the colonies ; so that there is no danger, in case of another war, of any colony's failing of its duty.

But, admitting the proposition in its full force, that it is absolutely necessary there should be a supreme power, co-extensive with all the dominions, will it follow that parliament, as now constituted, has a right to assume this supreme jurisdiction ? By no means.

A union of the colonies might be projected, and an American legislature ; for, if America has three millions of people, and the whole dominions, twelve millions, she ought to send a quarter part of all the members to the House of Commons ; and, instead of holding parliaments always at Westminster, the haughty members for Great Britain must humble themselves, one session in four, to cross the Atlantic, and hold the parliament in America.

There is no avoiding all inconveniences in human affairs. The greatest possible, or conceivable, would arise from ceding to Parliament power over us without a representation in it. The next greatest would accrue from any plan that can be devised for a representation there. The least of all would arise from going on as we began, and fared well for one hundred and fifty years, by letting Parliament regulate trade, and our own assemblies all other matters.

. . . .

We are a part of the British dominions, that is, of the King of Great Britain, and it is our interest and duty to continue so. It is equally our interest and duty to continue subject to the authority of Parliament in the regulation of our trade, as long as she shall leave us to govern our internal policy, and to give and grant our own money, and no longer.

This letter concludes with an agreeable flight of fancy.[1] The time may not be so far off, however, as this writer imagines, when the colonies may have the balance of numbers and wealth in their favor. But when that shall happen, if we should attempt to rule her by an American Parliament, without an adequate representation in it, she will infallibly resist us by her arms.

[1] ' After many more centuries shall have rolled away, long after we, who are now bustling upon the stage of life, shall have been received to the bosom of mother earth, and our names are forgotten, the colonies may be so far increased as to have the balance of wealth, numbers, and power in their favor ; the good of the empire may make it necessary to fix the seat of government here ; and some future George, equally the friend of mankind with him that now sways the British sceptre, may cross the Atlantic, and rule Great Britain by an American parliament.'—Massachusettensis.

FRANKLIN ON THE GALLOWAY PLAN AND THE NORTH RESOLUTION [1]

To Joseph Galloway

LONDON, 25 February 1775.

DEAR FRIEND,—In my last I mentioned to you my showing your plan of union to Lords Chatham and Camden. I now hear that you had sent it to Lord Dartmouth. Lord Gower, I believe, alluded to it when in the House he censured the Congress severely as first resolving to receive a plan for uniting the colonies to the mother country, and afterwards rejecting it, and ordering their first resolution to be erased out of their minutes. Permit me to hint to you that it is whispered here by ministerial people that yourself and Mr. Jay, of New York, are friends to their measures, and give them private intelligence of the views of the popular or country part in America. I do not believe this ; but I thought it a duty of friendship to acquaint you with the report.

I have not heard what objections were made to the plan in the Congress, nor would I make more than this one, that, when I consider the extreme corruption prevalent among all orders of men in this old, rotten state, and the glorious public virtue so predominant in our rising country, I cannot but apprehend more mischief than benefit from a closer union. I fear they will drag us after them in all the plundering wars which their desperate circumstances, injustice, and rapacity may prompt them to undertake ; and their wide-wasting prodigality and profusion is a gulf that will swallow up every aid we may distress ourselves to afford them.

Here numberless and needless places, enormous salaries, pensions, perquisites, bribes, groundless quarrels, foolish expeditions, false accounts or no accounts, contracts and jobs, devour all revenue, and produce continual necessity in the midst of natural plenty. I apprehend, therefore, that to unite us intimately will only be to corrupt and poison us also. It seems like Mezentius' coupling and binding together the dead and the living.

> Tormenti genus, et sanie taboque fluentes,
> Complexu in misero, longa sic morte necabat.

[1] *Works of Franklin* (Bigelow ed.), v. 435–9.

However, I would try anything, and bear anything that can be borne with safety to our just liberties, rather than engage in a war with such relations, unless compelled to it by dire necessity in our own defence.

But should that plan be again brought forward, I imagine that before establishing the union, it would be necessary to agree on the following preliminary articles.

(1) The Declaratory Act ; (2) all Acts of Parliament, or parts of Acts laying duties on the colonies ; (3) all Acts of Parliament altering the charters, or constitutions, or laws of any colony ; (4) all Acts of Parliament restraining manufactures ; to be repealed. (5) Those parts of the Navigation Acts, which are for the good of the whole Empire, such as require that ships in the trade should be British or Plantation built, and navigated by three-fourths British subjects, with the duties necessary for regulating commerce, to be re-enacted by both Parliaments. (6) Then, to induce the Americans to see the regulating Acts faithfully executed, it would be well to give the duties collected in each colony to the treasury of that colony, and let the Governor and Assembly appoint the officers to collect them, and proportion their salaries. Thus the business will be cheaper and better done, and the misunderstandings between the two countries, now created and fomented by the unprincipled wretches generally appointed from England, be entirely prevented.

These are hasty thoughts submitted to your consideration. You will see the new proposal of Lord North,[1] made on

---

[1] Submitted to the House of Commons on 20 February and adopted on the 27th : 'That it is the opinion of this Committee, that when the Governor, Council and Assembly or General Court, of any of His Majesty's provinces or colonies in America, shall propose to make provision, according to the condition, circumstances, and situation of such province or colony, for contributing their proportion to the common defence (such proportion to be raised under the authority of the General Court, or General Assembly of such province or colony, and disposable by Parliament), and shall engage to make provision also for the support of the civil government and the administration of justice in such province or colony, it will be proper, if such proposal shall be approved by His Majesty and the two Houses of Parliament, and for so long as such provision shall be made accordingly, to forbear, in respect of such province or colony, to levy any duty, tax, or assessment, or to impose any farther duty, tax, or assessment, except only such duties as it may be expedient to continue to levy or to impose for the regulation of commerce ; the nett produce of the duties last mentioned to be carried to the account of such province or colony respectively.' See the debate on it in *Parliamentary History*, xviii. 319–23.

Monday last, which I have sent to the committee. Those in administration, who are for violent measures, are said to dislike it. The others rely upon it as a means of dividing, and by that means subduing us. But I cannot conceive that any colony will undertake to grant a revenue to a government that holds a sword over their heads with a threat to strike the moment they cease to give or do not give so much as it is pleased to expect. In such a situation, where is the right of giving our own property freely or the right to judge of our own ability to give ? It seems to me the language of a highwayman who, with a pistol in your face, says : ' Give me your purse, and then I will not put my hand into your pocket. But give me all your money, or I will shoot you through the head.' With great and sincere esteem, I am, etc.,

B. FRANKLIN.

LETTERS OF JOSEPH WARREN TO ARTHUR LEE [1]

BOSTON, February 20, 1775.

DEAR SIR,—My friend Mr. Adams favoured me with the sight of your last letter. I am sincerely glad of your return to England, as I think your assistance was never more wanted there than at present. It is truly astonishing that Administration should have a doubt of the resolution of the Americans to make the last appeal rather than submit to wear the yoke prepared for their necks. We have waited with a degree of patience which is seldom to be met with : but I will venture to assert that there has not been any great alloy of cowardice, though both friends and enemies seem to suspect us of want of courage. I trust the event, which I confess I think is near at hand, will confound our enemies, and rejoice those who wish well to us. It is time for Britain to take some serious steps towards a reconciliation with her colonies. The people here are weary of watching the measures of those who are endeavouring to enslave them : they say they have been spending their time for ten years in counteracting the plans

---

[1] Richard Frothingham, *Life of Joseph Warren* (1865), pp. 418, 447. Joseph Warren, a Boston physician, was a prominent Radical, and Samuel Adams's right-hand man. He was killed at Bunker Hill. Arthur Lee, of Virginia, was practising law in London, and acting as joint agent, with Franklin, of the Massachusetts Assembly.

of their adversaries. They, many of them, begin to think that the difference between [them] will never be amicably settled ; but that they shall always be subject to new affronts from the caprice of every British minister. They even some-times speak of an open rupture with Great Britain, as a state preferable to the present uncertain condition of affairs. And although it is true that the people have yet a very warm affection for the British nation, yet it sensibly decays. They are loyal subjects to the King ; but they conceive that they do not swerve from their allegiance by opposing any measures taken by any man or set of men to deprive them of their liberties. They conceive that they are the King's enemies who would destroy the Constitution ; for the King is annihilated when the Constitution is destroyed.

It is not yet too late to accommodate the dispute amicably. But I am of opinion that, if once General Gage should lead his troops into the country, with design to enforce the late Acts of Parliament, Great Britain may take her leave, at least of the New-England colonies, and, if I mistake not, of all America. If there is any wisdom in the nation, God grant it may be speedily called forth ! Every day, every hour, widens the breach. A Richmond, a Chatham, a Shelburne, a Camden, with their noble associates, may yet repair it ; it is a work which none but the greatest of men can conduct. May you be successful and happy in your labors for the public safety !

BOSTON, April 3, 1775.

DEAR SIR,—Your favor of the 21st of December came opportunely to hand, as it enabled me to give the Provincial Congress, now sitting at Concord, a just view of the measures pursued by the tools of the Administration, and effectually to guard them against that state of security into which many have endeavored to lull them. If we ever obtain a redress of grievances from Great Britain, it must be by the influence of those illustrious personages whose virtue now keeps them out of power. The King never will bring them into power until the ignorance and frenzy of the present administration make the throne on which he sits shake under him. If America is an humble instrument of the salvation of Britain, it will give us the sincerest joy ; but, if Britain must lose her liberty, she must lose it alone. America must and will be free. The contest may be severe ; the end will be glorious. We would not boast, but we think, united and prepared as we are, we have no reason to doubt of success, if we should be compelled to the last appeal ; but we mean not to make that appeal until we can be justified in doing it in the sight of God and man. Happy shall we be if the mother country will allow us the free enjoyment of our rights, and indulge us in the pleasing employment of aggrandizing her.

. . . .

DECLARATION OF CAUSES OF TAKING UP ARMS [1]

6 July 1775

A Declaration by the Representatives of the United Colonies of North America, now met in Congress at Philadelphia, setting forth the causes and necessity of their taking up arms.

. . . .

BUT why should we enumerate our injuries in detail ? By one statute it is declared that Parliament can ' of right make laws to bind us in all cases whatsoever '. What is to defend us against so enormous, so unlimited a power ? Not a single man of those who assume it, is chosen by us ; or is subject to our controul or influence ; but, on the contrary, they are all of them exempt from the operation of such laws, and an American revenue, if not diverted from the ostensible purposes for which it is raised, would actually lighten their own burdens in proportion as they increase ours. We saw the misery to which such despotism would reduce us. We for ten years incessantly and ineffectually besieged the throne as supplicants ; we reasoned, we remonstrated with Parliament, in the most mild and decent language.

Administration, sensible that we should regard these oppressive measures as freemen ought to do, sent over fleets and armies to enforce them. The indignation of the Americans was roused, it is true, but it was the indignation of a virtuous, loyal, and affectionate people. A Congress of delegates from the United Colonies was assembled at Philadelphia on the fifth day of last September. We resolved again to offer an humble and dutiful petition to the king, and also addressed our fellow-subjects of Great Britain. We have pursued every

[1] 4 Force's *American Archives*, ii. 1867-9.

temperate, every respectful measure : we have even proceeded to break off our commercial intercourse with our fellow-
subjects, as the last peaceable admonition that our attachment to no nation upon earth should supplant our attachment
to liberty. This, we flattered ourselves, was the ultimate step
of the controversy ; but subsequent events have shewn how
vain was this hope of finding moderation in our enemies.

Several threatening expressions against the Colonies were
inserted in His Majesty's speech ; our petition, though we
were told it was a decent one, and that His Majesty had been
pleased to receive it graciously, and to promise laying it
before his Parliament, was huddled into both Houses among
a bundle of American papers, and there neglected.   The
Lords and Commons, in their address in the month of February,
said that ' a rebellion at that time actually existed within the
province of Massachusetts-Bay ; and that those concerned
in it had been countenanced and encouraged by unlawful
combinations and engagements, entered into by His Majesty's
subjects in several of the other colonies ; and therefore they
besought His Majesty that he would take the most effectual
measures to enforce due obedience to the laws and authority
of the supreme Legislature '.   Soon after the commercial
intercourse of whole colonies with foreign countries and with
each other was cut off by an Act of Parliament ; by another
several of them were intirely prohibited from the fisheries in
the seas near their coasts, on which they always depended
for their sustenance ; and large reinforcements of ships and
troops were immediately sent over to General Gage.

Fruitless were all the entreaties, arguments, and eloquence
of an illustrious band of the most distinguished peers and
commoners, who nobly and strenuously asserted the justice
of our cause, to stay or even to mitigate the heedless fury
with which these accumulated and unexampled outrages were
hurried on. Equally fruitless was the interference of the City
of London, of Bristol, and many other respectable towns in
our favour. Parliament adopted an insidious manœuvre
calculated to divide us, to establish a perpetual auction of
taxations where colony should bid against colony, all of them
uninformed what ransom would redeem their lives ; and thus
to extort from us, at the point of the bayonet, the unknown
sums that should be sufficient to gratify, if possible to gratify
ministerial rapacity, with the miserable indulgence left to us

of raising, in our own mode, the prescribed tribute. What terms more rigid and humiliating could have been dictated by remorseless victors to conquered enemies ? in our circumstances to accept them would be to deserve them.

Soon after the intelligence of these proceedings arrived on this continent, General Gage, who in the course of the last year had taken possession of the town of Boston in the province of Massachusetts-Bay, and still occupied it as a garrison, on the 19th day of April sent out from that place a large detachment of his army, who made an unprovoked assault on the inhabitants of the said Province, at the town of Lexington, as appears by the affidavits of a great number of persons, some of whom were officers and soldiers of that detachment, murdered eight of the inhabitants, and wounded many others. From thence the troops proceeded in warlike array to the town of Concord, where they set upon another party of the inhabitants of the same Province, killing several and wounding more, until compelled to retreat by the country people suddenly assembled to repel this cruel aggression.[1] Hostilities, thus commenced by the British troops, have been since prosecuted by them without regard to faith or reputation. The inhabitants of Boston being confined within that town by the General, their Governour, and having, in order to procure their dismission, entered into a treaty with him, it was stipulated that the said inhabitants having deposited their arms with their own magistrates, should have liberty to depart, taking with them their other effects. They accordingly delivered up their arms ; but in open violation of honour, in defiance of the obligation of treaties, which even savage nations esteemed sacred, the Governour ordered the arms deposited as aforesaid, that they might be preserved for their owners, to be seized by a body of soldiers ; detained the greatest part of the inhabitants in the town, and compelled the few who were permitted to retire, to leave their most valuable effects behind.

By this perfidy, wives are separated from their husbands, children from their parents, the aged and the sick from their relations and friends, who wish to attend and comfort them ; and those who have been used to live in plenty and even elegance, are reduced to deplorable distress.

[1] This account of Lexington and Concord is naturally biased. For a collection of sources on the Lexington affair, see A. C. McLaughlin's *Source Problems in U.S. History* (Harper's Parallel Source Problems, 1918).

The General, further emulating his ministerial masters, by a proclamation bearing date on the 12th day of June, after venting the grossest falsehoods and calumnies against the good people of these Colonies, proceeds to ' declare them all, either by name or description, to be rebels and traitors, to supersede the course of the common law, and instead thereof to publish and order the use and exercise of the law martial '. His troops have butchered our countrymen, have wantonly burnt Charlestown, besides a considerable number of houses in other places; our ships and vessels are seized; the necessary supplies of provisions are intercepted, and he is exerting his utmost power to spread destruction and devastation around him.

We have received certain intelligence that General Carleton, the Governour of Canada, is instigating the people of that Province, and the Indians, to fall upon us; and we have but too much reason to apprehend that schemes have been formed to excite domestick enemies against us. In brief, a part of these colonies now feel, and all of them are sure of feeling, as far as the vengeance of administration can inflict them, the complicated calamities of fire, sword, and famine.[1] We are reduced to the alternative of choosing an unconditional submission to the tyranny of irritated ministers or resistance by force. The latter is our choice. We have counted the cost of this contest, and find nothing so dreadful as voluntary slavery. Honour, justice, and humanity forbid us tamely to surrender that freedom which we received from our gallant ancestors, and which our innocent posterity have a right to receive from us. We cannot endure the infamy and guilt of resigning succeeding generations to that wretchedness which inevitably awaits them, if we basely entail hereditary bondage upon them.

Our cause is just. Our union is perfect. Our internal resources are great, and, if necessary, foreign assistance is undoubtedly attainable. We gratefully acknowledge, as signal instances of the Divine favour towards us, that His Providence would not permit us to be called into this severe controversy until we were grown up to our present strength, had been previously exercised in warlike operations, and possessed of the means of defending ourselves. With hearts fortified with these animating reflections, we most solemnly, before God and the world, *declare*, that exerting the utmost energy of

---

[1] The rest of the declaration was drafted by Jefferson.

those powers which our beneficent Creator hath graciously bestowed upon us, the arms we have been compelled by our enemies to assume, we will, in defiance of every hazard, with unabating firmness and perseverance, employ for the preservation of our liberties ; being with one mind resolved to die freemen, rather then to live slaves.

Lest this declaration should disquiet the minds of our friends and fellow-subjects in any part of the Empire, we assure them that we mean not to dissolve that union which has so long and so happily subsisted between us, and which we sincerely wish to see restored. Necessity has not yet driven us into that desperate measure, or induced us to excite any other nation to war against them. We have not raised armies with ambitious designs of separating from Great Britain, and establishing independent States. We fight not for glory or for conquest. We exhibit to mankind the remarkable spectacle of a people attacked by unprovoked enemies, without any imputation or even suspicion of offence. They boast of their privileges and civilization, and yet proffer no milder conditions than servitude or death.

In our own native land, in defence of the freedom that is our birthright, and which we ever enjoyed till the late violation of it ; for the protection of our property, acquired solely by the honest industry of our forefathers and ourselves, against violence actually offered, we have taken up arms. We shall lay them down when hostilities shall cease on the part of the aggressors, and all danger of their being renewed shall be removed, and not before.

With an humble confidence in the mercies of the supreme and impartial Judge and Ruler of the Universe, we most devoutly implore His divine goodness to protect us happily through this great conflict, to dispose our adversaries to reconciliation on reasonable terms, and thereby to relieve the Empire from the calamities of civil war.

By order of Congress.

JOHN HANCOCK, *President.*

APPROACHING INDEPENDENCE

(a) *John Adams to James Warren.*[1]

[PHILADELPHIA,] April 22, 1776.

THE management of so complicated and mighty a machine as the United Colonies requires the meekness of Moses, the patience of Job, and the wisdom of Solomon, added to the valour of David.

They are advancing by slow but sure steps, to that mighty Revolution which you and I have expected for some time. Forced attempts to accellerate their motions would have been attended with discontent and perhaps convulsions.

The news from South Carolina [2] has aroused and animated all the continent. It has spread a visible joy, and if North Carolina and Virginia should follow the example, it will spread through the rest of the colonies like electric fire.

The Royal Proclamation [3] and the late Act of Parliament [4] have convinced the doubting and confirmed the timorous and wavering. The two proprietary colonies only are still cool, but I hope a few weeks will alter their temper.

I think it is now the precise point of time for our Council and House of Representatives either to proceed to make such alterations in our Constitution as they may judge proper, or to send a petition to Philadelphia for the consent of Congress to do it. It will be considered as a fresh evidence of our spirit and vigour, and will give life and activity and energy to all the other colonies. Four months ago, or indeed at any time since you assumed a government,[5] it might have been disagreeable and perhaps dangerous ; but it is quite otherwise now. Another thing, if you are so unanimous in the

[1] *Warren–Adams Letters,* i (*Collections* of the Mass. Hist. Soc., lxxii), 232–4. James Warren was in the revolted Massachusetts government.

[2] The Provincial Congress of South Carolina on 26 March 1776 had adopted a constitution for that ' colony ', elected and set up a government independent of all royal authorities.

[3] The Proclamation of Rebellion, 23 August 1775. Macdonald's *Documentary Source Book,* 188.

[4] ' To prohibit all trade or intercourse with ' the Thirteen Colonies, 22 December 1775. 16 Geo. III, c. 5.

[5] Since 19 July 1775 Massachusetts had carried on as if the Province Charter were still unamended, and the Governor absent. Cf. below, p. 176.

measure of independency, and wish for a declaration of it, now is the proper time to instruct your delegates to that effect. It would have been productive of jealousies perhaps, and animosities, a few months ago ; but would have a contrary tendency now. The Colonies are all at this moment turning their eyes that way. Vast majorities in all the colonies now see the propriety and necessity of taking the decisive steps, and those who are averse to it are afraid to say much against it, and therefore such an instruction at this time would comfort and cheer the spirits of your friends, and would discourage and dishearten your enemies. . . .

After all, my friend, I do not att all wonder that so much reluctance has been shewn to the measure of independency. All great changes are irksome to the human mind, especially those which are attended with great dangers and uncertain effects. No man living can forsee the consequences of such a measure, and therefore I think it ought not to have been undertaken untill the design of Providence by a series of great events had so plainly marked out the necessity of it, that he who runs might read.

We may feel a sanguine confidence of our strength ! Yet in a few years it may be put to the tryal.

We may please ourselves with the prospect of free and popular governments, but there is great danger that these governments will not make us happy. God grant they may ! But I fear that in every Assembly members will obtain an influence by noise, not sense ; by meanness, not greatness ; by ignorance, not learning ; by contracted hearts, not large souls. I fear, too, that it will be impossible to convince and persuade people to establish wise regulations.

There is one thing, my dear sir, that must be attempted and sacredly observed, or we are all undone. There must be decency and respect and veneration introduced for persons in authority, of every rank, or we are undone. In a popular government this is the only way of supporting order, and in our circumstances, as our people have been so long without any government att all, it is more necessary than in any other. The United Provinces were so sensible of this that they carried it to a burlesque extream.

I hope your election [1] in May will be the most solemn

---

[1] ' Election ', in New England, meant the annual inauguration of the newly elected representatives and councillors.

and joyfull that ever took place in the Province. I hope everybody will attend. Clergy and laity should go to Boston, everybody should be gratefully pious and happy. It should be conducted with a solemnity that may make an impression on the whole people.

(b) *Congress recommends the formation of State Governments.*[1]

10–15 May 1776

WHEREAS, His Britannic Majesty, in conjunction with the Lords and Commons of Great Britain, has, by a late Act of Parliament, excluded the inhabitants of these United Colonies from the protection of his Crown ; and whereas, no answer whatever to the humble petitions of the colonies for redress of grievances and reconciliation with Great Britain [2] has been or is likely to be given ; but the whole force of that kingdom, aided by foreign mercenaries, is to be exerted for the destruction of the good people of these colonies ; and whereas, it appears absolutely irreconcileable to reason and good conscience for the people of these colonies now to take the oaths and affirmations necessary for the support of any government under the Crown of Great Britain, and it is necessary that every kind of authority under the said Crown should be totally suppressed, and all the powers of government exerted, under the authority of the people of these colonies, for the preservation of internal peace, virtue, and good order, as well as for the defence of their lives, liberties, and properties against the hostile invasions and cruel depredations of their enemies ; therefore

Resolved, That it be recommended to the respective Assemblies and Conventions of the United Colonies, where no government sufficient to the exigencies of their affairs have been hitherto established, to adopt such a government as shall, in the opinion of the representatives of the people, best conduce to the happiness and safety of their constituents in particular, and America in general.

[1] *Journals of Congress* (Ford ed.), iv. 352, 357. The preamble was adopted on 15 May and the resolve on 10 May. John Adams considered the passage of this resolve a personal triumph.

[2] The petition to the king from the Continental Congress, 8 July 1775, is particularly referred to. Macdonald's *Select Charters,* 381.

THE VIRGINIA BILL OF RIGHTS [1]

12 June 1776

AT A GENERAL CONVENTION of Delegates and Representatives, from the several counties and corporations of Virginia, held at the Capitol in the City of Williamsburg on Monday the 6th May 1776.

A Declaration of Rights made by the representatives of the good people of Virginia, assembled in full and free Convention ; which rights do pertain to them and their posterity, as the basis and foundation of government.

1. That all men are by nature equally free and independent, and have certain inherent rights, of which, when they enter into a state of society, they cannot by any compact deprive or divest their posterity ; namely, the enjoyment of life and liberty, with the means of acquiring and possessing property, and pursuing and obtaining happiness and safety.

2. That all power is vested in, and consequently derived from, the people ; that magistrates are their trustees and servants, and at all times amenable to them.

3. That government is, or ought to be instituted for the common benefit, protection, and security of the people, nation, or community ; of all the various modes and forms of government, that is best which is capable of producing the greatest degree of happiness and safety, and is most effectually secured against the danger of maladministration ; and that when any government shall be found inadequate or contrary to these purposes, a majority of the community hath an indubitable, unalienable and indefeasible right to reform, alter or abolish it, in such manner as shall be judged most conducive to the public weal.

4. That no man, or set of men, are entitled to exclusive or separate emoluments or privileges from the community, but in consideration of publick services ; which, not being descendible, neither ought the offices of magistrate, legislator or judge to be hereditary.

5. That the legislative and executive powers of the state should be separate and distinct from the judiciary ; and that

[1] *Statutes at Large of Virginia* (W. W. Hening, ed. 1821), ix. 110.

the members of the two first may be restrained from oppression, by feeling and participating the burthens of the people, they should, at fixed periods, be reduced to a private station, return into that body from which they were originally taken, and the vacancies be supplied by frequent, certain, and regular elections, in which all, or any part of the former members to be again eligible or ineligible, as the laws shall direct.

6. That elections of members to serve as representatives of the people in assembly, ought to be free ; and that all men having sufficient evidence of permanent common interest with, and attachment to the community, have the right of suffrage, and cannot be taxed or deprived of their property for publick uses, without their own consent, or that of their representatives so elected, nor bound by any law to which they have not, in like manner, assented for the public good.

7. That all power of suspending laws, or the execution of laws, by any authority without consent of the representatives of the people, is injurious to their rights, and ought not to be exercised.

8. That in all capital or criminal prosecutions a man hath a right to demand the cause and nature of his accusation, to be confronted with the accusers and witnesses, to call for evidence in his favour, and to a speedy trial by an impartial jury of his vicinage, without whose unanimous consent he cannot be found guilty ; nor can he be compelled to give evidence against himself ; that no man be deprived of his liberty, except by the law of the land or the judgment of his peers.

9. That excessive bail ought not to be required, nor excessive fines imposed, nor cruel and unusual punishments inflicted.

10. That general warrants, whereby an officer or messenger may be commanded to search suspected places without evidence of a fact committed, or to seize any person or persons not named, or whose offence is not particularly described and supported by evidence, are grievous and oppressive, and ought not to be granted.

11. That in controversies respecting property, and in suits between man and man, the ancient trial by jury is preferable to any other, and ought to be held sacred.

12. That the freedom of the press is one of the great

bulwarks of liberty, and can never be restrained but by despotick governments.

13. That a well-regulated militia, composed of the body of the people trained to arms, is the proper, natural and safe defence of a free state ; that standing armies in time of peace should be avoided as dangerous to liberty ; and that in all cases the military should be under strict subordination to, and governed by, the civil power.

14. That the people have a right to uniform government ; and, therefore, that no government separate from, or independent of the government of Virginia, ought to be erected or established within the limits thereof.

15. That no free government, or the blessings of liberty, can be preserved to any people, but by a firm adherence to justice, moderation, temperance, frugality and virtue, and by frequent recurrence to fundamental principles.

16. That religion, or the duty which we owe to our Creator, and the manner of discharging it, can be directed only by reason and conviction, not by force or violence ; and therefore all men are equally entitled to the free exercise of religion, according to the dictates of conscience ; and that it is the mutual duty of all to practise Christian forbearance, love, and charity towards each other.

THE CONSTITUTION OF VIRGINIA[1]

29 June 1776

The Constitution, or Form of Government, agreed to and resolved upon by the Delegates and Representatives of the several counties and corporations of Virginia.

1. WHEREAS George the third [a digest of the Declaration of Independence follows]. . . . By which several acts of misrule, the government of this country, as formerly exercised under the crown of Great Britain, is TOTALLY DISSOLVED.

2. WE, the Delegates and Representatives of the good people of Virginia, having maturely considered the premises, and viewing with great concern the deplorable conditions to which this once happy country must be reduced, unless some

---

[1] Hening's *Statutes* (1821), ix. 117. The paragraphs are not numbered in the original.

regular adequate mode of civil polity is speedily adopted, and in compliance with a recommendation of the General Congress, do ordain and declare the future form of government of Virginia to be as followeth :

3. The legislative, executive, and judiciary departments shall be separate and distinct, so that neither exercise the powers properly belonging to the other : nor shall any person exercise the powers of more than one of them at the same time ; except that the justices of the county courts shall be eligible to either House of Assembly.

4. The legislative shall be formed of two distinct branches, who, together, shall be a complete Legislature. They shall meet once, or oftener, every year, and shall be called the GENERAL ASSEMBLY OF VIRGINIA.

5. One of these shall be called the HOUSE OF DELEGATES, and consist of two representatives, to be chosen for each county, and for the district of West-Augusta, annually, of such men as actually reside in, and are freeholders of the same, or duly qualified according to law, and also of one delegate or representative to be chosen annually for the city of Williamsburg, and one for the borough of Norfolk, and a representative for each of such other cities and boroughs, as may hereafter be allowed particular representation by the legislature ; but when any city or borough shall so decrease as that the number of persons having right of suffrage therein shall have been for the space of seven years successively less than half the number of voters in some one county in Virginia, such city or borough thenceforward shall cease to send a delegate or representative to the Assembly.

6. The other shall be called the SENATE, and consist of twenty-four members, of whom thirteen shall constitute a House to proceed on business ; for whose election the different counties shall be divided into twenty-four districts, and each county of the respective district, at the time of the election of its delegates, shall vote for one Senator, who is actually a resident and freeholder within the district, or duly qualified according to law, and is upwards of twenty-five years of age ; and the Sheriffs of each county, within five days at farthest after the last county election in the district, shall meet at some convenient place, and from the poll so taken in their respective counties return as a Senator the man who shall have the greatest number of votes in the whole district. To

keep up this Assembly by rotation, the districts shall be equally divided into four classes and numbered by lot. At the end of one year after the general election, the six members elected by the first division shall be displaced, and the vacancies thereby occasioned supplied from such class or division, by new election, in the manner aforesaid. This rotation shall be applied to each division, according to its number, and continued in due order annually.

7. The right of suffrage in the election of members for both Houses shall remain as exercised at present, and each House shall choose its own speaker, appoint its own officers, settle its own rules of proceeding, and direct writs of election, for the supplying intermediate vacancies.

8. All laws shall originate in the House of Delegates, to be approved or rejected by the Senate, or to be amended with consent of the House of Delegates ; except money bills, which in no instance shall be altered by the Senate, but wholly approved or rejected.

9. A Governour, or chief magistrate, shall be chosen annually, by joint ballot of both Houses to be taken in each House respectively, deposited in the conference room, the boxes examined jointly by a committee of each House, and the numbers severally reported to them, that the appointments may be entered (which shall be the mode of taking the joint ballot of both Houses, in all cases) who shall not continue in that office longer than three years successively, nor be eligible until the expiration of four years after he shall have been out of that office. An adequate, but moderate salary shall be settled on him, during his continuance in office ; and he shall, with the advice of a Council of State, exercise the executive powers of government according to the laws of this Commonwealth ; and shall not, under any pretence, exercise any power or prerogative by virtue of any law, statute or custom of England. But he shall, with the advice of the Council of State, have the power of granting reprieves or pardons, except where the prosecution shall have been carried on by the House of Delegates, or the law shall otherwise particularly direct ; in which cases, no reprieve or pardon shall be granted, but by resolve of the House of Delegates.

10. Either House of the General Assembly may adjourn themselves respectively. The Governour shall not prorogue

or adjourn the Assembly during their sitting, nor dissolve them at any time; but he shall, if necessary, either by advice of the Council of State, or on application of a majority of the House of Delegates, call them before the time to which they shall stand prorogued or adjourned.

11. A Privy Council, or Council of State, consisting of eight members, shall be chosen by joint ballot of both Houses of Assembly, either from their own members or the people at large, to assist in the administration of government. They shall annually choose, out of their own members, a president, who, in case of death, inability, or absence of the Governour from the government, shall act as Lieutenant-Governour. Four members shall be sufficient to act, and their advice and proceedings shall be entered on record, and signed by the members present (to any part whereof, any member may enter his dissent) to be laid before the General Assembly, when called for by them. This Council may appoint their own clerk, who shall have a salary settled by law, and take an oath of secrecy in such matters as he shall be directed by the board to conceal. A sum of money appropriated to that purpose shall be divided annually among the members, in proportion to their attendance; and they shall be incapable, during their continuance in office, of sitting in either House of Assembly. Two members shall be removed, by joint ballot of both Houses of Assembly, at the end of every three years, and be ineligible for the three next years. These vacancies, as well as those occasioned by death or incapacity, shall be supplied by new elections, in the same manner.

12. The Delegates for Virginia to the Continental Congress shall be chosen annually, or superseded in the meantime by joint ballot of both Houses of Assembly.

13. The present militia officers shall be continued, and vacancies supplied by appointment of the Governour, with the advice of the Privy Council, on recommendations from the respective county courts; but the Governour and Council shall have a power of suspending any officer, and ordering a court-martial, on complaint of misbehaviour or inability, or to supply vacancies of officers, happening when in actual service. The Governour may embody the militia, with the advice of the Privy Council; and when embodied, shall alone have the direction of the militia, under the laws of the country.

14. The two Houses of Assembly shall, by joint ballot,

appoint Judges of the Supreme Court of Appeals, and General Court, Judges in Chancery, Judges of Admiralty, Secretary, and the Attorney-General, to be commissioned by the Governour, and continue in office during good behaviour. In case of death, incapacity, or resignation, the Governour, with the advice of the Privy Council, shall appoint persons to succeed in office, to be approved or displaced by both Houses. These officers shall have fixed and adequate salaries, and, together with all others holding lucrative offices, and all ministers of the Gospel of every denomination, be incapable of being elected members of either House of Assembly or the Privy Council.

15. The Governour, with the advice of the Privy Council, shall appoint Justices of the Peace for the counties ; and in case of vacancies, or a necessity of increasing the number hereafter, such appointments to be made upon the recommendation of the respective county courts. The present acting Secretary in Virginia, and clerks of all the county courts, shall continue in office. In case of vacancies, either by death, incapacity, or resignation, a Secretary shall be appointed as before directed, and the clerks by the respective courts. The present and future clerks shall hold their offices during good behaviour, to be judged of and determined in the General Court. The sheriffs and coroners shall be nominated by the respective courts, approved by the Governour, with the advice of the Privy Council, and commissioned by the Governour. The Justices shall appoint Constables ; and all fees of the aforesaid officers be regulated by law.

16. The Governour, when he is out of office, and others offending against the State, either by mal-administration, corruption, or other means by which the safety of the State may be endangered, shall be impeachable by the House of Delegates. Such impeachment to be prosecuted by the Attorney-General, or such other person or persons as the House may appoint in the General Court, according to the laws of the land. If found guilty, he or they shall be either forever disabled to hold any office under government, or be removed from such office *pro tempore*, or subjected to such pains or penalties as the law shall direct.

17. If all or any of the Judges of the General Court should on good grounds (to be judged of by the House of Delegates) be accused of any of the crimes or offences before mentioned, such House of Delegates may, in like manner, impeach the Judge or Judges so accused, to be prosecuted in the Court

of Appeals ; and he or they, if found guilty, shall be punished in the same manner as is prescribed in the preceding clause.

18. Commissions and grants shall run, *In the name of the* COMMONWEALTH *of* VIRGINIA, and bear test by the Governour, with the seal of the Commonwealth annexed. Writs shall run in the same manner, and bear test by the clerks of the several courts. Indictments shall conclude, *Against the peace and dignity of the Commonwealth.*

19. A Treasurer shall be appointed annually, by joint ballot of both Houses.

20. All escheats, penalties, and forfeitures, heretofore going to the King, shall go to the Commonwealth, save only such as the Legislature may abolish, or otherwise provide for.

21. The territories, contained within the Charters, erecting the Colonies of Maryland, Pennsylvania, North and South Carolina, are hereby ceded, released, and forever confirmed, to the people of these Colonies respectively, with all the rights of property, jurisdiction and government, and all other rights whatsoever, which might, at any time heretofore, have been claimed by Virginia, except the free navigation and use of the rivers Potowmack and Pokomoke, with the property of the Virginia shores or strands bordering on either of the said rivers, and all improvements which have been, or shall be made thereon. The western and northern extent of Virginia shall in all other respects, stand as fixed by the Charter of King James the First in the year one thousand six hundred and nine, and by the publick treaty of peace between the courts of Britain and France, in the year one thousand seven hundred and sixty-three ; unless by act of this legislature, one or more governments be established westward of the Allegheny mountains. And no purchases of lands shall be made of the Indian natives, but on behalf of the publick, by authority of the General Assembly.

22. In order to introduce this government, the representatives of the people met in Convention shall choose a Governour and Privy Council, also such other officers directed to be chosen by both Houses as may be judged necessary to be immediately appointed. The Senate to be first chosen by the people to continue until the last day of March next, and the other officers until the end of the succeeding session of Assembly. In case of vacancies, the speaker of either House shall issue writs for new elections.

THE DECLARATION OF INDEPENDENCE [1]

4 July 1776

The unanimous Declaration of the thirteen United States of America.

WHEN in the course of human events, it becomes necessary for one people to dissolve the political bands which have connected them with another, and to assume among the powers of the earth the separate and equal station to which the Laws of Nature and of Nature's God entitle them, a decent respect to the opinions of mankind requires that they should declare the causes which impel them to the separation.

We hold these truths to be self-evident, that all men are created equal, that they are endowed by their Creator with certain unalienable rights, that among these are life, liberty, and the pursuit of happiness. That to secure these rights, governments are instituted among men, deriving their just powers from the consent of the governed. That whenever any form of government becomes destructive of these ends, it is the right of the people to alter or to abolish it, and to institute new government, laying its foundation on such principles and organizing its powers in such form, as to them shall seem most likely to effect their safety and happiness. Prudence, indeed, will dictate that governments long established should not be changed for light and transient causes ; and accordingly all experience hath shown, that mankind are more disposed to suffer, while evils are sufferable, than to right themselves by abolishing the forms to which they are accustomed. But when a long train of abuses and usurpations, pursuing invariably the same object evinces a design to reduce them under absolute despotism, it is their right, it is their duty, to throw off such government, and to provide new guards for their future security. Such has been the patient sufferance of these Colonies ; and such is now the necessity which constrains them to alter their former systems of government. The history of the present King of Great

---

[1] For the drafting of the Declaration and its political philosophy, see Carl Becker, *The Declaration of Independence* (Harcourt, Brace & Co., N.Y., 1922) ; for the facts referred to in it, see H. Friedenwald, *The Declaration of Independence* (Macmillan, 1904).

Britain is a history of repeated injuries and usurpations, all having in direct object the establishment of an absolute tyranny over these States. To prove this, let facts be submitted to a candid world.

He has refused his assent to laws, the most wholesome and necessary for the public good.

He has forbidden his Governors to pass laws of immediate and pressing importance, unless suspended in their operation till his assent should be obtained ; and when so suspended, he has utterly neglected to attend to them.

He has refused to pass other laws for the accommodation of large districts of people, unless those people would relinquish the right of representation in the legislature, a right inestimable to them and formidable to tyrants only.

He has called together legislative bodies at places unusual, uncomfortable, and distant from the depository of their public records, for the sole purpose of fatiguing them into compliance with his measures.

He has dissolved representative houses repeatedly, for opposing with manly firmness his invasions on the rights of the people.

He has refused for a long time, after such dissolutions, to cause others to be elected ; whereby the legislative powers, incapable of annihilation, have returned to the people at large for their exercise ; the State remaining in the meantime exposed to all the dangers of invasion from without and convulsions within.

He has endeavoured to prevent the population of these States ; for that purpose obstructing the laws for naturalization of foreigners ; refusing to pass others to encourage their migration hither, and raising the conditions of new appropriations of lands.

He has obstructed the administration of justice, by refusing his assent to laws for establishing judiciary powers.

He has made judges dependent on his will alone, for the tenure of their offices, and the amount and payment of their salaries.

He has erected a multitude of new offices, and sent hither swarms of officers to harass our people, and eat out their substance.

He has kept among us, in times of peace, standing armies without the consent of our legislatures.

He has affected to render the military independent of and superior to the civil power.

He has combined with others to subject us to a jurisdiction foreign to our constitution, and unacknowledged by our laws ; giving his assent to their acts of pretended legislation :

For quartering large bodies of armed troops among us :

For protecting them, by a mock trial, from punishment for any murders which they should commit on the inhabitants of these States :

For cutting off our trade with all parts of the world :

For imposing taxes on us without our consent :

For depriving us in many cases of the benefits of trial by jury :

For transporting us beyond seas to be tried for pretended offences :

For abolishing the free system of English laws in a neighbouring Province, establishing therein an arbitrary government, and enlarging its boundaries so as to render it at once an example and fit instrument for introducing the same absolute rule into these Colonies :

For taking away our Charters, abolishing our most valuable laws, and altering fundamentally the forms of our governments :

For suspending our own Legislatures, and declaring themselves invested with power to legislate for us in all cases whatsoever.

He has abdicated government here, by declaring us out of his protection and waging war against us.

He has plundered our seas, ravaged our coasts, burnt our towns, and destroyed the lives of our people.

He is at this time transporting large armies of foreign mercenaries to compleat the works of death, desolation, and tyranny, already begun with circumstances of cruelty and perfidy scarcely paralleled in the most barbarous ages, and totally unworthy the head of a civilized nation.

He has constrained our fellow citizens taken captive on the high seas to bear arms against their country, to become the executioners of their friends and brethren, or to fall themselves by their hands.

He has excited domestic insurrections amongst us, and has endeavoured to bring on the inhabitants of our frontiers the merciless Indian savages, whose known rule of warfare is an undistinguished destruction of all ages, sexes, and conditions.

In every stage of these oppressions we have petitioned for redress in the most humble terms : our repeated petitions have been answered only by repeated injury. A prince whose character is thus marked by every act which may define a tyrant, is unfit to be the ruler of a free people.

Nor have we been wanting in attention to our Brittish brethren. We have warned them from time to time of attempts by their Legislature to extend an unwarrantable jurisdiction over us. We have reminded them of the circumstances of our emigration and settlement here. We have appealed to their native justice and magnanimity, and we have conjured them by the ties of our common kindred to disavow these usurpations, which would inevitably interrupt our connections and correspondence. They too have been deaf to the voice of justice and of consanguinity. We must, therefore, acquiesce in the necessity, which denounces our separation, and hold them, as we hold the rest of mankind, enemies in war, in peace friends.

We, therefore, the Representatives of the United States of America, in General Congress assembled, appealing to the Supreme Judge of the world for the rectitude of our intentions, do, in the name, and by authority of the good people of these Colonies, solemnly publish and declare, That these United Colonies are, and of right ought to be Free and Independent States ; that they are absolved from all allegiance to the British Crown, and that all political connection between them and the State of Great Britain is and ought to be totally dissolved ; and that as Free and Independent States they have full power to levy war, conclude peace, contract alliances establish commerce, and to do all other acts and things which independent States may of right do. And for the support of this declaration, with a firm reliance on the protection of Divine Providence, we mutually pledge to each other our lives, our fortunes and our sacred honor.

JOHN HANCOCK.[1]

[1] The Declaration was first published signed only by the President of Congress and the Secretary. The other members of Congress began to affix their signatures to the engrossed copy on 2 August. The signatures are grouped by States, but the names of the States are not in the original.

New Hampshire

JOSIAH BARTLETT,
WM. WHIPPLE,
MATTHEW THORNTON.

Massachusetts-Bay

SAML. ADAMS,
JOHN ADAMS,
ROBT. TREAT PAINE,
ELBRIDGE GERRY.

Rhode Island

STEP. HOPKINS,
WILLIAM ELLERY.

Connecticut

ROGER SHERMAN,
SAM'EL HUNTINGTON,
WM. WILLIAMS,
OLIVER WOLCOTT.

New York

WM. FLOYD,
PHIL. LIVINGSTON,
FRANS. LEWIS,
LEWIS MORRIS.

Pennsylvania

ROBT. MORRIS,
BENJAMIN RUSH,
BENJA. FRANKLIN,
JOHN MORTON,
GEO. CLYMER,
JAS. SMITH,
GEO. TAYLOR,
JAMES WILSON,
GEO. ROSS.

Delaware

CAESAR RODNEY,
GEO. READ,
THO. M'KEAN.

Georgia

BUTTON GWINNETT,
LYMAN HALL,
GEO. WALTON.

Maryland

SAMUEL CHASE,
WM. PACA,
THOS. STONE,
CHARLES CARROLL of Carroll-
ton.

Virginia

GEORGE WYTHE,
RICHARD HENRY LEE,
TH. JEFFERSON,
BENJA. HARRISON,
THS. NELSON, JR.,
FRANCIS LIGHTFOOT LEE,
CARTER BRAXTON.

North Carolina

WM. HOOPER,
JOSEPH HEWES,
JOHN PENN.

South Carolina

EDWARD RUTLEDGE,
THOS. HEYWARD, JUNR.,
THOMAS LYNCH, JUNR.,
ARTHUR MIDDLETON.

New Jersey

RICHD. STOCKTON,
JNO. WITHERSPOON,
FRAS. HOPKINSON,
JOHN HART,
ABRA. CLARK.

THE CONSTITUTION OF PENNSYLVANIA [1]

28 September 1776

The Constitution of the Commonwealth of Pennsylvania as established by the general convention elected for that purpose, and held at Philadelphia, 15 July 1776, and continued by adjournment, to 28 September 1776.

WHEREAS all government ought to be instituted and supported for the security and protection of the community as such, and to enable the individuals who compose it to enjoy their natural rights, and the other blessings which the author of existence has bestowed upon man ; and whenever these great ends of government are not obtained, the people have a right by common consent to change it, and take such measures as to them may appear necessary to promote their safety and happiness. AND WHEREAS the inhabitants of this Commonwealth have, in consideration of protection only, heretofore acknowledged allegiance to the king of Great Britain ; and the said king has not only withdrawn that protection, but commenced and still continues to carry on, with unabated vengeance, a most cruel and unjust war against them, employing therein not only the troops of Great Britain, but foreign mercenaries, savages and slaves, for the avowed purpose of reducing them to a total and abject submission to the despotic domination of the British Parliament (with many other acts of tyranny, more fully set forth in the Declaration of Congress) whereby all allegiance and fealty to the said king and his successors are dissolved and at an end, and all power and authority derived from him ceased in these colonies. AND WHEREAS it is absolutely necessary for the welfare and safety of the inhabitants of said colonies, that they be henceforth free and independent States, and that just, permanent and proper forms of government exist in every part of them, derived from and founded on the authority of the people only, agreeably to the directions of the honourable American Congress. WE, the representatives of the freemen of Pennsylvania, in general convention met,

[1] *The Proceedings relative to . . . the Conventions of 1776 and 1790,* &c. (Harrisburg, 1828), 57–65.

for the express purpose of framing such a government, confessing the goodness of the great Governour of the universe (who alone knows to what degree of earthly happiness mankind may attain by perfecting the arts of government) in permitting the people of this State, by common consent, and without violence, deliberately to form for themselves such just rules as they shall think best for governing their future society ; and being fully convinced that it is our indispensible duty to establish such original principles of government as will best promote the general happiness of the people of this State and their posterity, and provide for future improvements, without partiality for or prejudice against any particular class, sect, or denomination of men whatever, do, by virtue of the authority vested in us by our constituents, ordain, declare and establish the following *Declaration of Rights* and *Frame of Government*, to be the Constitution of this Commonwealth, and to remain in force therein for ever unaltered, except in such articles as shall hereafter, on experience, be found to require improvement, and which shall by the same authority of the people, fairly delegated as this frame of government directs, be amended or improved for the more effectual obtaining and securing the great end and design of all government, herein before mentioned.

CHAPTER I

A Declaration of the Rights of the Inhabitants of the Commonwealth or State of Pennsylvania.[1]

I. [Virginia Bill of Rights, s. 1.]

II. That all men have a natural and unalienable right to worship Almighty God, according to the dictates of their own consciences and understanding ; and that no man ought or of right can be compelled to attend any religious worship, or erect or support any place of worship, or maintain any ministry contrary to, or against, his own free will and consent ; nor can any man, who acknowledges the being of a God, be justly deprived or abridged of any civil right as a citizen, on account of his religious sentiments or peculiar mode of religious worship ; and that no authority can, or ought to be vested in,

---

[1] Sections of the same purport as clauses of the Virginia Bill of Rights are replaced by a reference to that document.

or assumed by any power whatever, that shall in any case interfere with, or in any manner controul the right of conscience in the free exercise of religious worship.

III. That the people of this State have the sole, exclusive and inherent right of governing and regulating the internal police of the same.

IV. [Virginia, s. 2.]

V. [Virginia, s. 3.]

VI. [Virginia, s. 5.]

VII. [Virginia, s. 6.]

VIII. That every member of society hath a right to be protected in the enjoyment of life, liberty, and property, and therefore is bound to contribute his proportion towards the expense of that protection, and yield his personal service when necessary, or an equivalent thereto ; but no part of a man's property can be justly taken from him, or applied to public uses, without his own consent or that of his legal representatives : Nor can any man who is conscientiously scrupulous of bearing arms be justly compelled thereto, if he will pay such equivalent ; nor are the people bound by any laws, but such as they have in like manner assented to, for their common good.

IX. [Virginia, s. 8.]

X. [Virginia, s. 10.]

XI. [Virginia, s. 11.]

XII. That the people have a right to freedom of speech, and of writing, and publishing their sentiments ; therefore the freedom of the press ought not to be restrained.

XIII. [Virginia, s. 13.]

XIV. [Virginia, s. 15.]

XV. That all men have a natural inherent right to emigrate from one State to another that will receive them, or to form a new State in vacant countries, or in such countries as they can purchase, whenever they think that thereby they may promote their own happiness.[1]

XVI. That the people have a right to assemble together, to consult for their common good, to instruct their representatives, and to apply to the legislature for redress of grievances, by address, petition, or remonstrance.

[1] Cf. Virginia Bill of Rights, s. 14. Pennsylvania had a definite western boundary, but Virginia claimed everything to the north and west !

Plan or Frame of Government for the Commonwealth or State of Pennsylvania.

1. The Commonwealth or State of Pennsylvania shall be governed hereafter by an assembly of the representatives of the freemen of the same, and a President and Council, in manner and form following—

2. The supreme legislative power shall be vested in a House of Representatives of the freemen of the Commonwealth or State of Pennsylvania.

3. The supreme executive power shall be vested in a President and Council.

4. Courts of justice shall be established in the city of Philadelphia, and in every county of this State.

5. The freemen of this Commonwealth and their sons shall be trained and armed for its defence, under such regulations, restrictions, and exceptions as the general assembly shall by law direct, preserving always to the people the right of choosing their colonels and all commissioned officers under that rank, in such manner and as often as by the said laws shall be directed.

6. Every freeman of the full age of twenty-one years, having resided in this State for the space of one whole year next before the day of election for Representatives, and paid public taxes during that time, shall enjoy the right of an elector : Provided always, that sons of freeholders of the age of twenty-one years shall be entitled to vote although they have not paid taxes.

7. The House of Representatives of the freemen of this Commonwealth shall consist of persons most noted for wisdom and virtue, to be chosen by the freemen of every city and county of this Commonwealth respectively, and no person shall be elected unless he has resided in the city or county for which he shall be chosen two years immediately before the said election, nor shall any member, while he continues such, hold any other office except in the militia.

8. No person shall be capable of being elected a member to serve in the House of Representatives of the freemen of this Commonwealth more than four years in seven.

9. The members of the House of Representatives shall be chosen annually by ballot, by the freemen of the Commonwealth, on the second Tuesday in October forever (except

this present year), and shall meet on the fourth Monday of the same month, and shall be stiled, *The General Assembly of the Representatives of the Freemen of Pennsylvania,* and shall have power to choose their speaker, the treasurer of the State, and their other officers ; sit on their own adjournments ; prepare bills and enact them into laws ; judge of the elections and qualifications of their own members ; they may expel a member, but not a second time for the same cause ; they may administer oaths or affirmations on examination of witnesses ; redress grievances ; impeach state criminals ; grant charters of incorporation ; constitute towns, boroughs, cities, and counties ; and shall have all other powers necessary for the legislature of a free state or commonwealth : but they shall have no power to add to, alter, abolish, or infringe any part of this Constitution.

10. A quorum of the House of Representatives shall consist of two-thirds of the whole number of members elected ; and having met and chosen their speaker, shall each of them before they proceed to business take and subscribe as well the oath or affirmation of fidelity and allegiance hereinafter directed, as the following oath or affirmation, viz. :

' I —— do swear (or affirm) that as a member of this Assembly, I will not propose or assent to any bill, vote, or resolution, which shall appear to me injurious to the people ; nor do or consent to any act or thing whatever, that shall have a tendency to lessen or abridge their rights and privileges as declared in the Constitution of this State ; but will in all things conduct myself as a faithful honest representative and guardian of the people, according to the best of my judgment and abilities.'

And each member, before he takes his seat, shall make and subscribe the following declaration, viz. :

' I do believe in one God, the Creator and Governour of the universe, the rewarder of the good and the punisher of the wicked, and I do acknowledge the Scriptures of the Old and New Testament to be given by Divine Inspiration.'

And no further or other religious test shall ever hereafter be required of any civil officer or magistrate in this State.

11. Delegates to represent this state in Congress shall be chosen by ballot by the future general assembly at their first meeting, and annually forever afterwards, as long as such representation shall be necessary. Any delegate may be

superseded at any time, by the general assembly appointing another in his stead. No man shall sit in Congress longer than two years successively, nor be capable of re-election for three years afterwards ; and no person who holds any office in the gift of the Congress shall hereafter be elected to represent this Commonwealth in Congress.

12. If any city or cities, county or counties shall neglect or refuse to elect and send Representatives to the General Assembly, two-thirds of the members from the cities or counties that do elect and send Representatives, provided they be a majority of the cities and counties of the whole State, when met, shall have all the powers of the General Assembly, as fully and amply as if the whole were present.

13. The doors of the House in which the Representatives of the Freemen of this State shall sit in General Assembly, shall be and remain open for the admission of all persons who behave decently, except only when the welfare of this State may require the doors to be shut.

14. The votes and proceedings of the General Assembly shall be printed weekly during their sitting, with the yeas and nays, on any question, vote or resolution, where any two members require it, except when the vote is taken by ballot ; and when the yeas and nays are so taken every member shall have a right to insert the reasons of his vote upon the minutes, if he desires it.

15. To the end that laws before they are enacted may be more maturely considered, and the inconvenience of hasty determinations as much as possible prevented, all bills of public nature shall be printed for the consideration of the people, before they are read in general assembly the last time for debate and amendment ; and, except on occasions of sudden necessity, shall not be passed into laws until the next session of assembly ; and for the more perfect satisfaction of the public, the reasons and motives for making such laws shall be fully and clearly expressed in the preambles.

16. The stile of the laws of this Commonwealth shall be, *Be it enacted, and it is hereby enacted by the Representatives of the Freemen of the Commonwealth of Pennsylvania in General Assembly met, and by the authority of the same.* And the General Assembly shall affix their seal to every bill, as soon as it is enacted into a law, which seal shall be kept by the assembly, and shall be called, THE SEAL OF THE LAWS

OF PENNSYLVANIA, and shall not be used for any other purpose.

17. The city of Philadelphia and each county of this Commonwealth respectively, shall on the first Tuesday in November in this present year, and on the second Tuesday in October annually for the two next succeeding years, viz. the year 1777, and the year 1778, choose six persons to represent them in General Assembly. But as representation in proportion to the number of taxable inhabitants is the only principle which can at all times secure liberty, and make the voice of a majority of the people the law of the land ; therefore the General Assembly shall cause complete lists of the taxable inhabitants in the city and each county in the Commonwealth respectively, to be taken and returned to them, on or before the last meeting of the assembly elected in the year 1778, who shall appoint a representation to each, in proportion to the number of taxables in such returns ; which representation shall continue for the next seven years afterwards, at the end of which, a new return of the taxable inhabitants shall be made, and a representation agreeable thereto appointed by the said Assembly, and so on septennially forever. The wages of the representatives in General Assembly and all other State charges shall be paid out of the State treasury.[1]

18. In order that the Freemen of this Commonwealth may enjoy the benefit of election as equally as may be until the representation shall commence, as directed in the foregoing section, each county at his own choice may be divided into districts, hold elections therein, and elect their representatives in the county, and their other elective officers, as shall be hereafter regulated by the General Assembly of this State. And no inhabitant of this State shall have more than one annual vote at the general election for representatives in assembly.

19. For the present the Supreme Executive Council of this State shall consist of twelve persons chosen in the following manner : The freemen of the city of Philadelphia, and of the counties of Philadelphia, Chester, and Bucks., respectively, shall choose by ballot one person for the city, and one for each county aforesaid, to serve for three years and no longer,

---

[1] Cf. *Remonstrance of the Frontier*, p. 9.

at the time and place for electing representatives in General Assembly. The freemen of the counties of Lancaster, York, Cumberland, and Berks., shall, in like manner elect one person for each county respectively, to serve as councillors for two years and no longer. And the counties of Northampton, Bedford, Northumberland and Westmoreland, respectively, shall, in like manner, elect one person for each county, to serve as councillors for one year, and no longer. And at the expiration of the time for which each councillor was chosen to serve, the freemen of the city of Philadelphia, and of the several counties in this state, respectively, shall elect one person to serve as councillor for three years and no longer ; and so on every third year forever. By this mode of election and continual rotation, more men will be trained to public business, there will in every subsequent year be found in the Council a number of persons acquainted with the proceedings of the foregoing years, whereby the business will be more consistently conducted, and moreover the danger of establishing an inconvenient aristocracy will be effectually prevented. All vacancies in the Council that may happen by death, resignation, or otherwise, shall be filled at the next general election for Representatives in General Assembly, unless a particular election for that purpose shall be sooner appointed by the President and Council. No member of the General Assembly or delegate in Congress, shall be chosen a member of the Council. The President and Vice-president shall be chosen annually by the joint ballot of the General Assembly and Council, of the members of the Council. Any person having served as a councillor for three successive years, shall be incapable of holding that office for four years afterwards. Every member of the Council shall be a justice of the peace for the whole Commonwealth, by virtue of his office.

In case new additional counties shall hereafter be erected in this State, such county or counties shall elect a councillor, and such county or counties shall be annexed to the next neighbouring counties, and shall take rotation with such counties.

The Council shall meet annually, at the same time and place with the General Assembly.

The treasurer of the state, trustees of the loan office, naval officers, collectors of customs or excise, judge of the admiralty, attornies general, sheriffs, and prothonotaries, shall not be capable of a seat in the General Assembly, Executive Council, or Continental Congress.

20. The President, and in his absence the Vice-president, with the Council, five of whom shall be a quorum, shall have power to appoint and commissionate judges, naval officers, judge of the admiralty, attorney-general, and all other officers, civil and military, except such as are chosen by the General Assembly or the people, agreeable to this Frame of Government, and the laws that may be made hereafter ; and shall supply every vacancy in any office, occasioned by death, resignation, removal or disqualification, until the office can be filled in the time and manner directed by law or this Constitution. They are to correspond with other States, and transact business with the officers of government, civil and military ; and to prepare such business as may appear to them necessary to lay before the General Assembly. They shall sit as judges, to hear and determine on impeachments, taking to their assistance for advice only, the Justices of the Supreme Court. And shall have power to grant pardons, and remit fines, in all cases whatsoever, except in cases of impeachment ; and in cases of treason and murder, shall have power to grant reprieves, but not to pardon, until the end of the next sessions of Assembly ; but there shall be no remission or mitigation of punishments on impeachments, except by act of the Legislature ; they are also to take care that the laws be faithfully executed ; they are to expedite the execution of such measures as may be resolved upon by the General Assembly ; and they may draw upon the treasury for such sums as shall be appropriated by the House : They may also lay embargoes, or prohibit the exportation of any commodity, for any time, not exceeding thirty days, in the recess of the House only : They may grant such licences, as shall be directed by law, and shall have power to call together the General Assembly when necessary, before the day to which they shall stand adjourned. The President shall be commander-in-chief of the forces of the State, but shall not command in person, except advised thereto by the Council, and then only so long as they shall approve thereof. The President and Council shall have a secretary, and keep fair books of their proceedings, wherein any councillor may enter his dissent, with his reasons in support of it.

21. All commissions shall be in the name, and by the

authority of the Freemen of the Commonwealth of Pennsylvania, sealed with the State seal, signed by the President or Vice-president, and attested by the secretary ; which seal shall be kept by the Council.

22. Every officer of state, whether judicial or executive, shall be liable to be impeached by the General Assembly, either when in office, or after his resignation or removal for mal-administration : All impeachments shall be before the President or Vice-president and Council, who shall hear and determine the same.

23. The Judges of the Supreme Court of Judicature shall have fixed salaries, be commissioned for seven years only, though capable of re-appointment at the end of that term, but removable for misbehaviour at any time by the General Assembly ; they shall not be allowed to sit as members in the Continental Congress, executive council, or general assembly, nor to hold any other office civil or military, nor to take or receive fees or perquisites of any kind.

24. The Supreme Court, and the several courts of common pleas of this Commonwealth, shall, besides the powers usually exercised by such courts, have the powers of a court of chancery, so far as relates to the perpetuating testimony, obtaining evidence from places not within this state, and the care of the persons and estates of those who are *non compotes mentis*, and such other powers as may be found necessary by future general assemblies, not inconsistent with this constitution.

25. Trials shall be by jury as heretofore : And it is recommended to the legislature of this State, to provide by law against every corruption or partiality in the choice, return, or appointment of juries.

26. Courts of sessions, common pleas, and orphans' courts shall be held quarterly in each city and county ; and the legislature shall have power to establish all such other courts as they may judge for the good of the inhabitants of the State. All courts shall be open, and justice shall be impartially administered without corruption or unnecessary delay : All their officers shall be paid an adequate but moderate compensation for their services : And if any officer shall take greater or other fees than the law allows him, either directly or indirectly, it shall ever after disqualify him from holding any office in this State.

27. All prosecutions shall commence in the name and by the authority of the Freemen of the Commonwealth of Pennsylvania ; and all indictments shall conclude with these words, *Against the peace and dignity of the same.* The style of all process hereafter in this State shall be, *The Commonwealth of Pennsylvania.*

28. The person of a debtor, where there is not a strong presumption of fraud, shall not be continued in prison, after delivering up, bona fide, all his estate real and personal, for the use of his creditors, in such manner as shall be hereafter regulated by law. All prisoners shall be bailable by sufficient sureties, unless for capital offences, when the proof is evident, or presumption great.

29. Excessive bail shall not be exacted for bailable offences : And all fines shall be moderate.

30. Justices of the peace shall be elected by the freeholders of each city and county respectively, that is to say, two or more persons may be chosen for each ward, township, or district, as the law shall hereafter direct : And their names shall be returned to the President in Council, who shall commissionate one or more of them for each ward, township, or district so returning, for seven years, removable for misconduct by the general assembly. But if any city or county, ward, township, or district in this Commonwealth, shall hereafter incline to change the manner of appointing their justices of the peace as settled in this article, the General Assembly may make laws to regulate the same, agreeable to the desire of a majority of the freeholders of the city or county, ward, township, or district so applying. No justice of the peace shall sit in the General Assembly unless he first resigns his commission ; nor shall he be allowed to take any fees, nor any salary or allowance, except such as the future legislature may grant.

31. Sheriffs and coroners shall be elected annually in each city and county, by the freemen ; that is to say, two persons for each office, one of whom for each, is to be commissioned by the president in council. No person shall continue in the office of sheriff more than three successive years, or be capable of being again elected during four years afterwards. The election shall be held at the same time and place appointed for the election of representatives : And the commissioners and assessors, and other officers chosen by the people, shall

also be then and there elected, as has been usual heretofore, until altered or otherwise regulated by the future legislature of this State.

32. All elections, whether by the people or in General Assembly, shall be by ballot, free and voluntary : And any elector who shall receive any gift or reward for his vote, in meat, drink, monies or otherwise, shall forfeit his right to elect for that time, and suffer such other penalties as future laws shall direct. And any person who shall directly or indirectly give, promise, or bestow any such rewards to be elected, shall be thereby rendered incapable to serve for the ensuing year.

33. All fees, licence money, fines and forfeitures heretofore granted, or paid to the governor, or his deputies for the support of government, shall hereafter be paid into the public treasury, unless altered or abolished by the future legislature.

34. A register's office for the probate of wills and granting letters of administration, and an office for the recording of deeds, shall be kept in each city and county ; the officers to be appointed by the General Assembly, removable at their pleasure, and to be commissioned by the President in Council.

35. The printing presses shall be free to every person who undertakes to examine the proceedings of the legislature, or any part of government.

36. As every freeman to preserve his independence (if without a sufficient estate), ought to have some profession, calling, trade or farm, whereby he may honestly subsist, there can be no necessity for, nor use in establishing offices of profit, the usual effects of which are dependence and servility unbecoming freemen, in the possessors and expectants ; faction, contention, corruption, and disorder among the people : but if any man is called into public service, to the prejudice of his private affairs, he has a right to a reasonable compensation. And whenever an office, through increase of fees or otherwise, becomes so profitable as to occasion many to apply for it, the profits ought to be lessened by the Legislature.

37. The future Legislature by this State shall regulate intails in such a manner as to prevent perpetuities.

38. The penal laws as heretofore used shall be reformed by the future Legislature of this State, as soon as may be, and punishments made in some cases less sanguinary, and in general more proportionate to the crimes.

39. To deter more effectually from the commission of crimes, by continued visible punishments of long duration, and to make sanguinary punishments less necessary; houses ought to be provided for punishing by hard labour, those who shall be convicted of crimes not capital; wherein the criminals shall be imployed for the benefit of the public, or for reparation of injuries done to private persons: And all persons at proper times shall be admitted to see the prisoners at their labour.

40. Every officer, whether judicial, executive or military, in authority under this commonwealth, shall take the following oath or affirmation of allegiance, and general oath of office before he enters on the execution of his office:

'I —— do swear (or affirm) that I will be true and faithful to the Commonwealth of Pennsylvania: And that I will not directly or indirectly do any act or thing prejudicial or injurious to the constitution or government thereof, as established by the convention.'

'I —— do swear (or affirm) that I will faithfully execute the office of —— for the —— of —— and will do equal right and justice to all men, to the best of my judgment and abilities, according to law.'

41. No public tax, custom, or contribution shall be imposed upon, or paid by the people of this State, except by a law for that purpose: And before any law be made for raising it, the purpose for which any tax is to be raised ought to appear clearly to the legislature to be of more service to the community than the money would be, if not collected; which being well observed, taxes can never be burthens.

42. Every foreigner of good character who comes to settle in this State, having first taken an oath or affirmation of allegiance to the same, may purchase, or by other just means acquire, hold, and transfer land or other real estate; and after one year's residence, shall be deemed a free denizen thereof, and entitled to all the rights of a natural born subject of this state, except that he shall not be capable of being elected a Representative until after two years' residence.

43. The inhabitants of this State shall have liberty to fowl and hunt in seasonable times on the lands they hold, and on all other lands therein not inclosed; and in like manner to fish in all boatable waters, and others not private property.

44. A school or schools shall be established in each county

by the legislature, for the convenient instruction of youth, with such salaries to the masters paid by the public as may enable them to instruct youth at low prices : And all useful learning shall be duly encouraged and promoted in one or more universities.

45. Laws for the encouragement of virtue, and prevention of vice and immorality, shall be made and constantly kept in force, and provision shall be made for their due execution : And all religious societies or bodies of men heretofore united or incorporated for the advancement of religion or learning, or for other pious and charitable purposes, shall be encouraged and protected in the enjoyment of the privileges, immunities, and estates which they were accustomed to enjoy, or could of right have enjoyed, under the laws and former constitution of this State.

46. The Declaration of Rights is hereby declared to be a part of the Constitution of this Commonwealth, and ought never to be violated on any pretence whatever.

47. In order that the freedom of the commonwealth may be preserved inviolate forever, there shall be chosen by ballot by the freemen in each city and county respectively, on the second Tuesday in October, in the year one thousand seven hundred and eighty-three, and on the second Tuesday in October, in every seventh year thereafter, two persons in each city and county of this State, to be called the COUNCIL OF CENSORS ; who shall meet together on the second Monday of November next ensuing their election ; the majority of whom shall be a quorum in every case, except as to calling a convention, in which two-thirds of the whole number elected shall agree : And whose duty it shall be to enquire whether the Constitution has been preserved inviolate in every part ; and whether the legislative and executive branches of government have performed their duty as guardians of the people, or assumed to themselves, or exercised other or greater powers than they are intitled to by the constitution : They are also to enquire whether the public taxes have been justly laid and collected in all parts of this Commonwealth, in what manner the public monies have been disposed of, and whether the laws have been duly executed. For these purposes they shall have power to send for persons, papers, and records ; they shall have authority to pass public censures, to order impeachments, and to recommend to the

legislature the repealing such laws as appear to them to have been enacted contrary to the principles of the Constitution. These powers they shall continue to have, for and during the space of one year from the day of their election and no longer : The said Council of Censors shall also have power to call a Convention, to meet within two years after their sitting, if there appear to them an absolute necessity of amending any article of the Constitution which may be defective, explaining such as may be thought not clearly expressed, and of adding such as are necessary for the preservation of the rights and happiness of the people ; but the articles to be amended, and the amendments proposed, and such articles as are proposed to be added or abolished, shall be promulgated at least six months before the day appointed for the election of such Convention, for the previous consideration of the people, that they may have an opportunity of instructing their delegates on the subject.

BENJ. FRANKLIN, *Prest.*

CONCORD TOWN MEETING DEMANDS A CONSTITUTIONAL CONVENTION [1]

21 October 1776

AT a meeting of the inhabitants of the town of Concord being free and twenty-one years of age and upwards, met by adjournment on the twenty-first day of October 1776 to take into consideration a Resolve of the Honourable House of Representatives of this State on the 17th of September last.[2]

[1] Massachusetts Archives ; facsimile in *Commonwealth of Massachusetts, Manual for the Constitutional Convention, 1917.* These resolves are the first known suggestion that a specially elected Convention was the proper body to draft a Constitution. They were drawn up by a committee consisting of two or three farmers (including the commanders of the minute-men at Concord fight), the village cordwainer, and a Harvard M.A.

[2] Massachusetts was governed by a popularly elected Provincial Congress from October 1774 to 19 July 1775 ; thereafter by a regularly elected General Court under the province charter, without the ' absent ' Governor. The lower House of this General Court requested the people, 17 September 1776, to empower it to go into convention with the Council (Upper House) and draft a State Constitution. This it proceeded to do, in spite of the objections of Concord and other towns ; but the Constitution thus drafted was rejected by the people. In 1779

Resolved as follows :

1. That this State being at present destitute of a properly established form of government, it is absolutely necessary that one should be immediatly formed and established.

2. That the Supreme Legislative, either in their proper capacity or in joint committee, are by no means a body proper to form and establish a constitution or form of government ; for reasons following. First, because we conceive that a Constitution in its proper idea intends a system of principles established to secure the subject in the possession and enjoyment of their rights and priviliges, against any encroachments of the governing part. Second, because the same body that forms a constitution have of consequence a power to alter it. Third, because a Constitution alterable by the Supreme Legislative is no security at all to the subject against any encroachment of the governing part on any, or on all of their rights and priviliges.

3. That it appears to this town highly necessary and expedient that a Convention or Congress be immediatly chosen, to form and establish a Constitution, by the inhabitents of the respective towns in this State, being free and twenty-one years of age and upwards, in proportion as the Representatives of this State formerly ware chosen : the Convention or Congress not to consist of a greater number than the House of Assembly of this State heretofore might consist of, except that each town and district shall have the liberty to send one Representative, or otherwise as shall appear meet to the inhabitants of this State in general.

4. That when the Convention or Congress have formed a Constitution, they adjourn for a short time and publish their proposed Constitution for the inspection and remarks of the inhabitents of this State.

5. That the honourable House of Assembly of this State be desired to recommend it to the inhabitents of the State to proceed to chuse a Convention or Congress for the purpas abovesaid as soon as possable.

CONCORD, October the 22d, 1776.

the advice of the Concord town meeting was followed. The *Manual* (note 1) contains a constitutional history of Massachusetts ; copies may be obtained from the Secretary of the Commonwealth, Boston.

ARTICLES OF CONFEDERATION [1]

1777 (1781) [2]

To all to whom these Presents shall come, we the undersigned Delegates of the States affixed to our Names, send greeting.

WHEREAS the Delegates of the United States of America, in Congress assembled, did, on the 15th day of November, in the year [1777] . . . agree to certain Articles of Confederation and perpetual Union between the States of . . . in the words following, viz. :

Articles of Confederation and perpetual Union between the states of New Hampshire, Massachusetts-Bay, Rhode Island and Providence Plantations, Connecticut, New-York, New-Jersey, Pennsylvania, Delaware, Maryland, Virginia, North-Carolina, South-Carolina, and Georgia.

I. The stile of this Confederacy shall be ' The United States of America '.

II. Each state retains its sovereignty, freedom, and independence, and every power, jurisdiction, and right, which is not by this Confederation expressly delegated to the United States, in Congress assembled.

III. The said states hereby severally enter into a firm league of friendship with each other, for their common defence, the security of their liberties, and their mutual and general welfare, binding themselves to assist each other, against all force offered to, or attacks made upon them, or any of them, on account of religion, sovereignty, trade, or any other pretence whatever.

IV. The better to secure and perpetuate mutual friendship and intercourse among the people of the different states in this union, the free inhabitants of each of these states, paupers, vagabonds, and fugitives from justice excepted, shall be entitled to all privileges and immunities of free citizens in the several states ; and the people of each state shall have free ingress and regress to and from any other state, and shall enjoy therein all the privileges of trade and commerce, subject

---

[1] *Journals of the Continental Congress* (G. Hunt ed.), xix. 214.

[2] The Articles of Confederation were drafted by a committee of Congress appointed 11 June 1776, and agreed to by Congress 15 November 1777. They did not go into force until ratified by the last of the Thirteen States, Maryland, on 1 March 1781.

to the same duties, impositions and restrictions as the inhabitants thereof respectively, provided that such restriction shall not extend so far as to prevent the removal of property imported into any state, to any other state, of which the owner is an inhabitant ; provided also that no imposition, duties or restriction shall be laid by any state, on the property of the United States, or either of them.

If any person guilty of, or charged with treason, felony, or other high misdemeanor in any state, shall flee from justice, and be found in any of the United States, he shall, upon demand of the Governor or executive power of the state from which he fled, be delivered up and removed to the state having jurisdiction of his offence.

Full faith and credit shall be given in each of these states to the records, acts and judicial proceedings of the courts and magistrates of every other state.

V. For the more convenient management of the general interests of the United States, delegates shall be annually appointed in such manner as the legislature of each state shall direct, to meet in Congress on the first Monday in November, in every year, with a power reserved to each state to recal its delegates, or any of them, at any time within the year, and to send others in their stead for the remainder of the year.

No state shall be represented in Congress by less than two, nor by more than seven members ; and no person shall be capable of being a delegate for more than three years in any term of six years ; nor shall any person, being a delegate, be capable of holding any office under the United States, for which he, or another for his benefit receives any salary, fees or emolument of any kind.

Each state shall maintain its own delegates in a meeting of the states, and while they act as members of the committee of the states.

In determining questions in the United States in Congress assembled, each state shall have one vote.

Freedom of speech and debate in Congress shall not be impeached or questioned in any court or place out of Congress, and the members of Congress shall be protected in their persons from arrests and imprisonments, during the time of their going to and from, and attendance on Congress, except for treason, felony, or breach of the peace.

VI. No state, without the consent of the United States in

Congress assembled, shall send any embassy to, or receive any embassy from, or enter into any conference, agreement, alliance or treaty with any king, prince or state ; nor shall any person holding any office of profit or trust under the United States, or any of them, accept of any present, emolument, office or title of any kind whatever from any king, prince or foreign state ; nor shall the United States in Congress assembled, or any of them, grant any title of nobility.

No two or more states shall enter into any treaty, confederation or alliance whatever between them, without the consent of the United States in Congress assembled, specifying accurately the purposes for which the same is to be entered into, and how long it shall continue.

No state shall lay any imposts or duties, which may interfere with any stipulations in treaties, entered into by the United States in Congress assembled, with any king, prince or state, in pursuance of any treaties already proposed by Congress, to the courts of France and Spain.

No vessels of war shall be kept up in time of peace by any state, except such number only, as shall be deemed necessary by the United States in Congress assembled, for the defence of such state, or its trade ; nor shall any body of forces be kept up by any state in time of peace, except such number only, as in the judgment of the United States in Congress assembled, shall be deemed requisite to garrison the forts necessary for the defence of such state ; but every state shall always keep up a well regulated and disciplined militia, sufficiently armed and accoutred, and shall provide and constantly have ready for use, in public stores, a due number of field pieces and tents, and a proper quantity of arms, ammunition, and camp equipage.

No state shall engage in any war without the consent of the United States in Congress assembled, unless such state be actually invaded by enemies, or shall have received certain advice of a resolution being formed by some nation of Indians to invade such state, and the danger is so imminent as not to admit of a delay till the United States in Congress assembled can be consulted : nor shall any state grant commissions to any ships or vessels of war, nor letters of marque or reprisal, except it be after a declaration of war by the United States in Congress assembled, and then only against the kingdom or state and the subjects thereof, against which war has been so declared, and under such regulations as shall be established by the United States in Congress assembled, unless such state be infested by pirates, in which case vessels of war may be fitted out for that occasion, and kept so long as the danger shall continue, or until the United States in Congress assembled, shall determine otherwise.

VII. When land-forces are raised by any state for the common defence, all officers of or under the rank of colonel, shall be appointed by the legislature of each state respectively, by whom such forces shall be raised, or in such manner as such state shall direct, and all vacancies shall be filled up by the state which first made the appointment.

VIII. All charges of war, and all other expences that shall be incurred for the common defence or general welfare, and allowed by the United States in Congress assembled, shall be defrayed out of a common treasury, which shall be supplied by the several states in proportion to the value of all land within each state, granted to or surveyed for any person, as such land and the buildings and improvements thereon shall be estimated according to such mode as the United States in Congress assembled, shall from time to time direct and appoint.

The taxes for paying that proportion shall be laid and levied by the authority and direction of the legislatures of the several states within the time agreed upon by the United States in Congress assembled.

IX. The United States in Congress assembled, shall have the sole and exclusive right and power of determining on peace and war, except in the cases mentioned in the sixth article—of sending and receiving ambassadors—entering into treaties and alliances, provided that no treaty of commerce shall be made whereby the legislative power of the respective states shall be restrained from imposing such imposts and duties on foreigners, as their own people are subjected to, or from prohibiting the exportation or importation of any species of goods or commodities whatsoever—of establishing rules for deciding in all cases, what captures on land or water shall be legal, and in what manner prizes taken by land or naval forces in the service of the United States shall be divided or appropriated—of granting letters of marque and reprisal in times of peace—appointing courts for the trial of piracies and felonies committed on the high seas and establishing courts for receiving and determining finally appeals in all cases of captures, provided that no member of Congress shall be appointed a judge of any of the said courts.

The United States in Congress assembled shall also be the last resort on appeal in all disputes and differences now subsisting or that hereafter may arise between two or more states concerning boundary, jurisdiction or any other cause whatever ; which authority shall always be exercised in the manner following. Whenever the legislative or executive authority or lawful agent of any state in controversy with another shall present a petition to Congress stating the matter in question and praying for a hearing, notice thereof shall be given by order of Congress to the legislative or executive authority of the other state in controversy, and a day assigned for the appearance of the parties by their lawful agents, who shall then be directed to appoint by joint consent, commissioners or judges to constitute a court for hearing and determining the matter in question : but if they cannot agree, Congress shall name three persons out of each of the United States, and from the list of such persons each party shall alternately strike out one, the petitioners beginning, until the number shall be reduced to thirteen ; and from that number not less than seven, nor more than nine names as Congress shall direct, shall in the presence of Congress be drawn out by lot, and the persons whose names shall be so drawn or any five of them, shall be commissioners or judges, to hear and finally determine the controversy, so always as a major part of the judges who shall hear the cause shall agree in the determination : and if either party shall neglect to attend at the day appointed, without showing reasons, which Congress shall judge sufficient, or being present shall refuse to strike, the Congress shall proceed to nominate three persons out of each state, and the secretary of Congress shall strike in behalf of such party absent or refusing ; and the judgment and sentence of the court to be appointed, in the manner before prescribed, shall be final and conclusive ; and if any of the parties shall refuse to submit to the authority of such court, or to appear or defend their claim or cause, the court shall nevertheless proceed to pronounce sentence, or judgment, which shall in like manner be final and decisive, the judgment or sentence and other proceedings being in either case transmitted to Congress, and lodged among the acts of Congress for the security of the parties concerned : provided that every commissioner, before he sits in judgment, shall take an oath to be administred by one of the judges of the supreme or superior court of the state, where the cause shall be tried, ' well and truly to hear and determine the matter in question, according to the best of his judgment, without favour, affection or hope of reward ' : provided also, that no state shall be deprived of territory for the benefit of the United States.

All controversies concerning the private right of soil claimed under different grants of two or more states, whose jurisdictions as they may respect such lands, and the states which passed such grants are adjusted, the said grants or either of them being at the same time claimed to have originated antecedent to such settlement of jurisdiction, shall on the petition of either party to the Congress of the United States, be finally determined as near as may be in the same manner as is before prescribed for deciding disputes respecting territorial jurisdiction between different states.

The United States in Congress assembled shall also have the sole and exclusive right and power of regulating the alloy and value of coin struck by their own authority, or by that of the respective states—fixing the standard of weights and measures throughout the United States—regulating the trade and managing all affairs with the Indians, not members of any of the states, provided that the legislative right of any state within its own limits be not infringed or violated—establishing or regulating post-offices from one state to another, throughout all the United States, and exacting such postage on the papers passing thro' the same as may be requisite to defray the expences of the said office—appointing all officers of the land forces, in the service of the United States, excepting regimental officers—appointing all the officers of the naval forces, and commissioning all officers whatever in the service of the United States—making rules for the government and regulation of the said land and naval forces, and directing their operations.

The United States in Congress assembled shall have authority to appoint a committee, to sit in the recess of Congress, to be denominated ' A Committee of the States ', and to consist of one delegate from each state ; and to appoint such other committees and civil officers as may be necessary for managing the general affairs of the United States under their direction—to appoint one of their number to preside, provided that no person be allowed to serve in the office of president more than one year in any term of three years ; to ascertain the necessary sums of money to be raised for the service of the United States, and to appropriate and apply the same for defraying the public expences—to borrow money, or emit bills on the credit of the United States, transmitting every half-year to the respective states an account of the sums of money so borrowed or emitted—to build and equip a navy—to agree upon the number of land forces, and to make requisitions from each state for its quota, in proportion to the number of white inhabitants in such state ; which requisition shall be binding, and thereupon the legislature of each state shall appoint the regimental officers, raise the men and cloath, arm and equip them in a soldier-like manner, at the expence of the United States ; and the officers and men so cloathed, armed, and equipped shall march to the place appointed, and within the time agreed on by the United States in Congress assembled. But if the United States in Congress assembled shall, on consideration of circumstances judge proper that any state should not raise men, or should raise a smaller number than its quota, and that any other state should raise a greater number of men than the quota thereof, such extra number shall be raised, officered, cloathed, armed, and equipped in the same manner as the quota of such state, unless the legislature of such state shall judge that such extra number cannot be safely spared out of the same, in which case they shall raise, officer, cloath, arm, and equip as many of such extra number as they judge can be safely spared. And the officers and men so cloathed, armed, and equipped, shall march to the place appointed, and within the time agreed on by the United States in Congress assembled.

The United States in Congress assembled shall never engage in a war, nor grant letters of marque and reprisal in time of peace, nor enter into any treaties or alliances, nor coin money, nor regulate the value thereof, nor ascertain the sums and expences necessary for the defence and welfare of the United States, or any of them, nor emit bills, nor borrow money on the credit of the United States, nor appropriate money, nor agree upon the number of vessels of war, to be built or purchased, or the number of land or sea forces to be raised, nor appoint a commander in chief of the army or navy, unless nine states assent to the same : nor shall a question on any other point, except for adjourning from day to day be determined, unless by the votes of a majority of the United States in Congress assembled.

The Congress of the United States shall have power to adjourn to any time within the year, and to any place within the United States, so that no period of adjournment be for a longer duration than the space of six months, and shall publish the journal of their proceedings monthly, except such parts thereof relating to treaties, alliances or military operations, as in their judgment require secrecy ; and the yeas and nays of the delegates of each state on any question shall be entered on the journal, when it is desired by any delegate ; and the delegates of a state, or any of them, at his or their request shall be furnished with a transcript of the said journal, except such parts as are above excepted, to lay before the legislatures of the several states.

X. The Committee of the States, or any nine of them, shall be authorized to execute, in the recess of Congress, such of the powers of Congress as the United States in Congress assembled, by the consent of nine states, shall from time to time think expedient to vest them with ; provided that no power be delegated to the said Committee, for the exercise of which, by the Articles of Confederation, the voice of nine states in the Congress of the United States assembled is requisite.

XI. Canada acceding to this confederation, and joining in the measures of the United States, shall be admitted into, and entitled to all the advantages of this union : but no other colony shall be admitted into the same, unless such admission be agreed to by nine states.

XII. All bills of credit emitted, monies borrowed, and debts contracted by, or under the authority of Congress, before the assembling of the United States, in pursuance of the present confederation, shall be deemed and considered as a charge against the United States, for payment and satisfaction whereof the said United States, and the public faith are hereby solemnly pledged.

XIII. Every state shall abide by the determinations of the United States in Congress assembled, on all questions which by this confederation are submitted to them. And the Articles of this Confederation shall be inviolably observed by every state, and the union shall be perpetual ; nor shall any alteration at any time hereafter be made in any of them ; unless such alteration be agreed to in a Congress of the United States, and be afterwards confirmed by the legislatures of every state.

And Whereas it hath pleased the Great Governor of the World to incline the hearts of the legislatures we respectively represent in Congress, to approve of, and to authorize us to ratify the said articles of confederation and perpetual union. Know Ye that we the undersigned delegates, by virtue of the power and authority to us given for that purpose, do by these presents, in the name and in behalf of our respective constituents, fully and entirely ratify and confirm each and every of the said articles of confederation and perpetual union, and all and singular the matters and things therein contained : And we do further solemnly plight and engage the faith of our respective constituents, that they shall abide by the determinations of the United States in Congress assembled, on all questions, which by the said confederation are submitted to them. And that the articles thereof shall be inviolably observed by the states we respectively represent, and that the union shall be perpetual. In Witness whereof we have hereunto set our hands in Congress. Done at Philadelphia in the state of Pennsylvania the ninth day of July, in the year of our Lord one Thousand seven Hundred and Seventy-eight, and in the third year of the independence of America.[1]

ROYAL INSTRUCTIONS TO THE PEACE COMMISSION OF 1778 [2]

St. James's, 12 April 1778

George R.

Orders and Instructions to be observed by our right trusty and right well-beloved cousin and Councillor, Frederick, Earl of Carlisle, *Knight of the most antient Order of the Thistle ; our right trusty and wellbeloved cousin and councillor* Richard, Lord Viscount Howe, *of Our Kingdom of Ireland ; our trusty and wellbeloved* Sir William Howe, *Knight of the most honour-*

[1] The delegates of only eight States signed on this date. Signatures omitted.

[2] *Historical MSS. Commission, 15th Report, Appendix, Part VI* (Carlisle MSS.), 322–33. The Enabling Act (18 Geo. III, c. 13) authorizes

able Order of the Bath, Lieutenant General of our forces, General and Commander-in-Chief of all and singular our forces employed or to be employed within Our Colonies in North America, lying upon the Atlantic Ocean, from Nova Scotia on the north to West Florida on the south, both inclusive ; WILLIAM EDEN, *Esq., one of our Commissioners for Trade and Plantations ; and* GEORGE JOHNSTONE, *Esq., Captain in our Royal Navy ; being our Commissioners appointed by us with sufficient powers to treat, consult, and agree upon the means of quieting the disorders now subsisting in certain of our colonies, plantations, and provinces in North America. Given at our Court at St. James's, the twelfth day of April 1778, in the eighteenth year of our reign.*

With these our Instructions, you will receive our commission under the great seal of Great Britain, constituting you, or any three of you, our Commissioners, with certain powers to treat, consult, and agree upon the means of quieting the disorders now subsisting in certain of our colonies, plantations, and provinces in North America. You are therefore to repair, with all convenient speed, to New York, or such other place in North America as you shall judge most proper ; and when you shall have arrived in any of them, you are to proceed to the execution of the trust we have reposed in you, and for that purpose you, or any three of you, are to communicate your arrival to the Commander-in-Chief of the American forces, or to any body of men, by whatever name known or distinguished, who may be supposed to represent the different provinces, colonies, and plantations in America.

And you are hereby directed to address them by any style or title which may describe them, and to lay before them a copy of the Act of Parliament by virtue of which we are enabled to appoint Commissioners, together with a copy of our commission ; and we do direct you, or any three of you, to express your desire and readiness to receive or meet them or any of them authorized for that purpose, at New York, or any place which shall be mutually agreed upon ; and that upon notice of the intention of all or any such persons constituting such body

the Commissioners to grant pardons, to arrange a suspension of arms, to suspend, up to 1 June 1779, the operation of any Act passed since 10 February 1763 in so far as it relates to America, to make temporary arrangements for colonial governments, and to conclude a ' treaty ', in accordance with royal instructions ; said treaty to require confirmation by Parliament.

as aforesaid to confer with you, or any three of you, upon the subject of this our commission and these our instructions, you do immediately dispatch safe conduct for them to the place at which it may be agreed to consult and confer.

You may likewise assure them that, as soon as peace is established, they shall thenceforth be protected in the antient course of their trade and commerce by the power of Great Britain ; and we authorize you to admit of any claim or title to independency in any description of men, during the time of treaty, and for the purpose of treaty.

If, under pretence of diffidence and distrust, they should decline treating upon the ground that you are not authorized finally to conclude any treaty or agreement, inasmuch as any resolution must be reserved for the future approbation or disapprobation of us and our two Houses of Parliament, after observing that the Legislature might reasonably imagine that the matters to be discussed were of too great concernment to be delegated to individuals, especially as you could not expect to meet with equal and corresponding powers in those persons who might act for and on the behalf of the thirteen revolted colonies, who may remind them that as a proof of the good faith and sincerity of the intentions of Great Britain, to promote a full and permanent reconciliation between Great Britain and the said colonies, the Legislature have spontaneously passed ' An Act for removing all doubts and apprehensions concerning taxation by the Parliament of Great Britain in any of the colonies, provinces, and plantations in North America and the West Indies ; and for repealing so much of an Act made in the 7th year of our reign as imposes a duty upon tea imported from Great Britain into any colony or plantation in America, or relates thereto.' [1]   And they have also passed ' An Act for repealing an Act passed in the 14th year of our reign, intitled, An Act for the better regulating the Government of the Province of Massachusetts Bay, in New England ; ' [2] and also the Act enabling us to vest you, or any three of you, with the powers and authorities with which we have entrusted you and

---

[1] 18 Geo. III, c. 12. This Act declares that the King and Parliament ' will not impose any duty, tax or assessment whatever . . . in any of His Majesty's colonies . . . in North America or the West Indies, except only such duties as it may be expedient to impose for the regulation of commerce ; the net produce of such duties to be always paid . . . for the use of the colony . . . in which . . . levied '.

[2] 18 Geo. III, c. 11.

do intrust you, of suspending all Acts passed since 1763, and for other purposes therein mentioned.

And as a further proof of such sincerity, you, or any three of you, are authorized to consent, as you are hereby authorized to consent, to make any propositions that they can offer, and that you shall think reasonable and fit to be entertained, the subject of an immediate reference to us and our two Houses of Parliament, separate from the other points of the treaty, in which the disposition of us and our two said Houses of Parliament to promote, by every proper concession, the restoration of peace and union can with no probability be doubted. You may particularly agree to a proposal that if, in the ensuing treaty, any mode can be settled of providing by provincial forces for the sufficient security and protection of our subjects, no standing army shall be raised or kept within the said Colonies in time of Peace without their consent. And also that none of the antient governments or constitutions in the said colonies shall be changed or varied without the consent or request of such of our respective colonies, signified by their general assemblies.

If this should likewise fail to produce the desired effect of entering into a treaty, it may be proper that such propositions and offers should, in such manner as you shall see fit, be made public and known as generally as possible ; and the first appearance of a desire in any Province to revert to the antient form of government must be watched with the utmost attention ; but, nevertheless, if an Assembly could be formed under your power of appointing a Governor, in the case in which you are at liberty to enter upon such detached treaty, the good consequences and the extensive effects in the operations of such Assembly are obvious. You are, however, to avoid giving umbrage or jealousy to the powers with which you are publicly treating, and you are not to make any public appeal to the inhabitants of America at large until you shall be satisfied that such public body of men, and the Commander-in-Chief of the American forces, shall refuse to enter into or proceed in such treaty.

But such caution is not to prevent you, or any three of you, from entering into any correspondence or treaty with particular colonies, bodies of men, or individual persons, to answer the purposes of the commission wherewith we have entrusted you, if your attempt to enter into a treaty, or come to any conclusion, with such representative body of men, as we have before described, should fail or miscarry.

And if you should at length despair of bringing such body or bodies of men to a treaty, or effectually to proceed in such treaty, you are, if you find it proper, finally to set forth a declaration, for the information of our well-disposed subjects at large, in which, after reciting the Act and the commission with which we have thought fit to empower you, or any three of you, you shall, if you think proper, publish a proclamation, containing a declaration of the earnest wishes of us and our Parliament for composing any differences that have unhappily subsisted between Great Britain and our said colonies, and for the re-establishment of peace and union upon firm and lasting foundations, and the means which have been used to obtain such salutary and happy purposes.

The propriety, nature, and extent of a suspension of arms will be best determined upon the spot in conjunction with the commanders-in-chief of our Army and Navy; but in the present apparent situation of things it does not seem to us to be necessary or advantageous that the first overture should come from you; nevertheless you, or any three of you, are to determine on this point as you shall deem most expedient on due deliberation.

If it should be proposed to accede to either a local cessation of hostilities within a certain district round the place of treaty, or in general by land, and on rivers, or entirely by sea and land, with such provisions as are usual or proper for the security and accommodation of the persons assembled and for the facilitating the treaty, you, or any three of you, are at liberty to agree to the same.

The proposals which among others appear to us to deserve your attention, are, as to the operations at land :

That a line of quarters shall be marked out for the respective forces beyond which neither side shall advance during the truce, except with leave given by the respective commanders of the opposite forces.

That there shall be a free and open communication for provisions to the respective quarters, and no persons supplying provisions to be molested in going or returning, except only as to such restrictions as the commanders may think fit to impose in their respective quarters, for the more orderly supply of their forces.

That no new levies shall be made, nor any augmentation to the force of either army, during the truce.

That the militia shall not be called out and trained during that interval.

And that a removal of our troops cannot be required till peace shall be restored ; and

That no arrays or drafts shall be made of the militia, or any military works whatever carried on, pending such treaty.

The naval operations cannot be put under similar terms. A cessation of arms supposes no augmentation of force during that period. It would be incongruous with that idea to permit military stores to be imported. The only provision that can be made, consistent with the seizure and detention of such vessels as are employed in carrying military stores is, that you should permit, and you, or any three of you, have hereby our royal authority, to permit all vessels sailing from America to have passes from you, or any three of you, for their protection, and that all vessels under sixty tons burthen shall pass from place to place in North America without interruption, and all other vessels above sixty tons, without passes, or seized and detained as having arms or ammunition on board, shall be restored to the owners, if the accommodation shall take place, otherwise to be proceeded against as prize.

You will also require and insist, as far as circumstances will admit, that after the commencement of any truce, no person shall be molested in any of the provinces for declaring his opinion upon any point of government, or for refusing to sign any test or association, or to take any oath.

That all persons now confined for any of the above causes, shall be restored to their liberty.

That no person shall be punished from the above period, but for some crime, and according to the known laws of the land, or for military offences, if that exception must be admitted.

That all proceedings on forfeitures, sequestrations and confiscations against persons for their attachment to the antient connexion with Great Britain, or against the estates of such persons, should be discontinued during the treaty, and in the progress of the treaty you will make it a condition, that they shall be annulled and revoked.

And you are to agree to the same with regard to any similar proceedings on our part, if any such shall have taken place against any of our revolted American subjects.

You will also insist that all persons may reside freely at their dwelling houses, and remain in quiet possession of their estates.

That all churches and places of legal and tolerated worship shall be opened, and the ministers and congregations protected in the exercise of their religion.

It is our will and pleasure that you should make these demands with due earnestness, even if upon some or all of them there should be found a necessity of relaxing.

It being to be understood that the design expressed by our subjects in America, to return to their condition in 1763, is the principle of the present negociation, that proposition, in general terms, must be agreed to at once. But the explanation of it will lead into some discussion, and it is very essential not only to evince the good faith of Great Britain, but, for the successful result of the treaty, to proceed by ascertaining in the first place the demands of our subjects in America, and the extent to which we mean to acquiesce in those demands, reserving the terms to be proposed to them as a subsequent consideration.

If they should require any security that the benefits held out to them by the 11th and 12th ch. of the 18th of our reign, should not be at any future time annulled or revoked, the demand is not to be rejected. But it would be proper to place it in the class of those demands which have been made to us and our two Houses of Parliament for the alteration and improvement of their Constitution, which Great Britain is desirous to consider with the utmost attention ; and it will be reasonable to put them upon proposing the security they may require.

As to contribution, it is just and reasonable that you should remind those with whom you treat that you are led to hope they will now make good, in the name and on the part of our subjects in America, their own repeated declarations of their readiness to contribute to the public charge, in common with all our other subjects, seeing they are to enjoy the common privileges of all our other subjects ; and they are the rather called upon to exercise this act of justice, as such contribution would now be a mere act of free will.

If they are disposed to consider that idea without prejudice, they will find their advantage in fixing upon a ratio by which the amount of a contribution may be regulated.

The sum required will be moderate. It may be taken upon a ratio of their numbers, their tonnage, or exports. The increase of the payment can only be in proportion to the increase of their abilities; and it becomes the interest of Great Britain to promote the industry, the trade, or the population of our subjects in America. If, however, no such specific measure should be agreed upon, they will probably be easily brought to see that it would be their own interest to maintain some force at their own charge; and as it was granted in the preliminary articles, that no standing army should be raised or kept within the said colonies, except in the cases therein mentioned, you may urge the propriety of providing for the establishment and maintenance of a provincial force, regular or militia, for the defence of the said colonies, the preservation of the public peace, and the protection and security of our subjects.

You will therefore enter into the consideration, and settle the number of troops proper to be kept on foot in each colony, together with all regulations necessary for the raising, exercising, clothing, and paying the same. But they are to be under our command, or under the command of those whom we may think to appoint, and all commissions are to be in our name, and by our authority.

If obstacles should arise to either of the modes in which the point of the contribution to the common defence hath been stated, there is still another mode in which the proposition may be put.

There are duties payable in the colonies under Acts of the Legislature, passed long before 1763, to which they never made any objection: the port duties, postage, the escheats, the forfeited grants of lands, and the quit-rents. These, tho' not considerable in the state of collection which will ever prevail while they are to be accounted for here, would form a very considerable article of revenue, if collected under a vigilant authority upon the spot. In lieu of all these, and upon a cession of them to the respective colonies, let their assemblies grant a certain sum for the service of the public, and for a certain term.

If all these points should fail, you must then propose to let the question rest in oblivion, and to secure them in fact, by concessions upon the repeal of such Acts as you have power to suspend, and such others as they may represent as fit to be repealed. And if the suspension of the Declaratory Act should be urged as a condition on their part, you may propose to supersede the necessity of it by a declaration to be framed upon the close of the whole treaty of the respective rights of Great Britain and America.

These four expedients, in the order in which they are placed, will afford you the means of avoiding the difficulties of settling this important and delicate point. But tho' we have suggested them in this place, you are always to remember that it will be more advantageous to postpone the discussion of them, or at least the decision upon them, to the second part of the treaty, concerning those terms which may be required from our subjects in America.

If, however, they should propose to fall into any other measures for the purpose of contributing to the public charge, in common with all our other subjects, or should entertain a prejudice in favour of the mode adopted by their Articles of Confederation lately proposed in Congress, and signed ' Henry Laurens, President ', you will so frame your discussions upon that matter as to facilitate the same, in such mode as you shall judge most advisable.

But if you find them peremptorily fixed on coming to no resolution favourable to any proposition of contribution at all, you, or any three of you, have hereby our royal authority ultimately to declare your acquiescence.

The preservation of their charters is another article upon which our subjects in America may require some security. It is not to be supposed that they will desire that in no case any alteration shall ever be made in any of their charters, because it is certain that numbers of them wish some charters to be materially altered ; but if the example of the repeal of the Act for altering the Government of the Massachusetts Bay,[1] and our royal declaration made, or to be made, in the preliminaries to this treaty, are not sufficient to quiet all their alarms on this head, you may admit, as a stipulation on their part, to be declared by us and our two Houses of Parliament, that no bill for the alteration of any of the constitutions of the colonies shall be brought into Parliament, but upon petition from the Assembly of such colony or colonies, as is declared in the preliminaries above referred to.

It is to be presumed then, that the proposition of restoring our colonies to the same situation in which they stood in the year 1763, may lead to an examination of the several

[1] 18 Geo. III, c. 11.

Acts passed since that period, of which they have desired a repeal.

You may therefore consent to the suspension of all or any part of them, in manner hereinafter mentioned. The 15th ch. of the 4th of our reign,[1] and the 52nd ch. of the 6th . . ., and the 2nd ch. of the 7th . . . ; as far as these Acts concern the regulations of trade, they ought to be postponed to the general head of the advantages of commerce to be allowed to America, which advantages must be taken up upon a larger view of things, than merely upon the Acts of our reign passed since 1763. [4 Geo. III, c. 29] is for the benefit of our colonies, and falls under the regulations of trade.[2]

[4 Geo. III, c. 34] regulates and restrains paper bills of credit. It is impossible to agree to so unjust a regulation, as that paper bills of credit should be a legal tender in private payment, nor can it be seriously demanded. If the great extent of paper currency issued since the rupture began, is urged in support of such an Act, it will be competent to you to point out a mode of relief which we will more fully explain, in the course of these our instructions, and which may be adopted for that evil without the injustice of admitting so many creditors to suffer. The Act above mentioned has been varied and explained by ch. 35 of the 10th of our reign, and the 57th ch. of the 13th,[3] . . . which, from their date, have also been stated as grievances, but the restraint now subsisting extends no farther than strict justice requires : bills may be issued, may pass at the treasury of the particular colony in which they are issued, but are not to be legal tender in private payment. Beyond this line it cannot be expected that any further concession should be made, in justice to private rights ; but this article need occasion no specific difficulty in the settlement of the treaty. If, on other grounds, the provincial legislatures are finally allowed to have the power of passing Acts of a local nature, the regulation of a paper currency is one of these Acts, and the evils which will arise from an improper exercise of the power in this instance are of a sort to correct themselves.

The next Act is the 18th ch. of the 6th of our reign, for

---

[1] The Revenue Acts of 1764 and 1766, and Act requiring non-enumerated bonds for vessels bound to Ireland.

[2] Act for encouragement of whaling in the Gulf of St. Lawrence.

[3] Act enabling New York to issue paper money to a certain amount, and to make it legal tender for taxes ; and Act extending the same.

quartering troops. This, which is now expired, and the several Acts continuing it, including the only one that now subsists, are in fact annulled by the rebellion, and it will become matter of new regulation to provide for the military force to be hereafter maintained in America.

[7 Geo. III, c. 41, c. 46, c. 56] may likewise be suspended, as may be the 44th ch. of the 13th of our reign.[1] The 22nd ch. of the 8th of our reign, relating to the courts of admiralty, may be referred to the regulations of trade. The 24th ch. of the 12th of our reign is a general and necessary law, not pointed at America, but that part of it which affects America it may be proposed to repeal.[2] [14 Geo. III, c. 19 and c. 45 are] repealed, [c. 39] is already expired.[3]

[15 Geo. III, c. 10, c. 18 ; 16 Geo. III, c. 5 ;[4] 17 Geo. III, c. 7, c. 9, c. 40,[5] are] measures of war, and must be treated as such, and will of course determine on a peace being established. [15 Geo. III, c. 15] is also a measure of war, and is in fact expired. The law subsisting on this subject will cease when the pacification takes place. [c. 31][6] is a regulation of the trade of the British European dominions. The 4th and 19th sections of it affect America, and you may consent to a suspension, and treat for a repeal of them if necessary.

One of the most important objects of these considerations is the large quantity of paper currency issued since the beginning of these unfortunate disputes.

From the first opening of the negociation you will have opportunities of pointing out the possibility of an immediate provision for the liquidation and discharge of that debt by various methods.

It may be proposed to erect a corporation in America upon the plan of a bank, composed of a certain number of proprietors, subscribing their shares, to be made in paper currency at a certain rate of depreciation, and converted into the stock of

[1] Act of 1767 creating the Commissioners of Customs in America ; the unrepealed customs regulations of the Townshend Act ; and the East India Tea Act.

[2] See Resolves of Continental Congress, p. 121.

[3] Boston Port Act, Mass. Government Act, and Administration of Justice Act. See pp. xxxiv, 100, above.

[4] Prohibitory Acts of 1775-6.

[5] Acts regulating privateers and prizes, Act of 1777 authorizing the trying for piracy of rebels engaged in privateering.

[6] Mutiny Act of 1775.

that country ; the corporation to receive from each of the British colonies a certain annuity towards the payment of an interest upon this fund, and to have the privilege of a banking company, besides which, any other advantages that they may propose, and that can reasonably be granted.

Another plan may be that each colony shall proceed to a liquidation of the paper bills issued within its district, and after providing a fund to discharge the interest, that the capital ascertained shall be created into a fund, to be charged on the amount of all the American revenues, and to be paid in Great Britain.

Another plan may be to leave to each colony the discharge of its peculiar debt, by creating within itself a particular fund to sink the interest and principal of the debt, and to accomplish the payment by lotteries.

Or it may be more eligible to adopt the plan proposed by themselves, in the Articles of Confederation before referred to by us, by which they are to erect a public treasury, and to assess such sums themselves, in the representative body, as each colony should pay respectively, each colony being to raise such sum in the mode and manner they think most convenient and least burthensome.

The best of the plans seems to be to transfer the fund and the payment to Great Britain, provided it can be done without engaging the credit of this country beyond the application of American duties ; and this plan would also be the most lucrative to the holders of the paper.

You are also at liberty to concert with the persons with whom you are to treat, the mode in which the expense, not only already incurred, but which is to be incurred for the public service in America, shall be raised from time to time.

But you are not to consent that the charges of the war, incurred by our colonies in America, should, in any manner whatever, be defrayed by Great Britain, though you may concur in any of the above-named propositions, or in any measures which may be proposed, and which should appear reasonable to you, for securing and discharging the same by the said colonies.

The appointment of Governors being left to you, and the recommendation to other situations in your power, if proper persons occur it would be our royal wish that some of the first and most considerable offices in America should be bestowed on our American subjects. Or otherwise, that such Governors and judicial and ministerial officers, the appointment and nomination of whom was received from us before the troubles broke out, should continue in their respective appointments, but with such variations and regulations, as well in the civil and criminal, as in the courts of admiralty, as you shall think most conducive to the due administration of justice, and to have the best tendency to give all reasonable content and satisfaction to our subjects there.

If it appears to you that no pacification can take place except upon a condition that the office of Governor, which has heretofore in most of the provinces made a part of our royal prerogative, should become elective, even this point may in such case be conceded ; but it must always be provided that the election shall be approved and the commission to such Governor or Governors issued under our authority. And the same instruction may be understood to extend to the appointment of all or any judicial and civil magistrates.

It is also our will and pleasure, for a further satisfaction to the minds of our subjects in America, that such offices there, as they can show to be burthensome shall be suppressed ; and the offices held under us shall be granted under such restrictions as may secure the performance of the duty.

The advantages that may be offered to our subjects of America at large, beyond the renewal of the rights they formerly exercised, and as an improvement of their situation, must in some measure depend upon the terms they are willing, on their part, to yield to Great Britain.

If a proper contribution could be obtained, it is obvious that all laws of revenue would then be reduced into a very small compass. The custom-house officers, though appointed by us, would in truth be officers of the Province, to whose treasury the amount of the duties would be carried ; and if they desired the appointment, in such case, to be by their Assemblies, there seems to be no objection to give this testimony of a desire on our part to comply with their wishes.

The admiralty courts may be restrained in such manner as will satisfy our subjects in America, as far as it can be made consistent with a reasonable security, and an impartial administration of justice on the subject matter of such jurisdiction in causes maritime.

An extension of the trade of America would also be an object that might be very fairly put in discussion. The principle of the Act of Navigation, and of the 22nd ch. of the 7th and 8th of King William has been relaxed in favour of many articles of American production, which are allowed to be carried directly to an European market upon condition only of touching at an English port.

It is impossible to foresee the particular demands which may [be] made to you in behalf of particular branches of trade. This only we direct you to observe in general, that no check should be given to any of them. One caution, however, should be attended to, that of all advantages, that of bounties should be the least favoured.

Upon the subject of commercial regulations, the prevailing principle has always been to secure a monopoly of American commerce.

The fetters of custom-house regulations are but a weak security for this monopoly in practice, and it should seem that the most effectual way to insure its continuance would be to lay upon articles of foreign produce, not imported from Great Britain, the amount of the provincial duties, whether collected for general or local purposes. This is a point to be watched in the course of the treaty ; and if there is, on the one hand, a relaxation from antient restraints, that new stipulation may reasonably be required on the other. The articles agreed upon by you, under the head of regulations of trade, must necessarily pass into an Act of Parliament, and to avoid the revival of any question upon right and authority, a representation from our colonies may precede the Act.

There are, however, some advantages, unconnected with this subject, which you will have in your power to offer immediately.

The regulation of the judicatures in America is a point in which it would be very easy to improve the condition of our subjects there, but upon which it is very difficult to give pointed instructions. They have objected to the judges holding commissions during good behaviour. If they are disposed to think differently, and also to give an independent provision to the judges, there could be no objection on our part to giving them commissions, if they are to receive their commissions from us, during good behaviour.

You will likewise acquiesce in any just and proper regulations that may be proposed relative to the courts of justice, and the mode of practice there, and to such regulations as you may think proper, to render appeals to us more speedy and less expensive.

If it should be proposed that a general assembly, in nature of the present Congress, or similar thereto, consisting of delegates from the said several colonies, should be constituted or established by authority, to meet in Congress for the better management of the general concerns and interests of the said colonies, you are not to decline entering into the consideration of the said proposal, and to see whether any such plan can be so settled and digested as to contribute to the welfare of our colonies, and preserve and secure their connection with Great Britain. But the greatest attention should be given that, in ascertaining the powers and functions of that Assembly, the sovereignty of the mother country should not be infringed, nor any powers given or ascribed to it that should be capable of being construed into an impeachment of the sovereign rights of His Majesty, and the constitutional control of this country. And if it should appear to you that such a plan may be formed as shall be likely to serve the good purpose of establishing a lasting confidence and reconciliation, yet, after it shall be so digested and matured, as it will make so great an alteration in the Constitution of America, it may be more advisable, if circumstances will admit, to refer the approbation of it to the Legislature of Great Britain, previous to inserting it as a concluded article of the treaty.

If it should be desired that our subjects in America should have any share of representation in our House of Commons, such a proposal may be admitted by you, so far as to refer the same to the consideration of our two Houses of Parliament ; and it will be proper that in stating such a proposition, the mode of representation, the number of the representatives, which ought to be very small, and the considerations offered on their part, in return for so great a distinction and benefit, should be precisely and distinctly stated.

You may also offer to our American subjects a release from us of all arrears of quit rents whatever.

And it is our royal intention that a full pardon, without any exception, should be offered to all that have been in rebellion. An amnesty, and also an indemnity, shall follow such pardon.

And finally, as the trial in England of treasons committed abroad, tho' unquestionably legal, has been a matter of complaint to our subjects in America, you may treat of, and agree upon any law to be proposed to us and our two Houses of Parliament, similar to that which has been occasionally made in England, in times of rebellion, authorizing a trial out of the county, where the treason hath been committed, but in some place adjoining, where justice may conveniently be administered.

In return for all you give, you are, if possible, to attain a reasonable contribution and compensation directly from the several provinces.

A duty to be imposed on all articles not British, or sent from Britain.

A duty on the foreign trade of America paid in Europe, if it shall be further extended.

These are all the demands that immediately affect the revenue of Great Britain ; but the honour and security of Great Britain require other terms, equally important. For instance :

A restoration of all rights of private property, and a full restitution for all violations of such rights, in the most ample manner, ought to be made good by the said colonies ; and perhaps the most eligible method might be of adding the amount of such losses to the debt contracted by the said colonies during the war, and discharged in the same manner, unless some more speedy and advantageous method could be pointed out for discharging the same.

Many particular cases of distress and losses sustained by our British merchants and proprietors of estates, during these commotions, have excited our most serious attention and concern ; and you will receive with these instructions several memorials on this head, to which you will give all possible consideration ; and throughout the whole progress of this treaty, as far as circumstances will admit, you will anxiously lay hold of every opportunity to exert every means of providing for them that relief which justice requires, and which it is our earnest wish to obtain in their behalf.

It is likewise to be observed that the conduct of the clergy of the Church of England has been so worthy of the profession and principles inculcated by the doctrine which has ever distinguished it amongst all the Reformed Churches, that particular attention must be paid to the care of all established clergymen dispossessed of their benefices, and for the preservation of their just rights, in the respective colonies where there is an established maintenance provided for the clergy. It must, therefore, be your particular care, and we do especially recommend it to you, to attend to every possible occasion of repairing their losses, and establishing their situations in the same condition in which they formerly held them.

It should also be agreed, amongst those points which they should concede to us, that no vessels of war should be kept up but such as shall be employed and commissioned by us.

All forts and fortifications should be delivered up to us, and the command of them should be in such Governors, or officers, as we shall, from time to time, appoint, garrisoned, however, by American troops.

No coin should be struck, or coinage established, but by our orders, and in our name.

All prisoners of war, and persons in custody, should be discharged.

As to the Declaration of Independence dated the 4th of July 1776, and all votes, resolutions, and orders passed since the rupture began, it is not necessary to insist on a formal revocation of them, as such declaration, votes, orders and resolutions, not being legal acts, will be in effect rescinded by the conclusion of the treaty.

Supposing upon the whole that the negociation should fall chiefly into the hands of the Congress, it will still be highly expedient, before the close of the negociation, that the several Assemblies should be called.

The proper time to propose this would be when the material concessions on the part of Great Britain are settled, and when it becomes necessary to fix terms on the part of America. To give sanction and effect to these terms, each Legislature should empower persons to engage on behalf of the colonies, as it is proposed to do by the Articles of Confederation before mentioned.

As it is impossible to foresee and enumerate all the matters which may arise during such an inquiry, you are not to consider these instructions as precluding you from entering into the examination and decision of any matters not contained herein, nor of any additional circumstances relative to such things as are the subject matter of these instructions. But you are at liberty to proceed upon every matter within the compass of your commission, and to give all possible satisfaction to the minds of our subjects in America, consistent with that degree of connection which is essentially necessary for preserving the relation between us and our subjects there.

Lastly. If there should be a reasonable prospect of bringing the treaty to a happy conclusion, you are not to lose so desirable an end, by breaking off the negociation on the adverse party absolutely insisting on some point which you are hereby directed, or which, from your own judgment and discretion, you should be disposed, not to give up or yield to, provided the same be short of open and avowed Independence (except such independence as relates only to the purpose of treaty).

But in such case you will suspend coming to any final resolution till you shall have received our further orders thereupon.

And you are upon all occasions to send unto us, by one of our principal secretaries of state, a particular account of all your proceedings, relative to the great object of these our instructions, and to such other objects as you may think worthy of our royal attention.—G.R.

RESOLUTION OF CONGRESS ON PUBLIC LANDS AND NEW STATES [1]

10 October 1780

Resolved, that the unappropriated lands that may be ceded or relinquished to the United States, by any particular States, pursuant to the recommendation of Congress of the 6 day of September last, shall be disposed of for the common benefit of the United States, and be settled and formed into distinct republican States, which shall become members of the Federal Union, and shall have the same rights of sovereignty, freedom and independence, as the other States : that each State which shall be so formed shall contain a suitable extent of territory, not less than one hundred nor more than one hundred and fifty miles square, or as near thereto as circumstances will admit ;

That the necessary and reasonable expences which any particular State shall have incurred since the commencement

---

[1] *Journals of the Continental Congress* (G. Hunt ed.), xviii. 915. A clause to the effect that no purchases from Indians within the ceded territory, ' which shall not have been ratified by lawful authority, shall be deemed valid or ratified by Congress ', was lost on an even division. Cf. Constitution of Virginia, s. 21.

of the present war, in subduing any of the British posts, or in maintaining forts or garrisons within and for the defence, or in acquiring any part of the territory that may be ceded or relinquished to the United States, shall be reimbursed ;

That the said lands shall be granted and settled at such times and under such regulations as shall hereafter be agreed on by the United States in Congress assembled, or any nine or more of them.

ORDINANCE OF CONGRESS ON PUBLIC LANDS [1]

20 May 1785

An Ordinance for ascertaining the mode of disposing of Lands in the Western Territory.

BE it ordained by the United States in Congress assembled, that the territory ceded by individual States to the United States, which has been purchased of the Indian inhabitants, shall be disposed of in the following manner :

A surveyor from each State shall be appointed by Congress or a Committee of the States, who shall take an oath for the faithful discharge of his duty, before the geographer of the United States, who . . . shall occasionally form such regulations for their conduct, as he shall deem necessary ; and shall have authority to suspend them for misconduct in office, and shall make report of the same to Congress, . . .

The surveyors, as they are respectively qualified, shall proceed to divide the said territory into townships of six miles square, by lines running due north and south, and others crossing these at right angles, as near as may be, unless where the boundaries of the late Indian purchases may render the same impracticable, . . .

The first line, running due north and south as aforesaid, shall begin on the river Ohio, at a point that shall be found to be due north from the western termination of a line, which has been run as the southern boundary of the State of Pennsylvania ; and the first line, running east and west, shall begin at the same point, and shall extend throughout the whole territory ; provided, that nothing herein shall be construed, as fixing the western boundary of the State of Penn-

[1] *Journal of the United States in Congress Assembled . . . from the first Monday in November 1784* (Philadelphia, 1785), 167–75.

sylvania. The geographer shall designate the townships, or fractional parts of townships, by numbers progressively from south to north; always beginning each range with No. 1; and the ranges shall be distinguished by their progressive numbers to the westward. The first range, extending from the Ohio to the lake Erie, being marked No. 1. The geographer shall personally attend to the running of the first east and west line; and shall take the latitude of the extremes of the first north and south line, and of the mouths of the principal rivers.

The lines shall be measured with a chain; shall be plainly marked by chaps on the trees, and exactly described on a plat; whereon shall be noted by the surveyor, at their proper distances, all mines, salt-springs, salt-licks and mill-seats, that shall come to his knowledge; and all water-courses, mountains and other remarkable and permanent things, over and near which such lines shall pass, and also the quality of the lands.

The plats of the townships respectively, shall be marked by subdivisions into lots of one mile square, or 640 acres, in the same direction as the external lines, and numbered from 1 to 36; always beginning the succeeding range of the lots with the number next to that with which the preceding one concluded.

.   .   .   .

The board of treasury shall transmit a copy of the original plats, previously noting thereon the townships and fractional parts of townships, which shall have fallen to the several States, by the distribution aforesaid,[1] to the commissioners of the loan-office of the several States, who, after giving notice . . . shall proceed to sell the townships or fractional parts of townships, at public vendue, in the following manner, viz.: The township or fractional part of a township No. 1, in the first range, shall be sold entire; and No. 2, in the same range, by lots; and thus in alternate order through the whole of the first range . . . provided, that none of the lands, within the said territory, be sold under the price of one dollar the acre, to be paid in specie, or loan-office certificates, reduced to specie value, by the scale of depreciation, or certificates of liquidated debts of the United States, including interest,

---

[1] One-seventh of the townships, chosen by lot, to be distributed by the States among their veterans.

besides the expense of the survey and other charges thereon, which are hereby rated at 36 dollars the township, . . . on failure of which payment, the said lands shall again be offered for sale.

There shall be reserved for the United States out of every township the four lots, being numbered 8, 11, 26, 29, and out of every fractional part of a township, so many lots of the same numbers as shall be found thereon, for future sale. There shall be reserved the lot No. 16, of every township, for the maintenance of public schools within the said township ; also one-third part of all gold, silver, lead and copper mines, to be sold, or otherwise disposed of as Congress shall hereafter direct. . . .

THE VIRGINIA STATUTE OF RELIGIOUS LIBERTY [1]

October 1785

An Act for establishing Religious Freedom.

I. WHEREAS Almighty God hath created the mind free ; that all attempts to influence it by temporal punishments or burthens, or by civil incapacitations, tend only to beget habits of hypocrisy and meanness, and are a departure from the plan of the Holy author of our religion, who being Lord both of body and mind, yet chose not to propagate it by coercions on either, as was in his Almighty power to do ; that the impious presumption of legislators and rulers, civil as well as ecclesiastical, who being themselves but fallible and uninspired men, have assumed dominion over the faith of others, setting up their own opinions and modes of thinking as the only true and infallible, and as such endeavouring to impose them on others, hath established and maintained false religions over the greatest part of the world, and through all time ; that to compel a man to furnish contributions of money for the propagation of opinions which he disbelieves, is sinful and tyrannical ; that even the forcing him to support this or that teacher of his own religious persuasion, is depriving him of the comfortable liberty of giving his contributions to the

[1] *Statutes at Large of Virginia* (W. W. Hening ed., Richmond, 1823), xii. 84–6.

particular pastor whose morals he would make his pattern, and whose powers he feels most persuasive to righteousness, and is withdrawing from the ministry those temporary rewards, which proceeding from an approbation of their personal conduct, are an additional incitement to earnest and unremitting labours for the instruction of mankind ; that our civil rights have no dependence on our religious opinions, any more than our opinions in physics or geometry ; that therefore the proscribing any citizen as unworthy the public confidence by laying upon him an incapacity of being called to offices of trust and emolument, unless he profess or renounce this or that religious opinion, is depriving him injuriously of those privileges and advantages to which in common with his fellow-citizens he has a natural right ; that it tends only to corrupt the principles of that religion it is meant to encourage, by bribing with a monopoly of worldly honours and emoluments, those who will externally profess and conform to it ; that though indeed these are criminal who do not withstand such temptation, yet neither are those innocent who lay the bait in their way ; that to suffer the civil magistrate to intrude his powers into the field of opinion, and to restrain the profession or propagation of principles on supposition of their ill tendency, is a dangerous fallacy, which at once destroys all religious liberty, because he being of course judge of that tendency will make his opinions the rule of judgment, and approve or condemn the sentiments of others only as they shall square with or differ from his own ; that it is time enough for the rightful purposes of civil government, for its officers to interfere when principles break out into overt acts against peace and good order ; and finally, that truth is great and will prevail if left to herself, that she is the proper and sufficient antagonist to error, and has nothing to fear from the conflict, unless by human interposition disarmed of her natural weapons, free argument and debate, errors ceasing to be dangerous when it is permitted freely to contradict them.

II. Be it enacted by the General Assembly, that no man shall be compelled to frequent or support any religious worship, place or ministry whatsoever, nor shall be enforced, restrained, molested, or burthened in his body or goods, nor shall otherwise suffer on account of his religious opinions or belief ; but that all men shall be free to profess, and by argument to maintain their opinion in matters of religion, and that the same shall in no wise diminish, enlarge or affect their civil capacities.

III. And though we well know that this Assembly, elected by the people for the ordinary purposes of legislation only, have no power to restrain the acts of succeeding Assemblies, constituted with powers equal to our own, and that therefore to declare this Act to be irrevocable would be of no effect in law ; yet as we are free to declare, and do declare, that the rights hereby asserted are of the natural rights of mankind, and that if any Act shall hereafter be passed to repeal the present, or to narrow its operation, such Act will be an infringement of natural right.

THE BACKGROUND OF SHAYS'S REBELLION [1]

(a) *Petition from the Town of Greenwich, Massachusetts*

16 January 1786

To the Honourable Senate and the House of Representatives in General Court assembled att their next session :

A Petition of the Subscribers humbly sheweth—

That in the time of the late war, being desirous to defend secure and promote the wrights and liberties of the people, we spared no pains but freely granted all that aid and assistance of every kind that our civel fathers required of us.

We are sencable also that a great debt is justly brought upon us by the war and are as willing to pay our shares towards itt as we are to injoy our shars in independancy and constatutional priviledges in the Commonwealth, if itt was in our power. And we beleve that if prudant mesuers ware taken and a moderate quantety of medium to circulate so that our property might sel for the real value we mite in proper time pay said debt.

But with the greatest submission we beg leave to informe your Honours that unles something takes place more favourable to the people, in a little time att least, one half of our inhabitants in our oppinion will become banckerupt—how can itt be otherwise—the constables are dayly vandering [2] our property both real and personal, our land after itt is prised by the best judges under oath is sold for about one third of

---

[1] MSS. in American Antiquarian Society, Worcester, Massachusetts.
[2] vendueing.

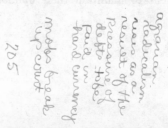

the value of itt, our cattle about one half the value, the best inglesh [1] hay thirteen shilings per tone, intervale hay att six shilings per tone, and other things att the same rate. And we beg leave further to informe your honours that sutes att law are very numerous and the atturneys in our oppinion very extravigent and oppressive in their demands. And when we compute the taxes laid upon us the five preceeding years: the state and county, town and class [2] taxes, the amount is equil to what our farms will rent for. Sirs, in this situation what have we to live on—no money to be had; our estates dayly posted and sold, as above described. What can your honours ask of us unles a paper curancy or some other medium be provided so that we may pay our taxes and debts. Suerly your honours are not strangers to the distresses of the people but doe know that many of our good inhabitants are now confined in gole for det and for taxes: maney have fled, others wishing to flee to the State of New York or some other State; and we believe that for two years past four inhabitants have removed from this State to some other State to one that has come from some other State to settle in this State.

Honoured Sirs, are not these imprisonments and fleeing away of our good inhabitents very injurious to the credit or honour of the Commonwealth? will not the people in the neighbouring States say of this State: altho' the Massachusets bost of their fine constatution, their government is such that itt devours their inhabitants? Notwithstanding all these distresses, we hear of no abatement of sallerys, but his Excellency the Governor must be paid eleven hundred a year out of the moneys collected as before mentoned, and other sallerys and grants to other gentlemen, as your honours very well know. Iff these things are honest, just and rite, we sincearly wish to be convinced of itt: but we honestly confess itt is beyond our skill to reconsile these sallerys and grants with the principles of our Constatution (viz.) piaty, justice, moderation, temperance, etc.

We observe in the proclamation lately sent out by his Excellency that the promotion of piaty and virtue is highly

---

[1] English hay, i.e. hay grown from seed, as distinguished from the wild native grasses in the intervales or river meads.

[2] During the war the inhabitants of Massachusetts townships were divided into as many classes as that township had to supply men for the army, and each class taxed itself to provide a soldier.

recommended. We rejoice att the recommendation, and beg leave to mention that maxim, example is stronger than pre-cipt ; and who can be more likely to bring forward a reforma-tion by example than the honourable members of the General Court, by a line of conduct agreeable to Scripture and the precipts of the Constatution. If your honours finde anything above mentioned worthy of notice, we earnestly pray that they may be candedly considered, for we have weighted, hoped and expected that the present General Court would point out sum way whereby the people might be releaved. We therefore most humbly pray your honours to admitt a paper currancy and make itt a tender in all payments whatsoever, or some other way to releave your petitioners as your honours in your grate wisdom shall think most proper. And iff no other can be found out, pray send us such a com-mitee as your honours can confide in to apprise our estates and take them att your own price. And as in duty bound shall ever pray

JEREMIAH POWERS.
NEHEMIAH STEBBINS.
ZEBEDEE OSBORN

January 16th 1786.   [and 57 other signatures].

(b) *Petition of a County Convention.*

28 September 1786

To the Honourable the Senate and the House of Representatives in General Court assembled : The Petition of the Conven-tion in the County of Worcester humbly sheweth :

That your petitioners are delegates from forty and one towns in said county, chosen to meet in convention, to collect the sentiments of the county respecting their present grievances, and to petition the General Court for redress— after mature examination find by the collective sense of the county, that the inhabitents wish relief from the following grievances, viz. :

The sitting of the General Court in the town of Boston, in transacting the buisness of an infant nation embarrassed with debt, oeconomy and dispatch are absolutely necessary, for which purposes the town of Boston for obvious reasons is by no means adapted.

The want of a circulating medium subjects the inhabitants to the greatest inconveniences, the people in general are extremely embarrassed with publick and private debts—no money can be obtained either by the sale or mortgage of real estate. The produce of the present year and the remainder of our cattle even were we to sell the whole, are totally inadequate to the present demands for money—such has been our situation for a long time past—an amazing flood of law suits have taken place—many industrious members of community have been confined in goal—and many more are liable to the same calamity—in a word, without relief we have nothing before us but distress and ruin.

In this deplorable condition we humbly seek protection and redress from the wisdom of the honourable court and pray that a portable representation of property may be contrived for the relief of the people, and that such prudent laws may be framed as shall have a tendency to correct the evils arising from the present scarcity of cash and to induce the man of wealth to place his wealth in the lands and products of his country rather than in speculations of publick securities or a commercial line, and that our brethren in Boston and the other populous towns may be induced by premiums and encouragements to manufacture the products of our own country in lieu of vending foreign goods.

The existence of the Courts of Common Pleas and Courts of General Sessions in their present mode has given general disgust; these courts are an amazing expence to the subject and in the opinion of your petitioners without the least advantage—not more than one action in forty brou't to our lower courts is ever deigned for tryal, and in those cases that are disputable little dependance is placed on their decission— the feelings of the people are deeply wounded when they see the officers of these courts living in the elegance of eastern magnificence when they reflect that the money is extorted from their distress.

It is with indignation that the good people of this county have seen more money lavished by a single grant of the General Court on one officer of government who has rendered himself generally disagreeable to the people than can be obtained by a long life of industrious labour, and the fees of whose office we apprehend are fully adequate to his services.

We feel it a grievance that the revenue arising from the

impport and excise should be appropriated to the payment of the interest of state securities as we have no other resource of obtaining money adequate to the payment of the interest of the foreign debt.

Your petitioners also conceive that in the distress and poverty of the people absolute oeconomy should be introduced into all the branches of government, the servants of which are too noomerous and their salleries too high, and we cannot but think the examples of the neighbouring States in this respect worthy of imitation.

The present practice of Law and the exorbitance of the fee table are universally complained off and we believe not without reason. We trust your honors will be of the same opinion if you turn your attention to the records of clerks, offices, the rules of the bar, of the insolence, influence and increasing wealth of the practitioners.

We further pray the honourable Court will use their earnest endeavours that the accounts between this commonwealth and the continent may be spedily settled—as we apprehend that we have been disproportionably burthened—and think it a great hardship that we have no relief from the expenses of the Penobscot expedition.

We pray your honors to pay attention to the situation of the holders of old continental money which lays dead on their hands without interest while they are taxed to pay the anual interest of securities the holders of which are exempted from taxes thereon ; we conceive the grant of the suppli-mentary fund inconsistent with republican principles and is very grievous to this people. We pray that the [time] for payment of the first part of the present tax may be prolonged.

We further pray that the Probate Courts may be regulated so as to be more expeditious and decisive in their opperation and less grievous to the subject as in the present mode. Many small estates are nearly swallowed up by the expences and time and travail in attendance. The present mode of registring deeds is inconvenient and we conceive it may be done with much less expence in the respective towns.

And whereas there are many actions commenced by the absentees [1] against the good people of this county and no doubt from the policy of our subtle enemies, and we conceive

---

[1] Absentee tories, who were suing for the recovery of their debts under the treaty of peace.

the creditor has too great advantage of the debtor by reason of the great scarcity of money. Therefore we pray your attention to every means proposed for the relief of debtors as far as is consistent with the treaty of peace of national faith.

And your petitioners earnestly pray the honourable Court as soon as may be to issue precepts to the selectmen of the several towns, and to the assessors of unincorporated plantations, directing them to convene the qualified voters of their respective towns and plantations for the purpose of collecting their sentiments on the necessity or expediency of revising the constitution in order to [obtain] amendments, and if it shall appear by the returns made that two thirds of the qualified voters throughout the State, who shall assemble and vote in consequence of the said precepts, are in favour of such revision or amendment, the General Court is hereby instructed to issue precepts or direct them to be issued from the secretary's office to the several towns to elect delegates to meet in convention for the purpose afforesaid.[1]

We pray the attention of the honourable Court to these our grievances, in order to their speedy redress, and your petitioners as in duty bound will ever pray.

PAXTON, September 28th, 1786.

By order of and in behalf of
the Convention.

WILLIS HALL, *Chairman.*

[endorsed] In the House of Representatives, Oct. 4, 1786. Read and committed to the committee of both Houses appointed the 29th ult. on the petition of the town of Dracut. Sent up for concurrence.

ARTEMAS WARD, *Speaker.*

Thursday morning. Assign'd for consideration, November 3d, 1786. To lie.

[1] The Constitution of 1780 provided that this might be done in 1795, but not before.

LETTERS ON THE INTERNAL SITUATION
1786-1787
(a) John Jay to Washington.[1]

PHILADELPHIA, June 27, 1786.

DEAR SIR,

. . . It is too true that the treaty has been violated. On such occasions I think it better fairly to confess and correct errors than attempt to deceive ourselves and others by fallacious, though plausible, palliations and excuses. To oppose popular prejudices, to censure the proceedings, and expose the improprieties of States, is an unpleasant task, but it must be done. Our affairs seem to lead to some crisis, some revolution—something that I cannot foresee or conjecture. I am uneasy and apprehensive; more so than during the war. Then we had a fixed object, and though the means and time of obtaining it were often problematical, yet I did firmly believe we should ultimately succeed, because I was convinced that justice was with us. The case is now altered; we are going and doing wrong, and therefore I look forward to evils and calamities, but without being able to guess at the instrument, nature, or measure of them.

That we shall again recover, and things again go well, I have no doubt. Such a variety of circumstances would not, almost miraculously, have combined to liberate and make us a nation for transient and unimportant purposes. I therefore believe that we are yet to become a great and respectable people; but when or how, the spirit of prophecy can only discern.

There doubtless is much reason to think and to say that we are wofully and, in many instances, wickedly misled. Private rage for property suppresses public considerations, and personal rather than national interests have become the great objects of attention. Representative bodies will ever be faithful copies of their originals, and generally exhibit a checkered assemblage of virtue and vice, of abilities and weakness.

The mass of men are neither wise nor good, and the virtue

[1] *Correspondence and Public Papers of John Jay* (H. P. Johnston ed.), iii. 203-5. Jay at this time was Secretary of Foreign Affairs of the Confederation.

like the other resources of a country, can only be drawn to a point and exerted by strong circumstances ably managed, or a strong government ably administered. New governments have not the aid of habit and hereditary respect, and being generally the result of preceding tumult and confusion do not immediately acquire stability or strength. Besides, in times of commotion, some men will gain confidence and importance, who merit neither, and who, like political mountebanks, are less solicitous about the health of their nostrums and prescriptions.

New York was rendered less federal by the opinions of the late President of Congress. This is a singular, though not unaccountable fact—indeed, human actions are seldom inexplicable.

What I most fear is, that the better kind of people, by which I mean the people who are orderly and industrious, who are content with their situations and not uneasy in their circumstances, will be led by the insecurity of property, the loss of confidence in their rulers, and the want of public faith and rectitude, to consider the charms of liberty as imaginary and delusive. A state of fluctuation and uncertainty must disgust and alarm such men, and prepare their minds for almost any change that may promise them quiet and security.

Be pleased to make my compliments to Mrs. Washington, and be assured that I am, with the greatest respect and esteem, dear sir,

Your obedient and humble servant,
JOHN JAY.

(b) *Washington to John Jay.*[1]

MOUNT VERNON, 1 August 1786.

DEAR SIR,

I have to thank you very sincerely for your interesting letter of the 27th of June, as well as for the other communication you had the goodness to make at the same time. I am sorry to be assured of what I had little doubt before, that we have been guilty of violating the treaty in some instances. What a misfortune it is, the British should have so well grounded a pretext for their palpable infractions! And what

---

[1] *Writings of Washington* (W. C. Ford ed.), xi. 53–6.

a disgraceful part, out of the choice of difficulties before us, are we to act !

Your sentiments, that our affairs are drawing rapidly to a crisis, accord with my own. What the event will be, is also beyond the reach of my foresight. We have errors to correct. We have probably had too good an opinion of human nature in forming our Confederation. Experience has taught us, that men will not adopt and carry into execution measures the best calculated for their own good, without the intervention of a coercive power. I do not conceive we can exist long as a nation without having lodged somewhere a power, which will pervade the whole Union in as energetic a manner as the authority of the State governments extends over the several States.

To be fearful of investing Congress, constituted as that body is, with ample authorities for national purposes, appears to me the very climax of popular absurdity and madness. Could Congress exert them for the detriment of the public, without injuring themselves in an equal or greater proportion ? Are not their interests inseparably connected with those of their constituents ? By the rotation of appointment, must they not mingle frequently with the mass of citizens ? Is it not rather to be apprehended, if they were possessed of the power before described, that their individual members would be induced to use them, on many occasions, very timidly and inefficaciously for fear of losing their popularity and future election ? We must take human nature as we find it. Perfection falls not to the share of mortals. Many are of opinion, that Congress have too frequently made use of the suppliant, humble tone of requisition in applications to the States, when they had a right to assert their imperial dignity and command obedience. Be that as it may, requisitions are a perfect nullity where thirteen sovereign, independent, disunited States are in the habit of discussing and refusing compliance with them at their option. Requisitions are actually little better than a jest and a by-word throughout the land. If you tell the legislatures they have violated the treaty of peace, and invaded the prerogatives of the confederacy, they will laugh in your face. What then is to be done ? Things cannot go in the same train forever. It is much to be feared, as you observe, that the better kind of people, being disgusted with the circumstances, will have their minds prepared for any revolution whatever. We are apt to run from one extreme into another. To anticipate and prevent disastrous contingencies would be the part of wisdom and patriotism.

What astonishing changes a few years are capable of producing. I am told that even respectable characters speak of a monarchical form of government without horror. From thinking proceeds speaking ; thence to acting is often but a single step. But how irrevocable and tremendous ! What a triumph for our enemies to verify their predictions ! What a triumph for the advocates of despotism to find that we are incapable of governing ourselves, and that systems founded on the basis of equal liberty are merely ideal and fallacious ! Would to God that wise measures may be taken in time to avert the consequences we have but too much reason to apprehend.

Retired as I am from the world, I frankly acknowledge I cannot feel myself an unconcerned spectator. Yet, having happily assisted in bringing the ship into port, and having been fairly discharged, it is not my business to embark again on a sea of troubles. Nor could it be expected, that my sentiments and opinions would have much weight on the minds of my countrymen. They have been neglected, though given as a last legacy in the most solemn manner. I had then perhaps some claim to public attention. I consider myself as having none at present.

With sentiments of sincere esteem and friendship, I am, dear sir, etc.

(c) Washington to Henry Lee, in Congress.[1]

MOUNT VERNON, 31 October 1786.

MY DEAR SIR,

. . . The picture which you have exhibited, and the accounts which are published of the commotions and temper of numerous bodies in the eastern States, are equally to be lamented and deprecated. They exhibit a melancholy proof of what our transatlantic foe has predicted ; and of another thing perhaps, which is still more to be regretted, and is yet more unaccountable, that mankind, when left to themselves, are unfit for their own government. I am mortified beyond

[1] *Writings of Washington* (W. C. Ford ed.), **xi**. 76–8.

expression when I view the clouds that have spread over the brightest morn that ever dawned upon any country. In a word, I am lost in amazement when I behold what intrigue, the interested views of desperate characters, ignorance, and jealousy of the minor part, are capable of effecting, as a scourge on the major part of our fellow citizens of the Union ; for it is hardly to be supposed that the great body of the people, though they will not act, can be so shortsighted or enveloped in darkness, as not to see rays of a distant sun through all this mist of intoxication and folly.

You talk, my good sir, of employing influence to appease the present tumults in Massachusetts. I know not where that influence is to be found, or, if attainable, that it would be a proper remedy for the disorders. *Influence* is no *government*. Let us have one by which our lives, liberties, and properties will be secured, or let us know the worst at once. Under these impressions, my humble opinion is, that there is a call for decision. Know precisely what the insurgents aim at. If they have *real* grievances, redress them if possible ; or acknowledge the justice of them, and your inability to do it in the present moment. If they have not, employ the force of government against them at once. If this is inadequate, *all* will be convinced that the superstructure is bad, or wants support. To be more exposed in the eyes of the world, and more contemptible than we already are, is hardly possible. To delay one or the other of these, is to exasperate on the one hand, or to give confidence on the other, and will add their numbers ; for, like snow-balls, such bodies increase by every movement, unless there is something in the way to obstruct and crumble them before the weight is too great and irresistible.

These are my sentiments. Precedents are dangerous things. Let the reins of government then be braced and held with a steady hand, and every violation of the Constitution be reprehended. If defective, let it be amended, but not suffered to be trampled upon whilst it has an existence.

. . . .

(d) *The French chargé d'affaires at New York, to the*
French Minister of Foreign Affairs.[1]

September–October 1786

No. 61.   NEW YORK, le 10 Septembre 1786.

MONSEIGNEUR,

. . . .

Ce projet[2] a essuyé une opposition vigoureuse de la part
des Etats du Nord ; ils ont observé que la conduite uniforme
de Sa Majesté pendant la guerre et depuis la paix leur avoit
inspiré la confiance la plus parfaite, mais que les pêcheries
étoient un article principal du traité futur et qu'ils ne sauroient
se flatter que la France voulût sacrifier ses propres avantages
pour procurer aux Etats Unis un débouché facile pour leur
poisson, que les derniers règlemens de la Cour prouvoient
assés combien elle étoit jalouse de ses pêcheries et combien
elle desiroit d'en étendre le commerce, non seulement aux
Antilles, mais dans le Sud de l'Europe ; qu'il n'étoit aucunement vraisemblable que Sa Majesté voulût se charger d'une
pareille médiation et qu'il seroit même dangereux pour l'alliance de s'exposer à un refus. Quant à la navigation du
Mississipi, ils ont remarqué que cet article, bien loin d'être
avantageux à la Confédération, ne serviroit qu'à détacher des
Etats-unis toutes les terres de l'intérieur ; que les habitans
du Kentuky ne sentant plus la nécessité d'entretenir des
liaisons de commerce avec les Etats maritimes, et ayant
d'ailleurs une politique tout à fait différente de celle de leurs
voisins, ne songeroient qu'à se rendre entièrement indépendans
du Congrès, comme d'un corps Souverain dont ils ne pouvoient
tirer aucune utilité ; que la fertilité de ces contrées attireroit
insensiblement les habitans les plus industrieux des Etats du
Nord, qui ne balanceroient pas un instant d'échanger les
rochers arides du Massachussets et du Newhampshire contre

[1] Archives des Affaires Étrangères, Paris, ' Correspondance politique,
États-Unis ', t. 32, ff. 65–95. The writer, Louis-Guillaume Otto, went
to the United States in 1779 as secretary to the French minister, and
became chargé d'affaires in 1785. New York was then the seat of the
Federal Government.

[2] Of French mediation in the dispute between Spain and the United
States over the latter's southern boundary, and the navigation of the
Mississippi. Compare the ideas on the western problem reported by
Otto with those in the Plan of 1768, above.

les plaines riantes de l'Ohio et du Mississipi ; qu'une population bornée, répandue sur une surface immense, affoibliroit les ressorts du Gouvernement, et que l'anarchie et la discorde naîtroient inévitablement de cet état des choses ; que la politique du Congrès devoit être de fortiffier de plus en plus les Etats maritimes et d'attendre qu'une population surabondante s'écoule dans la suite des tems vers l'intérieur des terres ; qu'indépendamment de tous ces motifs on devoit éviter avec soin d'exciter la jalousie des hordes sauvages qui infestent encore ces terreins, qu'une guerre avec ces nations perfides seroit une des plus grandes calamités dans l'épuisement actuel des finances ; que les possessions des Etats Unis n'étoient déjà que trop étendues et qu'il falloit plutôt resserrer leurs territoires que les augmenter au delà de toute proportion ; que d'ailleurs la Cour d'Espagne ne paroissoit aucunement disposée à abandonner la navigation du Mississipi, qu'en insistant sur cet article on ne feroit qu'irriter Sa Majesté Catholique et la rendre moins indulgente à l'égard des points les plus essentiels du traité ; qu'en conséquence de ces principes il falloit non seulement rejeter le plan de médiation proposé par les Etats du Sud, mais rapeller l'article de l'Ultimatum qui proposoit l'ouverture du Mississipi comme une condition *Sine qua non*.

. . . .

No. 62. NEW YORK, le 20 Septembre 1786.

MONSEIGNEUR,

Le défaut d'énergie dans les gouvernemens individuels des Etats avoit jusqu'ici occasionné peu de commotions prejudiciables au repos et à la sûreté des Citoyens, et l'on se flattoit que le Congrès prendroit insensiblement la consistance qu'on croyoit observer dans l'organisation intérieure des Etats ; mais la licence d'une populace avide vient d'ébranler la base du Gouvernement, qui avoit été regardé jusqu'ici comme le plus solide et le plus parfait de toute la confédération, et l'on s'aperçoit trop tard que les Constitutions américaines, si généralement admirées, sont bien loin d'être exemptes de défauts. Le bas peuple du Massachussets, indigné de n'avoir pu obtenir l'émission d'un papier monnoyé, vient de s'attrouper dans plusieurs districts, les armes à la main, pour suspendre les cours de justice et pour empêcher le recouvrement des dettes. Le Gouverneur Bowdoin, ayant négligé de rassembler sur le champ la milice, les insurgens sont parvenus à disperser les juges et les avocats. Ils demandent à hauts cris l'abolition des cours de justice, la tenue de l'Assemblée Législative dans toute autre ville qu'à Boston, la réduction des salaires accordés aux Officiers publics, l'émission d'un nouveau papier monnoye, l'élargissement des prisonniers pour dettes, l'apurement des comptes des Etats Unis, la prohibition de tout objet de luxe importé de pays étranger, la diminution des taxes, la liberté absolue de la presse, et l'abolition du Sénat ou de la chambre haute. Ce dernier article attaque la basse même de la Constitution, et tend à établir à l'instar de l'Etat de Pensylvanie, une démocratie parfaite. Les cours de justice sont actuellement protégées par des troupes et par plusieurs compagnies d'artillerie. Le Congrès étant informé que les séditieux s'étoient raprochés de Springfield, et que les arsenaux des Etats Unis étoient en danger, le Général Knox, ministre de la guerre, a reçu ordre de s'y rendre sur le champ, et d'y faire marcher un corps respectable de milice. La proclamation du Gouverneur du Massachussets, les lettres circulaires de la ville de Boston et des autres villes principales, les procédés des différentes Assemblées municipales, et les mesures prises par les séditieux pour disperser les cours de justice, se trouvent dans les gazettes que j'ai l'honneur de vous adresser. Je me borne à ajouter à ces details les reflexions que cet événement fâcheux a fait faire aux patriotes les plus éclairés. Ils s'aperçoivent qu'en formant les différentes constitutions ils avoient eu un trop grand besoin de l'assistance du bas peuple pour ne pas lui accorder beaucoup plus que le repos de la république, la sûreté du citoyen et l'énergie du gouvernement ne pouvoient comporter ; qu'une liberté entière et illimitée est un phantôme qui n'a jamais pu exister qu'aux dépens de la tranquillité publique ; que la théorie des trois pouvoirs, également distribués, est sublime, mais que la pratique offre mille difficultés qu'on auroit dû prévoir ; que le pouvoir exécutif est beaucoup trop foible en Amérique, que la simplicité des chefs les rend méprisables aux yeux d'une multitude qui ne juge que d'après ses sens ; et qu'il faut des coups d'authorité, des armes, des luteurs, pour faire respecter le gouvernement.

Ces principes, Monseigneur, se trouvent confirmés par une scène pareille à celle du Massachussets, qui vient d'avoir lieu dans le Newhampshire. Environ 300 séditieux s'étoient assemblés près d'Exeter pour dissoudre la cour de justice, mais le Gouverneur Sullivan, officier distingué pendant la guerre, s'est mis sur le champ à la tête de la milice, a dispersé les insurgens et fait emprisonner les chefs de cette révolte.

Le peuple du Connecticut a également fait quelques efforts pour faire abolir les dettes et disperser les cours de justice, mais la vigilance du Gouverneur a empêché jusqu'ici toute voye de fait.

On ne peut disconvenir, Monseigneur, que ces insurrections ne soient dues en grande partie à la rareté des espèces. Dans le petit Etat de Connecticut seulement, on a vu plus de cinq cent fermes mises en vente pour payer les arrérages des taxes. Comme ces ventes n'ont lieu que pour de l'argent comptant, elles se font au plus vil prix, et les propriétaires ne reçoivent souvent qu'un dixième de la valeur. Le peuple sent les suites funestes de cette oppression, mais en pouvant en découvrir la véritable cause, il s'en prend aux juges et aux avocats. Dans les Etats qui ont du papier monnoye, la rigueur des loix est moins désolante pour le cultivateur, puisqu'il peut toujours se procurer assés de papier pour satisfaire à ses engagemens, et que d'ailleurs les créanciers sont moins pressans.

Ces détails, Monseigneur, ne prouvent que trop l'impuissance des Etats Unis de remplir dans ce moment-ci les engagemens pris envers la France. Non seulement le Congrès n'a pas le pouvoir d'user de voyes de fait pour faire rentrer les sommes portées dans ses différentes réquisitions, mais les Etats individuels sont dépourvus de la vigueur nécessaire pour contraindre leurs citoyens, et ceux-ci n'ont pas de quoi payer en espèces les taxes modiques qui leur sont imposées. L'épuisement du trésor fédéral est porté à un point inconcevable, et l'on n'a pas même pu me remettre plusieurs sommes infiniment modiques dues à des officiers françois.

L'Assemblée de Pensylvanie, Monseigneur, voulant faire passer à la posterité un témoignage de sa reconnoissance pour les services que M. le Chevalier de la Luzerne a rendus à l'union, vient de donner son nom à un nouveau comté.

Je suis avec un profond respect, Monseigneur, votre très humble et très obéissant serviteur,

OTTO.

No. 64.   NEW YORK, 10 Octobre 1786.

MONSEIGNEUR,

Les Commissaires nommés par differens Etats pour proposer
un plan général de commerce, et donner au Congrès les pouvoirs nécessaires pour l'exécuter, se sont assemblés à Annapolis
dans le courant du mois dernier. Mais cinq Etats seulement
se trouvant representés, ils n'ont pas cru devoir entamer la
question principale, et ils se sont bornés à adresser au Congrès
et aux différentes Législatures un raport, qui caractérise
l'esprit actuel de la politique de ce pays-ci. En traduisant
ce raport je n'ai pas seulement eu soin de le mettre en françois,
mais de le rendre intelligible. On s'est efforcé de donner
à l'original une obscurité que le peuple pénétrera difficilement,
mais dont les citoyens puissans et éclairés ne manqueront pas
de tirer parti.[1]

Depuis très longtems, Monseigneur, on sent la nécessité de
donner au gouvernement fédéral plus d'énergie et de vigueur,
mais on sent également que l'indépendance excessive accordée
aux citoyens à l'égard des Etats, et aux Etats à l'égard du
Congrès, est trop chère aux individus pour qu'on puisse les
en dépouiller sans de grandes précautions. Le peuple n'ignore
pas que les suites naturelles d'un plus grand pouvoir accordé
au Gouvernement, seroient une perception régulière des taxes,
une administration sévère de la justice, des droits extra-
ordinaires sur les importations, des exécutions rigoureuses
contre les débiteurs, enfin une préponderance marquée des
hommes riches et des grands propriétaires. Il est donc de
l'intérêt du peuple de conserver autant qu'il est possible la
liberté absolue qu'on lui a accordé dans un tems, où l'on ne
connoissoit d'autre loi que la nécessité et où une armée angloise
posoit, pour ainsi dire, les fondemens de la Constitution
politique. C'est dans ces tems orageux qu'il a fallu convenir
que tout pouvoir ne devoit émaner que du peuple, que tout
étoit soumis à sa volonté suprême et que les magistrats
n'étoient que ses serviteurs.

Quoiqu'il n'y ait point de patriciens en Amérique, il s'y
trouve une classe d'hommes connus sous la dénomination de
gentlemen, qui par leurs richesses, par leurs talens, par leur

---

[1] The report of the Annapolis Convention may be found in *Debates
in the Federal Convention* (G. Hunt and J. B. Scott eds., Oxford Univ.
Press, American Branch, 1920), pp. xlix–lii.

éducation, par leurs familles, ou par les places qu'ils remplissent, aspirent à une préeminence que le peuple refuse de leur accorder ; et quoique plusieurs de ces hommes ayent trahi les intérêts de leur ordre pour acquérir de la popularité, il règne entre eux une liaison d'autant plus intime qu'ils redoutent presque tous les efforts du peuple pour les dépouiller de leurs possessions, et qu'ils sont d'ailleurs créanciers et par conséquent intéressés à fortiffier le Gouvernement et à veiller à l'exécution des loix. Ces hommes payent ordinairement les taxes les plus fortes, tandis que les petits propriétaires échapent à la vigilance des collecteurs. La plupart d'entre eux étant négocians, il leur importe d'établir solidement le crédit des Etats Unis en Europe par le payement exact des dettes, et de faire donner au Congrès des pouvoirs assés étendus pour y faire contribuer le peuple.

On a vainement essayé, Monseigneur, par des pamplets et par d'autres publications de répandre des notions de justice et de droiture, et de dépouiller le peuple d'une liberté dont il fait un si mauvais usage. En proposant une nouvelle organisation du Gouvernement fédéral, on auroit révolté tous les esprits. Des circonstances ruineuses pour le commerce de l'Amérique sont heureusement survenues pour fournir aux réformateurs un prétexte d'introduire quelques innovations. Ils ont représenté au peuple que le nom Américain étoit devenu un opprobre parmi toutes les nations de l'Europe, que le pavillon des Etats Unis étoit exposé partout à des insultes et à des vexations, que le cultivateur ne pouvant plus exporter librement ses denrées seroit bientôt réduit à la dernière misère, qu'il étoit tems d'user de répressailles et de prouver aux nations étrangères que les Etats Unis ne souffriroient pas impunément cette violation de la liberté du commerce, mais que des mesures vigoureuses ne pouvoient être prises que du consentement unanime des treize Etats, et que le Congrès n'ayant pas les pouvoirs nécessaires, il étoit essentiel de former une assemblée générale chargée de lui présenter le plan qu'il doit adopter, et de lui indiquer les moyens de l'exécuter. Les peuples, généralement mécontens des difficultés du commerce, et ne soupçonnant guère les motifs de leurs antagonistes, ont embrassé avec ardeur cette mesure, et ont nommé des commissaires qui ont dû s'assembler à Annapolis au commencement de septembre.

Les auteurs de cette proposition, Monseigneur, n'avoient

aucune espérance ni même aucun désir de voir réussir cette Assemblée de Commissaires qui ne devoit que préparer une question beaucoup plus importante que celle du commerce. Les mesures étoient si bien prises qu'à la fin de Septembre il n'y avoit pas plus de cinq Etats représentes à Annapolis, et les Commissaires des Etats du Nord se sont arrêtés plusieurs jours à Newyork afin de retarder leur arrivée. Les Etats assemblés, après avoir attendu près de trois semaines, se sont séparés sous prétexte qu'ils n'étoient pas assés nombreux pour entrer en matière et pour justiffier cette dissolution ils ont addressé aux différentes Législatures et au Congrès un raport, dont j'ai l'honneur de vous addresser ci-joint la traduction. Dans cette pièce les Commissaires se servent d'une infinité de circonlocutions et de phrases ambiques, pour exposer à leurs constituans l'impossibilité de prendre en consideration un plan général de commerce, et les pouvoirs qui y sont relatifs sans toucher en même tems à d'autres objets intimement liés avec la prosperité et l'importance nationale des Etats Unis. Sans nommer ces objets les commissaires s'étendent sur la crise actuelle des affaires publiques, sur les dangers auxquels la confédération se trouve exposée, sur le discrédit des Etats Unis en pays étranger, et sur la nécessité de réunir sous un seul point de vue, les intérêts de tous les Etats. Ils finissent par proposer pour le mois de May prochain une nouvelle Assemblée de Commissaires chargés non seulement de délibérer sur un plan général de commerce, mais sur d'autres matières qui pourront intéresser l'harmonie et le bien-être des Etats, et sur les moyens de proportionner le Gouvernement fédéral aux besoins de l'union. Malgré l'obscurité de cette pièce, Vous Vous appercevrés, Monseigneur, que les Commissaires ne veulent prendre en considération les griefs du commerce infiniment intéressans pour le peuple, sans perfectionner en même tems la constitution fondamentale du Congrès. On espère que de nouveaux Commissaires seront nommés avec des pouvoirs assès étendus pour délibérer sur ces objets importans et pour mettre le Congrès en état non seulement de prendre des résolutions pour la prosperité de l'union, mais de les exécuter.

Je suis avec un profond respect, Monseigneur, votre très humble et très obéissant serviteur,

OTTO.

THE NORTHWEST ORDINANCE [1]

13 July 1787

An Ordinance for the government of the Territory of the United States northwest of the River Ohio.

Be it ordained by the United States in Congress assembled, That the said territory, for the purposes of temporary government, be one district, subject, however, to be divided into two districts, as future circumstances may, in the opinion of Congress, make it expedient.

Be it ordained by the authority aforesaid, That the estates, both of resident and non-resident proprietors in the said Territory, dying intestate, shall descend to, and be distributed among their children, and the descendants of a deceased child, in equal parts ; the descendants of a deceased child or grandchild to take the share of their deceased parent in equal parts among them : And where there shall be no children or descendants, then in equal parts to the next of kin in equal degree ; and among collaterals, the children of a deceased brother or sister of the intestate shall have, in equal parts among them, their deceased parents' share ; and there shall in no case be a distinction between kindred of the whole and half-blood ; saving, in all cases, to the widow of the intestate her third part of the real estate for life, and one-third part of the personal estate ; and this law relative to descents and dower, shall remain in full force until altered by the legislature of the district. And until the Governor and Judges shall adopt laws as hereinafter mentioned, estates in the said Territory may be devised or bequeathed by wills in writing, signed and sealed by him or her in whom the estate may be (being of full age), and attested by three witnesses ; and real estates may be conveyed by lease and release, or bargain and sale, signed sealed and delivered by the person, being of full age, in whom the estate may be, and attested by two witnesses, provided such wills be duly proved, and such conveyances be acknowledged, or the execution thereof duly proved, and be recorded within one year after proper magistrates, courts, and registers shall be appointed for that

---

[1] *Journals of Congress, 1774–88* (Washington, 1823), 754–6.

purpose; and personal property may be transferred by delivery; saving, however to the French and Canadian inhabitants, and other settlers of the Kaskaskies, St. Vincents and the neighboring villages who have heretofore professed themselves citizens of Virginia, their laws and customs now in force among them, relative to the descent and conveyance, of property.[1]

Be it ordained by the authority aforesaid, That there shall be appointed from time to time by Congress, a Governor, whose commission shall continue in force for the term of three years, unless sooner revoked by Congress; he shall reside in the district, and have a freehold estate therein in 1,000 acres of land, while in the exercise of his office.

There shall be appointed from time to time by Congress, a Secretary, whose commission shall continue in force for four years unless sooner revoked; he shall reside in the district, and have a freehold estate therein in 500 acres of land, while in the exercise of his office; it shall be his duty to keep and preserve the Acts and Laws passed by the Legislature, and the public records of the district, and the proceedings of the governor in his Executive department; and transmit authentic copies of such acts and proceedings, every six months, to the Secretary of Congress: There shall also be appointed a Court to consist of three Judges, any two of whom to form a court, who shall have a common law jurisdiction, and reside in the district, and have each therein a freehold estate in 500 acres of land while in the exercise of their offices; and their commissions shall continue in force during good behavior.

The Governor and Judges, or a majority of them, shall adopt and publish in the district such laws of the original States, criminal and civil, as may be necessary and best suited to the circumstances of the district, and report them to Congress from time to time: which laws shall be in force in the district until the organization of the General Assembly therein, unless disapproved of by Congress; but afterwards the Legislature shall have authority to alter them as they shall think fit.

The Governor, for the time being, shall be commander-in-chief of the militia, appoint and commission all officers in the

[1] See Channing, *United States*, iii. 545–7, on the significance of this section, and the constitutional status of the Ordinance.

same below the rank of general officers; all general officers shall be appointed and commissioned by Congress.

Previous to the organization of the General Assembly, the Governor shall appoint such magistrates and other civil officers in each county or township, as he shall find necessary for the preservation of the peace and good order in the same: After the General Assembly shall be organized, the powers and duties of the magistrates and other civil officers shall be regulated and defined by the said Assembly; but all magistrates and other civil officers not herein otherwise directed, shall, during the continuance of this temporary government, be appointed by the Governor.

For the prevention of crimes and injuries, the laws to be adopted or made shall have force in all parts of the district, and for the execution of process, criminal and civil, the Governor shall make proper divisions thereof; and he shall proceed from time to time as circumstances may require, to lay out the parts of the district in which the Indian titles shall have been extinguished, into counties and townships, subject however to such alterations as may thereafter be made by the Legislature.

So soon as there shall be 5,000 free male inhabitants of full age in the district, upon giving proof thereof to the Governor, they shall receive authority, with time and place, to elect representatives from their counties or townships to represent them in the General Assembly: *Provided*, That, for every 500 free male inhabitants, there shall be one representative, and so on progressively with the number of free male inhabitants shall the right of representation increase, until the number of representatives shall amount to 25; after which, the number and proportion of representatives shall be regulated by the Legislature: *Provided*, That no person be eligible or qualified to act as a representative unless he shall have been a citizen of one of the United States three years, and be a resident in the district, or unless he shall have resided in the district three years; and, in either case, shall likewise hold in his own right, in fee simple, 200 acres of land within the same: *Provided, also*, That a freehold in 50 acres of land in the district, having been a citizen of one of the States, and being resident in the district, or the like freehold and two years residence in the district, shall be necessary to qualify a man as an elector of a representative.

The representatives thus elected, shall serve for the term of two years; and, in case of the death of a representative, or removal from office, the Governor shall issue a writ to the county or township for which he was a member, to elect another in his stead, to serve for the residue of the term.

The General Assembly or Legislature shall consist of the Governor, Legislative Council, and a House of Representatives. The Legislative Council shall consist of five members, to continue in office five years, unless sooner removed by Congress; any three of whom to be a quorum: and the members of the Council shall be nominated and appointed in the following manner, to wit: As soon as representatives shall be elected, the Governor shall appoint a time and place for them to meet together; and, when met, they shall nominate ten persons, residents in the district, and each possessed of a freehold in 500 acres of land, and return their names to Congress; five of whom Congress shall appoint and commission to serve as aforesaid; and, whenever a vacancy shall happen in the Council, by death or removal from office, the House of Representatives shall nominate two persons, qualified as aforesaid, for each vacancy, and return their names to Congress; one of whom Congress shall appoint and commission for the residue of the term. And every five years, four months at least before the expiration of the time of service of the members of Council, the said House shall nominate ten persons, qualified as aforesaid, and return their names to Congress; five of whom Congress shall appoint and commission to serve as members of the Council five years, unless sooner removed. And the Governor, Legislative Council, and House of Representatives, shall have authority to make laws in all cases, for the good government of the district, not repugnant to the principles and articles in this ordinance established and declared. And all bills, having passed by a majority in the House, and by a majority in the Council, shall be referred to the Governor for his assent; but no bill, or legislative act whatever, shall be of any force without his assent. The Governor shall have power to convene, prorogue, and dissolve the General Assembly, when, in his opinion, it shall be expedient.

The Governor, Judges, Legislative Council, Secretary, and such other officers as Congress shall appoint in the district, shall take an oath or affirmation of fidelity and of office; the

Governor before the President of Congress, and all other officers before the Governor. As soon as a Legislature shall be formed in the district, the Council and House assembled in one room, shall have authority, by joint ballot, to elect a delegate to Congress, who shall have a seat in Congress, with a right of debating but not of voting during this temporary government.

And, for extending the fundamental principles of civil and religious liberty, which form the basis whereon these republics, their laws and constitutions are erected ; to fix and establish those principles as the basis of all laws, constitutions, and governments, which forever hereafter shall be formed in the said territory : to provide also for the establishment of States, and permanent government therein, and for their admission to a share in the federal councils on an equal footing with the original States, at as early periods as may be consistent with the general interest :

It is hereby ordained and declared by the authority aforesaid, That the following articles shall be considered as articles of compact between the original States and the people and States in the said territory and forever remain unalterable, unless by common consent, to wit :

ART. 1st. No person, demeaning himself in a peaceable and orderly manner, shall ever be molested on account of his mode of worship or religious sentiments, in the said territory.

ART. 2d. The inhabitants of the said territory shall always be entitled to the benefits of the writ of habeas corpus, and of the trial by jury ; of a proportionate representation of the people in the Legislature ; and of judicial proceedings according to the course of the common law. All persons shall be bailable, unless for capital offences, where the proof shall be evident or the presumption great. All fines shall be moderate ; and no cruel or unusual punishments shall be inflicted. No man shall be deprived of his liberty or property, but by the judgment of his peers or the law of the land ; and, should the public exigencies make it necessary, for the common preservation, to take any person's property, or to demand his particular services, full compensation shall be made for the same. And, in the just preservation of rights and property, it is understood and declared, that no law ought ever to be made, or have force in the said territory, that shall, in any manner whatever, interfere with or affect private contracts or engagements, bona fide, and without fraud, previously formed.

ART. 3d. Religion, morality, and knowledge, being necessary to good government and the happiness of mankind, schools and the means of education shall forever be encouraged. The utmost good faith shall always be observed towards the Indians ; their lands and property shall never be taken from them without their consent ; and, in their property, rights, and liberty, they shall never be invaded or disturbed, unless in just and lawful wars authorized by Congress ; but laws founded in justice and humanity, shall from time to time be made for preventing wrongs being done to them, and for preserving peace and friendship with them.

ART. 4th. The said Territory, and the States which may be formed therein, shall forever remain a part of this Confederacy of the United States of America, subject to the Articles of Confederation, and to such alterations therein as shall be constitutionally made ; and to all the Acts and Ordinances of the United States in Congress assembled, conformable thereto. The inhabitants and settlers in the said Territory shall be subject to pay a part of the federal debts contracted or to be contracted, and a proportional part of the expenses of government, to be apportioned on them by Congress according to the same common rule and measure by which apportionments thereof shall be made on the other States ; and the taxes for paying their proportion shall be laid and levied by the authority and direction of the Legislatures of the district or districts, or new States, as in the original States, within the time agreed upon by the United States in Congress assembled. The Legislatures of those districts or new States, shall never interfere with the primary disposal of the soil by the United States in Congress assembled, nor with any regulations Congress may find necessary for securing the title in such soil to the bona fide purchasers. No tax shall be imposed on lands the property of the United States ; and, in no case, shall non-resident proprietors be taxed higher than residents. The navigable waters leading into the Mississippi and St. Lawrence, and the carrying places between the same, shall be common highways and forever free, as well to the inhabitants of the said Territory as to the citizens of the United States, and those of any other

States that may be admitted into the Confederacy, without any tax, impost, or duty therefor.

ART. 5th. There shall be formed in the said Territory, not less than three nor more than five States ; and the boundaries of the States, as soon as Virginia shall alter her act of cession, and consent to the same, shall become fixed and established as follows, to wit : The Western State in the said territory, shall be bounded by the Mississippi, the Ohio, and Wabash rivers ; a direct line drawn from the Wabash and Post Vincent's,[1] due North, to the territorial line between the United States and Canada ; and, by the said territorial line, to the Lake of the Woods and Mississippi. The middle State [2] shall be bounded by the said direct line, the Wabash from Post Vincent's to the Ohio ; by the Ohio, by a direct line, drawn due north from the mouth of the Great Miami, to the said territorial line, and by the said territorial line. The eastern State [3] shall be bounded by the last mentioned direct line, the Ohio, Pennsylvania, and the said territorial line : *Provided, however*, and it is further understood and declared, that the boundaries of these three States shall be subject so far to be altered, that, if Congress shall hereafter find it expedient, they shall have authority to form one or two States in that part of the said territory which lies north of an east and west line drawn through the southerly bend or extreme of lake Michigan. And, whenever any of the said States shall have 60,000 free inhabitants therein, such State shall be admitted, by its delegates, into the Congress of the United States, on an equal footing with the original States in all respects whatever, and shall be at liberty to form a permanent Constitution and State government : *Provided*, the Constitution and government so to be formed, shall be republican, and in conformity to the principles contained in these articles ; and, so far as it can be consistent with the general interest of the Confederacy, such admission shall be allowed at an earlier period, and when there may be a less number of free inhabitants in the State than 60,000.

ART. 6th. There shall be neither slavery nor involuntary servitude in the said territory, otherwise than in the punish-

---

[1] Vincennes, Indiana. The State described includes Illinois, Wisconsin, and parts of Minnesota and Michigan.

[2] Indiana and part of Michigan.

[3] Ohio and part of Michigan.

ment of crimes whereof the party shall have been duly convicted : *Provided, always,* That any person escaping into the same, from whom labor or service is lawfully claimed in any one of the original States, such fugitive may be lawfully reclaimed and conveyed to the person claiming his or her labor or service as aforesaid.

Be it ordained by the authority aforesaid, That the resolutions of the 23rd of April 1784, relative to the subject of this ordinance, be, and the same are hereby repealed and declared null and void.

SELECTIONS FROM NOTES OF THE DEBATES IN THE FEDERAL CONVENTION AT PHILADELPHIA [1]

May–September 1787

(a) *The Randolph, or Virginia Resolutions.*

29 May (Madison's notes)

Mr. RANDOLPH then opened the main business. He expressed his regret, that it should fall to him, rather than those, who were of longer standing in life and political experience, to open the great subject of their mission. But, as the convention had originated from Virginia, and his colleagues supposed that some proposition was expected from them, they had imposed this task on him.

He then commented on the difficulty of the crisis, and the

[1] The sessions of the Federal Convention were secret, and no official report was made of the debates ; but several members made notes of the proceedings. Madison's notes were first published in 1840, and have many times been reprinted, the best edition being that of Gaillard Hunt and J. B. Scott (*Debates in the Federal Convention of 1787,* Oxford Univ. Press, American Branch, 1920). Next in importance are the notes of Robert Yates of New York, published as *Secret Proceedings and Debates* (Albany, 1821 : a cheap reprint may be obtained from the Superintendent of Documents, Washington). Madison's and Yates's notes, with briefer memoranda by other delegates, the official journal, and many illustrative documents, are published by the Department of State as the *Documentary History of the Constitution* (5 vols., Washington, 1894–1905, obtainable from same source). A handier but more expensive compilation is *Records of the Federal Convention* (Max Farrand ed.), 3 vols., Yale University Press and Oxford, 1911. See also note to Virginia Convention, below, p. 307.

necessity of preventing the fulfilment of the prophecies of the American downfall.

He observed that in revising the fœderal system we ought to inquire (1) into the properties which such a government ought to possess, (2) the defects of the Confederation, (3) the danger of our situation, and (4) the remedy.

1. The character of such a government ought to secure (1) against foreign invasion ; (2) against dissentions between members of the Union, or seditions in particular States ; (3) to procure to the several States various blessings, of which an isolated situation was incapable ; (4) to be able to defend itself against incroachment ; and (5) to be paramount to the State Constitutions.

2. In speaking of the defects of the Confederation he professed a high respect for its authors, and considered them as having done all that patriots could do, in the then infancy of the science of constitutions and of confederacies—when the inefficiency of requisitions was unknown—no commercial discord had arisen among any States—no rebellion had appeared as in Massachusetts—foreign debts had not become urgent—the havoc of paper money had not been foreseen—treaties had not been violated—and perhaps nothing better could be obtained from the jealousy of the States with regard to their sovereignty.

He then proceeded to enumerate the defects : (1) that the Confederation produced no security against foreign invasion ; Congress not being permitted to prevent a war nor to support it by their own authority. Of this he cited many examples ; most of which tended to shew that they could not cause infractions of treaties or of the law of nations to be punished ; that particular States might by their conduct provoke war without controul ; and that neither militia nor drafts being fit for defence on such occasions, enlistments only could be successful, and these could not be executed without money. (2) That the fœderal government could not check the quarrels between States, nor a rebellion in any, not having constitutional power nor means to interpose according to the exigency. (3) That there were many advantages which the United States might acquire, which were not attainable under the Confederation—such as a productive impost, counteraction of the commercial regulations of other nations, pushing of commerce ad libitum, etc., etc. (4) That the fœderal government could not defend itself against incroachments from the States. (5) That it was not even paramount to the State Constitutions, ratified, as it was in many of the States.

3. He next reviewed the danger of our situation, and appealed to the sense of the best friends of the United States —the prospect of anarchy from the laxity of government everywhere ; and to other considerations.

4. He then proceeded to the remedy ; the basis of which he said must be the republican principle.

He proposed as conformable to his ideas the following resolutions, which he explained one by one.

RESOLUTIONS PROPOSED BY MR. RANDOLPH IN CONVENTION

1. *Resolved*, that the Articles of Confederation ought to be so corrected and enlarged as to accomplish the objects proposed by their institution ; namely, ' common defence, security of liberty and general welfare.'

2. *Resolved therefore*, that the rights of suffrage in the National Legislature ought to be proportioned to the quotas of contribution, or to the number of free inhabitants, as the one or the other rule may seem best in different cases.

3. *Resolved*, that the National Legislature ought to consist of two branches.

4. *Resolved*, that the members of the first branch of the National Legislature ought to be elected by the people of the several States every   for the term of   ; to be of the age of   years at least, to receive liberal stipends by which they may be compensated for the devotion of their time to the public service ; to be ineligible to any office established by a particular State, or under the authority of the United States, except those peculiarly belonging to the functions of the first branch, during the term of service, and for the space of   after its expiration ; to be incapable of re-election for the space of   after the expiration of their term of service,[1] and to be subject to recall.

5. *Resolved*, that the members of the second branch of the National Legislature ought to be elected by those of the first, out of a proper number of persons nominated by the individual Legislatures, to be of the age of   years at least ; to

[1] Cf. Constitution, art. i, s. vi, § 2.

hold their offices for a term sufficient to ensure their independence ; to receive liberal stipends, by which they may be compensated for the devotion of their time to the public service ; and to be ineligible to any office established by a particular State, or under the authority of the United States, except those peculiarly belonging to the functions of the second branch, during the term of service, and for the space of after the expiration thereof.[1]

6. *Resolved*, that each branch ought to possess the right of originating Acts ; that the National Legislature ought to be impowered to enjoy the legislative rights vested in Congress by the Confederation, and moreover to legislate in all cases to which the separate States are incompetent, or in which the harmony of the United States may be interrupted by the exercise of individual legislation ; to negative all laws passed by the several States, contravening, in the opinion of the National Legislature the articles of Union ; [2] and to call forth the force of the Union against any member of the Union failing to fulfil its duty under the articles thereof.

7. *Resolved*, that a National Executive be instituted ; to be chosen by the National Legislature for the term of years, to receive punctually at stated times, a fixed compensation for the services rendered, in which no increase nor diminution shall be made so as to affect the magistracy, existing at the time of increase or diminution, and to be ineligible a second time ; [3] and that besides a general authority to execute the national laws, it ought to enjoy the executive rights vested in Congress by the Confederation.

8. *Resolved*, that the Executive and a convenient number of the National Judiciary, ought to compose a Council of Revision with authority to examine every Act of the National Legislature before it shall operate, and every Act of a particular Legislature before a negative thereon shall be final ; and that the dissent of the said Council shall amount to a rejection, unless the Act of the National Legislature be again passed, or that of a particular Legislature be again negatived by   of the members of each branch.

9. *Resolved*, that a National Judiciary be established to

[1] Cf. Constitution, art. i, s. vi, § 2.
[2] The phrase ' or any treaty subsisting under the authority of the Union ' is here added in the transcript.
[3] Cf. Constitution, art. i, s. i, § 7.

consist of one or more supreme tribunals, and of inferior tribunals to be chosen by the National Legislature, to hold their offices during good behaviour ; and to receive punctually at stated times fixed compensation for their services, in which no increase or diminution shall be made so as to affect the persons actually in office at the time of such increase or diminution. That the jurisdiction of the inferior tribunals shall be to hear and determine in the first instance, and of the supreme tribunal to hear and determine in the dernier resort, all piracies and felonies on the high seas, captures from an enemy, cases in which foreigners or citizens of other States applying to such jurisdictions may be interested, or which respect the collection of the national revenue ; impeachments of any National officers, and questions which may involve the national peace and harmony.[1]

10. *Resolved,* that provision ought to be made for the admission of States lawfully arising within the limits of the United States, whether from a voluntary junction of government and territory or otherwise, with the consent of a number of voices in the National Legislature less than the whole.[2]

11. *Resolved,* that a republican government and the territory of each State, except in the instance of a voluntary junction of Government and territory, ought to be guarantied by the United States to each State.[3]

12. *Resolved,* that provision ought to be made for the continuance of Congress and their authorities and privileges, until a given day after the reform of the articles of Union shall be adopted, and for the completion of all their engagements.

13. *Resolved,* that provision ought to be made for the amendment of the Articles of Union whensoever it shall seem necessary, and that the assent of the National Legislature ought not to be required thereto.[4]

14. *Resolved,* that the legislative, executive and judiciary powers within the several States ought to be bound by oath to support the articles of Union.

15. *Resolved,* that the amendments which shall be offered to the Confederation by the Convention, ought at a proper time or times, after the approbation of Congress, to be submitted to an assembly or assemblies of representatives

---

[1] Ibid., art. iii.   [2] Ibid., art. iv, s. iii.
[3] Ibid., art. iv, s. iv.   [4] Ibid., art. v.

recommended by the several Legislatures to be expressly chosen by the people, to consider and decide thereon.[1]

He concluded with an exhortation, not to suffer the present opportunity of establishing general peace, harmony, happiness and liberty in the United States to pass away unimproved.

It was then *resolved*—That the House will to-morrow resolve itself into a committee of the whole house to consider of the state of the American Union, and that the propositions moved by Mr. Randolph be referred to the said committee.

Mr. CHARLES PINCKNEY laid before the House the draft of a federal government which he had prepared, to be agreed upon between the free and independent States of America.— Mr. Pinckney's plan [2] ordered that the same be referred to the committee of the whole appointed to consider the state of the American Union.

Adjourned.

(b) Democracy and the Lower House.

31 May (Madison)

In committee of the whole on Mr. Randolph's propositions.

The 3d Resolution ' that the National Legislature ought to consist of two branches ' was agreed to without debate or dissent, except that of Pennsylvania, given probably from complaisance to Doctor Franklin, who was understood to be partial to a single House of legislation.

Resolution 4, first clause ' that the members of the first branch of the National Legislature ought to be elected by the people of the several States ' being taken up,

Mr. SHERMAN [Conn.] opposed the election by the people, insisting that it ought to be by the State Legislatures. The people, he said, immediately should have as little to do as may be about the government. They want information, and are constantly liable to be misled.

Mr. GERRY [Mass.]. The evils we experience flow from the excess of democracy. The people do not want virtue, but are

[1] Cf. Constitution, art. vii.

[2] For the Pinckney plan, see *Debates in the Federal Convention* (Hunt and Scott ed.), pp. 596–8. Charles Pinckney (b. 1758) was the youngest member of the Convention. His cousin, Charles Cotesworth Pinckney, also on the South Carolina delegation, is referred to in the debates as General Pinckney.

the dupes of pretended patriots. In Massachusetts it had been fully confirmed by experience that they are daily misled into the most baneful measures and opinions by the false reports circulated by designing men, and which no one on the spot can refute. One principal evil arises from the want of due provision for those employed in the administration of government. It would seem to be a maxim of democracy to starve the public servants. He mentioned the popular clamour in Massachusetts for the reduction of salaries [1] and the attack made on that of the Governor, though secured by the spirit of the Constitution itself. He had he said been too republican heretofore : he was still however republican, but had been taught by experience the danger of the levilling spirit.

Mr. MASON [Va.] argued strongly for an election of the larger branch by the people. It was to be the grand depository of the democratic principle of the Government. It was, so to speak, to be our House of Commons. It ought to know and sympathise with every part of the community ; and ought therefore to be taken not only from different parts of the whole republic, but also from different districts of the larger members of it, which had in several instances, particularly in Virginia, different interests and views arising from difference of produce, of habits, etc., etc. He admitted that we had been too democratic, but was afraid we should incautiously run into the opposite extreme. We ought to attend to the rights of every class of the people. He had often wondered at the indifference of the superior classes of society to this dictate of humanity and policy ; considering that however affluent their circumstances, or elevated their situations might be, the course of a few years not only might but certainly would distribute their posterity throughout the lowest classes of society. Every selfish motive, therefore, every family attachment, ought to recommend such a system of policy as would provide no less carefully for the rights and happiness of the lowest than of the highest orders of citizens.

Mr. WILSƆN [Penn.] contended strenuously for drawing the most numerous branch of the Legislature immediately from the people. He was for raising the federal pyramid to a considerable altitude, and for that reason wished to give it as

[1] Cf. above, pp. 209–12, 221.

broad a basis as possible. No government could long subsist without the confidence of the people. In a republican government this confidence was peculiarly essential. He also thought it wrong to increase the weight of the State Legislatures by making them the electors of the National Legislature. All interference between the general and local governments should be obviated as much as possible. On examination it would be found that the opposition of States to federal measures had proceded much more from the officers of the States, than from the people at large.

Mr. MADISON considered the popular election of one branch of the National Legislature as essential to every plan of free government. He observed that in some of the States one branch of the Legislature was composed of men already removed from the people by an intervening body of electors. That if the first branch of the general legislature should be elected by the State Legislatures, the second branch elected by the first, the Executive by the second together with the first ; and other appointments again made for subordinate purposes by the Executive, the people would be lost sight of altogether ; and the necessary sympathy between them and their rulers and officers, too little felt. He was an advocate for the policy of refining the popular appointments by successive filtrations, but thought it might be pushed too far. He wished the expedient to be resorted to only in the appointment of the second branch of the Legislature, and in the executive and judiciary branches of the government. He thought, too, that the great fabric to be raised would be more stable and durable, if it should rest on the solid foundation of the people themselves, than if it should stand merely on the pillars of the Legislatures.

Mr. GERRY did not like the election by the people. The maxims taken from the British Constitution were often fallacious when applied to our situation which was extremely different. Experience he said had shewn that the State legislatures drawn immediately from the people did not always possess their confidence. He had no objection, however, to an election by the people, if it were so qualified that men of honor and character might not be unwilling to be joined in the appointments. He seemed to think the people might nominate a certain number out of which the State legislatures should be bound to choose.

Mr. BUTLER [S. C.] thought an election by the people an impracticable mode.

On the question for an election of the first branch of the National Legislature by the people : [1]

Mass. ay. Conn. div. N. Y. ay. N. J. no. Penn. ay. Del. div. Va. ay. N. C. ay. S. C. no. Geo. ay.

(c) *Monarchy and the Executive.*

1 June (Madison)

The committee of the whole proceeded to Resolution 7, ' that a National Executive be instituted, to be chosen by the National Legislature ', etc. . . .

Mr. PINCKNEY was for a vigorous Executive but was afraid the executive powers of the existing Congress might extend to peace and war, etc., which would render the Executive a monarchy of the worst kind, to wit, an elective one.

Mr. WILSON moved that the Executive consist of a single person. Mr. C. PINCKNEY seconded the motion, so as to read ' that a National Executive, to consist of a single person, be instituted '.

A considerable pause ensuing, and the chairman asking if he should put the question, Dr. FRANKLIN observed that it was a point of great importance, and wished that the gentlemen would deliver their sentiments on it before the question was put.

Mr. RUTLEDGE [S. C.] animadverted on the shyness of gentlemen on this and other subjects. He said it looked as if they supposed themselves precluded by having frankly disclosed their opinions from afterwards changing them, which he did not take to be at all the case. He said he was for vesting the Executive Power in a single person, tho' he was not for giving him the power of war and peace. A single man would feel the greatest responsibility and administer the public affairs best.

Mr. SHERMAN said he considered the executive magistracy as nothing more than an institution for carrying the will of the Legislature into effect, that the person or persons ought to be appointed by and accountable to the Legislature only, which

---

[1] The Convention voted, as had the Continental Congress, by States, a majority ballot of each State delegation determining the vote of that State.

was the depositary of the supreme will of the society. As they were the best judges of the business which ought to be done by the executive department, and consequently of the number necessary from time to time for doing it, he wished the number might not be fixed, but that the legislature should be at liberty to appoint one or more as experience might dictate.

Mr. WILSON preferred a single magistrate, as giving most energy, dispatch, and responsibility to the office. He did not consider the prerogatives of the British monarch as a proper guide in defining the executive powers. Some of these prerogatives were of a legislative nature. Among others, that of war and peace, etc. The only powers he considered strictly executive were those of executing the laws and appointing officers, not appertaining to and appointed by the Legislature.

Mr. GERRY favored the policy of annexing a Council to the executive, in order to give weight and inspire confidence.

Mr. RANDOLPH strenuously opposed a unity in the executive magistracy. He regarded it as the fetus of monarchy. We had he said no motive to be governed by the British government as our prototype. He did not mean, however, to throw censure on that excellent fabric. If we were in a situation to copy it, he did not know that he should be opposed to it ; but the fixed genius of the people of America required a different form of government. He could not see why the great requisites for the executive department, vigor, despatch, and responsibility, could not be found in three men, as well as in one man. The Executive ought to be independent. It ought, therefore, in order to support its independence to consist of more than one.

Mr. WILSON said that unity in the Executive, instead of being the fetus of monarchy, would be the best safeguard against tyranny. He repeated that he was not governed by the British model, which was inapplicable to the situation of this country ; the extent of which was so great, and the manners so republican, that nothing but a great confederated republic would do for it.

Mr. Wilson's motion for a single magistrate was postponed by common consent, the committee seeming unprepared for any decision on it ; and the first part of the clause agreed to, viz., ' that a National Executive be instituted.'

Mr. MADISON thought it would be proper, before a choice should be made between a unity and a plurality in the Executive, to fix the extent of the executive authority ; that as certain powers were in their nature executive, and must be given to that department whether administered by one or more persons, a definition of their extent would assist the judgment in determining how far they might be safely entrusted to a single officer. He accordingly moved that so much of the clause before the committee as related to the powers of the Executive should be struck out, and that after the words ' that a National Executive ought to be instituted ' there be inserted the words following, viz., ' with power to carry into effect the national laws, to appoint to offices in cases not otherwise provided for, [and to execute such other powers not Legislative nor Judiciary in their nature, as may from time to time be delegated by the national Legislature.] ' [1] . . .

The next clause in Resolution 7, relating to the mode of appointing, and the duration of, the Executive, being under consideration,

Mr. WILSON said he was almost unwilling to declare the mode which he wished to take place, being apprehensive that it might appear chimerical. He would say, however, at least that in theory he was for an election by the people. Experience, particularly in New York and Massachusetts, shewed that an election of the first magistrate by the people at large, was both a convenient and successful mode. The objects of choice in such cases must be persons whose merits have general notoriety.

Mr. SHERMAN was for the appointment by the Legislature, and for making him absolutely dependent on that body, as it was the will of that which was to be executed. An independence of the Executive on the Supreme Legislature, was in his opinion the very essence of tyranny, if there was any such thing.

Mr. WILSON moves that the blank for the term of duration should be filled with three years, observing at the same time that he preferred this short period, on the supposition that a re-eligibility would be provided for.

Mr. PINCKNEY moves for seven years.

Mr. SHERMAN was for three years, and against the doctrine of rotation, as throwing out of office the men best qualified to execute its duties.

Mr. MASON was for seven years at least, and for prohibiting a re-eligibility as the best expedient both for preventing the

---

[1] The motion was carried, with the bracketed words struck out.

effect of a false complaisance on the side of the Legislature towards unfit characters ; and a temptation on the side of the Executive to intrigue with the Legislature for a re-appointment.

Mr. BEDFORD [Del.] was strongly opposed to so long a term as seven years. He begged the committee to consider what the situation of the country would be, in case the first magistrate should be saddled on it for such a period and it should be found on trial that he did not possess the qualifications ascribed to him, or should lose them after his appointment. An impeachment he said would be no cure for this evil, as an impeachment would reach misfeasance only. not incapacity. He was for a triennial election, and for an ineligibility after a period of nine years.

On the question for seven years,

Mass. divided. Conn. no. N. Y. ay. N. J. ay. Penn. ay. Del. ay. Va. ay. N. C. no. S. C. no. Geo. no. There being 5 ays, 4 noes, 1 divided, a question was asked whether a majority had voted in the affirmative ? The President decided that it was an affirmative vote.

(d) Safety and the Senate.

7 June. IN COMMITTEE OF THE WHOLE (Madison)

Mr. DICKINSON [Del.] now moved ' that the members of the second branch [of the Legislature] ought to be chosen by the individual legislatures '.

Mr. SHERMAN seconded the motion ; observing that the particular States would thus become interested in supporting the national government, and that a due harmony between the two governments would be maintained. He admitted that the two ought to have separate and distinct jurisdictions, but that they ought to have a mutual interest in supporting each other.

Mr. PINCKNEY. If the small States should be allowed one Senator only, the number will be too great, there will be 80 at least.

Mr. DICKINSON had two reasons for his motion. 1. Because the sense of the States would be better collected through their governments, than immediately from the people at large. 2. Because he wished the Senate to consist of the most distinguished characters, distinguished for their rank in life and their weight of property, and bearing as strong a likeness to the British House of Lords as possible ; and he thought such characters more likely to be selected by the State Legislatures than in any other mode. The greatness of the number was no objection with him. He hoped there would be 80, and twice 80 of them. If their number should be small the popular branch could not be balanced by them. The legislature of a numerous people ought to be a numerous body.

Mr. WILLIAMSON [N. C.] preferred a small number of Senators, but wished that each State should have at least one. He suggested 25 as a convenient number. The different modes of representation in the different branches will serve as a mutual check.

Mr. BUTLER was anxious to know the ratio of representation before he gave any opinion.

Mr. WILSON. If we are to establish a national government, that government ought to flow from the people at large. If one branch of it should be chosen by the Legislatures, and the other by the people, the two branches will rest on different foundations, and dissensions will naturally arise between them. He wished the Senate to be elected by the people as well as the other branch, and the people might be divided into proper districts for the purpose, and he moved to postpone the motion of Mr. Dickinson, in order to take up one of that import.

Mr. MORRIS [Penn.] seconded him.

Mr. READ [Del.] proposed ' that the Senate should be appointed by the Executive Magistrate out of a proper number of persons to be nominated by the individual legislatures '. He said he thought it his duty to speak his mind frankly. Gentlemen he hoped would not be alarmed at the idea. Nothing short of this approach towards a proper model of government would answer the purpose, and he thought it best to come directly to the point at once. His proposition was not seconded nor supported.

Mr. MADISON. If the motion [of Mr. Dickinson] should be agreed to, we must either depart from the doctrine of proportional representation or admit into the Senate a very large number of members. The first is inadmissible, being evidently unjust. The second is inexpedient. The use of the Senate is to consist in its proceeding with more coolness, with more system, and with more wisdom, than the popular branch. Enlarge their number, and you communicate to them the vices which they are meant to correct. He differed from Mr. D. who thought that the additional number would give additional weight to the body. On the contrary, it appeared to him that their weight would be in an inverse ratio to their numbers. The example of the Roman Tribunes was applicable. They lost their influence and power, in proportion as their number was augmented. The reason seemed to be obvious : they were appointed to take care of the popular interests and pretensions at Rome, because the people by reason of their numbers could not act in concert, and were liable to fall into factions among themselves, and to become a prey to their aristocratic adversaries. The more the representatives of the people, therefore, were multiplied, the more they partook of the infirmities of their constituents, the more liable they became to be divided among themselves either from their own indiscretions or the artifices of the opposite faction, and of course the less capable of fulfilling their trust. When the weight of a set of men depends merely on their personal characters, the greater the number the greater the weight. When it depends on the degree of political authority lodged in them, the smaller the number the greater the weight. These considerations might perhaps be combined in the intended Senate ; but the latter was the material one.

Mr. GERRY. Four modes of appointing the Senate have been mentioned. 1. By the first branch of the National Legislature. This would create a dependence contrary to the end proposed. 2. By the National Executive. This is a stride towards monarchy that few will think of. 3. By the people. The people have two great interests, the landed interest, and the commercial, including the stockholders. To draw both branches from the people will leave no security to the latter interest ; the people being chiefly composed of the landed interest, and erroneously supposing that the other interests are adverse to it. 4. By the individual legislatures. The elections being carried thro' this refinement, will be most likely to provide some check in favor of the commercial interest against the landed ; without which oppression will take place, and no free Government can last long where that is the case. He was therefore in favor of this last.

Mr. DICKINSON.* The preservation of the States in a certain

---

* It will throw light on this discussion to remark that an election by the State Legislatures involved a surrender of the principle insisted

degree of agency is indispensable. It will produce that collision between the different authorities which should be wished for in order to check each other. To attempt to abolish the States altogether would degrade the councils of our country, would be impracticable, would be ruinous. He compared the proposed national system to the solar system, in which the States were the planets, and ought to be left to move freely in their proper orbits. The gentleman from Pennsylvania wished, he said, to extinguish these planets. If the State Governments were excluded from all agency in the national one, and all power drawn from the people at large, the consequence would be that the national Government would move in the same direction as the State Governments now do, and would run into all the same mischiefs. The reform would only unite the thirteen small streams into one great current pursuing the same course without any opposition whatever. He adhered to the opinion that the Senate ought to be composed of a large number, and that their influence from family, weight, and other causes would be increased thereby. He did not admit that the Tribunes lost their weight in proportion as their number was augmented, and gave a historical sketch of this institution. If the reasoning of Mr. Madison was good, it would prove that the number of the Senate ought to be reduced below ten, the highest number of the tribunitial corps.

Mr. WILSON. The subject it must be owned is surrounded with doubts and difficulties. But we must surmount them. The British government cannot be our model. We have no materials for a similar one. Our manners, our laws, the abolition of entails and of primogeniture, the whole genius of the people are opposed to it. He did not see the danger of the States being devoured by the national government. On the contrary, he wished to keep them from devouring the national government. He was not, however, for extinguishing these planets as was supposed by Mr. D. Neither did he, on the other hand, believe that they would warm or enlighten the sun. Within their proper orbits they must still be suffered to act for subordinate purposes for which their existence is made essential by the great extent of our country. He could not comprehend

on by the large States and dreaded by the small ones, namely that of a proportional representation in the Senate. Such a rule would make the body too numerous, as the smallest State must elect one member at least.

in what manner the landed interest would be rendered less predominant in the Senate by an election through the medium of the Legislatures, than by the people themselves. If the Legislatures, as was now complained, sacrificed the commercial to the landed interest, what reason was there to expect such a choice from them as would defeat their own views? He was for an election by the people in large districts which would be most likely to obtain men of intelligence and uprightness; subdividing the districts only for the accommodation of voters.

Mr. MADISON could as little comprehend in what manner family weight, as desired by Mr. D., would be more certainly conveyed into the Senate through elections by the State Legislatures, than in some other modes. The true question was in what mode the best choice would be made? If an election by the people, or thro' any other channel than the State Legislatures promised as uncorrupt and impartial a preference of merit, there could surely be no necessity for an appointment by those Legislatures. Nor was it apparent that a more useful check would be derived thro' that channel than from the people thro' some other. The great evils complained of were that the State Legislatures run into schemes of paper money, etc., whenever solicited by the people, and sometimes without even the sanction of the people. Their influence, then, instead of checking a like propensity in the National Legislature, may be expected to promote it. Nothing can be more contradictory than to say that the National Legislature without a proper check, will follow the example of the State Legislatures, and in the same breath, that the State Legislatures are the only proper check.

Mr. SHERMAN opposed elections by the people in districts, as not likely to produce such fit men as elections by the State Legislatures.

Mr. GERRY insisted that the commercial and monied interests would be more secure in the hands of the State Legislatures, than of the people at large. The former have more sense of character, and will be restrained by that from injustice. The people are for paper money when the Legislatures are against it. In Massachusetts the county conventions had declared a wish for a depreciating paper that would sink itself. Besides, in some States there are two branches in the Legislature, one of which is somewhat aristocratic. There would therefore be so far a better chance of refinement in the choice. There seemed, he thought, to be three powerful objections against elections by districts. 1. It is impracticable; the people cannot be brought to one place for the purpose; and whether brought to the same place or not, numberless frauds would be unavoidable. 2. Small States forming part of the same district with a large one, or a large part of a large one, would have no chance of gaining an appointment for its citizens of merit. 3. A new source of discord would be opened between different parts of the same district.

Mr. PINCKNEY thought the second branch ought to be permanent and independent, and that the members of it would be rendered more so by receiving their appointments from the State Legislatures. This mode would avoid the rivalships and discontents incident to the election by districts. He was for dividing the States into three classes according to their respective sizes, and for allowing to the first class three members, to the second, two, and to the third, one.

On the question for postponing Mr. Dickinson's motion referring the appointment of the Senate to the State Legislatures, in order to consider Mr. Wilson's for referring it to the people,

Mass. no. Conn. no. N. Y. no. N. J. no. Pa. ay. Del. no. Md. no. Va. no. N. C. no. S. C. no. G. no.

Col. MASON. Whatever power may be necessary for the National Government a certain portion must necessarily be left in the States. It is impossible for one power to pervade the extreme parts of the United States so as to carry equal justice to them. The State Legislatures also ought to have some means of defending themselves against encroachments of the National Government. In every other department we have studiously endeavored to provide for its self-defence. Shall we leave the States alone unprovided with the means for this purpose? And what better means can we provide than the giving them some share in, or rather to make them a constituent part of, the national establishment? There is danger on both sides no doubt; but we have only seen the evils arising on the side of the State Governments. Those on the other side remain to be displayed. The example of Congress does not apply. Congress had no power to carry their acts into execution as the national government will have.

On Mr. DICKINSON's motion for an appointment of the Senate by the State Legislatures:

Mass. ay. Conn. ay. N. Y. ay. Pa. ay. Del. ay. Md. ay. Va. ay. N. C. ay. S. C. ay. Geo. ay.

(e) *The New Jersey Plan.*[1] *Small States* v. *Large States.*

16 June. IN COMMITTEE OF THE WHOLE (Madison)

Mr. PATERSON [N. J.] said as he had on a former occasion given his sentiments on the plan proposed by Mr. R. he would now, avoiding repetition as much as possible, give his reasons in favor of that proposed by himself. He preferred it because it accorded, first, with the powers of the Convention, second, with the sentiments of the people. If the Confederacy was radically wrong, let us return to our States, and obtain larger powers, not assume them of ourselves. I came here not to speak my own sentiments, but the sentiments of those who sent me. Our object is not such a government as may be best in itself, but such a one as our constituents have authorized us to prepare, and as they will approve. If we argue the matter on the supposition that no Confederacy at present exists, it can not be denied that all the States stand on the footing of equal sovereignty. All, therefore, must concur before any can be bound. If a proportional representation be right, why do we not vote so here ? If we argue on the fact that a federal compact actually exists, and consult the articles of it, we still find an equal sovereignty to be the basis of it. He reads the 5th art. of [the Articles of] Confederation, giving each State a vote, and the 13th, declaring that no alteration shall be made without unanimous consent. This is the nature of all treaties.

What is unanimously done must be unanimously undone. It was observed that the larger States gave up the point, not because it was right, but because the circumstances of the moment urged the concession. Be it so. Are they for that reason at liberty to take it back ? Can the donor resume his gift without the consent of the donee ? This doctrine may be convenient, but it is a doctrine that will sacrifice the lesser States. The large States acceded readily to the Confederacy. It was the small ones that came in reluctantly and slowly. New Jersey and Maryland were the two last, the former objecting to the want of power in Congress over trade : both of them to the want of power to appropriate the vacant territory to the benefit of the whole. If the sovereignty of the States is to be maintained, the Representatives must be drawn immediately from the States, not from the people ; and we

[1] See Introduction.

have no power to vary the idea of equal sovereignty. The only expedient that will cure the difficulty is that of throwing the States into hotchpot. To say that this is impracticable will not make it so. Let it be tried, and we shall see whether the citizens of Massachusetts, Pennsylvania, and Virginia accede to it. It will be objected that coercion will be impracticable. But will it be more so in one plan than the other? Its efficacy will depend on the quantum of power collected, not on its being drawn from the States, or from the individuals; and according to his plan it may be exerted on individuals as well as according to that of Mr. R. A distinct executive and judiciary also were equally provided by his plan. It is urged that two branches in the Legislature are necessary. Why? for the purpose of a check. But the reason for the precaution is not applicable to this case. Within a particular State, where party heats prevail, such a check may be necessary. In such a body as Congress it is less necessary, and besides, the delegations of the different States are checks on each other. Do the people at large complain of Congress? No, what they wish is that Congress may have more power. If the power now proposed be not eno', the people hereafter will make additions to it. With proper powers, Congress will act with more energy and wisdom than the proposed National Legislature; being fewer in number and more secreted and refined by the mode of election. The plan of Mr. R. will also be enormously expensive. Allowing Georgia and Delaware two representatives each in the popular branch, the aggregate number of that branch will be 180. Add to it half as many for the other branch and you have 270 members coming once at least a year from the most distant as well as the most central parts of the republic. In the present deranged state of our finances can so expensive a system be seriously thought of? By enlarging the powers of Congress the greatest part of this expence will be saved, and all purposes will be answered. At least a trial ought to be made.

Mr. WILSON entered into a contrast of the principal points of the two plans so far, he said, as there had been time to examine the one last proposed. These points were: 1. In the Virginia plan there are two, and in some degree three branches in the Legislature: in the plan from New Jersey there is to be a *single* legislature only. 2. Representation of the people at large is the basis of the one: the State Legislatures the pillars of the other.   3. Proportional representation prevails in one : equality of suffrage in the other.   4. A single Executive Magistrate is at the head of the one : a plurality is held out in the other.   5. In the one a majority of the people of the United States must prevail : in the other a minority may prevail. 6. The National Legislature is to make laws in all cases to which the separate States are incompetent and, in place of this Congress are to have additional power in a few cases only. 7. A negative on the laws of the States : in place of this coercion to be substituted.   8. The Executive to be removeable on impeachment and conviction in one plan : in the other to be removeable at the instance of a majority of the executives of the States.   9. Revision of the laws provided for in one : no such check in the other.   10. Inferior national tribunals in one : none such in the other.   11. In the one, jurisdiction of National tribunals to extend, etc. : an appellate jurisdiction only allowed in the other.   12. Here the jurisdiction is to extend to all cases affecting the national peace and harmony : there, a few cases only are marked out.   13. Finally, the ratification is in this to be by the people themselves : in that by the legislative authorities according to the 13th Article of Confederation.

With regard to the power of the Convention he conceived himself authorized to conclude nothing, but to be at liberty to propose anything.   In this particular he felt himself perfectly indifferent to the two plans.

With regard to the sentiments of the people he conceived it difficult to know precisely what they are.   Those of the particular circle in which one moved were commonly mistaken for the general voice.   He could not persuade himself that the State governments and sovereignties were so much the idols of the people, nor a national government so obnoxious to them, as some supposed.   Why should a national government be unpopular ?   Has it less dignity ?   Will each citizen enjoy under it less liberty or protection ?   Will a citizen of Delaware be degraded by becoming a citizen of the United States ? Where do the people look at present for relief from the evil of which they complain ?   Is it from an internal reform of their governments ?   No, Sir.   It is from the national councils that relief is expected.   For these reasons he did not fear that the people would not follow us into a national government, and it will be a further recommendation of Mr. R.'s plan that it is to be submitted to them, and not to the Legislatures, for ratification.

Proceeding now to the first point on which he had contrasted the two plans, he observed that anxious as he was for some augmentation of the federal powers, it would be with extreme reluctance indeed that he could ever consent to give powers to Congress : [1] he had two reasons either of which was sufficient. 1. Congress as a legislative body does not stand on the people. ... He would not repeat the remarks he had formerly made on the principles of Representation ; he would only say that an inequality in it has ever been a poison contaminating every branch of government. In Great Britain, where this poison has had a full operation, the security of private rights is owing entirely to the purity of her tribunals of justice, the judges of which are neither appointed nor paid by a venal Parliament. The political liberty of that nation, owing to the inequality of representation, is at the mercy of its rulers. He means not to insinuate that there is any parallel between the situation of that country and ours at present. But it is a lesson we ought not to disregard, that the smallest bodies in Great Britain are notoriously the most corrupt. Every other source of influence must also be stronger in small than large bodies of men. When Lord Chesterfield had told us that one of the Dutch provinces had been seduced into the views of France, he need not have added, that it was not Holland, but one of the smallest of them. There are facts among ourselves which are known to all. Passing over others, he will only remark that the Impost,[2] so anxiously wished for by the public, was defeated not by any of the larger States in the Union. 2. Congress is a single Legislature. Despotism comes on mankind in different shapes, sometimes in an executive, sometimes in a military one. Is there no danger of a legislative despotism ? Theory and practice both proclaim it. If the legislative authority be not restrained there can be neither liberty nor stability ; and it can only be restrained by dividing it within itself, into distinct and independent branches. In a single house there is no check, but the inadequate one, of the virtue and good sense of those who compose it.

On another great point the contrast was equally favorable

---

[1] The Congress of the Confederation.

[2] A proposed amendment to the Articles of Confederation, defeated by the single dissenting vote of Rhode Island.

to the plan reported by the committee of the whole. It vested the executive powers in a single magistrate. The plan of New Jersey vested them in a plurality. In order to controul the legislative authority you must divide it. In order to controul the executive, you must unite it. One man will be more responsible than three. Three will contend among themselves till one becomes the master of his colleagues. In the triumvirates of Rome, first Caesar, then Augustus, are witnesses of this truth. The Kings of Sparta and the Consuls of Rome prove also the factious consequences of dividing the Executive Magistracy. Having already taken up so much time he would not, he said, proceed to any of the other points. Those on which he had dwelt, are sufficient of themselves : and on a decision of them the fate of the others will depend.

Mr. PINCKNEY, the whole comes to this, as he conceived. Give New Jersey an equal vote, and she will dismiss her scruples, and concur in the National system. He thought the Convention authorized to go any length in recommending, which they found necessary to remedy the evils which produced this Convention.

(f) *Alexander Hamilton's ideas.*

18 June (Yates's notes) [1]

Mr. HAMILTON. To deliver my sentiments on so important a subject, when the first characters in the Union have gone before me, inspires me with the greatest diffidence, especially when my own ideas are so materially dissimilar to the plans now before the committee. My situation is disagreeable, but it would be criminal not to come forward on a question of such magnitude. I have well considered the subject, and am convinced that no amendment of the Confederation can answer the purpose of a good government, so long as State sovereignties do, in any shape, exist ; and I have great doubts whether a national government on the Virginia plan can be made effectual. What is federal ? An association of several independent states into one. How or in what manner this association is formed, is not so clearly distinguishable. We find the Diet of Germany has in some instances the power of legislation on individuals. We find the United States of America have it in an extensive degree in the cases of piracies.

[1] See p. 233, note.

Let us now review the powers with which we are invested. We are appointed for the sole and express purpose of revising the Confederation, and to alter or amend it, so as to render it effectual for the purposes of a good government. Those who suppose it must be federal, lay great stress on the terms *sole* and *express*, as if these words intended a confinement to a federal government ; when the manifest import is no more than that the institution of a good government must be the sole and express object of your deliberations. Nor can we suppose an annihilation of our powers by forming a national government, as many of the States have made in their constitutions no provision for any alteration ; and thus much I can say for the State I have the honor to represent, that when our credentials were under consideration in the Senate, some members were for inserting a restriction in the powers, to prevent an encroachment on the Constitution : it was answered by others, and thereupon the resolve carried on the credentials, that it might abridge some of the constitutional powers of the State, and that possibly in the formation of a new Union it would be found necessary. This appears reasonable, and therefore leaves us at liberty to form such a national government as we think best adapted for the good of the whole. I have therefore no difficulty as to the extent of our powers, nor do I feel myself restrained in the exercise of my judgment under them. We can only propose and recommend—the power of ratifying or rejecting is still in the States. But on this great question I am still greatly embarrassed. I have before observed my apprehension of the inefficacy of either plan, and I have great doubts whether a more energetic government can pervade this wide and extensive country. I shall now show that both plans are materially defective.

(1) A good government ought to be constant, and ought to contain an active principle. (2) Utility and necessity. (3) An habitual sense of obligation. (4) Force. (5) Influence.

I hold it, that different societies have all different views and interests to pursue, and always prefer local to general concerns. For example : New York legislature made an external compliance lately to a requisition of Congress ; but do they not at the same time counteract their compliance by gratifying the local objects of the State so as to defeat their concession ? And this will ever be the case. Men always love power, and States will prefer their particular concerns to the general welfare ; and as the States become large and important, will they not be less attentive to the general government ? What in process of time will Virginia be ? She contains now half a million of inhabitants—in twenty-five years she will double the number. Feeling her own weight and importance, must she not become indifferent to the concerns of the Union ? And where, in such a situation, will be found national attachment to the general government ?

By *force*, I mean the *coercion* of law and the coercion of arms. Will this remark apply to the power intended to be vested in the government to be instituted by their plan ? A delinquent must be compelled to obedience by force of arms. How is this to be done ? If you are unsuccessful, a dissolution of your government must be the consequence ; and in that case the individual legislatures will reassume their powers ; nay, will not the interest of the States be thrown into the State governments ?

By *influence*, I mean the regular weight and support it will receive from those who will find it their interest to support a government intended to preserve the peace and happiness of the community of the whole. The State governments, by either plan, will exert the means to counteract it. They have their State judges and militia all combined to support their State interests ; and these will be influenced to oppose a national government. Either plan is therefore precarious. The national government cannot long exist when opposed by such a weighty rival. The experience of ancient and modern confederacies evince this point, and throw considerable light on the subject. The Amphyctionic Council of Greece had a right to require of its members troops, money, and the force of the country. Were they obeyed in the exercise of those powers ? Could they preserve the peace of the greater States and Republics ? or where were they obeyed ? History shows that their decrees were disregarded, and that the stronger States, regardless of their power, gave law to the lesser.

Let us examine the federal institution of Germany. It was instituted upon the laudable principle of securing the independency of the several States of which it was composed, and to protect them against foreign invasion. Has it answered these good intentions ? Do we not see that their councils are weak and distracted, and that it cannot prevent the wars and confusions which the respective electors carry on against each other ? The Swiss cantons, or the Helvetic union, are equally inefficient.

Such are the lessons which the experience of others affords us, and from whence results the evident conclusion that all federal governments are weak and distracted. To avoid the evils deducible from these observations, we must establish a general and national government, completely sovereign, and annihilate the State distinctions and State operations ; and unless we do this, no good purpose can be answered. What does the Jersey plan propose ? It surely has not this for its object. By this we grant the regulation of trade and a more effectual collection of the revenue, and some partial duties. These, at five or ten per cent., would only perhaps amount to a fund to discharge the debt of the corporation.

Let us take a review of the variety of important objects, which must necessarily engage the attention of a national government. You have to protect your rights against Canada on the north, Spain on the south, and your western frontier against the savages. You have to adopt necessary plans for the settlement of your frontiers, and to institute the mode in which settlements and good government are to be made.

How is the expense of supporting and regulating these important matters to be defrayed ? By requisition on the States, according to the Jersey plan ? Will this do it ? We have already found it ineffectual. Let one State prove delinquent, and it will encourage others to follow the example ; and thus the whole will fail. And what is the standard to quota among the States their respective proportions ? Can lands be the standard ? How would that apply between Russia and Holland ? Compare Pennsylvania with North Carolina, or Connecticut with New York. Does not commerce or industry in the one or other make a great disparity between these different countries, and may not the comparative value of the States from these circumstances make an unequal disproportion when the data is numbers ? I therefore conclude that either system would ultimately destroy the Confederation, or any other government which is established on such fallacious principles. Perhaps imposts, taxes on specific articles, would produce a more equal system of drawing a revenue.

Another objection against the Jersey plan is, the unequal representation. Can the great States consent to this? If they did it would eventually work its own destruction. How are forces to be raised by the Jersey plan? By quotas? Will the States comply with the requisition? As much as they will with the taxes.

Examine the present Confederation, and it is evident they can raise no troops nor equip vessels before war is actually declared. They cannot therefore take any preparatory measure before an enemy is at your door. How unwise and inadequate their powers! and this must ever be the case when you attempt to define powers.—Something will always be wanting. Congress, by being annually elected and subject to recall, will ever come with the prejudices of their States rather than the good of the Union. Add therefore additional powers to a body thus organized, and you establish a sovereignty of the worst kind, consisting of a single body. Where are the checks? None. They must either prevail over the State governments, or the prevalence of the State governments must end in their dissolution. This is a conclusive objection to the Jersey plan.

Such are the insuperable objections to both plans: and what is to be done on this occasion? I confess I am at a loss. I foresee the difficulty on a consolidated plan of drawing a representation from so extensive a continent to one place. What can be the inducements for gentlemen to come six hundred miles to a national legislature? The expense would at least amount to £100,000. This, however, can be no conclusive objection if it eventuates in an extinction of State governments. The burthen of the latter would be saved, and the expense then would not be great. State distinctions would be found unnecessary, and yet I confess, to carry government to the extremities, the State governments reduced to corporations, and with very limited powers, might be necessary, and the expense of the national government become less burthensome.

Yet, I confess, I see great difficulty of drawing forth a good representation. What, for example, will be the inducements for gentlemen of fortune and abilities to leave their houses and business to attend annually and long? It cannot be the wages; for these, I presume, must be small. Will not the power, therefore, be thrown into the hands of the demagogue or middling politician, who, for the sake of a small stipend and the hopes of advancement, will offer himself as a candidate, and the real men of weight and influence, by remaining at home, add strength to the State governments? I am at a loss to know what must be done—I despair that a republican form of government can remove the difficulties. Whatever may be my opinion, I would hold it, however, unwise to change that form of government. I believe the British government forms the best model the world ever produced, and such has been its progress in the minds of the many, that this truth gradually gains ground. This government has for its object public strength and individual security. It is said with us to be unattainable. If it was once formed it would maintain itself. All communities divide themselves into the few and the many. The first are the rich and well born, the other the mass of the people. The voice of the people has been said to be the voice of God ; and however generally this maxim has been quoted and believed, it is not true in fact. The people are turbulent and changing ; they seldom judge or determine right. Give therefore to the first class a distinct, permanent share in the government. They will check the unsteadiness of the second, and as they cannot receive any advantage by a change, they therefore will ever maintain good government. Can a democratic assembly, who annually revolve in the mass of the people, be supposed steadily to pursue the public good? Nothing but a permanent body can check the imprudence of democracy. Their turbulent and uncontrouling disposition requires checks. The Senate of New York, although chosen for four years, we have found to be inefficient. Will, on the Virginia plan, a continuance of seven years do it ? It is admitted that you cannot have a good executive upon a democratic plan. See the excellency of the British executive—he is placed above temptation—he can have no distinct interests from the public welfare. Nothing short of such an executive can be efficient. The weak side of a republican government is the danger of foreign influence. This is unavoidable, unless it is so constructed as to bring forward its first characters in its support. I am therefore for a general government, yet would wish to go the full length of republican principles.

Let one body of the Legislature be constituted during good behaviour or life.

Let one Executive be appointed who dares execute his powers.

It may be asked is this a republican system ? It is strictly so, as long as they remain elective.

And let me observe, that an Executive is less dangerous to the liberties of the people when in office during life, than for seven years.

It may be said this constitutes an elective monarchy ? Pray what is a monarchy ? May not the Governors of the respective States be considered in that light ? But by making the Executive subject to impeachment, the term monarchy cannot apply. These elective monarchs have produced tumults in Rome, and are equally dangerous to peace in Poland ; but this cannot apply to the mode in which I would propose the election. Let electors be appointed in each of the States to elect the Executive—[*Here Mr. H. produced his plan, a copy whereof is hereunto annexed*] [1] to consist of two branches—and I would give them the unlimited power of passing *all laws* without exception. The Assembly to be elected for three years by the people in districts—the Senate to be elected by electors to be chosen for that purpose by the people, and to remain in office during life. The Executive to have the power of negativing all laws—to make war or peace with the advice of the Senate—to make treaties with their advice, but to have the sole direction of all military operations, and to send ambassadors and appoint all military officers, and to pardon all offenders, treason excepted, unless by advice of the Senate. On his death or removal, the President of the Senate to officiate, with the same powers, until another is elected. Supreme judicial officers to be appointed by the Executive and the Senate. The Legislature to appoint courts in each State, so as to make the State governments unnecessary to it.

All State laws to be absolutely void which contravene the general laws. An officer to be appointed in each State to have a negative on all State laws. All the militia and the appointment of officers to be under the national government.

I confess that this plan and that from Virginia are very remote from the idea of the people. Perhaps the Jersey plan is nearest their expectation. But the people are gradually ripening in their opinions of government—they begin to be tired of an excess of democracy—and what even is the Virginia plan, but *pork still, with a little change of the sauce.*

[1] See Farrand, *Records of Federal Convention*, i. 291–3, iii. 617–30.

(g) *Corruption and Government.*

22 June (Yates)

The clause, to be ineligible to any office, etc.,[1] came next to be considered. . . .

Mr. MASON. It seems as if it was taken for granted, that all offices will be filled by the Executive, while I think many will remain in the gift of the Legislature. In either case, it is necessary to shut the door against corruption. If otherwise, they may make or multiply offices, in order to fill them. Are gentlemen in earnest when they suppose that this exclusion will prevent the first characters from coming forward? Are we not struck at seeing the luxury and venality which has already crept in among us? If not checked we shall have ambassadors to every petty State in Europe—the little republic of St. Marino not excepted. We must in the present system remove the temptation. I admire many parts of the British Constitution and government, but I detest their corruption. Why has the power of the crown so remarkably increased the last century? A stranger, by reading their laws, would suppose it considerably diminished; and yet, by the sole power of appointing the increased officers of government, corruption pervades every town and village in the kingdom. If such a restriction should abridge the right of election, it is still necessary, as it will prevent the people from ruining themselves; and will not the same causes here produce the same effects? I consider this clause as the corner-stone on which our liberties depend—and if we strike it out we are erecting a fabric for our destruction.

Mr. GORHAM [Mass.]. The corruption of the English government cannot be applied to America. This evil exists there in the venality of their boroughs; but even this corruption has its advantage, as it gives stability to their government. We do not know what the effect would be if Members of Parliament were excluded from offices. The great bulwark of our liberty is the frequency of elections, and their great danger is the septennial Parliaments.

Mr. HAMILTON. In all general questions which become the subjects of discussion, there are always some truths mixed

---

[1] See Randolph's Resolutions, No. 5, of 29 May.

with falsehoods. I confess there is danger where men are capable of holding two offices. Take mankind in general, they are vicious—their passions may be operated upon. We have been taught to reprobate the danger of influence in the British Government, without duly reflecting how far it was necessary to support a good government. We have taken up many ideas upon trust, and at last, pleased with our own opinions, establish them as undoubted truths. Hume's opinion of the British Constitution confirms the remark, that there is always a body of firm patriots, who often shake a corrupt administration. Take mankind as they are, and what are they governed by ? Their passions. There may be in every government a few choice spirits, who may act from more worthy motives. One great error is that we suppose mankind more honest than they are. Our prevailing passions are ambition and interest ; and it will ever be the duty of a wise government to avail itself of those passions, in order to make them subservient to the public good—for these ever induce us to action. Perhaps a few men in a State, may, from patriotic motives, or to display their talents, or to reap the advantage of public applause, step forward ; but if we adopt the clause we destroy the motive. I am therefore against all exclusions and refinements, except only in this case ; that when a member takes his seat, he should vacate every other office. It is difficult to put any exclusive regulation into effect. We must in some degree submit to the inconvenience.

The question was then put for striking out—4 ayes—4 noes —3 States divided. New York of the number.

(h) Senators' Term of Office.

26 June (Yates)

Mr. GORHAM. My motion for 4 years' continuance, was not put yesterday. I am still of opinion that classes will be necessary, but I would alter the time. I therefore move that the Senators be elected for 6 years, and that the rotation be triennial.[1]

Mr. PINCKNEY. I oppose the time, because of too long a continuance. The members will by this means be too long separated from their constituents, and will imbibe attach-

---

[1] Subsequently adopted. See Constitution, art. i, s. iii.

ments different from that of the State,[1] nor is there any danger that members, by a shorter duration of office, will not support the interest of the Union, or that the States will oppose the general interest. The State of South Carolina was never opposed in principle to Congress, nor thwarted their views in any case, except in the requisition of money, and then only for want of power to comply—for it was found there was not money enough in the State to pay their requisition.

Mr. READ moved that the term of nine years be inserted, in triennial rotation.

Mr. MADISON. We are now to determine whether the republican form shall be the basis of our government. I admit there is weight in the objection of the gentleman from South Carolina ; but no plan can steer clear of objections. That great powers are to be given, there is no doubt ; and that those powers may be abused is equally true. It is also probable that members may lose their attachments to the States which sent them—yet the first branch will control them in many of their abuses. But we are now forming a body on whose wisdom we mean to rely, and their permanency in office secures a proper field in which they may exert their firmness and knowledge. Democratic communities may be unsteady, and be led to action by the impulses of the moment. Like individuals they may be sensible of their own weakness, and may desire the counsels and checks of friends to guard them against the turbulency and weakness of unruly passions. Such are the various pursuits of this life, that in all civilized countries, the interest of a community will be divided. There will be debtors and creditors,[2] and an unequal possession of property, and hence arises different views and different objects in government. This indeed is the ground-work of aristocracy ; and we find it blended in every government, both ancient and modern. Even where titles have survived property, we discover the noble beggar haughty and assuming.

The man who is possessed of wealth, who lolls on his sofa

---

[1] ' The States, he said, had different interests. Those of the southern and of South Carolina in particular, were different from the northern.' —Madison's notes of same speech.

[2] ' Farmers, merchants, and manufacturers ' inserted here in Madison's notes.

or rolls in his carriage, cannot judge of the wants or feelings of the day laborer.   The government we mean to erect is intended to last for ages.   The landed interest, at present, is prevalent ; but in process of time, when we approximate to the states and kingdoms of Europe ; when the number of landholders shall be comparatively small, through the various means of trade and manufactures, will not the landed interest be overbalanced in future elections, and unless wisely provided against, what will become of your government ?   In England, at this day, if elections were open to all classes of people, the property of the landed proprietors would be insecure.   An agrarian law would soon take place.   If these observations be just, our government ought to secure the permanent interests of the country against innovation.   Landholders ought to have a share in the government, to support these invaluable interests and to balance and check the other. They ought to be so constituted as to protect the minority of the opulent against the majority.   The Senate, therefore, ought to be this body ; and to answer these purposes, they ought to have permanency and stability.   Various have been the propositions ; but my opinion is, the longer they continue in office, the better will these views be answered.

Mr. SHERMAN.   The two objects of this body are permanency and safety to those who are to be governed.   A bad government is the worse for being long.   Frequent elections give security and even permanency.   In Connecticut we have existed 132 years under an annual government ; and as long as a man behaves himself well, he is never turned out of office.   Four years to the Senate is quite sufficient when you add to it the rotation proposed.

Mr. HAMILTON.   This question has already been considered in several points of view.   We are now forming a republican government.   Real liberty is neither found in despotism or the extremes of democracy, but in moderate governments.

Those who mean to form a solid republican government, ought to proceed to the confines of another government.[1]   As long as offices are open to all men, and no constitutional rank is established, it is pure republicanism.   But if we incline too

---

[1] ' He acknowledged himself not to think favorably of republican government ;   but addressed his remarks to those who did think favorably of it, in order to prevail on them to tone their government as high as possible.'—Madison.

much to democracy, we shall soon shoot into a monarchy. The difference of property is already great amongst us. Commerce and industry will still increase the disparity. Your government must meet this state of things, or combinations will in process of time, undermine your system. What was the tribunitial power of Rome ? It was instituted by the plebeans as a guard against the patricians. But was this a sufficient check ? No—the only distinction which remained at Rome was, at last, between the rich and poor. The gentleman from Connecticut forgets that the democratic body is already secure in a representation. As to Connecticut, what were the little objects of their government before the revolution ? Colonial concerns merely. They ought now to act on a more extended scale, and dare they do this ? Dare they collect the taxes and requisitions of Congress ? Such a government may do well, if they do not tax, and this is precisely their situation.

Mr. GERRY. It appears to me that the American people have the greatest aversion to monarchy, and the nearer our government approaches to it, the less chance have we for their approbation. Can gentlemen suppose that the reported system can be approved of by them ?[1] Demagogues are the great pests of our government, and have occasioned most of our distresses. If four years are insufficient, a future convention may lengthen the time.

Mr. WILSON. The motion is now for nine years, and a triennial rotation. Every nation attends to its foreign intercourse—to support its commerce—to prevent foreign contempt and to make war and peace. Our Senate will be possessed of these powers, and therefore ought to be dignified and permanent. What is the reason that Great Britain does not enter into a commercial treaty with us ? Because Congress has not the power to enforce its observance. But give them those powers, and give them the stability proposed by the motion, and they will have more permanency than a monarchical government. The great objection of many is,

[1] ' He did not deny the position of Mr. Madison that the majority will generally violate justice when they have an interest in so doing ; but he did not think there was any such temptation in this country. Our situation was different from that of Great Britain, and the great majority of lands yet to be parcelled out and settled would very much prolong the difference.'—Madison.

that this duration would give birth to views inconsistent with the interests of the union. This can have no weight, if the triennial rotation is adopted; and this plan may possibly tend to conciliate the minds of the members of the Convention on this subject, which have varied more than on any other question.

The question was then put on Mr. Read's motion, and lost, 8 noes—3 ayes.

The question on 5 years, and a biennial rotation, was carried—7 ayes—4 noes. New York in the minority.

(i) *Sectional Interests and the Federal Ratio.*

11 July (Madison)

Mr. Randolph's motion requiring the Legislature to take a periodical census for the purpose of redressing inequalities in the representation, was resumed.

Mr. SHERMAN was against shackling the Legislature too much. We ought to choose wise and good men, and then confide in them.

Mr. MASON. The greater the difficulty we find in fixing a proper rule of representation, the more unwilling ought we to be, to throw the task from ourselves, on the General Legislature. He did not object to the conjectural ratio which was to prevail in the outset; but considered a revision from time to time according to some permanent and precise standard as essential to the fair representation required in the first branch. According to the present population of America, the northern part of it had a right to preponderate, and he could not deny it. But he wished it not to preponderate hereafter when the reason no longer continued. From the nature of man we may be sure that those who have power in their hands will not give it up while they can retain it. On the contrary we know they will always when they can rather increase it. If the southern States therefore should have three-quarters of the people of America within their limits, the Northern will hold fast the majority of representatives. One quarter will govern the three-quarters. The southern States will complain: but they may complain from generation to generation without redress. Unless some principle therefore which will do justice to them hereafter shall be inserted in the Constitution, disagreeable as the declaration was to him, he must declare he could neither vote for the system here, nor support it in his State. Strong objections had been drawn from the danger to the Atlantic interests from new western States. Ought we to sacrifice what we know to be right in itself, lest it should prove favorable to States which are not yet in existence ? If the western States are to be admitted into the Union, as they arise, they must, he would repeat, be treated as equals, and subjected to no degrading discriminations. They will have the same pride and other passions which we have, and will either not unite with or will speedily revolt from the Union, if they are not in all respects placed on an equal footing with their brethren. It has been said they will be poor, and unable to make equal contributions to the general treasury. He did not know but that in time they would be both more numerous and more wealthy than their Atlantic brethren. The extent and fertility of their soil made this probable ; and though Spain might for a time deprive them of the natural outlet for their productions, yet she will, because she must, finally yield to their demands. He urged that numbers of inhabitants, though not always a precise standard of wealth, was sufficiently so for every substantial purpose.

Mr. WILLIAMSON was for making it the duty of the Legislature to do what was right and not leaving it at liberty to do or not do it. He moved that Mr. Randolph's proposition be postponed in order to consider the following : ' that in order to ascertain the alterations that may happen in the population and wealth of the several States, a census shall be taken of the free white inhabitants and three-fifths of those of other descriptions on the first year after this Government shall have been adopted, and every   year thereafter ; and that the representation be regulated accordingly.'

Mr. RANDOLPH agreed that Mr. Williamson's proposition should stand in the place of his. He observed that the ratio fixt for the first meeting was a mere conjecture, that it placed the power in the hands of that part of America, which could not always be entitled to it ; that this power would not be voluntarily renounced ; and that it was consequently the duty of the Convention to secure its renunciation when justice might so require ; by some constitutional provisions. If equality between great and small States be inadmissible, because in that case unequal numbers of constituents would be represented by equal numbers of votes ; was it not equally inadmissible that a larger and more populous district of America should hereafter have less representation, than a smaller and less populous district. If a fair representation of the people be not secured, the injustice of the Government will shake it to its foundations. What relates to suffrage is justly stated by the celebrated Montesquieu as a fundamental article in republican governments. If the danger suggested by Mr. Gouverneur Morris be real, of advantage being taken of the Legislature in pressing moments, it was an additional reason for tying their hands in such a manner that they could not sacrifice their trust to momentary considerations. Congress have pledged the public faith to new States, that they shall be admitted on equal terms.[1] They never would nor ought to accede on any other. The census must be taken under the direction of the General Legislature. The States will be too much interested to take an impartial one for themselves.

Mr. Butler and General [C. C.] Pinckney insisted that blacks be included in the rule of representation, *equally* with the whites : and for that purpose moved that the words ' three-fifths ' be struck out.

Mr. Gerry thought that three-fifths of them was to say the least the full proportion that could be admitted.

Mr. Gorham. This ratio was fixed by Congress as a rule of taxation. Then it was urged by the delegates representing the States having slaves that the blacks were still more inferior to freemen. At present when the ratio of representation is to be established, we are assured that they are equal to freemen. The arguments on the former occasion had convinced him that three-fifths was pretty near the just proportion, and he should vote according to the same opinion now.

Mr. Butler insisted that the labour of a slave in South Carolina was as productive and valuable as that of a freeman in Massachusetts, that as wealth was the great means of defence and utility to the nation they were equally valuable to it with freemen ; and that consequently an equal representation ought to be allowed for them in a government which was instituted principally for the protection of property, and was itself to be supported by property.

---

[1] The Resolution of 1780, see above, p. 203.

Mr. MASON could not agree to the motion, notwithstanding it was favorable to Virginia, because he thought it unjust. It was certain that the slaves were valuable, as they raised the value of land, increased the exports and imports, and of course the revenue ; would supply the means of feeding and supporting an army, and might in cases of emergency become themselves soldiers. As in these important respects they were useful to the community at large, they ought not to be excluded from the estimate of representation. He could not, however, regard them as equal to freemen, and could not vote for them as such. He added as worthy of remark, that the southern States have this peculiar species of property, over and above the other species of property common to all the States.

Mr. WILLIAMSON reminded Mr. Gorham that if the southern States contended for the inferiority of blacks to whites when taxation was in view, the eastern States on the same occasion contended for their equality. He did not, however, either then or now, concur in either extreme, but approved of the ratio of three-fifths.

On Mr. Butler's motion for considering blacks as equal to whites in the apportionment of representation.

Mass. no. Conn. no. [N. Y. not on floor.] N. J. no. Pa. no. Del. ay. Md. no. Va. no. N. C. no. S. C. ay. Geo. ay.

Mr. GOUVERNEUR MORRIS said he had several objections to the proposition of Mr. Williamson. 1. It fettered the legislature too much. 2. It would exclude some States altogether who would not have a sufficient number to entitle them to a single representative. 3. It will not consist with the resolution passed on Saturday last authorising the Legislature to adjust the representation from time to time on the principles of population and wealth, or with the principles of equity. If slaves were to be considered as inhabitants, not as wealth, then the said resolution would not be pursued : if as wealth, then why is not other wealth but slaves included ? These objections may perhaps be removed by amendments. His great objection was that the number of inhabitants was not a proper standard of wealth. The amazing difference between the comparative numbers and wealth of different countries, rendered all reasoning superfluous on the subject. Numbers might with greater propriety be deemed a measure of strength, than of wealth ; yet the late defence made by Great Britain against her numerous enemies proved in the clearest manner, that it is entirely fallacious even in this respect.

Mr. KING thought there was great force in the objections of Mr. Gouverneur Morris : he would however accede to the proposition for the sake of doing something.

Mr. RUTLEDGE contended for the admission of wealth in the estimate by which representation should be regulated. The western States will not be able to contribute in proportion to their numbers ; they should not therefore be represented in that proportion. The Atlantic States will not concur in such a plan. He moved that ' at the end of   years after the first meeting of the Legislature, and of every
years thereafter, the Legislature shall proportion the Representation according to the principles of wealth and population '.

. . . .

Mr. GOUVERNEUR MORRIS. The arguments of others and his own reflections had led him to a very different conclusion. If we can't agree on a rule that will be just at this time, how can we expect to find one that will be just in all times to come ? Surely those who come after us will judge better of things present than we can of things future. He could not persuade himself that numbers would be a just rule at any time. The remarks of [Mr. Mason] relative to the western country had not changed his opinion on that head. Among other objections, it must be apparent they would not be able to furnish men equally enlightened, to share in the administration of our common interests. The busy haunts of men, not the remote wilderness, was the proper school of political talents. If the western people get the power into their hands, they will ruin the Atlantic interests. The back members are always most averse to the best measures. He mentioned the case of Pennsylvania formerly. The lower part of the State had the power in the first instance. They kept it in their own hands, and the country was the better for it.[1] Another objection with him against admitting the blacks into the census, was that the people of Pennsylvania would revolt at the idea of being put on a footing with slaves. They would reject any plan that was to have such an effect. Two objections had been raised against leaving the adjustment of the representation from time to time to the discretion of the

---

[1] See above, p. 9.

Legislature. The first was they would be unwilling to revise it at all. The second, that by referring to *wealth* they would be bound by a rule which if willing, they would be unable to execute. The first objection distrusts their fidelity. But if their duty, their honor and their oaths will not bind them, let us not put into their hands our liberty and all our other great interests : let us have no Government at all. 2. If these ties will bind them, we need not distrust the practicability of the rule. It was followed in part by the committee in the apportionment of representatives yesterday reported to the House. The best course that could be taken would be to leave the interests of the people to the representatives of the people.

Mr. MADISON was not a little surprised to hear this implicit confidence urged by a member who on all occasions had inculcated so strongly the political depravity of men, and the necessity of checking one vice and interest by opposing to them another vice and interest. If the Representatives of the people would be bound by the ties he had mentioned, what need was there of a Senate ? What of a revisionary power ? But his reasoning was not only inconsistent with his former reasoning, but with itself. At the same time that he recommended this implicit confidence to the southern States in the northern majority, he was still more zealous in exhorting all to a jealousy of a western majority. To reconcile the gentleman with himself, it must be imagined that he determined the human character by the points of the compass. The truth was that all men having power ought to be distrusted to a certain degree. The case of Pennsylvania had been mentioned, where it was admitted that those who were possessed of the power in the original settlement, never admitted the new settlements to a due share of it. England was a still more striking example. The power there had long been in the hands of the boroughs, of the minority ; who had opposed and defeated every reform which had been attempted. Virginia was in a less degree another example. With regard to the western States, he was clear and firm in opinion that no unfavorable distinctions were admissible either in point of justice or policy. He thought also that the hope of contributions to the Treasury from them had been much underrated. Future contributions it seemed to be understood on all hands would be principally levied on imports and exports. The extent and fertility of the western soil would for a long time give to agriculture a preference over manufactures. Trials would be repeated till some articles could be raised from it that would bear a transportation to places where they could be exchanged for imported manufactures. Whenever the Mississippi should be opened to them, which would of necessity be the case, as soon as their population would subject them to any considerable share of the public burden, imposts on their trade could be collected with less expence and greater certainty, than on that of the Atlantic States. In the meantime, as their supplies must pass thro' the Atlantic States, their contributions would be levied in the same manner with those of the Atlantic States. He could not agree that any substantial objection lay against fixing numbers for the perpetual standard of Representation. It was said that Representation and taxation were to go together ; that taxation and wealth ought to go together, that population and wealth were not measures of each other. He admitted that in different climates, under different forms of Government, and in different stages of civilization, the inference was perfectly just. He would admit that in no situation numbers of inhabitants were an accurate measure of wealth. He contended however that in the United States it was sufficiently so for the object in contemplation. Altho' their climate varied considerably, yet as the governments, the laws, and the manners of all were nearly the same, and the intercourse between different parts perfectly free, population, industry, arts, and the value of labour, would constantly tend to equalize themselves. The value of labour might be considered as the principal criterion of wealth and ability to support taxes ; and this would find its level in different places where the intercourse should be easy and free, with as much certainty as the value of money or any other thing. Wherever labour would yield most people would resort, till the competition should destroy the inequality. Hence it is that the people are constantly swarming from the more to the less populous places—from Europe to America, from the northern and middle parts of the United States to the southern and western. They go where land is cheaper, because there labour is dearer. If it be true that the same quantity of produce raised on the banks of the Ohio is of less value than on the Delaware, it is also true that the same labor will raise twice or thrice the quantity in the former, that it will raise in the latter situation.

Col. MASON agreed with Mr. Gouverneur Morris that we ought to leave the interests of the people to the representatives of the people : but the objection was that the Legislature would cease to be the representatives of the people. It would continue so no longer than the States now containing a majority of the people should retain that majority. As soon as the southern and western population should predominate, which must happen in a few years, the power would be in the hands of the minority, and would never be yielded to the majority, unless provided for by the Constitution.

On the question for postponing Mr. Williamson's motion, in order to consider that of Mr. Rutledge, it passed in the negative. Mass. ay. Cont. no. N. J. no. Pa. ay. Del. ay. Md. no. Va. no. N. C. no. S. C. ay. Geo. ay.

On the question on the first clause of Mr. Williamson's motion as to taking a census of the *free* inhabitants, it passed in the affirmative. Mass. ay. Cont. ay. N. J. ay. Pa. ay. Del. no. Md. no. Va. ay. N. C. ay. S. C. no. Geo. no.

The next clause as to three-fifths of the negroes being considered,

Mr. KING, being much opposed to fixing numbers as the rule of representation, was particularly so on account of the blacks. He thought the admission of them along with whites at all, would excite great discontents among the States having no slaves. He had never said as to any particular point that he would in no event acquiesce in and support it ; but he would say that if in any case such a declaration was to be made by him, it would be in this. He remarked that in the temporary allotment of Representatives made by the committee, the southern States had received more than the number of their white and three-fifths of their black inhabitants entitled them to.

.   .   .   .

Mr. WILSON did not well see on what principle the admission of blacks in the proportion of three-fifths could be explained. Are they admitted as citizens ? then why are they not admitted on an equality with white citizens ? are they admitted as property ? then why is not other property admitted into the computation ? These were difficulties however which he thought must be overruled by the necessity of compromise. He had some apprehensions also from the tendency of the blending of the blacks with the whites, to give disgust to the people of Pennsylvania as had been intimated by his colleague. But he differed from him in thinking numbers of inhabitants so incorrect a measure of wealth. He had seen the western settlements of Pennsylvania, and on a comparison of them with the city of Philadelphia could discover little other difference, than that property was more unequally divided among individuals here than there. Taking the same number in the aggregate in the two situations he believed there would be little difference in their wealth and ability to contribute to the public wants.

Mr. GOUVERNEUR MORRIS was compelled to declare himself reduced to the dilemma of doing injustice to the southern States or to human nature, and he must therefore do it to the former. For he could never agree to give such encouragement to the slave trade as would be given by allowing them a representation for their negroes, and he did not believe those States would ever confederate on terms that would deprive them of that trade.

On the question for agreeing to include three-fifths of the blacks :

Mass. no. Cont. ay. N. J. no. Pa. no. Del. no. Md. no. Va. ay. N. C. ay. S. C. no. Geo. ay.[1]

(j) *Qualifications for Suffrage.*

7 August (Madison)

Art. iv, Sect. 1 [2] was then taken up.

Mr. GOUVERNEUR MORRIS moved to strike out the last member of the section beginning with the words ' qualifications of electors ', in order that some other provision might be substituted which would restrain the right of suffrage to freeholders.

Mr. FITZSIMONS [Penn.] seconded the motion.

Mr. WILLIAMSON was opposed to it.

Mr. WILSON. This part of the report was well considered by the Committee, and he did not think it could be changed

---

[1] But subsequently carried : see Constitution, art. i, s. ii, § 3.

[2] Of the report of the Committee of Detail. Equivalent to art. i, s. ii, § 1 of the Constitution.

for the better. It was difficult to form any uniform rule of qualifications for all the States. Unnecessary innovations he thought too should be avoided. It would be very hard and disagreeable for the same persons at the same time to vote for Representatives in the State Legislature and to be excluded from a vote for those in the National Legislature.

Mr. GOUVERNEUR MORRIS. Such a hardship would be neither great nor novel. The people are accustomed to it and not dissatisfied with it in several of the States. In some the qualifications are different for the choice of the Governor and of the Representatives ; in others for different houses of the Legislature. Another objection against the clause as it stands is that it makes the qualifications of the National Legislature depend on the will of the States, which he thought not proper.

Mr. ELLSWORTH [Conn.] thought the qualifications of the electors stood on the most proper footing. The right of suffrage was a tender point, and strongly guarded by most of the State Constitutions. The people will not readily subscribe to the National Constitution if it should subject them to be disfranchised. The States are the best judges of the circumstances and temper of their own people.

Col. MASON. The force of habit is certainly not attended to by those gentlemen who wish for innovations on this point. Eight or nine States have extended the right of suffrage beyond the freeholders ; what will the people there say if they should be disfranchised ? A power to alter the qualifications would be a dangerous power in the hands of the Legislature.

Mr. BUTLER. There is no right of which the people are more jealous than that of suffrage. Abridgments of it tend to the same revolution as in Holland where they have at length thrown all power into the hands of the Senates, who fill up vacancies themselves, and form a rank aristocracy.

Mr. DICKINSON had a very different idea of the tendency of vesting the right of suffrage in the freeholders of the country. He considered them as the best guardians of liberty ; and the restriction of the right to them as a necessary defence against the dangerous influence of those multitudes without property and without principle with which our country like all others, will in time abound. As to the unpopularity of the innovation, it was in his opinion chimerical. The great mass of our citizens is composed at this time of freeholders, and will be pleased with it.

Mr. ELLSWORTH. How shall the freehold be defined? Ought not every man who pays a tax, to vote for the representative who is to levy and dispose of his money? Shall the wealthy merchants and manufacturers, who will bear a full share of the public burdens, be not allowed a voice in the imposition of them? Taxation and representation ought to go together.

Mr. GOUVERNEUR MORRIS. He had long learned not to be the dupe of words. The sound of aristocracy, therefore, had no effect on him. It was the thing, not the name, to which he was opposed, and one of his principal objections to the Constitution as it is now before us, is that it threatens this country with an aristocracy. The aristocracy will grow out of the House of Representatives. Give the votes to people who have no property, and they will sell them to the rich who will be able to buy them. We should not confine our attention to the present moment. The time is not distant when this country will abound with mechanics and manufacturers who will receive their bread from their employers. Will such men be the secure and faithful guardians of liberty? Will they be the impregnable barrier against aristocracy? He was as little duped by the association of the words ' taxation and representation '. The man who does not give his vote freely is not represented. It is the man who dictates the vote. Children do not vote. Why? because they want prudence, because they have no will of their own. The ignorant and the dependent can be as little trusted with the public interest. He did not conceive the difficulty of defining ' freeholders ' to be insuperable. Still less, that the restriction could be unpopular. Nine-tenths of the people are at present freeholders, and these will certainly be pleased with it. As to merchants, etc., if they have wealth and value the right, they can acquire it. If not, they don't deserve it.

Col. MASON. We all feel too strongly the remains of antient prejudices, and view things too much through a British medium. A freehold is the qualification in England, and hence it is imagined to be the only proper one. The true idea in his opinion was that every man having evidence of attachment to and permanent common interest with the society ought to share in all its rights and privileges. Was this qualification restrained to freeholders ? Does no other kind of property but land evidence a common interest in the proprietor ? Does nothing besides property mark a permanent attachment ? Ought the merchant, the monied man, the parent of a number of children whose fortunes are to be pursued in his own country, to be viewed as suspicious characters, and unworthy to be trusted with the common rights of their fellow citizens ?

Mr. MADISON. The right of suffrage is certainly one of the fundamental articles of republican government, and ought not to be left to be regulated by the Legislature. A gradual abridgment of this right has been the mode in which aristocracies have been built on the ruins of popular forms. Whether the Constitutional qualification ought to be a freehold, would with him depend much on the probable reception such a change would meet with in States where the right was now exercised by every description of people. In several of the States a freehold was now the qualification. Viewing the subject in its merits alone, the freeholders of the country would be the safest depositories of Republican liberty. In future times a great majority of the people will not only be without landed, but any other sort of, property. These will either combine under the influence of their common situation ; in which case, the rights of property and the public liberty will not be secure in their hands : or what is more probable, they will become the tools of opulence and ambition, in which case there will be equal danger on another side. The example of England has been misconceived [by Col. Mason]. A very small proportion of the Representatives are there chosen by freeholders. The greatest part are chosen by the cities and boroughs, in many of which the qualification of suffrage is as low as it is in any one of the United States, and it was in the boroughs and cities rather than the counties, that bribery most prevailed, and the influence of the Crown on elections was most dangerously exerted.

Dr. FRANKLIN. It is of great consequence that we should not depress the virtue and public spirit of our common people ; of which they displayed a great deal during the war, and which contributed principally to the favorable issue of it. He related the honorable refusal of the American seamen who were carried in great numbers into the British prisons during the war, to redeem themselves from misery or to seek their fortunes, by entering on board the ships of the enemies to their country; contrasting their patriotism with a contemporary instance in which the British seamen made prisoners by the Americans, readily entered on the ships of the latter on being promised a share of the prizes that might be made out of their own country. This proceeded he said from the different manner in which the common people were treated in America and Great Britain. He did not think that the elected had any right in any case to narrow the privileges of the electors. He quoted as arbitrary the British statute setting forth the danger of tumultuous meetings, and under that pretext narrowing the right of suffrage to persons having freeholds of a certain value; observing that this statute was soon followed by another under the succeeding Parliament subjecting the people who had no votes to peculiar labors and hardships. He was persuaded also that such a restriction as was proposed would give great uneasiness in the populous States. The sons of a substantial farmer, not being themselves freeholders, would not be pleased at being disfranchised, and there are a great many persons of that description.

Mr. MERCER [Md.]. The Constitution is objectionable in many points, but in none more than the present. He objected to the footing on which the qualification was put, but particularly to the mode of election by the people. The people can not know and judge of the characters of candidates. The worse possible choice will be made. He quoted the case of the Senate in Virginia as an example in point. The people in towns can unite their votes in favor of one favorite; and by that means always prevail over the people of the country, who being dispersed will scatter their votes among a variety of candidates.

Mr. RUTLEDGE thought the idea of restraining the right of suffrage to the freeholders a very unadvised one. It would create division among the people and make enemies of all those who should be excluded.

On the question for striking out as moved by Mr. Gouverneur Morris, from the word ' qualifications ' to the end of the article,

N. H. no. Mass. no. Conn. no. Pa. no. Del. ay. Md. divided. Va. no. N. C. no. S. C. no. Geo. not present.

(k) *Foreigners and the Senate.*

9 August (Madison)

Art. v, sect. 3 [1] was then taken up.

Mr. GOUVERNEUR MORRIS moved to insert 14 instead of 4 years citizenship as a qualification for Senators : urging the danger of admitting strangers into our public councils. Mr. PINCKNEY seconds him.

Mr. ELLSWORTH was opposed to the motion as discouraging meritorious aliens from emigrating to this country.

Mr. PINCKNEY. As the Senate is to have the power of making treaties and managing our foreign affairs, there is peculiar danger and impropriety in opening its door to those who have foreign attachments. He quoted the jealousy of the Athenians on this subject, who made it death for any stranger to intrude his voice into their legislative proceedings.

Col. MASON highly approved of the policy of the motion. Were it not that many, not natives of this country, had acquired great credit during the Revolution, he should be for restraining the eligibility into the Senate to natives.

Mr. MADISON was not averse to some restrictions on this subject, but could never agree to the proposed amendment. He thought any restriction however in the Constitution unnecessary, and improper. Unnecessary, because the National Legislature is to have the right of regulating naturalization, and can by virtue thereof fix different periods of residence as conditions of enjoying different privileges of citizenship ; improper, because it will give a tincture of illiberality to the Constitution, because it will put out of the power of the National Legislature even by special acts of naturalization to confer the full rank of citizens on meritorious strangers, and because it will discourage the most desireable class of people from emigrating to the United States. Should the proposed Constitution have the intended effect of giving stability and reputation to our governments, great numbers of respectable Europeans : men who love liberty and wish to partake its blessings, will be ready to transfer their fortunes hither. All such would feel the mortification of being marked with suspicious incapacitations,

---

[1] Of the report of the Committee of Detail. Equivalent to art. i, s. iii, § 3 of the Constitution.

though they should not covet the public honors. He was not apprehensive that any dangerous number of strangers would be appointed by the State Legislatures, if they were left at liberty to do so : nor that foreign powers would make use of strangers as instruments for their purposes. Their bribes would be expended on men whose circumstances would rather stifle than excite jealousy and watchfulness in the public.

Mr. Butler was decidedly opposed to the admission of foreigners without a long residence in the country. They bring with them, not only attachments to other countries, but ideas of government so distinct from ours that in every point of view they are dangerous. He acknowledged that if he himself had been called into public life within a short time after his coming to America, his foreign habits, opinions, and attachments would have rendered him an improper agent in public affairs. He mentioned the great strictness observed in Great Britain on this subject.

Dr. Franklin was not against a reasonable time, but should be very sorry to see anything like illiberality inserted in the Constitution. The people in Europe are friendly to this country. Even in the country with which we have been lately at war, we have now and had during the war, a great many friends, not only among the people at large, but in both Houses of Parliament. In every other country in Europe all the people are our friends. We found in the course of the Revolution that many strangers served us faithfully, and that many natives took part against their country. When foreigners, after looking about for some other country in which they can obtain more happiness, give a preference to ours, it is a proof of attachment which ought to excite our confidence and affection.

Mr. Randolph did not know but it might be problematical whether emigrations to this country were on the whole useful or not : but he could never agree to the motion for disabling them for fourteen years to participate in the public honours. He reminded the Convention of the language held by our patriots during the Revolution and the principles laid down in all our American Constitutions. Many foreigners may have fixed their fortunes among us under the faith of these invitations. All persons under this description, with all others who would be affected by such a regulation, would enlist themselves under the banners of hostility to the proposed system. He would go as far as seven years, but no farther.

Mr. WILSON said he rose with feelings which were perhaps peculiar ; mentioning the circumstance of his not being a native, and the possibility, if the ideas of some gentlemen should be pursued, of his being incapacitated from holding a place under the very Constitution which he had shared in the trust of making. He remarked the illiberal complexion which the motion would give to the system, and the effect which a good system would have in inviting meritorious foreigners among us, and the discouragement and mortification they must feel from the degrading discrimination, now proposed. He had himself experienced this mortification. On his removal into Maryland, he found himself, from defect of residence, under certain legal incapacities which never ceased to produce chagrin, though he assuredly did not desire and would not have accepted the offices to which they related. To be appointed to a place may be matter of indifference. To be incapable of being appointed, is a circumstance grating and mortifying.

Mr. GOUVERNEUR MORRIS. The lesson we are taught is that we should be governed as much by our reason, and as little by our feelings as possible. What is the language of reason on this subject ? That we should not be polite at the expence of prudence. There was a moderation in all things. It is said that some tribes of Indians carried their hospitality so far as to offer to strangers their wives and daughters. Was this a proper model for us ? He would admit them to his house, he would invite them to his table, would provide for them comfortable lodgings ; but would not carry the complaisance so far as to bed them with his wife. He would let them worship at the same altar, but did not choose to make priests of them. He ran over the privileges which emigrants would enjoy among us, though they should be deprived of that of being eligible to the great offices of government ; observing that they exceeded the privileges allowed to foreigners in any part of the world ; and that as every society from a great nation down to a club had the right of declaring the conditions on which new members should be admitted, there could be no room for complaint. As to those philosophical gentlemen, those citizens of the world as they call themselves, he owned he did not wish to see any of them in our public councils. He would not trust them. The men who can shake off their attachments to their own country can never love any other. These attachments are the wholesome prejudices which uphold all governments. Admit a Frenchman into your Senate, and he will study to increase the commerce of France : an Englishman, and he will feel an equal bias in favor of that of England. It has been said that the Legislatures will not chuse foreigners, at least improper ones. There was no knowing what Legislatures would do. Some appointments made by them proved that everything ought to be apprehended from the cabals practised on such occasions. He mentioned the case of a foreigner who left this State in disgrace, and worked himself into an appointment from another to Congress.[1]

(*l*) *Slave Trade and Navigation Acts.*

22 August (Madison)

Art. vii, sect. 4,[2] was resumed. Mr. SHERMAN was for leaving the clause as it stands. He disapproved of the slave trade ; yet as the States were now possessed of the right to import slaves, as the public good did not require it to be taken from them, and as it was expedient to have as few objections as possible to the proposed scheme of government, he thought it best to leave the matter as we find it. He observed that the abolition of slavery seemed to be going on in the United States, and that the good sense of the several States would probably by degrees compleat it. He urged on the Convention the necessity of despatching its business.

Col. MASON. This infernal trafic originated in the avarice of British merchants. The British Government constantly checked the attempts of Virginia to put a stop to it. The present question concerns not the importing States alone but the whole Union. The evil of having slaves was experienced during the late war. Had slaves been treated as they might have been by the enemy, they would have proved dangerous instruments in their hands. But their folly dealt by the slaves, as it did by the tories. He mentioned the dangerous

---

[1] The Convention compromised on a period of nine years.
[2] Of the report of the Committee of Detail. Equivalent to art. i, s. ix, § 1 of the Constitution, without the limitation to 1808.

insurrections of the slaves in Greece and Sicily ; and the instructions given by Cromwell to the Commissioners sent to Virginia, to arm the servants and slaves, in case other means of obtaining its submission should fail. Maryland and Virginia he said had already prohibited the importation of slaves expressly. North Carolina had done the same in substance. All this would be in vain if South Carolina and Georgia be at liberty to import. The western people are already calling out for slaves for their new lands, and will fill that country with slaves if they can be got thro' South Carolina and Georgia. Slavery discourages arts and manufactures. The poor despise labor when performed by slaves. They prevent the immigration of whites, who really enrich and strengthen a country. They produce the most pernicious effect on manners. Every master of slaves is born a petty tyrant. They bring the judgment of Heaven on a country. As nations cannot be rewarded or punished in the next world, they must be in this. By an inevitable chain of causes and effects, Providence punishes national sins, by national calamities. He lamented that some of our eastern brethren had from a lust of gain embarked in this nefarious traffic. As to the States being in possession of the right to import, this was the case with many other rights, now to be properly given up. He held it essential in every point of view that the General Government should have power to prevent the increase of slavery.

Mr. ELLSWORTH. As he had never owned a slave could not judge of the effects of slavery on character : he said, however, that if it was to be considered in a moral light we ought to go farther and free those already in the country. As slaves also multiply so fast in Virginia and Maryland that it is cheaper to raise than import them, whilst in the sickly rice swamps foreign supplies are necessary ; if we go no farther than is urged, we shall be unjust towards South Carolina and Georgia. Let us not intermeddle. As population increases, poor laborers will be so plenty as to render slaves useless. Slavery in time will not be a speck in our country. Provision is already made in Connecticut for abolishing it, and the abolition has already taken place in Massachussets. As to the danger of insurrections from foreign influence, that will become a motive to kind treatment of the slaves.

Mr. PINCKNEY. If slavery be wrong, it is justified by the

example of all the world. He cited the case of Greece, Rome, and other antient States ; the sanction given by France, England, Holland, and other modern States. In all ages one half of mankind have been slaves. If the southern States were let alone they will probably of themselves stop importations. He would himself as a citizen of South Carolina vote for it. An attempt to take away the right as proposed will produce serious objections to the Constitution, which he wished to see adopted.

General PINCKNEY declared it to be his firm opinion that if himself and all his colleagues were to sign the Constitution and use their personal influence, it would be of no avail towards obtaining the assent of their constituents. South Carolina and Georgia cannot do without slaves. As to Virginia, she will gain by stopping the importations. Her slaves will rise in value, and she has more than she wants. It would be unequal to require South Carolina and Georgia to confederate on such unequal terms. He said the royal assent before the Revolution had never been refused to South Carolina as to Virginia. He contended that the importation of slaves would be for the interest of the whole Union. The more slaves, the more produce to employ the carrying trade, the more consumption also ; and the more of this, the more of revenue for the common treasury. He admitted it to be reasonable that slaves should be dutied like other imports, but should consider a rejection of the clause as an exclusion of South Carolina from the Union.

Mr. BALDWIN had conceived national objects alone to be before the Convention, not such as like the present were of a local nature. Georgia was decided on this point. That State has always hitherto supposed a General Government to be the pursuit of the central States, who wished to have a vortex for every thing, that her distance would preclude her from equal advantage, and that she could not prudently purchase it by yielding national powers. From this it might be understood in what light she would view an attempt to abridge one of her favorite prerogatives. If left to herself, she may probably put a stop to the evil. As one ground for this conjecture, he took notice of the sect of   which he said was a respectable class of people, who carried their ethics beyond the mere equality of men, extending their humanity to the claims of the whole animal creation.

Mr. WILSON observed that if South Carolina and Georgia were themselves disposed to get rid of the importation of slaves in a short time as had been suggested, they would never refuse to unite because the importation might be prohibited. As the section now stands, all articles imported are to be taxed. Slaves alone are exempt. This is in fact a bounty on that article.

Mr. GERRY thought we had nothing to do with the conduct of the States as to slaves, but ought to be careful not to give any sanction to it.

Mr. DICKINSON considered it as inadmissible on every principle of honor and safety that the importation of slaves should be authorised to the States by the Constitution. The true question was whether the national happiness would be promoted or impeded by the importation, and this question ought to be left to the National Government, not to the States particularly interested. If England and France permit slavery, slaves are at the same time excluded from both those kingdoms. Greece and Rome were made unhappy by their slaves. He could not believe that the southern States would refuse to confederate on the account apprehended; especially as the power was not likely to be immediately exercised by the General Government.

.   .   .   .

Mr. RUTLEDGE. If the Convention thinks that North Carolina, South Carolina, and Georgia will ever agree to the plan, unless their right to import slaves be untouched, the expectation is vain. The people of those States will never be such fools as to give up so important an interest. He was strenuous against striking out the section, and seconded the motion of General Pinckney for a commitment.

Mr. GOUVERNEUR MORRIS wished the whole subject to be committed, including the clauses relating to taxes on exports and to a navigation act. These things may form a bargain among the northern and southern States.

Mr. BUTLER declared that he never would agree to the power of taxing exports.

Mr. SHERMAN said it was better to let the southern States import slaves than to part with them, if they made that a *sine qua non*. He was opposed to a tax on slaves imported as making the matter worse, because it implied they were *property*. He acknowledged that if the power of prohibiting the importation should be given to the General Government that it would be exercised. He thought it would be its duty to exercise the power.

Mr. READ was for the commitment provided the clause concerning taxes on exports should also be committed.

Mr. SHERMAN observed that that clause had been agreed to and therefore could not be committed.

Mr. RANDOLPH was for committing in order that some middle ground might, if possible, be found. He could never agree to the clause as it stands. He would sooner risk the Constitution. He dwelt on the dilemma to which the Convention was exposed. By agreeing to the clause, it would revolt the Quakers, the Methodists, and many others in the States having no slaves. On the other hand, two States might be lost to the Union. Let us then, he said, try the chance of a commitment.

On the question for committing the remaining part of Sect. 4 and 5 [1] of art. vii. N. H. no. Mass. abs. Conn. ay. N. J. ay. Pa. no. Del. no. Md. ay. Va. ay. N. C. ay. S. C. ay. Geo. ay.

Mr. PINCKNEY and Mr. LANGDON [N. H.] moved to commit sect. 6 as to [no] navigation act [being passed without assent] by two-thirds of each House.

Mr. GORHAM did not see the propriety of it. Is it meant to require a greater proportion of votes? He desired it to be remembered that the eastern States had no motive to Union but a commercial one. They were able to protect themselves. They were not afraid of external danger, and did not need the aid of the southern States.

Mr. WILSON wished for a commitment in order to reduce the proportion of votes required.

Mr. ELLSWORTH was for taking the plan as it is. This widening of opinions has a threatening aspect. If we do not agree on this middle and moderate ground, he was afraid we should lose two States, with such others as may be disposed to stand aloof, should fly into a variety of shapes and directions, and most probably into several confederations, and not without bloodshed.

On the question for committing sect. 6 as to a navigation act, to a member from each State—N. H. ay. Mass. ay.

---

[1] No export duties, no interference with the slave trade, and no capitation tax, unless in proportion to the census.

Conn. no. N. J. no. Pa. ay. Del. ay. Md. ay. Va. ay. N. C. ay. S. C. ay. Geo. ay. . . .

To this committee were referred also the two clauses above-mentioned, of the sect. 4 and 5 of art. vii.

. . . .

25 August (Madison)

The Report of the committee of eleven being taken up,

General PINCKNEY moved to strike out the words ' the year eighteen hundred ' as the year limiting the importation of slaves, and to insert the words ' the year eighteen hundred and eight '.

Mr. GORHAM seconded the motion.

Mr. MADISON. Twenty years will produce all the mischief that can be apprehended from the liberty to import slaves. So long a term will be more dishonorable to the national character, than to say nothing about it in the Constitution.

On the motion ; which passed in the affirmative.

N. H. ay. Mass. ay. Conn. ay. N. J. no. Pa. no. Del. no. Md. ay. Va. no. N. C. ay. S. C. ay. Geo. ay.

Mr. GOUVERNEUR MORRIS was for making the clause read at once, ' importation of slaves into North Carolina, South Carolina, and Georgia shall not be prohibited, etc.' This, he said, would be most fair and would avoid the ambiguity by which, under the power with regard to naturalization, the liberty reserved to the States might be defeated. He wished it to be known also that this part of the Constitution was a compliance with those States. If the change of language, however, should be objected to by the members from those States, he should not urge it.

. . . .

The first part of the report was then agreed to, amended as follows,

' The migration or importation of such persons as the several States now existing shall think proper to admit, shall not be prohibited by the Legislature prior to the year 1808.'

N. H. Mass. Conn. Md. N. C. S. C. Geo. : ay
N. J. Pa. Del. Va. . . . . no

. . . .

29 August (Madison)

Art. vii, sect. 6,[1] by the Committee of eleven reported to be struck out (see the 24 instant) being now taken up,

Mr. PINCKNEY moved to postpone the Report in favor of the following proposition—'That no act of the Legislature for the purpose of regulating the commerce of the United States with foreign powers, or among the several States, shall be passed without the assent of two thirds of the members of each House.' He remarked that there were five distinct commercial interests. (1) The fisheries and West India trade, which belonged to the New England States. (2) The interest of New York lay in a free trade. (3) Wheat and flour the staples of the two middle States (N. J. and Penn.). (4) Tobacco the staple of Maryland and Virginia, and partly of North Carolina. (5) Rice and indigo, the staples of South Carolina and Georgia. These different interests would be a source of oppressive regulations if no check to a bare majority should be provided. States pursue their interests with less scruple than individuals. The power of regulating commerce was a pure concession on the part of the southern States. They did not need the protection of the northern States at present.

Mr. MARTIN [Md.] seconded the motion.

General PINCKNEY said it was the true interest of the southern States to have no regulation of commerce; but considering the loss brought on the commerce of the eastern States by the Revolution, their liberal conduct towards the views * of South Carolina, and the interest the weak southern States had in being united with the strong eastern States, he thought it proper that no fetters should be imposed on the power of making commercial regulations; and that his constituents, though prejudiced against the eastern States, would be reconciled to this liberality. He had himself, he said, prejudices against the eastern States before he came here, but would acknowledge that he had found them as liberal and candid as any men whatever.

Mr. CLYMER [Penn.]. The diversity of commercial interests

[1] The requirement of a two-thirds majority for a navigation Act.

* He meant the permission to import slaves. An understanding on the two subjects of *navigation* and *slavery* had taken place between those parts of the Union, which explains the vote on the motion depending, as well as the language of General Pinckney and others.— Madison.

of necessity creates difficulties, which ought not to be increased by unnecessary restrictions. The northern and middle States will be ruined, if not enabled to defend themselves against foreign regulations.

Mr. SHERMAN, alluding to Mr. Pinckney's enumeration of particular interests as requiring a security against abuse of the power, observed that the diversity was of itself a security, adding that to require more than a majority to decide a question was always embarrassing, as had been experienced in cases requiring the votes of nine States in Congress.

Mr. PINCKNEY replied that his enumeration meant the five minute interests. It still left the two great divisions of northern and southern interests.

Mr. GOUVERNEUR MORRIS opposed the object of the motion as highly injurious. Preferences to American ships will multiply them, till they can carry the southern produce cheaper than it is now carried. A navy was essential to security, particularly of the southern States, and can only be had by a Navigation Act encouraging American bottoms and seamen. In those points of view then alone, it is the interest of the southern States that navigation acts should be facilitated. Shipping, he said, was the worst and most precarious kind of property, and stood in need of public patronage.

Mr. WILLIAMSON was in favor of making two-thirds instead of a majority requisite, as more satisfactory to the southern people. No useful measure he believed had been lost in Congress for want of nine votes. As to the weakness of the southern States, he was not alarmed on that account. The sickliness of their climate for invaders would prevent their being made an object. He acknowledged that he did not think the motion requiring two-thirds necessary in itself, because if a majority of the northern States should push their regulations too far, the southern States would build ships for themselves : but he knew the southern people were apprehensive on this subject and would be pleased with the precaution. . . .

Mr. BUTLER differed from those who considered the rejection of the motion as no concession on the part of the southern States. He considered the interests of these and of the eastern States to be as different as the interests of Russia and Turkey. Being notwithstanding desirous of conciliating the affections of the eastern States, he should vote against requiring two-thirds instead of a majority.

Col. MASON. If the government is to be lasting, it must be founded in the confidence and affections of the people, and must be so constructed as to obtain these. The majority will be governed by their interests. The southern States are the minority in both Houses. Is it to be expected that they will deliver themselves bound hand and foot to the eastern States, and enable them to exclaim, in the words of Cromwell on a certain occasion—' the Lord hath delivered them into our hands ' ?

Mr. WILSON took notice of the several objections and remarked that if every peculiar interest was to be secured, unanimity ought to be required. The majority, he said, would be no more governed by interest than the minority. It was surely better to let the latter be bound hand and foot than the former. Great inconveniences had, he contended, been experienced in Congress from the Articles of Confederation requiring nine votes in certain cases.

Mr. MADISON went into a pretty full view of the subject. He observed that the disadvantage to the southern States from a Navigation Act lay chiefly in a temporary rise of freight, attended, however, with an increase of southern as well as northern shipping, with the emigration of northern seamen and merchants to the southern States, and with a removal of the existing and injurious retaliations among the States on each other. The power of foreign nations to obstruct our retaliating measures on them by a corrupt influence would also be less, if a majority should be made competent than if two-thirds of each House should be required to legislative acts in this case. An abuse of the power would be qualified with all these good effects. But he thought an abuse was rendered improbable by the provision of two branches, by the independence of the Senate, by the negative of the Executive, by the interest of Connecticut and New Jersey, which were agricultural, not commercial States ; by the interior interest which was also agricultural in the most commercial States, and by the accession of western States which would be altogether agricultural. He added that the southern States would derive an essential advantage in the general security afforded by the increase of our maritime strength. He stated the vulnerable situation of them all, and of Virginia in particular. The increase of the coasting trade, and of seamen, would also be favorable to the southern States, by increasing the consumption of their produce. If the wealth of the eastern should in a still greater proportion be augmented, that wealth would contribute the more to the public wants, and be otherwise a national benefit.

Mr. RUTLEDGE was against the motion of his colleague. It did not follow from a grant of the power to regulate trade, that it would be abused. At the worst a Navigation Act could bear hard a little while only on the southern States. As we are laying the foundation for a great empire, we ought to take a permanent view of the subject and not look at the present moment only. He reminded the House of the necessity of securing the West India trade to this country. That was the great object, and a Navigation Act was necessary for obtaining it.

Mr. RANDOLPH said that there were features so odious in the Constitution as it now stands, that he doubted whether he should be able to agree to it. A rejection of the motion would compleat the deformity of the system. He took notice of the argument in favor of giving the power over trade to a majority, drawn from the opportunity foreign powers would have of obstructing retaliatory measures, if two-thirds were made requisite. He did not think there was weight in that consideration. The difference between a majority and two-thirds did not afford room for such an opportunity. Foreign influence would also be more likely to be exerted on the President, who could require three-fourths by his negative. He did not mean, however, to enter into the merits. What he had in view was merely to pave the way for a declaration which he might be hereafter obliged to make if an accumulation of obnoxious ingredients should take place, that he could not give his assent to the plan.

Mr. GORHAM. If the Government is to be so fettered as to be unable to relieve the eastern States, what motive can they have to join in it, and thereby tie their own hands from measures which they could otherwise take for themselves? The eastern States were not led to strengthen the Union by fear for their own safety. He deprecated the consequences of disunion, but if it should take place it was the southern part of the Continent that had most reason to dread them. He urged the improbability of a combination against the interest of the southern States, the different situations of the northern and middle States being a security against it. It was moreover certain that foreign ships would never be altogether excluded, especially those of nations in treaty with us.

On the question to postpone in order to take up Mr. Pinckney's motion,

N. H. no. Mass. no. Conn. no. N. J. no. Pa. no. Del. no. Md. ay. Va. ay. N. C. ay. S. C. no. Geo. ay.

The Report of the Committee for striking out sect. 6, requiring two-thirds of each House to pass a Navigation Act, was then agreed to, *nem. con.*

THE CONSTITUTION OF THE UNITED STATES

As adopted by the Convention, 17 September 1787, and ratified in 1788 [1]

WE, the people of the United States, in order to form a more perfect Union, establish justice, insure domestic tranquility, provide for the common defence, promote the general welfare, and secure the blessings of liberty to ourselves and our posterity, do ordain and establish this Constitution for the United States of America.

ARTICLE I

SECTION I

All legislative powers herein granted shall be vested in a Congress of the United States, which shall consist of a Senate and House of Representatives.

SECTION II

1.[2] The House of Representatives shall be composed of Members chosen every second year by the people of the several States, and the electors in each State shall have the qualifications requisite for electors of the most numerous branch of the State Legislature.[3]

2. No person shall be a representative who shall not have

---

[1] For subsequent Amendments, see Appendix.
[2] The numbers prefixed to the paragraphs are added by the editor.
[3] See also Amendments xv and xix.

attained to the age of twenty-five years, and been seven years a citizen of the United States, and who shall not, when elected, be an inhabitant of that State in which he shall be chosen.

3. Representatives and direct taxes shall be apportioned among the several States which may be included within this Union, according to their respective numbers, which shall be determined by adding to the whole number of free persons, including those bound to service for a term of years, and excluding Indians not taxed, three-fifths of all other persons. The actual enumeration shall be made within three years after the first meeting of the Congress of the United States, and within every subsequent term of ten years, in such manner as they shall by law direct. The number of Representatives shall not exceed one for every thirty thousand, but each State shall have at least one Representative ; and until such enumeration shall be made, the State of New Hampshire shall be entitled to chuse three, Massachusetts eight, Rhode Island and Providence Plantations one, Connecticut five, New York six, New Jersey four, Pennsylvania eight, Delaware one, Maryland six, Virginia ten, North Carolina five, South Carolina five, and Georgia three.

4. When vacancies happen in the representation from any State, the executive authority thereof shall issue writs of election to fill such vacancies.

5. The House of Representatives shall chuse their Speaker and other officers ; and shall have the sole power of impeachment.

Section III

1. The Senate of the United States shall be composed of two Senators from each State, chosen by the Legislature [1] thereof, for six years ; and each Senator shall have one vote.

2. Immediately after they shall be assembled in consequence of the first election, they shall be divided as equally as may be into three classes. The seats of the Senators of the first class shall be vacated at the expiration of the second year, of the second class at the expiration of the fourth year, and of the third class at the expiration of the sixth year, so that one-third may be chosen every second year ; and if vacancies happen by resignation, or otherwise, during the recess of the

[1] See Amendment xvii.

Legislature of any State, the Executive thereof may make temporary appointments until the next meeting of the Legislature,[1] which shall then fill such vacancies.

3. No person shall be a Senator who shall not have attained to the age of thirty years, and been nine years a Citizen of the United States, and who shall not, when elected, be an inhabitant of that State for which he shall be chosen.

4. The Vice President of the United States shall be President of the Senate, but shall have no vote, unless they be equally divided.

5. The Senate shall chuse their other officers, and also a President *pro tempore*, in the absence of the Vice President, or when he shall exercise the office of President of the United States.

6. The Senate shall have the sole power to try all impeachments. When sitting for that purpose, they shall be on oath or affirmation. When the President of the United States is tried, the Chief Justice shall preside : and no person shall be convicted without the concurrence of two-thirds of the members present.

7. Judgment in cases of impeachment shall not extend further than to removal from office, and disqualification to hold and enjoy any office of honor, trust, or profit under the United States ; but the party convicted shall nevertheless be liable and subject to indictment, trial, judgment, and punishment, according to law.

SECTION IV

1. The times, places, and manner of holding elections for Senators and Representatives shall be prescribed in each State by the Legislature thereof ; but the Congress may at any time by law make or alter such regulations, except as to the places of chusing Senators.

2. The Congress shall assemble at least once in every year, and such meeting shall be on the first Monday in December, unless they shall by law appoint a different day.

SECTION V

1. Each House shall be the judge of the elections, returns, and qualifications of its own Members, and a majority of each shall constitute a quorum to do business ; but a smaller number may adjourn from day to day, and may be authorized

[1] See Amendment xvii.

to compel the attendance of absent Members, in such manner, and under such penalties as each House may provide.

2. Each House may determine the rules of its proceedings, punish its Members for disorderly behaviour, and, with the concurrence of two-thirds, expel a Member.

3. Each House shall keep a journal of its proceedings, and from time to time publish the same, excepting such parts as may in their judgment require secrecy ; and the yeas and nays of the Members of either House on any question shall, at the desire of one-fifth of those present, be entered on the journal.

4. Neither House, during the session of Congress, shall, without the consent of the other, adjourn for more than three days, nor to any other place than that in which the two Houses shall be sitting.

Section VI

1. The Senators and Representatives shall receive a compensation for their services, to be ascertained by law, and paid out of the Treasury of the United States. They shall in all cases, except treason, felony, and breach of the peace, be privileged from arrest during their attendance at the session of their respective Houses, and in going to and returning from the same ; and for any speech or debate in either House, they shall not be questioned in any other place.

2. No Senator or Representative shall, during the time for which he was elected, be appointed to any civil office under the authority of the United States, which shall have been created, or the emoluments whereof shall have been encreased during such time ; and no person holding any office under the United States, shall be a Member of either House during his continuance in office.

Section VII

1. All bills for raising revenue shall originate in the House of Representatives ; but the Senate may propose or concur with amendments as on other bills.

2. Every bill which shall have passed the House of Representatives and the Senate, shall, before it become a law, be presented to the President of the United States ; if he approve he shall sign it, but if not he shall return it, with his objections, to that House in which it shall have originated, who

shall enter the objections at large on their journal, and proceed to reconsider it. If after such reconsideration two-thirds of that House shall agree to pass the bill, it shall be sent, together with the objections, to the other House, by which it shall likewise be reconsidered, and if approved by two-thirds of that House, it shall become a law. But in all such cases the votes of both Houses shall be determined by yeas and nays, and the names of the persons voting for and against the bill shall be entered on the journal of each House respectively. If any bill shall not be returned by the President within ten days (Sundays excepted) after it shall have been presented to him, the same shall be a law, in like manner as if he had signed it, unless the Congress by their adjournment prevent its return, in which case it shall not be a law.

3. Every order, resolution, or vote to which the concurrence of the Senate and House of Representatives may be necessary (except on a question of adjournment) shall be presented to the President of the United States; and before the same shall take effect, shall be approved by him, or being disapproved by him, shall be repassed by two-thirds of the Senate and House of Representatives, according to the rules and limitations prescribed in the case of a bill.

Section VIII

1. The Congress shall have power to lay and collect taxes, duties, imposts, and excises, to pay the debts and provide for the common defence and general welfare of the United States; but all duties, imposts, and excises shall be uniform throughout the United States;

2. To borrow money on the credit of the United States;

3. To regulate commerce with foreign nations, and among the several States, and with the Indian tribes;

4. To establish an uniform rule of naturalization, and uniform laws on the subject of bankruptcies throughout the United States;

5. To coin money, regulate the value thereof, and of foreign coin, and fix the standard of weights and measures;

6. To provide for the punishment of counterfeiting the securities and current coin of the United States;

7. To establish post offices and post roads;

8. To promote the progress of science and useful arts, by

securing for limited times to authors and inventors the exclusive right to their respective writings and discoveries ;

9. To constitute tribunals inferior to the Supreme Court ;

10. To define and punish piracies and felonies committed on the high seas, and offences against the Law of Nations ;

11. To declare war, grant letters of marque and reprisal, and make rules concerning captures on land and water ;

12. To raise and support armies, but no appropriation of money to that use shall be for a longer term than two years ;

13. To provide and maintain a navy ;

14. To make rules for the government and regulation of the land and naval forces ;

15. To provide for calling forth the militia to execute the laws of the Union, suppress insurrections, and repel invasions ;

16. To provide for organizing, arming, and disciplining the militia, and for governing such part of them as may be employed in the service of the United States, reserving to the States respectively, the appointment of the officers, and the authority of training the militia according to the discipline prescribed by Congress ;

17. To exercise exclusive legislation in all cases whatsoever over such district (not exceeding ten miles square) as may, by cession of particular States, and the acceptance of Congress, become the seat of the Government of the United States, and to exercise like authority over all places purchased by the consent of the Legislature of the State in which the same shall be, for the erection of forts, magazines, arsenals, dock-yards, and other needful buildings ;—And

18. To make all laws which shall be necessary and proper for carrying into execution the foregoing powers, and all other powers vested by this Constitution in the Government of the United States, or in any department or officer thereof.

Section IX

1. The migration or importation of such persons as any of the States now existing shall think proper to admit, shall not be prohibited by the Congress prior to the year one thousand eight hundred and eight, but a tax or duty may be imposed on such importation, not exceeding ten dollars for each person.

2. The privilege of the writ of habeas corpus shall not be suspended, unless when in cases of rebellion or invasion the public safety may require it.

3. No bill of attainder or *ex post facto* law shall be passed.

4. No capitation, or other direct, tax shall be laid, unless in proportion to the census or enumeration herein before directed to be taken.[1]

5. No tax or duty shall be laid on articles exported from any State.

6. No preference shall be given by any regulation of commerce or revenue to the ports of one State over those of another : nor shall vessels bound to, or from, one State, be obliged to enter, clear, or pay duties in another.

7. No money shall be drawn from the Treasury, but in consequence of appropriations made by law ; and a regular statement and account of the receipts and expenditures of all public money shall be published from time to time.

8. No title of nobility shall be granted by the United States : and no person holding any office of profit or trust under them, shall, without the consent of the Congress, accept of any present, emolument, office, or title, of any kind whatever, from any king, prince, or foreign State.

Section X

1. No State shall enter into any treaty, alliance, or confederation ; grant letters of marque and reprisal ; coin money ; emit bills of credit ; make anything but gold and silver coin a tender in payment of debts ; pass any bill of attainder, *ex post facto* law, or law impairing the obligation of contracts, or grant any title of nobility.

2. No State shall, without the consent of the Congress, lay any imposts or duties on imports or exports, except what may be absolutely necessary for executing its inspection laws : and the net produce of all duties and imposts, laid by any State on imports or exports, shall be for the use of the Treasury of the United States ; and all such laws shall be subject to the revision and controul of the Congress.

3. No State shall, without the consent of Congress, lay any duty of tonnage, keep troops, or ships of war in time of peace, enter into any agreement or compact with another State, or with a foreign power, or engage in war, unless actually invaded, or in such imminent danger as will not admit of delay.

[1] See Amendment xvi.

ARTICLE II

SECTION I

1. The executive power shall be vested in a President of the United States of America. He shall hold his office during the term of four years, and, together with the Vice President, chosen for the same term, be elected, as follows :

2. Each State shall appoint, in such manner as the Legislature thereof may direct, a number of Electors, equal to the whole number of Senators and Representatives to which the State may be entitled in the Congress ; but no Senator or Representative, or person holding an office of trust or profit under the United States, shall be appointed an Elector.

3. The Electors shall meet in their respective States, and vote by ballot for two persons, of whom one at least shall not be an inhabitant of the same State with themselves. And they shall make a list of all the persons voted for, and of the number of votes for each ; which list they shall sign and certify, and transmit sealed to the seat of the Government of the United States, directed to the President of the Senate. The President of the Senate shall, in the presence of the Senate and House of Representatives, open all the certificates, and the votes shall then be counted. The person having the greatest number of votes shall be the President, if such number be a majority of the whole number of Electors appointed ; and if there be more than one who have such majority and have an equal number of votes, then the House of Representatives shall immediately chuse by ballot one of them for President ; and if no person have a majority, then from the five highest on the list the said House shall in like manner chuse the President. But in chusing the President, the votes shall be taken by States, the Representation from each State having one vote ; a quorum for this purpose shall consist of a Member or Members from two-thirds of the States, and a majority of all the States shall be necessary to a choice. In every case, after the choice of the President, the person having the greatest number of votes of the Electors shall be the Vice President. But if there should remain two or more who have equal votes, the Senate shall chuse from them by ballot the Vice President.[1]

4. The Congress may determine the time of chusing the

---

[1] This paragraph was superseded by Amendment xii.

Electors, and the day on which they shall give their votes; which day shall be the same throughout the United States.

5. No person except a natural born Citizen, or a Citizen of the United States, at the time of the adoption of this Constitution, shall be eligible to the office of President; neither shall any person be eligible to that office who shall not have attained to the age of thirty-five years, and been fourteen years a resident within the United States.

6. In case of the removal of the President from office, or of his death, resignation, or inability to discharge the powers and duties of the said office, the same shall devolve on the Vice President, and the Congress may by law provide for the case of removal, death, resignation, or inability, both of the President and Vice President, declaring what officer shall then act as President, and such officer shall act accordingly, until the disability be removed, or a President shall be elected.

7. The President shall, at stated times, receive for his services, a compensation, which shall neither be encreased nor diminished during the period for which he shall have been elected, and he shall not receive within that period any other emolument from the United States, or any of them.

8. Before he enter on the execution of his office, he shall take the following oath or affirmation: ' I do solemnly swear (or affirm) that I will faithfully execute the office of President of the United States, and will to the best of my ability, preserve, protect, and defend the Constitution of the United States.'

Section II

1. The President shall be Commander-in-Chief of the Army and Navy of the United States, and of the militia of the several States, when called into the actual service of the United States; he may require the opinion, in writing, of the principal officer in each of the executive departments, upon any subject relating to the duties of their respective offices, and he shall have power to grant reprieves and pardons for offences against the United States, except in cases of impeachment.

2. He shall have power, by and with the advice and consent of the Senate, to make treaties, provided two-thirds of the Senators present concur; and he shall nominate, and by and with the advice and consent of the Senate, shall appoint

ambassadors, other public ministers, and consuls, Judges of the Supreme Court, and all other officers of the United States, whose appointments are not herein otherwise provided for, and which shall be established by law ; but the Congress may by law vest the appointment of such inferior officers, as they think proper, in the President alone, in the Courts of Law, or in the heads of departments.

3. The President shall have power to fill up all vacancies that may happen during the recess of the Senate, by granting commissions which shall expire at the end of their next session.

SECTION III

He shall from time to time give to the Congress information of the state of the Union, and recommend to their consideration such measures as he shall judge necessary and expedient ; he may, on extraordinary occasions, convene both Houses, or either of them, and in case of disagreement between them, with respect to the time of adjournment, he may adjourn them to such time as he shall think proper ; he shall receive ambassadors and other public ministers ; he shall take care that the laws be faithfully executed, and shall commission all the officers of the United States.

SECTION IV

The President, Vice President, and all civil officers of the United States, shall be removed from office on impeachment for, and conviction of, treason, bribery, or other high crimes and misdemeanors.

ARTICLE III

SECTION I

The judicial power of the United States, shall be vested in one Supreme Court, and in such inferior courts as the Congress may from time to time ordain and establish. The Judges, both of the Supreme and inferior courts, shall hold their offices during good behaviour, and shall, at stated times, receive for their services, a compensation, which shall not be diminished during their continuance in office.

SECTION II

1. The judicial power shall extend to all cases, in law and equity, arising under this Constitution, the laws of the United

States, and treaties made, or which shall be made, under their authority ;—to all cases affecting ambassadors, other public ministers and consuls ;—to all cases of admiralty and maritime jurisdiction ;—to controversies to which the United States shall be a party ;—to controversies between two or more States ;—between a State and Citizens of another State ; —between Citizens of different States ;—between Citizens of the same State claiming lands under grants of different States, and between a State, or the Citizens thereof, and foreign States, Citizens, or subjects.

2. In all cases affecting ambassadors, other public ministers, and consuls, and those in which a State shall be party, the Supreme Court shall have original jurisdiction. In all the other cases before mentioned, the Supreme Court shall have appellate jurisdiction, both as to law and fact, with such exceptions, and under such regulations as the Congress shall make.

3. The trial of all crimes, except in cases of impeachment, shall be by jury ; and such trial shall be held in the State where the said crimes shall have been committed ; but when not committed within any State, the trial shall be at such place or places as the Congress may by law have directed.

Section III

1. Treason against the United States shall consist only in levying war against them or in adhering to their enemies, giving them aid and comfort. No person shall be convicted of treason unless on the testimony of two witnesses to the same overt act, or on confession in open court.

2. The Congress shall have power to declare the punishment of treason, but no attainder of treason shall work corruption of blood, or forfeiture except during the life of the person attainted.

Article IV
Section I

Full faith and credit shall be given in each State to the public acts, records, and judicial proceedings of every other State. And the Congress may by general laws prescribe the manner in which such acts, records, and proceedings shall be proved, and the effect thereof.

SECTION II

1. The Citizens of each State shall be entitled to all privileges and immunities of Citizens in the several States.

2. A person charged in any State with treason, felony, or other crime, who shall flee from justice, and be found in another State, shall on demand of the executive authority of the State from which he fled, be delivered up to be removed to the State having jurisdiction of the crime.

3. No person held to service or labour in one State, under the laws thereof, escaping into another, shall, in consequence of any law or regulation therein, be discharged from such service or labour, but shall be delivered up on claim of the party to whom such service or labour may be due.

SECTION III

1. New States may be admitted by the Congress into this Union ; but no new State shall be formed or erected within the jurisdiction of any other State ; nor any State be formed by the junction of two or more States, or parts of States, without the consent of the Legislatures of the States concerned as well as of the Congress.

2. The Congress shall have power to dispose of and make all needful rules and regulations respecting the territory or other property belonging to the United States ; and nothing in this Constitution shall be so construed as to prejudice any claims of the United States, or of any particular State.

SECTION IV

The United States shall guarantee to every State in this Union a republican form of government, and shall protect each of them against invasion ; and on application of the Legislature, or of the Executive (when the Legislature cannot be convened) against domestic violence.

ARTICLE V

The Congress, whenever two-thirds of both Houses shall deem it necessary, shall propose Amendments to this Constitution, or, on the application of the Legislatures of two-thirds of the several States, shall call a Convention for proposing Amendments, which, in either case, shall be valid to all intents and purposes, as part of this Constitution, when ratified by the Legislatures of three-fourths of the several States, or by Conventions in three-fourths thereof, as the one or the other mode of ratification may be proposed by the Congress ; provided that no Amendment which may be made prior to the year one thousand eight hundred and eight shall in any manner affect the first and fourth clauses in the ninth section of the first Article ; and that no State, without its consent, shall be deprived of its equal suffrage in the Senate.

ARTICLE VI

1. All debts contracted and engagements entered into, before the adoption of this Constitution, shall be as valid against the United States under this Constitution, as under the Confederation.

2. This Constitution, and the laws of the United States, which shall be made in pursuance thereof ; and all treaties made, or which shall be made, under the authority of the United States, shall be the Supreme Law of the land ; and the judges in every State shall be bound thereby, any thing in the Constitution or laws of any State to the contrary notwithstanding.

3. The Senators and Representatives before mentioned, and the Members of the several State Legislatures, and all executive and judicial officers, both of the United States and of the several States, shall be bound by oath or affirmation, to support this Constitution ; but no religious test shall ever be required as a qualification to any office or public trust under the United States.

ARTICLE VII

The ratification of the Conventions of nine States, shall be sufficient for the establishment of this Constitution between the States so ratifying the same.

Done in Convention by the unanimous consent of the States present the seventeenth day of September in the year of our Lord one thousand seven hundred and eighty-seven and of the Independence of the United States of America the twelfth. In Witness whereof we have hereunto subscribed our names,

G⁰. WASHINGTON,
President, and Deputy from Virginia.

GOUVERNEUR MORRIS TO WASHINGTON [1]

PHILADELPHIA, 30 *October* 1787.

His Excellency Gen'l Washington.

DEAR SIR,—Shortly after your departure from this place, I went to my farm and returned hither last Sunday evening. Living out of the busy world I had nothing to say worth your attention, or I would earlier have given you the trouble you now experience. Altho not very inquisitive about political opinions, I have not been quite inattentive. The States eastward of New York appear to be almost unanimous in favor of the new Constitution ; for I make no account of the dissentients in Rhode Island. Their preachers are advocates for the adoption, and this circumstance coinciding with the steady support of the property and other abilities of the country makes the current set strongly, and I trust irresistibly, that way. Jersey is so near unanimity in her favorable opinion, that we may count with certainty on something more than votes should the state of affairs hereafter require the application of pointed arguments. New York, hemmed in between the warm friends of the Constitution, could not easily (unless supported by powerful States) make any important struggle, even tho her citizens were unanimous, which is by no means the case. Parties there are nearly balanced. If the assent or dissent of the New York Legislature were to decide on the fate of America there would still be a chance, tho I believe the force of Government would preponderate and effect a rejection. But the Legislature cannot assign to the people any good reason for not trusting them with a decision on their own affairs, and must therefore agree to a convention. In the choice of a convention it is not improbable that the fœderal party will prove strongest, for persons of every distinct and opposite interests have joined on this subject. With respect to this State I am far from being decided in my opinion that they will consent. True it is that the city and its neighbourhood are enthusiastic in the cause ; but I dread the cold and sour temper of the back counties, and still more the wicked industry of those who have long habituated themselves to live on the public, and cannot bear the idea of being removed from the power and

[1] Washington manuscripts, Library of Congress.

profit of State Government, which has been and still is the means of supporting themselves, their families and dependents ; and (which perhaps is more grateful) of depressing and humbling their political adversaries.   What opinions prevail more southward I cannot guess.   You are in condition better than any other person to judge of a great and important part of that country.

I have observed that your name to the new Constitution has been of infinite service.   Indeed I am convinced that if you had not attended the Convention, and the same paper had been handed out to the world, it would have met with a colder reception, with fewer and weaker advocates, and with more and more strenuous opponents.   As it is, should the idea prevail that you would not accept of the Presidency, it would prove fatal in many parts.   Truth is, that your great and decided superiority leads men willingly to put you in a place which will not add to your personal dignity, nor raise you higher than you already stand : but they would not willingly put any other person in the same situation, because they feel the elevation of others as operating (by comparison) the degredation of themselves.   And however absurd this idea, you will agree with me the men must be treated as men and not as machines, much less as philosophers, and least of all things as reasonable creatures ; seeing that in effect they reason not to direct but to excuse their conduct.

Thus much for the public opinion on these subjects, which must not be neglected in a country where opinion is everything.   I will add my conviction that of all men you are the best fitted to fill that office.   Your cool steady temper is *indispensibly necessary* to give firm and manly tone to the new Government.   To constitute a well poised political machine is the task of no common workman ; but to set it in motion requires still greater qualities.   When once agoing it will proceed a long time from the original impulse.   Time gives to primary institutions the mighty power of habit ; and custom, the law both of wise men and of fools, serves as the great commentator of human establishments, and like other commentators as frequently obscures as it explains the real. No Constitution is the same on paper and in life.   The exercise of authority depends on personal character ; and the whip and reins by which an able charioteer governs unruly steeds will only hurl the unskilful presumer with more speedy and headlong violence to the earth. The horses once trained may be managed by a woman or a child ; not so when they first feel the bit. And indeed among these thirteen horses now about to be coupled together, there are some of every race and character. They will listen to your voice, and submit to your control ; you therefore must, I say *must* mount the seat. But [that] the result may be as pleasing to you as it will be useful to them, I wish but do not expect. You will, however, on this, as on other occasions, feel that interior satisfaction and self-approbation which the world cannot give ; and you will have in every possible event the applause of those who know you enough to respect you properly. Indulge my vanity so far as to place in that number, dear General,

Yours

Gouv^r. Morris.

SELECTIONS FROM DEBATES IN THE VIRGINIA RATIFYING CONVENTION [1]

June 1788

(a) *The General Issue.*

4 June

Mr. Henry. Mr. Chairman, the public mind, as well as my own, is extremely uneasy at the proposed change of government. Give me leave to form one of the number of those who wish to be thoroughly acquainted with the reasons of this perilous and uneasy situation, and why we are brought hither to decide on this great national question. I consider myself as the servant of the people of this Commonwealth, as a sentinel over their rights, liberty, and happiness.

---

[1] *Debates and other Proceedings of the Convention of Virginia, Convened at Richmond, on Monday the 2nd day of June 1788, for the purpose of deliberating on the Constitution recommended by the Grand Federal Convention,* Petersburg (Va.), 1788–9, 3 vols. These debates, with those of the other State ratifying Conventions, Madison's and Yates's Notes, and other material on the Constitution, are printed (rather inaccurately) in *Elliot's Debates* (the ' second edition ', Washington, 1836–45, with many subsequent reprints, lately by Lippincott's, Philadelphia, is the best). They are not abridged, like the Federal Convention debates. The *Federalist* essays should be read at this point.

I represent their feelings when I say that they are exceedingly uneasy, being brought from that state of full security which they enjoyed, to the present delusive appearance of things. A year ago, the minds of our citizens were at perfect repose. Before the meeting of the late Federal Convention at Philadelphia, a general peace and a universal tranquillity prevailed in this country; but, since that period, they are exceedingly uneasy and disquieted. When I wished for an appointment to this Convention, my mind was extremely agitated for the situation of public affairs. I conceived the republic to be in extreme danger. If our situation be thus uneasy, whence has arisen this fearful jeopardy? It arises from this fatal system; it arises from a proposal to change our government—a proposal that goes to the utter annihilation of the most solemn engagements of the States. A proposal of establishing nine states into a confederacy, to the eventual exclusion of four states. It goes to the annihilation of those solemn treaties we have formed with foreign nations.

The present circumstances of France—the good offices rendered us by that kingdom—require our most faithful and most punctual adherence to our treaty with her. We are in alliance with the Spaniards, the Dutch, the Prussians. Those treaties bound us as thirteen states confederated together. Yet here is a proposal to sever that confederacy. Is it possible that we shall abandon all our treaties and national engagements?—and for what? I expected to hear the reasons for an event so unexpected to my mind and many others. Was our civil polity, or public justice, endangered or sapped? Was the real existence of the country threatened, or was this preceded by a mournful progression of events? This proposal of altering our federal government is of a most alarming nature. Make the best of this new government— say it is composed by anything but inspiration—you ought to be extremely cautious, watchful, jealous of your liberty; for instead of securing your rights, you may lose them for ever. If a wrong step be now made, the Republic may be lost for ever. If this new government will not come up to the expectation of the people, and they shall be disappointed, their liberty will be lost, and tyranny must and will arise I repeat it again, and I beg gentlemen to consider, that a wrong step made now will plunge us into misery, and our Republic will be lost.

It will be necessary for this Convention to have a faithful historical detail of the facts that preceded the session of the Federal Convention, and the reasons that actuated its members in proposing an entire alteration of government, and to demonstrate the dangers that awaited us. If they were of such awful magnitude as to warrant a proposal so extremely perilous as this, I must assert that this Convention has an absolute right to a thorough discovery of every circumstance relative to this great event. And here I would make this inquiry of those worthy characters who composed a part of the late Federal Convention. I am sure they were fully impressed with the necessity of forming a great consolidated government, instead of a confederation. That this is a consolidated government is demonstrably clear ; and the danger of such a government is, to my mind, very striking. I have the highest veneration for those gentlemen ; but, sir, give me leave to demand, What right had they to say, *We, the People ?* [1] My political curiosity, exclusive of my anxious solicitude for the public welfare, leads me to ask, Who authorized them to speak the language of, *We, the People,* instead of, *We, the States ?* States are the characteristics and the soul of a confederation. If the States be not the agents of this compact, it must be one great consolidated National Government, of the people of all the States. I have the highest respect for those gentlemen who formed the Convention, and, were some of them not here, I would express some testimonial of esteem for them. America had, on a former occasion, put the utmost confidence in them—a confidence which was well placed ; and I am sure, sir, I would give up anything to them ; I would cheerfully confide in them as my Representatives. But, sir, on this great occasion, I would demand the cause of their conduct. Even from that illustrious man who saved us by his valor, I would have a reason for his conduct : that liberty which he has given us by his valor, tells me to ask this reason ; and sure I am, were he here, he would give us that reason. But there are other gentlemen here, who can give us this information. The people gave them no power to use their name. That they exceeded their power is perfectly clear. It is not mere curiosity that actuates me. I wish to hear the real, actual, existing danger, which should lead us to take those steps so dangerous in my

[1] The preamble to the Constitution was under consideration.

conception. Disorders have arisen in other parts of America; but here, sir, no dangers, no insurrection or tumult has happened—everything has been calm and tranquil. But notwithstanding this, we are wandering on the great ocean of human affairs. I see no landmark to guide us. We are running we know not whither. Difference of opinion has gone to a degree of inflammatory resentment in different parts of the country which has been occasioned by this perilous innovation. The Federal Convention ought to have amended the old system—for this purpose they were solely delegated; the object of their mission extended to no other consideration. You must, therefore, forgive the solicitation of one unworthy member, to know what danger could have arisen under the present Confederation, and what are the causes of this proposal to change our government.

.   .   .   .

Mr. GEORGE MASON. Mr. Chairman, whether the Constitution be good or bad, the present clause clearly discovers that it is a national government, and no longer a Confederation. I mean that clause which gives the first hint of the general government laying direct taxes. The assumption of this power of laying direct taxes does, of itself, entirely change the Confederation of the States into one consolidated government. This power being at discretion, unconfined, and without any kind of control, must carry everything before it. The very idea of converting what was formerly a Confederation to a consolidated government, is totally subversive of every principle which has hitherto governed us. This power is calculated to annihilate totally the State governments. Will the people of this great community submit to be individually taxed by two different and distinct powers? Will they suffer themselves to be doubly harassed? These two concurrent powers cannot exist long together. The one will destroy the other. The general government being paramount to, and in every respect more powerful than the State governments, the latter must give way to the former. Is it to be supposed that one national government will suit so extensive a country, embracing so many climates, and containing inhabitants so very different in manners, habits, and customs? It is ascertained by history, that there never was a government over a very extensive country without destroying the liberties of the people. History also, supported by the opinions of the best writers, shows us that monarchy may suit a large territory, and despotic governments ever so extensive a country, but that popular governments can only exist in small territories. Is there a single example, on the face of the earth, to support a contrary opinion ? Where is there one exception to this general rule ? Was there ever an instance of a general national government extending over so extensive a country, abounding in such a variety of climates, etc., where the people retained their liberty ? I solemnly declare that no man is a greater friend to a firm union of the American States than I am ; but, sir, if this great end can be obtained without hazarding the rights of the people, why should we recur to such dangerous principles ? Requisitions have been often refused, sometimes from an impossibility of complying with them ; often from that great variety of circumstances which retard the collection of moneys ; and perhaps sometimes from a wilful design of procrastinating. But why shall we give up to the National Government this power, so dangerous in its nature, and for which its members will not have sufficient information ? Is it not well known that what would be a proper tax in one State would be grievous in another ? The gentleman who hath favored us with a eulogium in favor of this system, must, after all the encomiums he has been pleased to bestow upon it, acknowledge that our Federal Representatives must be unacquainted with the situation of their constituents. Sixty-five members cannot possibly know the situation and circumstances of all the inhabitants of this immense continent. When a certain sum comes to be taxed, and the mode of levying to be fixed, they will lay the tax on that article which will be most productive and easiest in the collection, without consulting the real circumstances or convenience of a country, with which in fact they cannot be sufficiently acquainted.

The mode of levying taxes is of the utmost consequence ; and yet here it is to be determined by those who have neither knowledge of our situation, nor a common interest with us, nor a fellow-feeling for us. The subjects of taxation differ in three-fourths, nay, I might say with truth, in four-fifths of the States. If we trust the National Government with an effectual way of raising the necessary sums, 'tis sufficient. Everything we do further is trusting the happiness and rights of the people. Why then should we give up this dangerous power of individual taxation? Why leave the manner of laying taxes to those, who in the nature of things, cannot be acquainted with the situation of those on whom they are to impose them, when it can be done by those who are well acquainted with it? If, instead of giving this oppressive power, we give them such an effectual alternative as will answer the purpose, without encountering the evil and danger that might arise from it, then I would chearfully acquiesce; and would it not be far more eligible? I candidly acknowledge the inefficacy of the Confederation; but requisitions have been made which were impossible to be complied with—requisitions for more gold and silver than were in the United States. If we give the general government the power of demanding their quotas of the States, with an alternative of laying direct taxes in case of non-compliance, then the mischief would be avoided; and the certainty of this conditional power would, in all human probability, prevent the application; and the sums necessary for the Union would be then laid by the States, by those who know how it can best be raised, by those who have a fellow-feeling for us. Give me leave to say that the sum raised one way with convenience and ease, would be very oppressive another way. Why then not leave this power to be exercised by those who know the mode most convenient for the inhabitants, and not by those who must necessarily apportion it in such manner as shall be oppressive?

With respect to the representation so much applauded, I cannot think it such a full and free one as it is represented; but I must candidly acknowledge that this defect results from the very nature of the government. It would be impossible to have a full and adequate representation in the general government; it would be too expensive and too unwieldy. We are then under the necessity of having this a very inadequate representation. Is this general representation to be compared with the real, actual, substantial representation of the State Legislatures? It cannot bear a comparison. To make representation real and actual, the number of Representatives ought to be adequate; they ought to mix with the people, think as they think, feel as they feel—ought to be perfectly amenable to them, and thoroughly acquainted with their interest and condition. Now, these great ingredients are either not at all, or in so small a degree, to be found in our Federal Representatives that we have no real, actual, substantial representation ; but I acknowledge it results from the nature of the government. The necessity of this inconvenience may appear a sufficient reason not to argue against it. But, sir, it clearly shows that we ought to give power with a sparing hand to a Government thus imperfectly constructed. To a Government which in the nature of things, cannot but be defective no powers ought to be given but such as are absolutely necessary. There is one thing in it which I conceive to be extremely dangerous. Gentlemen may talk of public virtue and confidence ; we shall be told that the House of Representatives will consist of the most virtuous men on the Continent, and that in their hands we may trust our dearest rights. This, like all other assemblies, will be composed of some bad and some good men ; and, considering the natural lust of power so naturally inherent in man, I fear the thirst of power will prevail to oppress the people. What I conceive to be so dangerous, is the provision with respect to the number of Representatives. It does not expressly provide that we shall have one for every thirty thousand, but that the number shall not exceed that proportion. The utmost that we can expect (and perhaps that is too much) is, that the present number shall be continued to us : ' the number of Representatives shall not exceed one for every thirty thousand.' . . .

But my principal objection is, that the Confederation is converted to one general consolidated government, which, from my best judgment of it (and which perhaps will be shewn, in the course of this discussion, to be really well founded), is one of the worst curses that can possibly befall a nation. Does any man suppose that one general national government can exist in so extensive a country as this ? I hope that a government may be framed which may suit us, by drawing a line between the General and State Governments, and prevent that dangerous clashing of interest and power which must, as it now stands, terminate in the destruction of one or the other When we come to the Judiciary, we shall be more convinced that this government will terminate in the annihilation of the State governments. The question then will be, whether a consolidated government can preserve the freedom and secure the great rights of the people.

If such amendments be introduced as shall exclude danger, I shall most gladly put my hand to it. When such amendments as shall, from the best information, secure the great essential rights of the people, shall be agreed to by gentlemen, I shall most heartily make the greatest concessions, and concur in any reasonable measure to obtain the desirable end of conciliation and unanimity. An indispensable amendment in this case is, that Congress shall not exercise the power of raising direct taxes till the States shall have refused to comply with the requisitions of Congress. On this condition it may be granted ; but I see no reason to grant it unconditionally, as the States can raise the taxes with more ease, and lay them on the inhabitants with more propriety than it is possible for the General Government to do. If Congress hath this power without controul, the taxes will be laid by those who have no fellow-feeling or acquaintance with the people. This is my objection to the article now under consideration. It is a very great and important one. I therefore beg gentlemen to consider it. Should this power be restrained, I shall withdraw my objections to this part of the Constitution ; but as it stands, it is an objection so strong in my mind, that its amendment is with me a *sine qua non* of its adoption. I wish for such amendments, and such only, as are necessary to secure the dearest rights of the people.

Mr. MADISON. Mr. Chairman, it would give me great pleasure to concur with my honorable colleague in any conciliatory plan. The clause to which the worthy member alludes is only explanatory of the proportion which representation and taxation shall respectively bear to one another. The power of laying direct taxes will be more properly discussed when we come to that part of the Constitution which vests that power in Congress. At present I must endeavour to reconcile our proceedings to the resolution we have taken by postponing the examination of this power till we come properly to it. With respect to converting the Confederation to a complete consolidation, I think no such consequence will follow from the Constitution ; and that with more attention, we shall see that he is mistaken. And with respect to the number of representatives, I reconcile it to my mind when I consider that it may be increased to the proportion fixed ; and that, as it may be so increased, it shall, because it is the interest of those who alone can prevent it, who are our Representatives, and who depend on their good behaviour for their reëlection. Let me observe also, that as far as the number of representatives may seem to be inadequate to discharge their duty, they will have sufficient information from the laws of particular States, from the State Legislatures, from their own experience, and from a great number of individuals. And as to our security against them, I conceive, sir, that the general limitation of their powers, and the general watchfulness of the States, will be a sufficient guard. As it is now late, I shall defer any further investigation till a more convenient time.

5 June

Mr. PENDLETON. . . . The expression, *We, the people*, is thought improper. Permit me to ask the gentleman who made this objection, who but the people can delegate powers? Who but the people have a right to form government? The expression is a common one, and a favorite one with me. The representatives of the people, by their authority, is a mode wholly inessential. If the objection be, that the Union ought to be not of the people, but of the State governments, then I think the choice of the former very happy and proper. What have the State governments to do with it? Were they to determine, the people would not in that case be the judges upon what terms it was adopted.

But the power of the Convention is doubted. What is the power? To propose, not to determine. This power of proposing was very broad. It extended to remove all defects in government. The members of that Convention, who were to consider all the defects in our General Government, were not confined to any particular plan. Were they deceived? This is the proper question here. Suppose the paper on your table dropped from one of the planets; the people found it, and sent us here to consider whether it was proper for their adoption. Must we not obey them? Then the question must be between this government and the Confederation. The latter is no government at all. It has been said that it has carried us through a dangerous war to a happy issue. Not that Confederation, but common danger, and the spirit of America, were bonds of our Union: Union and unanimity, and not that insignificant paper, carried us through that dangerous war. 'United, we stand—divided, we fall!' echoed and re-echoed through America—from Congress to the drunken carpenter—was effectual, and procured the end of our wishes, though now forgotten by gentlemen, if such there be, who incline to let go this stronghold to catch at feathers ; for such all substituted projects may prove.

This spirit had nearly reached the end of its power when relieved by peace. It was the spirit of America, and not the Confederation, that carried us through the war. Thus I prove it : the moment of peace showed the imbecility of the Federal Government. Congress was empowered to make war and peace ; a peace they made, giving us the great object, independence, and yielding us a territory that exceeded my most sanguine expectations. Unfortunately a single disagreeable clause, not the object of the war, has retarded the performance of the treaty on our part. Congress could only recommend its performance, not enforce it ; our last Assembly (to their honor be it said) put this on its proper grounds—on honorable grounds ; it was as much as they ought to have done. This single instance shews the imbecility of the Confederation ; the debts contracted by the war were unpaid. Demands were made on Congress ; all that Congress was able to do was to make an estimate of the debt, and proportion it among the several States ; they sent on the requisitions from time to time to the States for their respective quotas. These were either complied with partially, or not at all. Repeated demands on Congress distressed that honorable body ; but they were unable to fulfil those engagements, as they so earnestly wished. What was the idea of other nations respecting America ? What was the idea entertained of us by those nations to whom we were so much indebted ? The inefficacy of the General Government warranted an idea that we had no government at all. Improvements were proposed, and agreed to by twelve States, but were interrupted because the little State of Rhode Island refused to accede to them. This was a further proof of the imbecility of that government. Need I multiply instances to show that it is wholly ineffectual for the purposes of its institution ? Its whole progress since the peace proves it.

Shall we then, sir, continue under such a government, or shall we introduce that kind of government which shall produce the real happiness and security of the people ? When gentlemen say that we ought not to introduce this new government, but strengthen the hands of Congress, they ought to be explicit. In what manner shall this be done ? If the Union of the States be necessary, government must be equally so ; for without the latter, the former cannot be effected. Government must then have its complete powers or be ineffectual ; Legislative to fix rules, impose sanctions, and point out the punishment of the transgressors of these rules ; an Executive to watch over officers and bring them to punishment ; a Judiciary to guard the innocent, and fix the guilty, by a fair trial. Without an Executive, offenders would not be brought to punishment ; without a Judiciary, any man might be taken up, convicted and punished without a trial. Hence the necessity of having these three branches. Would any gentleman in this committee agree to vest these three powers in one body, Congress ? No ! Hence the necessity of a new organization and distribution of those powers. If there be any feature in this government which is not republican it would be exceptionable. From all the public servants responsibility is secured by their being representatives, mediate or immediate, for short terms, and their powers defined. It is on the whole complexion of it a government of laws, not of men.

But it is represented to be a consolidated government annihilating that of the States—a consolidated government which so extensive a territory as the United States cannot admit of, without terminating in despotism. If this be such a Government, I will confess with my worthy friend that it is inadmissible over such a territory as this country. Let us consider whether it be such a government or not. I should understand a consolidated government to be that which should have the sole and exclusive power, Legislative, Executive and Judicial, without any limitation. Is this such a government ? Or can it be changed to such a one ? It only extends to the general purposes of the Union. It does not intermeddle with the local, particular affairs of the States. Can Congress legislate for the State of Virginia ? Can they make a law altering the form of transferring property, or the rule of descents in Virginia ? In one word, can they make a single law for the individual exclusive purpose of any one State ? It is the interest of the Federal to preserve the State governments ; upon the latter the existence of the former depends. The Senate derives its existence immediately from the State Legislatures ; and the representatives and President are elected under their direction and controul; they also preserve order among the citizens of their respective States, and without order and peace no society can possibly exist. Unless, therefore, there be State Legislatures to continue the existence of Congress, and preserve order and peace among the inhabitants, this General Government, which gentlemen suppose will annihilate the State Governments, must itself be destroyed. When therefore the Federal Government is, in so many respects, so absolutely dependent on the State Governments, I wonder how any gentleman, reflecting on the subject, could have conceived an idea of a possibility of the former destroying the latter. But the power of laying direct taxes is objected to. Government must be supported; this cannot be done without a revenue. If a sufficient revenue be not otherwise raised, recurrence must be had to direct taxation. Gentlemen admit this, but insist on the propriety of first applying to the State Legislatures.

Let us consider the consequence that would result from this. In the first place, time would be lost by it. Congress would make requisitions in December; our legislature do not meet till October; here would be a considerable loss of time, admitting the requisitions to be fully complied with. But suppose the requisitions to be refused; would it not be dangerous to send a collector to collect the Congressional taxes, after the State Legislature had absolutely refused to comply with the demands of Congress? Would not resistance to collectors be the probable consequence? Would not this resistance terminate in confusion, and a dissolution of the Union? The concurrent power of two different bodies laying direct taxes is objected to. These taxes are for two different purposes, and cannot interfere with one another. I can see no danger resulting from this; and we must suppose that a very small sum more than the impost would be sufficient.

But the representation is supposed too small. I confess, I think with the gentleman who opened the debate (Mr. NICHOLAS) on this subject; and I think he gave a very satisfactory answer to this objection when he observed that, though the number might be insufficient to convey information of necessary local interests to a State Legislature, yet it was sufficient for the Federal Legislature, who are to act only on general subjects, in which this State is concerned in common with other States. The apportionment of representation and taxation by the same scale is just. It removes the objection that while Virginia paid one sixth part of the expences of the Union, she had no more weight in public counsels than Delaware, which paid but a very small proportion. By this just apportionment she is put on a footing with the small States, in point of representation and influence in counsels. I cannot imagine a more judicious principle than is here fixed by the Constitution—the number *shall not exceed* one for every thirty thousand. But it is objected that the number may be less. If Virginia sends in that proportion, I ask where is the power in Congress to reject them ? States might incline to send too many ; they are therefore restrained : but can it be doubted that they will send the number they are entitled to ? We may be therefore sure, from this principle unequivocally fixed in the Constitution, that the number of our Representatives shall be in proportion to the increase or decrease of our population. I can truly say that I am of no party, nor actuated by any influence, but the true interest and real happiness of those whom I represent ; and my age and situation, I trust, will sufficiently demonstrate the truth of this assertion. I cannot conclude without adding, that I am perfectly satisfied with this part of the system.

Mr. LEE of Westmoreland.[1] Mr. Chairman, I feel every power of my mind moved by the language of the honorable gentleman yesterday. The éclat and brilliancy which have distinguished that gentleman, the honors with which he has been dignified, and the brilliant talents which he has so often displayed, have attracted my respect and attention. On so important an occasion, and before so respectable a body, I expected a new display of his powers of oratory ; but instead of proceeding to investigate the merits of the new plan of government, the worthy character informed us of horrors which he felt, of apprehensions in his mind, which made him tremblingly fearful of the fate of the Commonwealth. Mr. Chairman, was it proper to appeal to the fear of this House ? The question before us belongs to the judgment of this House. I trust he is come to judge, and not to alarm. I trust that he, and every other gentleman in this House, comes with a firm resolution coolly and calmly to examine, and fairly and impartially to determine. He was pleased to pass an eulogium

[1] Henry Lee, the ' Light-Horse Harry ' of the war, and father of Robert H. Lee.

on that character who is the pride of peace and support of war ; and declared that even from him he would require the reason of proposing such a system. I cannot see the propriety of mentioning that illustrious character on this occasion ; we must be all fully impressed with a conviction of his extreme rectitude of conduct. But, sir, this system is to be examined by its own merit. He then adverted to the style of the government, and asked what authority they had to use the expression, ' We, the people,' and not ' We, the States '. This expression was introduced into that paper with great propriety. This system is submitted to the people for their consideration because on them it is to operate if adopted. It is not binding on the people until it becomes their act. It is now submitted to the people of Virginia. If we do not adopt it, it will be always null and void as to us. Suppose it was found to be proper for our adoption, and becoming the government of the people of Virginia ; by what style should it be done ? Ought we not to make use of the name of the people ? No other style would be proper. He then spoke of the characters of the gentlemen who framed it. This was inapplicable, strange, and unexpected : it was a more proper inquiry whether such evils existed as rendered necessary a change of government.

This necessity is evidenced by the concurrent testimony of almost all America. The legislative acts of different States avow it. It is acknowledged by the acts of this State ; under such an act we are here now assembled. If reference to the acts of the assemblies will not sufficiently convince him of this necessity, let him go to our seaports ; let him see our commerce languishing—not an American bottom to be seen ; let him ask the price of land and of produce in different parts of the country : to what cause shall we ascribe the very low prices of these ? To what cause are we to attribute the decrease of population and industry, and the impossibility of employing our tradesmen and mechanics ? To what cause will the gentleman impute these and a thousand other misfortunes our people labor under ? These, sir, are owing to the imbecility of the Confederation ; to that defective system which never can make us happy at home nor respectable abroad. The gentleman sat down as he began, leaving us to ruminate on the horrors which he opened with. Although I could trust to the argument of the gentleman who spoke yesterday in favor of the plan, permit me to make one observation on the weight of our representatives in the government. If the House of Commons in England, possessing less power, are now able to withstand the power of the Crown—if that House of Commons, which has been undermined by corruption in every age, and contaminated by bribery even in this enlightened age, with far less powers than our representatives possess, is still able to contend with the executive of that country—what danger have we to fear that our representatives cannot successfully oppose the encroachments of the other branches of government? Let it be remembered that in the year 1782 the East India Bill was brought into the House of Commons. Although the members of that House are only elected in part by the landed interest, yet in spite of ministerial influence that Bill was carried in that House by a majority of one hundred and thirty, and the king was obliged to dissolve the Parliament to prevent its effect. If, then, the House of Commons was so powerful, no danger can be apprehended that our House of Representatives is not amply able to protect our liberties. I trust that this representation is sufficient to secure our happiness, and that we may fairly congratulate ourselves on the superiority of our government to that I just referred to.

Mr. HENRY. Mr. Chairman, I am obliged to the very worthy gentleman for his encomium. I wish I was possessed of talents, or possessed of any thing that might enable me to elucidate this great subject. I am not free from suspicion: I am apt to entertain doubts. I rose yesterday to ask a question which arose in my own mind. When I asked that question, I thought the meaning of my interrogation was obvious. The fate of this question and of America may depend on this. Have they said, 'We, the States?' Have they made a proposal of a compact between States? If they had, this would be a confederation. It is otherwise most clearly a consolidated government. The question turns, sir, on that poor little thing —the expression, We, the *people*, instead of the *States*, of America. I need not take much pains to show that the principles of this system are extremely pernicious, impolitic, and dangerous. Is this a monarchy, like England—a compact between prince and people, with checks on the former to secure the liberty of the latter? Is this a confederacy, like Holland— an association of a number of independent States, each of which retains its individual sovereignty? It is not a democracy, wherein the people retain all their rights securely. Had these principles been adhered to, we should not have been brought to this alarming transition, from a confederacy to a consolidated government. We have no detail of those great considerations, which, in my opinion, ought to have abounded before we should recur to a government of this kind. Here is a revolution as radical as that which separated us from Great Britain. It is as radical if in this transition our rights and privileges are endangered, and the sovereignty of the States will be relinquished : and cannot we plainly see that this is actually the case ? The rights of conscience, trial by jury, liberty of the press, all your immunities and franchises, all pretensions to human rights and privileges, are rendered insecure, if not lost, by this change, so loudly talked of by some, and inconsiderately by others. Is this tame relinquishment of rights worthy of freemen ? Is it worthy of that manly fortitude that ought to characterize republicans ? It is said eight states have adopted this plan. I declare that if twelve states and a half had adopted it, I would, with manly firmness, and in spite of an erring world, reject it. You are not to inquire how your trade may be increased, nor how you are to become a great and powerful people, but how your liberties can be secured ; for liberty ought to be the direct end of your government.

Having premised these things, I shall, with the aid of my judgment and information, which I confess are not extensive, go into the discussion of this system more minutely. Is it necessary for your liberty that you should abandon those great rights by the adoption of this system ? Is the relinquishment of the trial by jury and the liberty of the press necessary for your liberty ? Will the abandonment of your most sacred rights tend to the security of your liberty ? Liberty, the greatest of all earthly blessings—give us that precious jewel, and you may take every thing else ! But I am fearful I have lived long enough to become an old-fashioned fellow. Perhaps an invincible attachment to the dearest rights of man may, in these refined, enlightened days, be deemed old-fashioned ; if so, I am contented to be so. I say the time has been when every pore of my heart beat for American liberty, and which, I believe, had a counterpart in the breast of every true American; but suspicions have gone forth—suspicions of my integrity—publicly reported that my professions are not real. Twenty-three years ago was I supposed a traitor to my country. I was then said to be a bane of sedition, because I supported the rights of my country. I may be thought suspicious when I say our privileges and rights are in danger. But, sir, a number of the people of this country are weak enough to think these things are too true. I am happy to find that the honorable gentleman on the other side declares they are groundless. But, sir, suspicion is a virtue as long as its object is the preservation of the public good, and as long as it stays within proper bounds. Should it fall on me, I am contented. Conscious rectitude is a powerful consolation. I trust there are many who think my professions for the public good to be real. Let your suspicion look to both sides. There are many on the other side who possibly may have been persuaded of the necessity of these measures, which I conceive to be dangerous to your liberty. Guard with jealous attention the public liberty. Suspect every one who approaches that jewel. Unfortunately, nothing will preserve it but downright force. Whenever you give up that force you are inevitably ruined. I am answered by gentlemen that, though I might speak of terrors, yet the fact was that we were surrounded by none of the dangers I apprehended. I conceive this new government to be one of those dangers : it has produced those horrors which distress many of our best citizens. We are come hither to preserve the poor Commonwealth of Virginia, if it can be possibly done : something must be done to preserve your liberty and mine. The Confederation, this same despised government, merits, in my opinion, the highest encomium. It carried us through a long and dangerous war ; it rendered us victorious in that bloody conflict with a powerful nation ; it has secured us a territory greater than any European monarch possesses : and shall a government which has been thus strong and vigorous, be accused of imbecility, and abandoned for want of energy ? Consider what you are about to do before you part with this government. Take longer time in reckoning things ; revolutions like this have happened in almost every country in Europe ; similar examples are to be found in ancient Greece and ancient Rome—instances of the people losing their liberty by their own carelessness, and the ambition of a few. We are cautioned by the honorable gentleman who presides against faction and turbulence. I acknowledge that licentiousness is dangerous, and that it ought to be provided against : I acknowledge, also, the new form of government may effectually prevent it : yet there is another thing it will as effectually do, it will oppress and ruin the people. There are sufficient guards placed against sedition and licentiousness ; for, when power is given to this government to suppress these, or for any other purpose, the language it assumes is clear, express, and unequivocal ; but when this Constitution speaks of privileges, there is an ambiguity, sir, a fatal ambiguity—an ambiguity which is very astonishing. In the clause under consideration there is the strangest language that I can conceive. I mean, when it says that there shall not be more representatives than one for every thirty thousand. Now, sir, how easy is it to evade this privilege ! ' The number shall not exceed one for every thirty thousand.' This may be satisfied by one representative from each State. Let our numbers be ever so great, this immense continent may, by this artful expression, be reduced to have but thirteen representatives. I confess this construction is not natural ; but the ambiguity of the expression lays a good ground for a quarrel. Why was it not clearly and unequivocally expressed, that they should be entitled to have one for every thirty thousand ? This would have obviated all disputes ; and was this difficult to be done ? What is the inference ? When population increases, and a State shall send representatives in this proportion, Congress *may* remand them, because the right of having one for every thirty thousand is not clearly expressed. This possibility of reducing the number to one for each State approximates to probability by that other expression—' but each State shall at least have one representative.' Now, is it not clear that, from the first expression, the number might be reduced so much that some States should have no representatives at all, were it not for the insertion of this last expression ? And as this is the only restriction upon them, we may fairly conclude that they *may* restrain the number to one from each State. Perhaps the same horrors may hang over my mind again. I shall be told I am continually afraid : but, sir, I have strong cause of apprehension. . . .

The honorable gentleman said that great danger would ensue if the Convention rose without adopting this system. I ask, where is that danger ? I see none Other gentlemen have told us within these walls, that the Union is gone, or that the Union will be gone. Is not this trifling with the judgment of their fellow-citizens ? Till they tell us the ground of their fears I will consider them as imaginary. I rose to make inquiry where those dangers were ; they could make no answer : I believe I never shall have that answer. Is there a disposition in the people of this country to revolt against the dominion of laws ? Has there been a single tumult in Virginia ? Have not the people of Virginia, when laboring under the severest pressure of accumulated distresses, manifested the most cordial acquiescence in the execution of the laws ? What could be more awful than their unanimous acquiescence under general distresses ? Is there any revolution in Virginia ? Whither is the spirit of America gone ? Whither is the genius of America fled ? It was but yesterday, when our enemies marched in triumph through our country. Yet the people of this country could not be appalled by their pompous armaments. They stopped their career and victoriously captured them. Where is the peril, now, compared to that ? Some minds are agitated by foreign alarms. Happily for us, there is no real danger from Europe ; that country is engaged in more arduous business. From that quarter there is no cause of fear ; you may sleep in safety for ever for them.

Where is the danger ? If, sir, there was any, I would recur to the American spirit to defend us ; that spirit which has enabled us to surmount the greatest difficulties. To that illustrious spirit I address my most fervent prayer to prevent our adopting a system destructive to liberty. Let not gentlemen be told that it is not safe to reject this government. Wherefore is it not safe ? We are told there are dangers, but those dangers are ideal ; they cannot be demonstrated. To encourage us to adopt it, they tell us that there is a plain, easy way of getting amendments. When I come to contemplate this part, I suppose that I am mad, or that my countrymen are so. The way to amendment is, in my conception, shut. Let us consider this plain, easy way. [Constitution, art. v.]

Hence it appears that three fourths of the States must ultimately agree to any amendments that may be necessary. Let us consider the consequence of this. However uncharitable it may appear, yet I must tell my opinion—that the most unworthy characters may get into power and prevent the introduction of amendments. Let us suppose—for the case is supposable, possible, and probable—that you happen to deal those powers to unworthy hands ; will they relinquish powers already in their possession, or agree to amendments ?

Two thirds of the Congress, or of the State legislatures, are necessary even to propose amendments. If one third of these be unworthy men, they may prevent the application for amendments ; but what is destructive and mischievous is that three fourths of the State legislatures, or of the State conventions, must concur in the amendments when proposed ! In such numerous bodies there must necessarily be some designing, bad men. To suppose that so large a number as three fourths of the States will concur is to suppose that they will possess genius, intelligence, and integrity, approaching to miraculous. It would, indeed, be miraculous that they should concur in the same amendments, or even in such as would bear some likeness to one another ; for four of the smallest States, that do not collectively contain one tenth part of the population of the United States, may obstruct the most salutary and necessary amendments. Nay, in these four States, six tenths of the people may reject these amendments ; and suppose that amendments shall be opposed to amendments, which is highly probable—is it possible that three fourths can ever agree to the same amendments ? A bare majority in these four small States may hinder the adoption of amendments ; so that we may fairly and justly conclude that one twentieth part of the American people may prevent the removal of the most grievous inconveniences and oppression, by refusing to accede to amendments. A trifling minority may reject the most salutary amendments. Is this an easy mode of securing the public liberty ? It is, sir, a most fearful situation, when the most contemptible minority can prevent the alteration of the most oppressive government ; for it may in many respects, prove to be such. Is this the spirit of republicanism ?

What, sir, is the genius of democracy ? Let me read that clause of the Bill of Rights of Virginia which relates to this :[1] ...

This, sir, is the language of democracy—that a majority of the community have a right to alter their government when found to be oppressive. But how different is the genius of your new Constitution from this ! How different from the sentiments of freemen, that a contemptible minority can prevent the good of the majority ! If, then, gentlemen, standing on this ground, are come to that point, that they are willing to bind themselves and their posterity to be oppressed, I am

[1] See above, p. 149, s. 3.

amazed and inexpressibly astonished. If this be the opinion of the majority, I must submit ; but to me, sir, it appears perilous and destructive. I cannot help thinking so. Perhaps it may be the result of my age. These may be feelings natural to a man of my years, when the American spirit has left him, and his mental powers, like the members of the body, are decayed. If, sir, amendments are left to the twentieth, or the tenth part of the people of America, your liberty is gone forever. We have heard that there is a great deal of bribery practised in the House of Commons in England, and that many of the members raise themselves to preferments by selling the rights of the people. But, sir, the tenth part of that body cannot continue oppressions on the rest of the people. English liberty is, in this case, on a firmer foundation than American liberty. It will be easily contrived to procure the opposition of one tenth of the people to any alteration, however judicious. The honorable gentleman who presides told us that, to prevent abuses in our government, we will assemble in Convention, recall our delegated powers, and punish our servants for abusing the trust reposed in them. O sir, we should have fine times indeed, if to punish tyrants it were only sufficient to assemble the people ! Your arms, wherewith you could defend yourselves, are gone ; and you have no longer an aristocratical, no longer a democratical spirit. Did you ever read of any revolution in any nation, brought about by the punishment of those in power, inflicted by those who had no power at all ? You read of a Riot Act in a country which is called one of the freest in the world, where a few neighbors cannot assemble without the risk of being shot by a hired soldiery, the engines of despotism. We may see such an Act in America.

A standing army we shall have, also, to execute the execrable commands of tyranny ; and how are you to punish them ? Will you order them to be punished ? Who shall obey these orders ? Will your mace-bearer be a match for a disciplined regiment ? In what situation are we to be ? The clause before you gives a power of direct taxation, unbounded and unlimited, exclusive power of legislation, in all cases whatsoever, for ten miles square, and over all places purchased for the erection of forts, magazines, arsenals, dockyards, etc. What resistance could be made ? The attempt would be madness. You will find all the strength of this country in the hands of your enemies ; those garrisons will naturally be the strongest places in the country. Your militia is given up to Congress, also in another part of this plan : they will therefore act as they think proper : all power will be in their own possession. You cannot force them to receive their punishment. Of what service would militia be to you, when, most probably, you will not have a single musket in the State ? For, as arms are to be provided by Congress, they may or may not furnish them.

Let me here call your attention to that part which gives the Congress power ' to provide for organizing, arming, and disciplining the militia, and for governing such part of them as may be employed in the service of the United States— reserving to the States, respectively, the appointment of the officers, and the authority of training the militia according to the discipline prescribed by Congress '. By this, sir, you see that their controul over our last and best defence is unlimited. If they neglect or refuse to discipline or arm our militia, they will be useless. The States can do neither—this power being exclusively given to Congress. The power of appointing officers over men not disciplined or armed is ridiculous ; so that this pretended little remains of power left to the States may, at the pleasure of Congress, be rendered nugatory. Our situation will be deplorable indeed : nor can we ever expect to get this government amended, since I have already shewn that a very small minority may prevent it, and that small minority interested in the continuance of the oppression. Will the oppressor let go the oppressed ? Was there ever an instance ? Can the annals of mankind exhibit one single example where rulers overcharged with power willingly let go the oppressed, though solicited and requested most earnestly ? The application for amendments will there-fore be fruitless. Sometimes the oppressed have got loose by one of those bloody struggles that desolate a country ; but a willing relinquishment of power is one of those things which human nature never was, nor ever will be, capable of. . . .

Shall we imitate the example of those nations who have gone from a simple to a splendid government ? Are those nations more worthy of our imitation ? What can make an adequate satisfaction to them for the loss they suffered in attaining such a government—for the loss of their liberty ? If we admit this consolidated government, it will be because we like a great, splendid one. Some way or other we must be a great and mighty empire ; we must have an army, and a navy, and a number of things. When the American spirit was in its youth, the language of America was different : liberty, sir, was then the primary object. We are descended from a people whose government was founded on liberty : our glorious forefathers of Great Britain made liberty the foundation of everything. That country is become a great, mighty, and splendid nation ; not because their government is strong and energetic, but, sir, because liberty is its direct end and foundation. We drew the spirit of liberty from our British ancestors : by that spirit we have triumphed over every difficulty. But now, sir, the American spirit, assisted by the ropes and chains of consolidation, is about to convert this country into a powerful and mighty empire. If you make the citizens of this country agree to become the subjects of one great consolidated empire of America, your government will not have sufficient energy to keep them together. Such a government is incompatible with the genius of republicanism. There will be no checks, no real balances, in this government. What can avail your specious, imaginary balances, your rope-dancing, chain-rattling, ridiculous ideal checks and contrivances ? But, sir, we are not feared by foreigners ; we do not make nations tremble. Would this, sir, constitute happiness, or secure liberty ? I trust, sir, our political hemisphere will ever direct their operations to the security of those objects.

Consider our situation, sir. Go to the poor man and ask him what he does. He will inform you that he enjoys the fruits of his labor, under his own fig-tree, with his wife and children around him, in peace and security. Go to every other member of society—you will find the same tranquil ease and content ; you will find no alarms or disturbances. Why, then, tell us of dangers, to terrify us into an adoption of this new government ? And yet who knows the dangers that this new system may produce ? They are out of the sight of the common people : they cannot foresee latent consequences. I dread the operation of it on the middling and lower class of people : it is for them I fear the adoption of this system. . . .

The next clause of the [Virginian] Bill of Rights tells you, ' that all power of suspending law, or the execution of laws, by any authority, without the consent of the representatives of the people, is injurious to their rights, and ought not to be exercised '. This tells us that there can be no suspension of government or laws without our own consent ; yet this

Constitution can counteract and suspend any of our laws that contravene its oppressive operation ; for they have the power of direct taxation, which suspends our Bills of Rights ; and it is expressly provided that they can make all laws necessary for carrying their powers into execution ; and it is declared paramount to the laws and Constitutions of the States. Consider how the only remaining defence we have left is destroyed in this manner. Besides the expenses of maintaining the Senate and other House in as much splendor as they please, there is to be a great and mighty President, with very extensive powers—the powers of a king. He is to be supported in extravagant magnificence ; so that the whole of our property may be taken by this American government, by laying what taxes they please, giving themselves what salaries they please, and suspending our laws at their pleasure. I might be thought too inquisitive, but I believe I should take up but very little of your time in enumerating the little power that is left to the government of Virginia ; for this power is reduced to little or nothing : their garrisons, magazines, arsenals, and forts, which will be situated in the strongest places within the States ; their ten miles square, with all the fine ornaments of human life, added to their powers, and taken from the States, will reduce the power of the latter to nothing. . . .

This Constitution is said to have beautiful features ; but when I come to examine these features, sir, they appear to me horribly frightful. Among other deformities, it has an awful squinting. It squints towards monarchy ; and does not this raise indignation in the breast of every true American ? Your President may easily become King. Your Senate is so imperfectly constructed that your dearest rights may be sacrificed by what may be a small minority ; and a very small minority may continue forever unchangeably this government, although horridly defective. Where are your checks in this government ? Your strongholds will be in the hands of your enemies. It is on a supposition that our American governors shall be honest, that all the good qualities of this government are founded ; but its defective and imperfect construction puts it in their power to perpetrate the worst of mischiefs, should they be bad men ; and, sir, would not all the world, from the eastern to the western hemisphere, blame our distracted folly in resting our rights upon the contingency of our rulers being good or bad ? Show me that age and country where the rights and liberties of the people were placed on the sole chance of their rulers being good men, without a consequent loss of liberty ! I say that the loss of that dearest privilege has ever followed, with absolute certainty, every such mad attempt.

If your American chief be a man of ambition and abilities, how easy is it for him to render himself absolute ! The army is in his hands, and if he be a man of address, it will be attached to him, and it will be the subject of long meditation with him to seize the first auspicious moment to accomplish his design ; and, sir, will the American spirit solely relieve you when this happens ? I would rather infinitely—and I am sure most of this Convention are of the same opinion—have a King, Lords, and Commons, than a government so replete with such insupportable evils. If we make a King, we may prescribe the rules by which he shall rule his people, and interpose such checks as shall prevent him from infringing them ; but the President, in the field, at the head of his army, can prescribe the terms on which he shall reign master, so far that it will puzzle any American ever to get his neck from under the galling yoke. I cannot with patience think of this idea. If ever he violates the laws, one of two things will happen : he shall come at the head of his army, to carry everything before him ; or he will give bail, or do what Mr. Chief Justice will order him. If he be guilty, will not the recollection of his crimes teach him to make one bold push for the American throne ? Will not the immense difference between being master of everything, and being ignominiously tried and punished, powerfully excite him to make this bold push ? But, sir, where is the existing force to punish him ? Can he not, at the head of his army, beat down every opposition ? Away with your President ! we shall have a King ! The army will salute him monarch : your militia will leave you, and assist in making him King, and fight against you : and what have you to oppose this force ? What will then become of you and your rights ? Will not absolute despotism ensue ? [Here Mr. HENRY strongly and pathetically expatiated on the probability of the President's enslaving America, and the horrid consequences that must result.] . . .

6 June

. . . .

Mr. MADISON then arose—[but he spoke so low that his exordium could not be heard distinctly.] I shall not attempt to make impressions by any ardent professions of zeal for the public welfare. We know the principles of every man will, and ought to be, judged, not by his professions and declarations, but by his conduct ; by that criterion I mean, in common with every other member, to be judged ; and should it prove unfavorable to my reputation, yet it is a criterion from which I will by no means depart. Comparisons have been made between the friends of this Constitution and those who oppose it : although I disapprove of such comparisons, I trust that, in point of truth, honor, candour, and rectitude of motives, the friends of this system, here and in other States, are not inferior to its opponents. But professions of attachment to the public good, and comparisons of parties, ought not to govern or influence us now. We ought, sir, to examine the Constitution on its own merits solely. We are to inquire whether it will promote the public happiness. Its aptitude to produce this desirable object ought to be the exclusive subject of our present researches. In this pursuit, we ought not to address our arguments to the feelings and passions, but to those understandings and judgments which were selected by the people of this country, to decide this great question by a calm and rational investigation. I hope that gentlemen, in displaying their abilities on this occasion, instead of giving opinions and making assertions, will condescend to prove and demonstrate, by a fair and regular discussion. It gives me pain to hear gentlemen continually distorting the natural construction of language ; for it is sufficient if any human production can stand a fair discussion. Before I proceed to make some additions to the reasons which have been adduced by my honorable friend over the way, I must take the liberty to make some observations on what was said by another gentleman (Mr. HENRY). He told us that this Constitution ought to be rejected because it endangered the public liberty, in his opinion, in many instances. Give me leave to make one answer to that observation. Let the dangers which this system is supposed to be replete with be clearly pointed out. If any dangerous and unnecessary powers be given to the general legislature, let them be plainly demonstrated, and let us not rest satisfied with general assertions of danger, without examination. If powers be necessary, apparent danger is not a sufficient reason against conceding them. . . .

I must confess I have not been able to find his usual consistency in the gentleman's arguments on this occasion. He informs us that the people of this country are at perfect repose, that every man enjoys the fruits of his labor peaceably and securely, and that everything is in perfect tranquillity and safety. I wish sincerely, sir, this were true. If this be their happy situation, why has every State acknowledged the contrary ? Why were deputies from all the States sent to the General Convention ? Why have complaints of national and individual distresses been echoed and re-echoed throughout the Continent ? Why has our general government been so shamefully disgraced and our Constitution violated ? Wherefore have laws been made to authorise a change, and wherefore are we now assembled here ? A federal government is formed for the protection of its individual members. Ours has attacked itself with impunity. Its authority has been disobeyed and despised. I think I perceive a glaring inconsistency in another of his arguments. He complains of this Constitution, because it requires the consent of at least three fourths of the States to introduce amendments which shall be necessary for the happiness of the people. The assent of so many, he urges as too great an obstacle to the admission of salutary amendments, which, he strongly insists, ought to be at the will of a bare majority. We hear this argument at the very moment we are called upon to assign reasons for proposing a Constitution which puts it in the power of nine States to abolish the present inadequate, unsafe, and pernicious Confederation ! In the first case, he asserts that a majority ought to have the power of altering the government, when found to be inadequate to the security of public happiness. In the last case, he affirms that even three fourths of the community have not a right to alter a government which experience has proved to be subversive of national felicity ! Nay, that the most necessary and urgent alterations cannot be made without the absolute unanimity of all the States. Does not the thirteenth article of the Confederation expressly require that no alteration shall be made without the unanimous consent of all the States ?   Could anything in theory be more perniciously improvident and injudicious than this submission of the will of the majority to the most trifling minority ? . . . Let me mention one fact, which I conceive must carry conviction to the mind of any one.   The smallest State in the Union has obstructed every attempt to reform the government.   That little member has repeatedly disobeyed and counteracted the general authority ;   nay, has even supplied the enemies of its country with provisions.   Twelve States had agreed to certain improvements which were proposed, being thought absolutely necessary to preserve the existence of the general government ;   but as these improvements, though really indispensable, could not by the Confederation be introduced into it without the consent of every State, the refractory dissent of that little State prevented their adoption.   The inconveniences resulting from this requisition, of unanimous concurrence in alterations in the Confederation, must be known to every member in this Convention ;   'tis therefore needless to remind them of them. Is it not self-evident that a trifling minority ought not to bind the majority ?   Would not foreign influence be exerted with facility over a small minority ?   Would the honorable gentleman agree to continue the most radical defects in the old system, because the petty State of Rhode Island would not agree to remove them ?

He next objects to the exclusive legislation over the district where the seat of government may be fixed.   Would he submit that the representatives of this State should carry on their deliberations under the controul of any other member of the Union ?   If any State had the power of legislation over the place where Congress should fix the general government, this would impair the dignity and hazard the safety of Congress. If the safety of the Union were under the controul of any particular State, would not foreign corruption probably prevail in such a State to induce it to exert its controuling influence over the members of the General Government ? Gentlemen cannot have forgotten the disgraceful insult which Congress received some years ago.[1]   When we also reflect that the previous cession of particular States is necessary before Congress can legislate exclusively anywhere, we must instead of being alarmed at this part, heartily approve of it.

[1] Forced to evacuate Philadelphia by mutinous troops.

But the honorable member sees great danger in the provision concerning the militia. This I conceive to be an additional security to our liberty, without diminishing the power of the States in any considerable degree. It appears to me so highly expedient that I should imagine it would have found advocates even in the warmest friends of the present system. The authority of training the militia, and appointing the officers, is reserved to the States. Congress ought to have the power to establish a uniform discipline through the States, and to provide for the execution of the laws, suppress insurrections, and repel invasions. These are the only cases wherein they can interfere with the militia ; and the obvious necessity of their having power over them in these cases must convince any reflecting mind. Without uniformity of discipline, military bodies would be incapable of action ; without a general controuling power to call forth the strength of the Union to repel invasions, the country might be overrun and conquered by foreign enemies ; without such a power to suppress insurrections, our liberties might be destroyed by domestic faction, and domestic tyranny be established.

The honorable member then told us that there was no instance of power once transferred being voluntarily renounced. Not to produce European examples, which may probably be done before the rising of this Convention, have we not seen already in seven States (and probably in an eighth State) legislatures surrendering some of the most important powers they possessed ? But, sir, by this government, powers are not given to any particular set of men ; they are in the hands of the people ; delegated to their representatives chosen for short terms : to representatives responsible to the people, and whose situation is perfectly similar to their own. As long as this is the case we have no danger to apprehend. When the gentleman called our recollection to the usual effects of the concession of powers, and imputed the loss of liberty generally to open tyranny, I wish he had gone on further. Upon his review of history, he would have found that the loss of liberty very often resulted from factions and divisions, from local considerations which eternally lead to quarrels ; he would have found internal dissensions to have more frequently demolished civil liberty than a tenacious disposition in rulers to retain any stipulated powers. [Here

Mr. MADISON enumerated the various means whereby nations had lost their liberty.]

The power of raising and supporting armies is exclaimed against as dangerous and unnecessary. I wish there were no necessity of vesting this power in the General Government. But suppose a foreign nation to declare war against the United States; must not the General Legislature have the power of defending the United States? Ought it to be known to foreign nations that the General Government of the United States of America has no power to raise and support an army, even in the utmost danger, when attacked by external enemies? Would not their knowledge of such a circumstance stimulate them to fall upon us? If, sir, Congress be not invested with this power, any powerful nation, prompted by ambition or avarice, will be invited by our weakness to attack us; and such an attack, by disciplined veterans, would certainly be attended with success, when only opposed by irregular, undisciplined militia. Whoever considers the peculiar situation of this country, the multiplicity of its excellent inlets and harbours, and the uncommon facility of attacking it, however much he may regret the necessity of such a power, cannot hesitate a moment in granting it. One fact may elucidate this argument. In the course of the late war, when the weak parts of the Union were exposed, and many States were in the most deplorable situation by the enemy's ravages, the assistance of foreign nations was thought so urgently necessary for our protection, that the relinquishment of territorial advantages was not deemed too great a sacrifice for the acquisition of one ally. This expedient was admitted with great reluctance even by those States who expected advantages from it. The crisis, however, at length arrived, when it was judged necessary for the salvation of this country to make certain cessions to Spain; whether wisely or otherwise is not for me to say; but the fact was, that instructions were sent to our representative at the court of Spain to empower him to enter into negotiations for that purpose. How it terminated is well known. This fact shows the extremities to which nations will go in cases of imminent danger, and demonstrates the necessity of making ourselves more respectable. The necessity of making dangerous cessions, and of applying to foreign aid, ought to be excluded.

. . . .

Give me leave to say something of the nature of the government, and to show that it is safe and just to vest it with the power of taxation. There are a number of opinions ; but the principal question is, whether it be a federal or consolidated government. In order to judge properly of the question before us, we must consider it minutely in its principal parts. I conceive myself that it is of a mixed nature ; it is in a manner unprecedented. We cannot find one express example in the experience of the world : it stands by itself. In some respects it is a government of a federal nature ; in others it is of a consolidated nature. Even if we attend to the manner in which the Constitution is investigated, ratified, and made the act of the people of America, I can say, notwithstanding what the honorable gentleman has alleged, that this government is not completely consolidated, nor is it entirely federal. Who are parties to it ? The people—but not the people as composing one great body ; but the people as composing thirteen sovereignties. Were it, as the gentleman asserts, a consolidated government, the assent of a majority of the people would be sufficient for its establishment ; and, as a majority have adopted it already, the remaining States would be bound by the act of the majority, even if they unanimously reprobated it. Were it such a government as is suggested, it would be now binding on the people of this State, without having had the privilege of deliberating upon it. But, sir, no State is bound by it as it is, without its own consent. Should all the States adopt it, it will be then a government established by the Thirteen States of America, not through the intervention of the legislatures, but by the people at large. In this particular respect, the distinction between the existing and proposed governments is very material. The existing system has been derived from the dependent derivative authority of the legislatures of the States ; whereas this is derived from the superior power of the people. If we look at the manner in which alterations are to be made in it, the same idea is, in some degree, attended to. By the new system, a majority of the States cannot introduce amendments ; nor are all the States required for that purpose : three fourths of them must concur in alterations ; in this there is a departure from the federal idea. The members to the national House of Representatives are to be chosen by the people at large, in proportion to the numbers in the respective districts. When we come to the Senate, its members are elected by the States in their equal and political capacity ; but had the government been completely consolidated, the Senate would have been chosen by the people in their individual capacity, in the same manner as the members of the other House. Thus it is of a complicated nature ; and this complication, I trust, will be found to exclude the evils of absolute consolidation, as well as of a mere confederacy. If Virginia were separated from all the States, her power and authority would extend to all cases. In like manner, were all powers vested in the General Government, it would be a consolidated government ; but the powers of the Federal Government are enumerated ; it can only operate in certain cases. It has legislative powers on defined and limited objects, beyond which it cannot extend its jurisdiction.

But the honorable member has satirized with peculiar acrimony the powers given to the General Government by this Constitution. I conceive that the first question on this subject is whether these powers be necessary ; if they be, we are reduced to the dilemma of either submitting to the inconvenience, or losing the Union. Let us consider the most important of these reprobated powers ; that of direct taxation is most generally objected to. With respect to the exigencies of government, there is no question but the most easy mode of providing for them will be adopted. When, therefore, direct taxes are not necessary, they will not be recurred to. It can be of little advantage to those in power to raise money in a manner oppressive to the people. To consult the conveniences of the people will cost them nothing, and in many respects will be advantageous to them. Direct taxes will only be recurred to for great purposes.[1] What has brought on other nations those immense debts, under the pressure of which many of them labour ? Not the expenses of their governments, but war. If this country should be engaged in war—and I conceive we ought to provide for the possibility of such a case—how would it be carried on ? By the usual means provided from year to year ? As our imposts will be necessary for the expenses of government and other common exigencies, how are we to carry on the means of defence ? How is it possible a war could be supported with-

[1] They have been, actually, only twice adopted.

out money or credit ? And would it be possible for a government to have credit without having the power of raising money ? No ; it would be impossible for any government in such a case to defend itself. Then, I say, sir, that it is necessary to establish funds for extraordinary exigencies, and to give this power to the General Government ; for the utter inutility of previous requisitions on the States is too well known. Would it be possible for those countries, whose finances and revenues are carried to the highest perfection, to carry on the operations of government on great emergencies, such as the maintenance of a war, without an uncontrouled power of raising money ? Has it not been necessary for Great Britain, notwithstanding the facility of the collection of her taxes, to have recourse very often to this and other extraordinary methods of procuring money ? Would not her public credit have been ruined if it was known that her power to raise money was limited ? Has not France been obliged on great occasions to use unusual means to raise funds ? It has been the case in many countries, and no government can exist unless its powers extend to make provisions for every contingency. If we were actually attacked by a powerful nation, and our general government had not the power of raising money, but depended solely on requisitions, our condition would be truly deplorable. If the revenue of this Commonwealth were to depend on twenty distinct authorities, it would be impossible for it to carry on its operations. This must be obvious to every member here ; I think, therefore, that it is necessary, for the preservation of the Union, that this power shall be given to the General Government.

But it is urged that its consolidated nature, joined to the power of direct taxation, will give it a tendency to destroy all subordinate authority ; that its increasing influence will speedily enable it to absorb the State Governments. I cannot think this will be the case. If the General Government were wholly independent of the governments of the particular States, then, indeed, usurpation might be expected to the fullest extent. But, sir, on whom does this General Government depend ? It derives its authority from these governments, and from the same sources from which their authority is derived. The members of the Federal Government are taken from the same men from whom those of the State legislatures are taken. If we consider the mode in which the federal representatives will be chosen, we shall be convinced that the general will never destroy the individual governments ; and this conviction must be strengthened by an attention to the construction of the Senate. The representatives will be chosen probably under the influence of the members of the State legislatures ; but there is not the least probability that the election of the latter will be influenced by the former. One hundred and sixty members represent this Commonwealth in one branch of the Legislature, are drawn from the people at large, and must ever possess more influence than the few men who will be elected to the General Legislature. . . .

(b) *The Judiciary.*

20 June

Mr. JOHN MARSHALL. Mr. Chairman, this part of the plan [1] before us is a great improvement on that system from which we are now departing. Here are tribunals appointed for the decision of controversies which were before either not at all, or improperly, provided for. That many benefits will result from this to the members of the collective society, every one confesses. Unless its organization be defective, and so constructed as to injure, instead of accommodating, the convenience of the people, it merits our approbation. After such a candid and fair discussion by those gentlemen who support it, after the very able manner in which they have investigated and examined it—I conceived it would be no longer considered as so very defective, and that those who opposed it would be convinced of the impropriety of some of their objections. But I perceive they still continue the same opposition. Gentlemen have gone on an idea that the federal courts will not determine the causes which may come before them with the same fairness and impartiality with which other courts decide. What are the reasons of this supposition ? Do they draw them from the manner in which the judges are chosen, or the tenure of their office ? What is it that makes us trust our judges ? Their independence in

---

[1] Art. III, ss. i, ii. This speech gains significance from the fact that Marshall became Chief Justice of the United States, and wrote the opinion of the Supreme Court in the case of Marbury *v.* Madison.

office, and manner of appointment. Are not the judges of
the federal court chosen with as much wisdom as the judges
of the State Governments? Are they not equally, if not
more independent? If so, shall we not conclude that they
will decide with equal impartiality and candour? If there
be as much wisdom and knowledge in the United States as
in a particular State, shall we conclude that the wisdom and
knowledge will not be equally exercised in the selection of
judges?

The principle on which they object to the federal jurisdiction seems, to me, to be founded on a belief that there will
not be a fair trial had in those courts. If this committee
will consider it fully they will find it has no foundation, and
that we are as secure there as anywhere else. What mischief
results from some causes being tried there? Is there not the
utmost reason to conclude that judges, wisely appointed,
and independent in their office, will never countenance any
unfair trial? What are the subjects of its jurisdiction?
Let us examine them with an expectation that causes will
be as candidly tried there as elsewhere, and then determine.
The objection which was made by the honorable member
who was first up yesterday (Mr. MASON) has been so fully
refuted that it is not worth while to notice it. He objected
to Congress having power to create a number of inferior
courts, according to the necessity of public circumstances.
I had an apprehension that those gentlemen who placed no
confidence in Congress would object that there might be no
inferior courts. I own that I thought that those gentlemen
would think there would be no inferior courts, as it depended
on the will of Congress, but that we should be dragged to the
centre of the Union. But I did not conceive that the power
of increasing the number of courts could be objected to by
any gentleman, as it would remove the inconvenience of
being dragged to the centre of the United States. I own
that the power of creating a number of courts is, in my
estimation, so far from being a defect, that it seems necessary
to the perfection of this system. After having objected to
the number and mode, he objected to the subject matter of
their cognizance. [Here Mr. Marshall read the 2d section.]

These, sir, are the points of federal jurisdiction to which
he objects, with a few exceptions. Let us examine each of
them with a supposition that the same impartiality will be

observed there as in other courts, and then see if any mischief will result from them. With respect to its cognizance in all cases arising under the Constitution and the laws of the United States, he says that the laws of the United States being paramount to the laws of the particular States, there is no case but what this will extend to. Has the government of the United States power to make laws on every subject ? Does he understand it so ? Can they make laws affecting the mode of transferring property, or contracts, or claims, between citizens of the same State ? Can they go beyond the delegated powers ? If they were to make a law not warranted by any of the powers enumerated, it would be considered by the judges as an infringement of the Constitution which they are to guard. They would not consider such a law as coming under their jurisdiction. They would declare it void. It will annihilate the State courts, says the honorable gentleman. Does not every gentleman here know that the causes in our courts are more numerous than they can decide, according to their present construction ? Look at the dockets. You will find them crowded with suits, which the life of man will not see determined. If some of these suits be carried to other courts, will it be wrong ? They will still have business enough.

Then there is no danger that particular subjects, small in proportion, being taken out of the jurisdiction of the State judiciaries, will render them useless and of no effect. Does the gentleman think that the State courts will have no cognizance of cases not mentioned here ? Are there any words in this Constitution which exclude the courts of the States from those cases which they now possess ? Does the gentleman imagine this to be the case ? Will any gentleman believe it ? Are not controversies respecting lands claimed under the grants of different States the only controversies between citizens of the same State which the federal judiciary can take cognizance of ? The case is so clear that to prove it would be a useless waste of time. The State courts will not lose the jurisdiction of the causes they now decide. They have a concurrence of jurisdiction with the federal courts in those cases in which the latter have cognizance.

How disgraceful is it that the State courts cannot be trusted ! says the honorable gentleman. What is the language of the Constitution ? Does it take away their jurisdiction ?

Is it not necessary that the federal courts should have cognizance of cases arising under the Constitution, and the laws of the United States ? What is the service or purpose of a judiciary, but to execute the laws in a peaceable, orderly manner, without shedding blood, or creating a contest, or availing yourselves of force ? If this be the case, where can its jurisdiction be more necessary than here ?

To what quarter will you look for protection from an infringement on the Constitution, if you will not give the power to the judiciary ? There is no other body that can afford such a protection. But the honorable member objects to it, because he says that the officers of the government will be screened from merited punishment by the federal judiciary. The federal sheriff, says he, will go into a poor man's house and beat him, or abuse his family, and the federal court will protect him. Does any gentleman believe this ? Is it necessary that the officers will commit a trespass on the property or persons of those with whom they are to transact business ? Will such great insults on the people of this country be allowable ? Were a law made to authorize them, it would be void. The injured man would trust to a tribunal in his neighborhood. To such a tribunal he would apply for redress, and get it. There is no reason to fear that he would not meet that justice there which his country will be ever willing to maintain. But, on appeal, says the honorable gentleman, what chance is there to obtain justice ? This is founded on an idea that they will not be impartial. There is no clause in the Constitution which bars the individual member injured from applying to the State courts to give him redress. He says that there is no instance of appeals as to fact in common law cases. The contrary is well known to you, Mr. Chairman, to be the case in this Commonwealth. With respect to mills, roads, and other cases, appeals lye from the inferior to the superior court, as to fact as well as law. Is it a clear case, that there can be no case in common law in which an appeal as to fact might be proper and necessary ? Can you not conceive a case where it would be productive of advantages to the people at large to submit to that tribunal the final determination, involving facts as well as law ? Suppose it should be deemed for the convenience of the citizens that those things which concerned foreign ministers should be tried in the inferior courts, if justice would be done, the decision would satisfy all. But if an appeal in matters of fact could not be carried to the superior court, then it would result that such cases could not be tried before the inferior courts, for fear of injurious and partial decisions.

But, sir, where is the necessity of discriminating between the three cases of chancery, admiralty, and common law? Why not leave it to Congress? Will it enlarge their powers? Is it necessary for them wantonly to infringe your rights? Have you anything to apprehend, when they can in no case abuse their power without rendering themselves hateful to the people at large? When this is the case, something may be left to the legislature freely chosen by ourselves, from among ourselves, who are to share the burdens imposed upon the community, and who can be changed at our pleasure. Where power may be trusted, and there is no motive to abuse it, it seems to me to be as well to leave it undetermined as to fix it in the Constitution.

With respect to disputes between a State and the citizens of another State, its jurisdiction has been decried with unusual vehemence. I hope that no gentleman will think that a State will be called at the bar of the federal court. Is there no such case at present? Are there not many cases in which the legislature of Virginia is a party, and yet the State is not sued? It is not rational to suppose that the sovereign power shall be dragged before a court. The intent is, to enable States to recover claims of individuals residing in other States. I contend this construction is warranted by the words. But, say they, there will be partiality in it if a State cannot be defendant—if an individual cannot proceed to obtain judgment against a State, though he may be sued by a State. It is necessary to be so, and cannot be avoided. I see a difficulty in making a State defendant, which does not prevent its being plaintiff. If this be only what cannot be avoided, why object to the system on that account? If an individual has a just claim against any particular State, is it to be presumed that, on application to its Legislature, he will not obtain satisfaction? But how could a State recover any claim from a citizen of another State, without the establishment of these tribunals?

The honorable member objects to suits being instituted in the federal courts, by the citizens of one State, against the citizens of another State. . . . It may be necessary with respect to the laws and regulations of commerce, which Congress may make. It may be necessary in cases of debt, and some other controversies. In claims for land, it is not necessary, but it is not dangerous. In the court of which State will it be instituted? said the honorable gentleman. It will be instituted in the court of the State where the defendant resides, where the law can come at him, and nowhere else. By the laws of which State will it be determined? said he. By the laws of the State where the contract was made. According to those laws, and those only, can it be decided. Is this a novelty? No; it is a principle in the jurisprudence of this Commonwealth. If a man contracted a debt in the East Indies, and it was sued for here, the decision must be consonant to the laws of that country. Suppose a contract made in Maryland, where the annual interest is at six per centum, and a suit instituted for it in Virginia; what interest would be given now, without any federal aid? The interest of Maryland most certainly; and if the contract had been made in Virginia, and suit brought in Maryland, the interest of Virginia must be given, without doubt. It is now to be governed by the laws of that State where the contract was made. The laws which governed the contract at its formation govern it in its decision. To preserve the peace of the Union only, its jurisdiction in this case ought to be recurred to. Let us consider that, when citizens of one State carry on trade in another State, much must be due to the one from the other, as is the case between North Carolina and Virginia. Would not the refusal of justice to our citizens, from the courts of North Carolina, produce disputes between the States? Should the federal judiciary swerve from their duty in order to give partial and unjust decisions? . . .

He objects, in the next place, to its jurisdiction in controversies between a State and a foreign State. Suppose, says he, in such a suit, a foreign State is cast; will she be bound by the decision? If a foreign State brought a suit against the Commonwealth of Virginia, would she not be barred from the claim if the federal judiciary thought it unjust? The previous consent of the parties is necessary; and, as the federal judiciary will decide, each party will acquiesce. It will be the means of preventing disputes with foreign nations. On an attentive consideration of these points, I trust every part will appear satisfactory to the committee.

The exclusion of trial by jury, in this case, he urged to prostrate our rights. Does the word *court* only mean the judges? Does not the determination of a jury necessarily lead to the judgment of the court? Is there anything here which gives the judges exclusive jurisdiction of matters of fact? What is the object of a jury trial? To inform the court of the facts. When a court has cognizance of facts does it not follow that they can make inquiry by a jury? It is impossible to be otherwise. I hope that in this country, where impartiality is so much admired, the laws will direct facts to be ascertained by a jury. But, says the honorable gentleman, the juries in the ten miles square will be mere tools of parties, with which he would not trust his person or property; which, he says, he would rather leave to the court. Because the government may have a district of ten miles square, will no man stay there but the tools and officers of the government? Will nobody else be found there? Is it so in any other part of the world, where a government has legislative power? Are there none but officers, and tools of the government of Virginia in Richmond? Will there not be independent merchants and respectable gentlemen of fortune within the ten miles square? Will there not be worthy farmers and mechanics? Will not a good jury be found there, as well as anywhere else? . . .

. . . .

The honorable gentleman says that unjust claims will be made, and the defendant had better pay them than go to the Supreme Court. Can you suppose such a disposition in one of your citizens, as that, to oppress another man, he will incur great expenses? What will he gain by an unjust demand? Does a claim establish a right? He must bring his witnesses to prove his claim. If he does not bring his witnesses, the expenses must fall upon him. Will he go on a calculation that the defendant will not defend it, or cannot produce a witness? Will he incur a great deal of expense, from a dependance on such a chance? Those who know human nature, black as it is, must know that mankind are too well attached to their interest to run such a risk. I conceive that this power is absolutely necessary, and not dangerous; that, should it be attended by little inconveniences, they will be altered, and that they can have no interest in not altering them. Is there any real danger? When I compare it to the exercise of the same power in the government of Virginia, I am persuaded there is not. The federal government has no other motive, and has every reason for doing right which the members of our State Legislature have. Will a man on the Eastern Shore [1] be sent to be tried in Kentucky, or a man from Kentucky be brought to the Eastern Shore to have his trial? A government, by doing this, would destroy itself. I am convinced the trial by jury will be regulated in the manner most advantageous to the community.

(c) *Personalities.*

23 June

Mr. HENRY. . . . The whole history of human nature cannot produce a government like that before you. The manner in which the judiciary and other branches of the government are formed, seems to me calculated to lay prostrate the States, and the liberties of the people. But, sir, another circumstance ought totally to reject that plan, in my opinion ; which is, that it cannot be understood, in many parts, even by the supporters of it. A Constitution, sir, ought to be, like a beacon, held up to the public eye, so as to be understood by every man. Some gentlemen have observed that the word *jury* implies a jury of the vicinage. There are so many inconsistencies in this, that, for my part, I cannot understand it. By the Bill of Rights of England, a subject has a right to a trial by his peers. What is meant by his peers ? Those who reside near him, his neighbours, and who are well acquainted with his character and situation in life. Is this secured in the proposed plan before you ? No, sir, I think not. But, sir, as I have observed before, what is to become of the purchases of the Indians ?—those unhappy nations who have given up their lands to private purchasers ; who, by being made drunk, have given a thousand, nay, I might say, ten thousand acres, for the trifling sum of sixpence ! It is with true concern, with grief, I tell you that I have waited with pain to come to this part of the plan ; because I observed gentlemen admitted its being defective, and, I had my hopes, would have proposed amendments. But this part they have defended ; and this convinces me of the necessity of obtaining amendments before it is adopted. They have defended it

[1] Of Chesapeake Bay.

with ingenuity and perseverance, but by no means satisfactorily. If previous amendments are not obtained, the trial by jury is gone. British debtors will be ruined by being dragged to the federal court, and the liberty and happiness of our citizens gone, never again to be recovered.

Mr. STEPHENS. Mr. Chairman : the gentleman, sir, means to frighten us by his bugbears and hobgoblins, his sale of lands to pay taxes, Indian purchases, and other horrors, that I think I know as much about as he does. I have travelled through the greater part of the Indian countries. I know them well, sir. I can mention a variety of resources by which the people may be enabled to pay their taxes. [He then went into a description of the Mississippi and its waters, Cook's River, the Indian tribes residing in that country, and the variety of articles which might be obtained to advantage by trading with these people.] I know, Mr. Chairman, of several rich mines of gold and silver in the western country ; and will the gentleman tell me that these precious metals will not pay taxes ? If the gentleman does not like this government, let him go and live among the Indians. I know of several nations that live very happy ; and I can furnish him with a vocabulary of their language.

Mr. GEORGE NICHOLAS observed, that he should only make a few observations on the objections that had been stated to the clauses now under consideration, and not renew the answer already given. The gentleman says he would admit some parts of the Constitution, but that he would never agree to that now before us. I beg gentlemen, when they retire from these walls, that they would take the Constitution, and strike out such parts as the honorable gentleman (Mr. HENRY) has given his approbation to, and they will find what a curious kind of government he would make of it. It appears to me, sir, that he has objected to the whole ; and that no part, if he had his way, would be agreed to.

It has been observed, sir, that the judges appointed under the British Constitution are more independent than those to be appointed under the Plan on the table. This, sir, like other assertions of honorable gentlemen, is equally groundless. May there not be a variety of pensions granted to the judges in England, so as to influence them ? and cannot they be removed by a vote of both Houses of Parliament ? This is not the case with our federal judges. They are to be appointed during good behaviour, and cannot be removed, and at stated times are to receive a compensation for their services. We are told, sir, of fraudulent assignments of bonds. Do gentlemen suppose that the federal judges will not see into such a conduct, and prevent it? Western claims are to be revived too—new suits commenced in the federal courts for disputes already determined in this State. This, sir, cannot be, for they are already determined under the laws of this State, and, therefore, are conclusive.

But, sir, we are told that two executions are to issue—one from the federal court and the other from the State court. Do not gentlemen know, sir, that the first execution is good, and must be satisfied, and that the debtor cannot be arrested under the second execution? Quitrents, too, sir, are to be sued for. To satisfy gentlemen, sir, I beg leave to refer them to an Act of Assembly passed in the year 1782, before the peace, which absolutely abolishes the quitrents, and discharges the holders of lands in the Northern Neck from any claim of that kind. [He then read the Act alluded to.] As to the claims of certain companies who purchased lands of the Indians, they were determined prior to the opening of the land-office by the Virginia Assembly; and it is not to be supposed they will again renew their claim. But, sir, there are gentlemen who have come by large possessions, that it is not easily to account for. [Here Mr. HENRY interfered, and hoped the honorable gentleman meant nothing personal.] Mr. NICHOLAS observed, I mean what I say, sir. But we are told of the blue laws of Massachusetts: are these to be brought in debate here? Sir, when the gentleman mentioned them the day before yesterday, I did not well understand what he meant; but from inquiry, I find, sir, they were laws made for the purpose of preserving the morals of the people, and took the name of *blue* laws from their being written on blue paper. But how does this apply to the subject before you? Is this to be compared to the plan now on the table? Sir, this puts me in mind of an observation I have heard out of doors; which was that, because the New Englandmen wore black stockings and plush breeches, there can be no union with them. We have heard a great deal of the trial by jury—a design to destroy the State judiciaries, and the destruction of the State governments. This, sir, has already been travelled over, and I think sufficiently explained to render it unnecessary for me to trouble the committee again on the subject.

Mr. HENRY. Mr. Chairman, if the gentleman means personal insinuations, or to wound my private reputation, I think this is an improper place to do so. If, on the other hand, he means to go on in the discussion of the subject, he ought not to apply arguments which might tend to obstruct the discussion. As to land matters, I can tell how I came by what I have; but I think that gentleman (Mr. NICHOLAS) has no right to make that inquiry of me. I mean not to offend any one. I have not the most distant idea of injuring any gentleman; my object was to obtain information. If I have offended in private life, or wounded the feelings of any man, I did not intend it. I hold what I hold in right, and in a just manner. I beg pardon, sir, for having intruded thus far.

Mr. NICHOLAS. Mr. Chairman, I meant no personality in what I said, nor did I mean any resentment. If such conduct meets the contempt of that gentleman, I can only assure him it meets with an equal degree of contempt from me. [Mr. President observed, that he hoped gentlemen would not be personal; that they would proceed to investigate the subject calmly, and in a peaceable manner.] Mr. NICHOLAS replied, that he did not mean the honorable gentleman (Mr. HENRY), but he meant those who had taken up large tracts of land in the western country. The reason he would not explain himself before was, that he thought some observations dropped from the honorable gentleman as ought not to have come from one gentleman to another.

. . . .

[Article IV, section iii was then read.]

Mr. GRAYSON. Mr. Chairman : it appears to me, sir, under this section, there never can be a southern State admitted into the Union. There are seven States, which are a majority, and whose interest it is to prevent it. The balance being actually in their possession, they will have the regulation of commerce, and the federal ten miles square wherever they please. It is not to be supposed, then, that they will admit any southern State into the Union, so as to lose that majority.

Mr. MADISON replied, that he thought this part of the plan

more favorable to the southern States than the present Confederation, as there was a greater chance of new States being admitted.

Mr. GEORGE MASON took a retrospective view of several parts which had been before objected to. He endeavored to demonstrate the dangers that must inevitably arise from the insecurity of our rights and privileges, as they depended on vague, indefinite, and ambiguous implications. The adoption of a system so replete with defects, he apprehended, could not but be productive of the most alarming consequences. He dreaded popular resistance to its operation. He expressed, in emphatic terms, the dreadful effects which must ensue, should the people resist ; and concluded by observing, that he trusted gentlemen would pause before they would decide a question which involved such awful consequences.

Mr. LEE (of Westmoreland). Mr. Chairman, my feelings are so oppressed with the declarations of my honorable friend, that I can no longer suppress my utterance. I respect the honorable gentleman, and never believed I should live to have heard fall from his lips opinions so injurious to our country, and so opposite to the dignity of this Assembly. If the dreadful picture which he has drawn be so abhorrent to his mind as he has declared, let me ask the honorable gentleman if he has not pursued the very means to bring into action the horrors which he deprecates. Such speeches within these walls, from a character so venerable and estimable, easily progress into overt acts, among the less thinking and the vicious. Then, sir, I pray you to remember, and the gentlemen in opposition not to forget, should these impious scenes commence, which my honorable friend might abhor, and which I execrate, whence and how they began. God of Heaven avert from my country the dreadful curse !

But if the madness of some, and the vice of others, should risk the awful appeal, I trust that the friends to the paper on your table, conscious of the justice of their cause, conscious of the integrity of their views, and recollecting their uniform moderation, will meet the afflicting call with that firmness and fortitude which become men summoned to defend what they conceive to be the true interest of their country, and will prove to the world that, although they boast not, in words, of love of country and affection for liberty, still they are not less attached to these invaluable objects than their vaunting opponents, and can, with alacrity and resignation, encounter every difficulty and danger in defence of them.

[The remainder of the Constitution was then read, and the several objectionable parts noticed by the opposition, particularly that which related to the mode pointed out by which amendments were to be obtained; and, after discussing it fully, the Committee then rose.]

(d) *Previous v. Subsequent Amendment.*

24 June

Mr. WYTHE arose, and addressed the chairman; but he spoke so very low that his speech could not be fully comprehended. He took a cursory view of the situation of the United States previous to the late war, their resistance to the oppression of Great Britain, and the glorious conclusion and issue of that arduous conflict. To perpetuate the blessings of freedom, happiness, and independence, he demonstrated the necessity of a firm, indissoluble union of the States. He expatiated on the defects and inadequacy of the Confederation, and the consequent misfortunes suffered by the people. He pointed out the impossibility of securing liberty without society, the impracticability of acting personally, and the inevitable necessity of delegating power to agents. He then recurred to the system under consideration. He admitted its imperfection, and the propriety of some amendments. But the excellency of many parts of it could not be denied by its warmest opponents. He thought that experience was the best guide, and could alone develop its consequences. Most of the improvements that had been made in the science of government, and other sciences, were the result of experience. He referred it to the advocates for amendments, whether, if they were indulged with any alterations they pleased, there might not still be a necessity of alteration.

He then proceeded to the consideration of the question of previous or subsequent amendments.[1] The critical situation

---

[1] i.e. whether Virginia should ratify the Constitution with amendments, in which case her ratification would be of no effect until the other States adopted the same amendments, or whether, like Massachusetts, she should ratify the Constitution as it stood, and at the same time recommend that certain amendments be adopted by the Constitutional mode.

of America, the extreme danger of dissolving the Union, rendered it necessary to adopt the latter alternative. He saw no danger from this. It appeared to him, most clearly, that any amendments which might be thought necessary would be easily obtained after ratification, in the manner proposed by the Constitution, as amendments were desired by all the States, and had already been proposed by the several States. He then *proposed* that the committee should *ratify the Constitution*, and that whatsoever amendments might be deemed necessary should be recommended to the consideration of the Congress which should first assemble under the Constitution, to be acted upon according to the mode prescribed therein. [The resolution of ratification proposed by Mr. Wythe was then read by the clerk.]

Mr. HENRY, after observing that the proposal of ratification was premature, and that the importance of the subject required the most mature deliberation, proceeded thus. . . .

With respect to that part of the proposal which says that every power not granted remains with the people,[1] it must be previous to adoption, or it will involve this country in inevitable destruction. To talk of it as a thing subsequent, not as one of your unalienable rights, is leaving it to the casual opinion of the Congress who shall take up the consideration of that matter. They will not reason with you about the effect of this Constitution. They will not take the opinion of this committee concerning its operation. They will construe it as they please. If you place it subsequently, let me ask the consequences. Among ten thousand *implied powers* which they may assume, they may, if we be engaged in war, liberate every one of your slaves if they please. And this must and will be done by men, a majority of whom have not a common interest with you. They will, therefore, have no feeling of your interests. It has been repeatedly said here, that the great object of a national government was national defence. That power which is said to be intended for security and safety may be rendered detestable and oppressive. If they give power to the general government to provide for the *general defence*, the means must be commensurate to the end. All the means in the possession of the people must be given to the government which is intrusted with the public defence. In this State there are two hundred and thirty-six

---

[1] Subsequently adopted as Amendment x.

thousand blacks, and there are many in several other States. But there are few or none in the northern States ; and yet, if the northern States shall be of opinion that our slaves are numberless, they may call forth every national resource. May Congress not say, *that every black man must fight ?* Did we not see a little of this last war ? We were not so hard pushed as to make emancipation general ; but Acts of Assembly passed that every slave who would go to the army should be free. Another thing will contribute to bring this event about. Slavery is detested. We feel its fatal effects—we deplore it with all the pity of humanity. Let all these considerations, at some future period, press with full force on the minds of Congress. Let that urbanity, which I trust will distinguish America, and the necessity of national defence— let all these things operate on their minds ; they will search that paper, and see if they have power of manumission. And have they not, sir ? Have they not power to provide for the general defence and welfare ? May they not think that these call for the abolition of slavery ? May they not pronounce all slaves free, and will they not be warranted by that power ? This is no ambiguous implication or logical deduction. The paper speaks to the point : they have the power in clear, unequivocal terms, and will clearly and certainly exercise it. As much as I deplore slavery, I see that prudence forbids its abolition. I deny that the general government ought to set them free, because a decided majority of the States have not the ties of sympathy and fellow-feeling for those whose interest would be affected by their emancipation. The majority of Congress is to the north, and the slaves are to the south.

In this situation, I see a great deal of the property of the people of Virginia in jeopardy, and their peace and tranquillity gone. I repeat it again, that it would rejoice my very soul that every one of my fellow-beings was emancipated. As we ought with gratitude to admire that decree of Heaven which has numbered us among the free, we ought to lament and deplore the necessity of holding our fellow-men in bondage. But is it practicable, by any human means, to liberate them without producing the most dreadful and ruinous consequences ? We ought to possess them in the manner we inherited them from our ancestors, as their manumission is incompatible with the felicity of our country. But we ought to soften, as much as possible, the rigor of their unhappy fate. I know that, in a variety of particular instances, the legislature, listening to complaints, have admitted their emancipation. Let me not dwell on this subject. I will only add that this, as well as every other property of the people of Virginia, is in jeopardy, and put in the hands of those who have no similarity of situation with us. This is a local matter, and I can see no propriety in subjecting it to Congress. . . .

Mr. MADISON. Mr. Chairman, nothing has excited more admiration in the world than the manner in which free governments have been established in America ; for it was the first instance, from the creation of the world to the American Revolution, that free inhabitants have been seen deliberating on a form of government, and selecting such of their citizens as possessed their confidence, to determine upon and give effect to it. But why has this excited so much wonder and applause ? Because it is of so much magnitude, and because it is liable to be frustrated by so many accidents. If it has excited so much wonder that the United States have, in the middle of war and confusion, formed free systems of government, how much more astonishment and admiration will be excited, should they be able, peaceably, freely, and satisfactorily, to establish one general government, when there is such a diversity of opinions and interests—when not cemented or stimulated by any common danger ! How vast must be the difficulty of concentrating, in one government, the interests, and conciliating the opinions, of so many different, heterogeneous bodies !

How have the confederacies of ancient and modern times been formed ? As far as ancient history describes the former to us, they were brought about by the wisdom of some eminent sage. How was the imperfect union of the Swiss cantons formed ? By danger. How was the confederacy of the United Netherlands formed ? By the same. They are surrounded by dangers. By these, and one influential character, they were stimulated to unite. How was the Germanic system formed ? By danger, in some degree, but principally by the overruling influence of individuals.

When we consider this government, we ought to make great allowances. We must calculate the impossibility that every State should be gratified in its wishes, and much less that every individual should receive this gratification. It has never been denied, by the friends of the paper on the table, that it has defects ; but they do not think that it contains any real danger. They conceive that they will, in all probability, be removed, when experience will show it to be necessary. I beg that gentlemen, in deliberating on this subject, would consider the alternative. Either nine States shall have ratified it, or they will not. If nine States will adopt it, can it be reasonably presumed, or required, that nine States, having freely and fully considered the subject, and come to an affirmative decision, will, upon the demand of a single State, agree that they acted wrong, and could not see its defects—tread back the steps which they have taken, and come forward, and reduce it to uncertainty whether a general system shall be adopted or not ? Virginia has always heretofore spoken the language of respect to the other States, and she has always been attended to. Will it be that language to call on a great majority of the States to acknowledge that they have done wrong ? Is it the language of confidence to say that we do not believe that amendments for the preservation of the common liberty, and general interests, of the States, will be consented to by them ? This is the language neither of confidence nor respect. Virginia, when she speaks respectfully, will be as much attended to as she has hitherto been when speaking this language.

It is a most awful thing that depends on our decision— no less than whether the thirteen States shall unite freely, peaceably, and unanimously, for security of their common happiness and liberty, or whether every thing is to be put in confusion and disorder. Are we to embark in this dangerous enterprise, uniting various opinions to contrary interests, with the vain hope of coming to an amicable concurrence ?

It is worthy of our consideration that those who prepared the paper on the table found difficulties not to be described in its formation : mutual deference and concession were absolutely necessary. Had they been inflexibly tenacious of their individual opinions, they would never have concurred. Under what circumstances was it formed ? When no party was formed, or particular proposition made, and men's minds were calm and dispassionate. Yet, under these circumstances, it was difficult, extremely difficult, to agree to any general system.

Suppose eight States only should ratify, and Virginia should propose certain alterations, as the previous condition of her accession. If they should be disposed to accede to her proposition, which is the most favorable conclusion, the difficulty attending it will be immense. Every State which has decided it, must take up the subject again. They must not only have the mortification of acknowledging that they had done wrong, but the difficulty of having a reconsideration of it among the people, and appointing new conventions to deliberate upon it. They must attend to *all* the amendments, which may be dictated by as great a diversity of political opinions as there are local attachments. When brought together in one assembly, they must go through, and accede to, every one of the amendments. The gentlemen who, within this house, have thought proper to propose previous amendments, have brought no less than forty amendments, a bill of rights which contains twenty amendments, and twenty other alterations, some of which are improper and inadmissible. Will not every State think herself equally entitled to propose as many amendments? And suppose them to be contradictory! I leave it to this Convention whether it be probable that they can agree, or agree to anything but the plan on the table; or whether greater difficulties will not be encountered than were experienced in the progress of the formation of the Constitution.

25 June

Mr. ZACHARIAH JOHNSON. Mr. Chairman, I am now called upon to decide the greatest of all questions—a question which may involve the felicity or misery of myself and posterity. I have hitherto listened attentively to the arguments adduced by both sides, and attended to hear the discussion of the most complicated parts of the system by gentlemen of great abilities. Having now come to the ultimate stage of the investigation, I think it my duty to declare my sentiments on the subject. When I view the necessity of government among mankind, and its happy operation when judiciously constructed; and when I view the principles of this Constitution, and the satisfactory and liberal manner in which they have been developed by the gentleman in the chair, and several other gentlemen; and when I view, on the other hand, the strained construction which has been put, by the gentlemen on the other side, on every word and syllable, in endeavoring to prove oppressions which can never possibly happen—my judgment is convinced of the safety and propriety of this system. This conviction has not arisen from a blind acquiescence or dependence on the assertions and opinions of others, but from a full persuasion of its rectitude, after an attentive and mature consideration of the subject ; the arguments of other gentlemen having only confirmed the opinion which I had previously formed, and which I was determined to abandon, should I find it to be ill founded.

As to the principle of representation, I find it attended to in this government in the fullest manner. It is founded on absolute equality. When I see the power of electing the Representatives—the principal branch—in the people at large, in those very persons who are the constituents of the State legislatures ; when I find that the other branch is chosen by the State legislature ; that the executive is eligible in a secondary degree by the people likewise, and that the terms of elections are short, and proportionate to the difficulty and magnitude of the objects which they are to act upon ; and when, in addition to this, I find that no person holding any office under the United States shall be a member of either branch, . . . I plainly see a security of the liberties of this country, to which we may safely trust. . . .

When gentlemen of high abilities in this house, and whom I respect, tell us that the militia may be subjected to martial law in time of peace, and whensoever Congress may please, I am much astonished. My judgment is astray, and exceedingly undiscerning, if it can bear such a construction. Congress has only the power of arming and disciplining them. The States have the appointment of the officers, and the authority of training the militia, according to the discipline prescribed by Congress. When called into the actual service of the United States, they shall be subject to the marching orders of the United States. Then, and then only, it ought to be so. When we advert to the plain and obvious meaning of the words, without twisting and torturing their natural signification, we must be satisfied that this objection is groundless. Had we adverted to the true meaning, and not gone farther, we should not be here to-day, but should have come to a decision long ago.

We are also told that religion is not secured ; that religious tests are not required. You will find that the exclusion of tests will strongly tend to establish religious freedom. If tests were required, and if the Church of England, or any other were established, I might be excluded from any office under the government, because my conscience might not permit me to take the test required. The diversity of opinions and variety of sects in the United States have justly been reckoned a great security with respect to religious liberty. The difficulty of establishing a uniformity of religion in this country is immense. The extent of the country is very great. The multiplicity of sects is very great likewise. The people are not to be disarmed of their weapons. They are left in full possession of them. The government is administered by the representatives of the people voluntarily and freely chosen. . . .

They object to this government because it is strong and energetic, and, with respect to the rich and poor, that it will be favorable to the one and oppressive to the other. It is right it should be energetic. This does not show that the poor shall be more oppressed than the rich. . . . As to the indolent and fraudulent, nothing will reclaim these but the hand of force and compulsion. Is there any thing in this government which will show that it will bear hardly and unequally on the honest and industrious part of the community ? I think not. As to the mode of taxation, the proportion of each State, being known, cannot be exceeded ; and such proportion will be raised, in the most equitable manner, of the people, according to their ability. There is nothing to warrant a supposition that the poor will be equally taxed with the wealthy and opulent.

I shall make a comparison, to illustrate my observations, between the State and the general government. In our State government, so much admired by the worthy gentleman over the way, though there are 1,700 militia in some counties, and but 150 in others, yet every county sends two members, to assist in legislating for the whole community. There is disproportion between the respectable county of Augusta, which I have the honor to represent, and the circumscribed, narrow county of Warwick. Will any gentleman tell us that this is a more equal representation than is fixed in the Constitution, whereby 30,000 are to send one representative, in whatever place they may reside ? By the same State system, the poor, in many instances, pay as much as the rich. Many laws occur to my mind where I could show you that the representation and taxation bear hard on those who live in large, remote, back counties. The mode of taxation is more oppressive to us than to the rest of the community. Last fall, when the principle of taxation was debated, it was determined that tobacco should be received in discharge of taxes ; but this did not relieve us, for it would not fetch what it cost us, as the distance is so great, and the carriage so difficult. Other specific articles were not received in payment of taxes ; so that we had no other alternative than to pay specie, which was a peculiar hardship. I could point out many other disadvantages which we labor under ; but I shall not now fatigue the House.

It is my lot to be among the poor people. The most that I can claim or flatter myself with, is to be of the middle rank. I wish no more, for I am contented. But I shall give my opinion unbiased and uninfluenced, without erudition or eloquence, but with firmness and candor ; and in so doing I will satisfy my conscience. If this Constitution be bad, it will bear equally as hard on me as on any other member of the society. It will bear hard on my children, who are as dear to me as any man's children can be to him. Having their felicity and happiness at heart, the vote I shall give in its favor can only be imputed to a conviction of its utility and propriety. . . .

They tell us that they see a progressive danger of bringing about emancipation. The principle has begun since the revolution. Let us do what we will, it will come round. Slavery has been the foundation of that impiety and dissipation which have been so much disseminated among our countrymen. If it were totally abolished, it would do much good. . . .

I am happy to see that happy day approaching when we lose sight of dissensions and discord, which are the greatest sources of political misfortunes. Division is a dreadful thing. This Constitution may have defects. There can be no human institution without defects. We must go out of this world to find it otherwise. The annals of mankind do not show us one example of a perfect constitution. . . .

Mr. HENRY. . . .

. . . .

I beg pardon of this house for having taken up more time than came to my share, and I thank them for the patience and polite attention with which I have been heard. If I shall be in the minority, I shall have those painful sensations which arise from a conviction of *being overpowered in a good cause.* Yet I will be a peaceable citizen. My head, my hand, and my heart, shall be at liberty to retrieve the loss of liberty, and remove the defects of that system in a constitutional way. I wish not to go to violence, but will wait with hopes that the spirit which predominated in the Revolution is not yet gone, nor the cause of those who are attached to the Revolution yet lost. I shall therefore patiently wait in expectation of seeing that government changed, so as to be compatible with the safety, liberty, and happiness, of the people.

Gov. RANDOLPH. Mr. Chairman, one parting word I humbly supplicate. The suffrage which I shall give in favor of the Constitution will be ascribed, by malice, to motives unknown to my breast. But, although for every other act of my life I shall seek refuge in the mercy of God, for this I request his justice only. Lest, however, some future annalist should, in the spirit of party vengeance, deign to mention my name, let him recite these truths—that I went to the federal Convention with the strongest affection for the Union ; that I acted there in full conformity with this affection ; that I refused to subscribe, because I had, as I still have, objections to the Constitution, and wished a free inquiry into its merits ; and that the accession of eight States reduced our deliberations to the single question of Union or no Union.

[The President now resumed the chair, and the committee reported a resolution of ratification. An attempt to make the ratification conditional upon previous amendments having passed in the negative, ayes 80, noes 88. The main question was then put, that the Convention do agree with the Committee's proposed resolution ' that the said Constitution be ratified '. This passed in the affirmative, ayes 89, noes 79.]

27 June

[The following engrossed form of ratification [1] was adopted by the Convention, to be transmitted to Congress, together with a series of amendments, that the first Congress under the Constitution, and the States, were recommended to adopt.]

We the Delegates of the People of Virginia duly elected in pursuance of a recommendation from the General Assembly and now met in Convention having fully and freely investi-

---

[1] *Documentary History of the Constitution,* ii. 145–6.

gated and discussed the proceedings of the Fœderal Convention and being prepared as well as the most mature deliberation hath enabled us to decide thereon Do in the name and in behalf of the People of Virginia declare and make known that the powers granted under the Constitution being derived from the People of the United States may be resumed by them whensoever the same shall be perverted to their injury or oppression and that every power not granted thereby remains with them and at their will[1]: that therefore no right of any denomination can be cancelled, abridged, restrained, or modified by the Congress by the Senate or House of Representatives, acting in any Capacity by the President or any Department or Officer of the United States except in those instances in which power is given by the Constitution for those purposes : and that among other essential rights the liberty of Conscience and of the Press cannot be cancelled, abridged, restrained, or modified by any authority of the United States. With these impressions with a solemn appeal to the Searcher of hearts for the purity of our intentions and under the conviction that whatsoever imperfections may exist in the Constitution ought rather to be examined in the mode prescribed therein than to bring the Union into danger by a delay with a hope of obtaining Amendments previous to the Ratification, We the said Delegates in the name and in behalf of the People of Virginia do by these presents assent to and ratify the Constitution recommended on the seventeenth day of September one thousand seven hundred and eighty seven by the Fœderal Convention for the Government of the United States hereby announcing to all those whom it may concern that the said Constitution is binding upon the said People according to an authentic Copy hereto annexed in the Words following. . . .[2]

[1] The question whether this clause reserved the ' right of secession ' is discussed in R. L. Schuyler, *The Constitution of the United States*, p. 164.

[2] There follows the text of the Constitution (see p. 292). The Convention ratified by a majority of 10 in a total vote of 168. Zachariah Johnson and the other members from the Shenandoah Valley were in the majority.

APPENDIX

AMENDMENTS TO THE CONSTITUTION OF THE UNITED STATES, WITH DATES OF ADOPTION

ARTICLE I, 1791

Congress shall make no law respecting an establishment of religion, or prohibiting the free exercise thereof; or abridging the freedom of speech or of the press; or the right of the people peaceably to assemble, and to petition the government for a redress of grievances.

ARTICLE II, 1791

A well-regulated militia being necessary to the security of a free State, the right of the people to keep and bear arms shall not be infringed.

ARTICLE III, 1791

No soldier shall, in time of peace, be quartered in any house without the consent of the owner, nor in time of war, but in a manner to be prescribed by law.

ARTICLE IV, 1791

The right of the people to be secure in their persons, houses, papers, and effects, against unreasonable searches and seizures, shall not be violated, and no warrants shall issue but upon probable cause, supported by oath or affirmation, and particularly describing the place to be searched, and the person or things to be seized.

ARTICLE V, 1791

No person shall be held to answer for a capital or otherwise infamous crime, unless on a presentment or indictment of a grand jury, except in cases arising in the land or naval forces, or in the militia, when in actual service in time of war or public danger; nor shall any person be subject for the same offense to be twice put in jeopardy of life or limb; nor shall be compelled in any criminal case to be a witness against himself, nor be deprived of life, liberty, or property, without due process of law; nor shall private property be taken for public use without just compensation.

ARTICLE VI, 1791

In all criminal prosecutions the accused shall enjoy the right to a speedy and public trial, by an impartial jury of the State and district wherein the crime shall have been committed, which district shall have been previously ascertained by law, and to be informed of the nature and cause of the accusation; to be confronted with the witnesses against him; to have compulsory process for obtaining witnesses in his favor, and to have the assistance of counsel for his defense.

ARTICLE VII, 1791

In suits at common law, where the value in controversy shall exceed twenty dollars, the right of trial by jury shall be preserved, and no fact tried by a jury shall be otherwise re-examined in any court of the United States, than according to the rules of the common law.

ARTICLE VIII, 1791

Excessive bail shall not be required, nor excessive fines imposed, nor cruel and unusual punishments inflicted.

ARTICLE IX, 1791

The enumeration in the Constitution of certain rights shall not be construed to deny or disparage others retained by the people.

ARTICLE X, 1791

The powers not delegated to the United States by the Constitution, nor prohibited by it to the States, are reserved to the States respectively or to the people.

ARTICLE XI, 1798

The judicial power of the United States shall not be construed to extend to any suit in law or equity, commenced or prosecuted against one of the United States by citizens of another State, or by citizens or subjects of any foreign State.

ARTICLE XII, 1804

The electors shall meet in their respective States and vote by ballot for President and Vice-President, one of whom, at least, shall not be an inhabitant of the same State with themselves; they shall name in their ballots the person voted for as President, and in distinct ballots the person voted for as Vice-President, and they shall make distinct lists of all persons voted for as President and of all persons voted for as Vice-President, and of the number of votes for each; which lists they shall sign and certify, and transmit sealed to the seat of the government of the United

States, directed to the President of the Senate. The President of the Senate shall, in the presence of the Senate and House of Representatives, open all the certificates and the votes shall then be counted. The person having the greatest number of votes for President shall be the President, if such number be a majority of the whole number of electors appointed ; and if no person have such majority, then from the persons having the highest numbers not exceeding three on the list of those voted for as President, the House of Representatives shall choose immediately, by ballot, the President. But in choosing the President the votes shall be taken by States, the representation from each State having one vote ; a quorum for this purpose shall consist of a member or members from two thirds of the States, and a majority of all the States shall be necessary to a choice. And if the House of Representatives shall not choose a President whenever the right of choice shall devolve upon them, before the fourth day of March next following, then the Vice-President shall act as President, as in the case of the death or other constitutional disability of the President.

The person having the greatest number of votes as Vice-President shall be the Vice-President, if such number be a majority of the whole number of electors appointed ; and if no person have a majority, then from the two highest numbers on the list the Senate shall choose the Vice-President ; a quorum for the purpose shall consist of two thirds of the whole number of Senators, and a majority of the whole number shall be necessary to a choice. But no person constitutionally ineligible to the office of President shall be eligible to that of Vice-President of the United States.

ARTICLE XIII, 1865

SECTION 1. Neither slavery nor involuntary servitude, except as a punishment for crime whereof the party shall have been duly convicted, shall exist within the United States or any place subject to their jurisdiction.

SECTION 2. Congress shall have power to enforce this article by appropriate legislation.

ARTICLE XIV, 1868

SECTION 1. All persons born or naturalized in the United States, and subject to the jurisdiction thereof, are citizens of the United States and of the State wherein they reside. No State shall make or enforce any law which shall abridge the privileges or immunities of citizens of the United States ; nor shall any State deprive any person of life, liberty, or property, without due process of law ; nor deny to any person within its jurisdiction the equal protection of the laws.

SECTION 2. Representatives shall be apportioned among the several States according to their respective numbers, counting the whole number of persons in each State, excluding Indians not taxed. But when the right to vote at any election for the choice of electors for President and Vice-President of the United States, Representatives in Congress, the executive and judicial officers of a State, or the members of the legislature thereof, is denied to any of the male inhabitants of such State, being twenty-one years of age, and citizens of the United States, or in any way abridged, except for participation in rebellion, or other crime, the basis of representation therein shall be reduced in the proportion which the number of such male citizens shall bear to the whole number of male citizens twenty-one years of age in such State.

SECTION 3. No person shall be a Senator or Representative in Congress, or elector of President and Vice-President, or hold any office, civil or military, under the United States or under any State, who, having previously taken an oath as a member of Congress, or as an officer of the United States, or as a member of any State legislature, or as an executive or judicial officer of any State, to support the Constitution of the United States, shall have engaged in insurrection or rebellion against the same, or given aid or comfort to the enemies thereof. But Congress may, by a vote of two thirds of each house, remove such disability.

SECTION 4. The validity of the public debt of the United States, authorized by law, including debts incurred for payment of pensions and bounties for services in suppressing insurrection or rebellion, shall not be questioned. But neither the United States nor any State shall assume or pay any debt or obligation incurred in aid of insurrection or rebellion against the United States, or any claim for the loss or emancipation of any slave ; but all such debts, obligations, and claims shall be held illegal and void.

SECTION 5. The Congress shall have power to enforce, by appropriate legislation, the provisions of this article.

ARTICLE XV, 1870

SECTION 1. The right of citizens of the United States to vote shall not be denied or abridged by the United States or by any State on account of race, color, or previous condition of servitude.

SECTION 2. The Congress shall have power to enforce this article by appropriate legislation.

ARTICLE XVI, 1913

The Congress shall have power to lay and collect taxes on incomes, from whatever source derived, without apportionment among the several States, and without regard to any census or enumeration.

ARTICLE XVII, 1913

The Senate of the United States shall be composed of two Senators from each State, elected by the people thereof, for six years ; and each Senator shall have one vote. The electors in each State shall have the qualifications requisite for electors of the most numerous branch of the State legislatures.

When vacancies happen in the representation of any State in the Senate, the executive authority of such State shall issue writs of election to fill such vacancies : *Provided*, That the legislature of any State may empower the executive thereof to make temporary appointments until the people fill the vacancies by election as the legislature may direct.

This amendment shall not be so construed as to affect the election or term of any Senator chosen before it becomes valid as part of the Constitution.

ARTICLE XVIII, 1919 (repealed 1933)

SECTION 1. After one year from the ratification of this article the manufacture, sale, or transportation of intoxicating liquors within, the importation thereof into, or the exportation thereof from the United States and all territory subject to the jurisdiction thereof for beverage purposes is hereby prohibited.

SECTION 2. The Congress and the several States shall have concurrent power to enforce this article by appropriate legislation.

ARTICLE XIX, 1920

The right of citizens of the United States to vote shall not be denied or abridged by the United States or by any State on account of sex.

Congress shall have power to enforce this article by appropriate legislation.

ARTICLE XX, 1933

SECTION 1. The terms of the President and Vice President shall end at noon on the twentieth day of January, and the terms of Senators and Representatives at noon on the third day of January, of the years in which such terms would have ended if this article had not been ratified ; and the terms of their successors shall then begin.

SECTION 2. The Congress shall assemble at least once in every year, and such meeting shall begin at noon on the third day of January, unless they shall by law appoint a different day.

SECTION 3. If, at the time fixed for the beginning of the term of the President, the President elect shall have died, the Vice President elect shall become President. If a President shall not have been chosen before the time fixed for the beginning of his term, or if the President elect shall have failed to qualify, then the Vice President elect shall act as President until a President shall have qualified; and the Congress may by law provide for the case wherein neither a President elect nor a Vice President elect shall have qualified, declaring who shall then act as President, or the manner in which one who is to act shall be selected, and such person shall act accordingly until a President or Vice President shall have qualified.

SECTION 4. The Congress may by law provide for the case of the death of any of the persons from whom the House of Representatives may choose a President whenever the right of choice shall have devolved upon them, and for the case of the death of any of the persons from whom the Senate may choose a Vice President whenever the right of choice shall have devolved upon them.

SECTION 5. Sections 1 and 2 shall take effect on the fifteenth day of October following the ratification of this article.

SECTION 6. This article shall be inoperative unless it shall have been ratified as an amendment to the Constitution by the legislatures of three-fourths of the several States within seven years from the date of its submission.

ARTICLE XXI, 1933

SECTION 1. The eighteenth article of amendment to the Constitution of the United States is hereby repealed.

SECTION 2. The transportation or importation into any State, Territory, or possession of the United States for delivery or use therein of intoxicating liquors, in violation of the laws thereof, is hereby prohibited.

SECTION 3. This article shall be inoperative unless it shall have been ratified as an amendment to the Constitution by conventions in the several States, as provided in the Constitution, within seven years from the date of the submission hereof to the States by the Congress.

ARTICLE XXII, 1951

SECTION 1. No person shall be elected to the office of the President more than twice, and no person who has held the office of President, or acted as President, for more than two years of a term to which some other person was elected President shall be elected to the office of the President more than once. But this Article shall not apply to any person holding the office of President when this Article was proposed by the Congress, and shall not prevent any person who may be holding the office of President, or acting as President, during the term within which this article becomes operative from holding the office of President or acting as President during the remainder of such term.

SECTION 2. This article shall be inoperative unless it shall have been ratified as an amendment to the Constitution by the legislatures of three-fourths of the several States within seven years from the date of its submission to the States by the Congress.

ARTICLE XXIII, 1961

SECTION 1. The District constituting the seat of Government of the United States shall appoint in such manner as the Congress may direct:

A number of electors of President and Vice President equal to the whole number of Senators and Representatives in Congress to which the District would be entitled if it were a State, but in no event more than the least populous State; they shall be in addition to those appointed by the States, but they shall be considered, for the purposes of the election of President and Vice President, to be electors appointed by a State; and they shall meet in the District and perform such duties as provided by the twelfth article of amendment.

SECTION 2. The Congress shall have power to enforce this article by appropriate legislation.

ARTICLE XXIV, 1964

SECTION 1. The right of citizens of the United States to vote in any primary or other election for President or Vice President, for electors for President or Vice President, or for Senator or Representative in Congress, shall not be denied or abridged by the United States or any State by reason of failure to pay any poll tax or other tax.

SECTION 2. The Congress shall have power to enforce this article by appropriate legislation.

INDEX